# DISCRETION AND VALOUR

Trevor Beeson

# DISCRETION AND VALOUR

*Religious Conditions in Russia
and Eastern Europe*

REVISED EDITION
with a Foreword
to the first edition by
Sir John Lawrence

FORTRESS PRESS                    PHILADELPHIA

———————

**Library of Congress Cataloging in Publication Data**

Beeson, Trevor.
  Discretion and valour.

  Bibliography: p.
  Includes index.
  1. Christianity—Soviet Union. 2. Christianity—
Europe, Eastern. 3. Communism and Christianity—Soviet
Union. 4. Communism and Christianity—Europe, Eastern.
I. Title.
  BR936.B34   1982     200′.947     81-70664
  ISBN 0-8006-1621-9

*33,961*

———————

9392G82   Printed in the United States of America   1-1621

# Contents

# Preface

The generous reception accorded to this book when its first edition was published in London in 1974 was a clear and welcome indication of concern for religious believers in Eastern Europe and of a widespread desire for information about their activities and their response to Communist rule. The subsequent translation of the book into French, German and Finnish, and its circulation in *samizdat* form in the Soviet Union, provided evidence that the concern and the thirst for knowledge were not confined to the English-speaking world.

Although *Discretion and Valour* was a pioneer venture, both in its subject and in the method of its writing, it has stood up well to critical examination inside and outside Eastern Europe. A few factual errors have been pointed out, but none of these has been serious enough to affect the broad picture of the countries concerned. The imbalance of the chapter on Hungary, caused by lack of information about the Roman Catholic Church in that country, was a problem which could not be solved at that time. The sufferings of Christians and others in Albania deserved more than an outline sketch, but the difficulty of obtaining reliable information from that beautiful but isolated country was – and remains – virtually insuperable.

The general position of religious believers in Eastern Europe is the same today as it was in 1974. The Communist governments of the Soviet Union and its satellite states are still in power, and still regard religious faith and religious institutions as a threat to their own sovereignty and an obstacle to the building of a truly socialist society. Conditions vary from place to place, and from time to time, but even in the most 'liberal' parts of Eastern Europe religious believers are still subjected to restrictions and to discrimination that would be regarded as quite intolerable in the Western democracies. Yet faith still abounds and in at least one country, Poland, it may well move mountains. Elsewhere, faith is taking a small but significant number of believers into the dissident movements which have become a new feature of the Eastern European landscape and which are still growing.

Faced by the persistence of religious faith and the apparent ability of some religious institutions to flourish under persecution, a few of the Communist regimes have modified their policies and are now seeking to co-operate with the churches and other religious bodies. In the German Democratic Republic and in Hungary, for example, there is rather more freedom today than there was a decade ago. In Yugoslavia the need to maintain the fragile unity of a federal republic has priority over Marxist-Leninist orthodoxy, so collaboration rather than confrontation is the main order of the day. The Orthodox Church continues to provide the most powerful focus of Romanian unity and independence, and is therefore encouraged as well as controlled. Poland is unique – fascinatingly and dangerously so. The Soviet Union and its most faithful allies, Czechoslovakia and Bulgaria, still tread heavily – and perhaps wearily – along their familiar totalitarian paths, conceding little, and ever-fearful of the slightest deviation. In all these situations Christians and others still have to decide whether their faith calls them to discreet compromise with the Communist powers that be or to valiant opposition to rulers who have forfeited any claim to their allegiance. Obviously, the decision is no easier today than it was a decade ago.

For a growing number of people in Eastern Europe, however, the sense of isolation and loneliness is decreasing. The religious element in the 1975 Helsinki Declaration on Human Rights (or, more correctly, the Final Act of the Conference on Security and Co-operation in Europe) placed the issue of religious freedom firmly on the world's agenda. And the election in 1978 of a Polish pope placed on the world's stage a personal embodiment of religious faith refined and invigorated by persecution, and committed to the cause of human freedom. This revised edition of *Discretion and Valour*, which takes account of events since 1974 and new sources of information about events since 1945, is offered in the hope that it may continue to encourage prayerful identification with all the people of Eastern Europe, and to stimulate the quest for justice and freedom everywhere.

*TREVOR BEESON*
*Westminster Abbey*
*February 1982*

# Acknowledgements

It will be apparent to the reader that no one person could have direct access to all the information contained in this book or possess the background knowledge and expertise required for its balanced interpretation. The author gladly and gratefully acknowledges the generous help of a large company of colleagues and friends whose commitment to the cause of religious freedom has enabled him to make considerable demands on their time and skill. For obvious reasons the names of those who live in Eastern Europe cannot be mentioned.

The British Council of Churches Working Party which played such a large part in the production of the first edition consisted of Sir John Lawrence (Chairman), Stella Alexander, Canon John Arnold, Professor Andrew Q. Blane, Dr Lucian Blit, the Rev. Walter Bottoms, the Rev. Michael Bourdeaux, Peter Hebblethwaite, Michael Hickling, the Rev. Michael Moore, the Rev. Paul Oestreicher, the Rev. Dr Ernest A. Payne, Peter Reddaway, Dr Janis Sapiets, the Rev. Alex Shillinglaw, and the Rev. Hugh Wilcox. Assistance was given by Professor Bohdan Bociurkiw, Christopher Cviic, the Rev. Dr C. R. Goulding, the Rev. Dr Blahoslav Hruby, Kenneth R. Johnstone, Dr Methodie Kusseff, Professor Jan Lochman, Pastor R. J. Patkai, Dr S. Pavlowitch, Professor Marin Pundeff, Professor V. S. Vardys and Father G. T. Vass, S.J.

In the compilation of this revised edition special thanks must go to Keston College, Kent, England, without whose scholarly research, made available in the *Keston News Service* and *Religion in Communist Lands*, and in the advice of its staff members, the task could not have been undertaken. Individuals who have helped include Stella Alexander, Dr Emmerich Andras, S.J., Janice Broun, the Rev. Brian Duckworth, Peter Hebblethwaite, Sir John Lawrence, Canon Michael Moore, Canon Paul Oestreicher, Dean R. J. Patkai, Dr Konrad Raiser, the Rt Rev. P. C. Rodger, Dr Michael Rowe, the Rev. Dr David S. Russell, Dr Walter Sawatsky, Marite Sapiets, Alan Scarfe, Dr

H. Spier, the Rev. Dr W. P. Stephens, Alexander Tomsky, Philip Walters, Dr Roger Williamson, and Canon Kenyon Wright.

All the members of the original Working Party, and all those who have given information and advice, have helped in a private capacity, and neither they nor the institutions and organizations with which they are connected accept any responsibility for the contents of this book. The author alone is responsible.

# Foreword to the First Edition

In the British churches there is growing concern about religious conditions throughout Eastern Europe. However, though there is material available about particular countries, there is as yet no single source which brings together information about each of the countries and which also introduces to the non-specialist the ambiguities and subtleties of the differing situations. The International Affairs Department of the British Council of Churches (BCC) and the Conference of British Missionary Societies had already shown by the work done over the last seven years by the East-West Relations Advisory Committee the value of people of differing expertise and views working together, and they therefore asked the BCC to set up a Working Party.

The present book is written by the Rev. Trevor Beeson with the advice and assistance of the BCC group. We deliberately chose Mr Beeson to write the book, since it was felt that a distinguished journalist with wide experience – but yet bringing a fresh mind to bear on the problems of Eastern Europe – would complement our own specialist expertise. Our method of work has been to leave him to write and order the material as he wanted, but to guide him to the most reliable sources and, when necessary, to provide him with specially written background papers. In this way we believe we have combined the advantages of single authorship with those of multiple expertise.

The memoranda prepared for the group have been first submitted to searching scrutiny by us and have sometimes been totally rewritten before being accepted as raw material on which Mr Beeson could work. He has then prepared drafts of the various chapters, which have in turn been submitted to a careful examination and rewritten by Mr Beeson in the light of the discussion, sometimes more than once. The material for each chapter has thus been before the working group several times. This process has been arduous for all concerned, but particularly for the author. The group wish to express their great appreciation of the unfailing good temper with which Mr Beeson has accepted successive criticisms of his drafts. They cannot claim for themselves quite the high standards of good temper which they gratefully recognize in him, but, in spite of great differences of experience and approach, their meetings have been harmonious. We have had to deal with a number of contentious and delicate matters, but in the end we have always been able to reach agreement about how each such matter should be treated.

In the nature of things, none of us would probably be happy with every sentence in this book, but we give unanimous support to *Discretion and Valour* as the expression of a sustained and single-minded effort by all of us to establish the truth and state it. There are no minority reports or minutes of dissent.

Our task is to describe the situation as it is today, with all its light and its dark. If we had been writing twenty years ago we should have had to paint a more sombre picture of concentration camps and brutal repression of religion in a number of countries. We are glad to record that many have now come out of the house of bondage, but we do not hesitate to refer to the suffering that still exists. One aim of our work has been to correct misunderstanding, inaccurate accounts, and propagandist distortions from whatever quarter they come. It is not commonly realized how much the situation has changed over twenty years in some of the East European countries. We do not accept that the only authentic Christianity is underground.

We were all appointed because we have some expert knowledge of some part of the field, but no one knows the situation of every religious body in every country of Eastern Europe. To begin with, even the greatest linguist would find it impossible to know all the languages of Eastern Europe from Albanian to Estonian. So we have all had to rely at some points on each other's special knowledge and on the many consultants and correspondents without whose help the book could not have been written. We have, however, acted as a team and all of us have done our best to be present at every meeting, even when the agenda lay outside the field that we knew personally.

This has been an education for all of us, and though we each started with considerable knowledge we have all been astonished by the great variety of conditions under which religious people are living in the East European countries. What is true of one country may be quite untrue of its neighbour. In all cases the churches and other religious bodies have difficulties, and in some cases one is obliged to speak of persecution, but the range is enormous. In Albania every open expression of religious belief, whether Muslim or Christian, is illegal and is severely punished, sometimes by death. In some other countries of Eastern Europe the churches have certainly not complete freedom, but more freedom than in some countries of what used to be called the mission field.

Our book is intended for the general reader. We believe that the information it conveys is reliable, but it is hardly possible that there are no mistakes of detail in a book that covers such a wide field. We have used statistics where they are available, and we believe that they give a rough guide. In some of the countries that we are dealing with, good sociological studies of religion have been made, but it should be realized that in other cases there is a wide margin of error. No one knows, for example, how many practising believers there are in the Soviet Union. In such cases we have given the best figures that we can, and we believe that these at least indicate the correct order of magnitude. We have described the situation as it was when we met.

We have been concerned to show the deep spiritual life that exists in so many East European countries and the remarkable theology that is to be found in some of them. But spirituality often eludes measurement or description, and an adequate account of new theological developments would need more space than we have at our disposal. Moreover, some important books known to exist in *samizdat* have not yet reached the West. There are heights and depths which could not be adequately treated in this book. But I personally believe that, when the West eventually learns the full story of those churches in Russia which I know best, their influence on the spiritual life of Western countries is likely to be profound.

For practical purposes we have been forced to limit ourselves to European Russia and Eastern Europe in the strict sense, stopping a little west of the Bosporus, at the Caspian Sea and at the Caucasus Mountains. For this reason we have been unable to describe the remarkable recent growth of the Baptist Church in Siberia and Central Asia, and signs of the equally remarkable life of the Orthodox Church in Siberia. It is with great regret that, for the same reason, we omit any mention of the Church in

Armenia, the first country in the world to embrace Christianity
as a national religion, and the Church in Georgia, which is almost
equally ancient. These churches have their special position in the
Soviet Union, and we should have liked to describe the vigorous
revival of Armenian church life after Stalin, and its links with the
Armenian diaspora throughout the world. Because we stop at the
western border of Turkey in Europe, we are unable to deal with
the great historic role of the Ecumenical Patriarchate in
South-East Europe or with its continuing influence.

The Christian religion is the majority religion of all the
countries with which we deal except Albania, which is two-thirds
Muslim, but our concern is with all religions. In the case of
Judaism our concern is with the religious life of Jews rather than
with any ethnic or political difficulties, but it is particularly
difficult in this case to draw the line between religion and
politics. There is a vast amount of political information
available, but we have not found it easy to get the material we
needed about the specifically religious life of observant Jews in
Eastern Europe.

The Kalmucks are the only Buddhists living within the
geographical boundaries of Europe. We regret that considerations of space have prevented us from devoting a section to
them. We regret equally that we have not been able to deal with
the religious life of the many Muslims who live in the European
part of the Soviet Union, though we have been able to say
something about the Muslims in Yugoslavia and in Albania. We
regret still more that we have not been able to describe the
religious life of the tens of millions of Muslims who are citizens
of the Soviet Union and live in Turkistan and Transcaucasia. I
can testify from my own experience that cultural Islam is
enormously strong in those regions, and I have no reason to
doubt the spiritual reality that lies behind it, but that would be
the subject of another book.

JOHN LAWRENCE
*Chairman of the BCC Working Party*
London 16 January 1974

# Chapter 1

# COMMUNISM, RELIGION AND THE CHURCHES

For well over half a century the Christian churches and other religious bodies in the Soviet Union have been confronted with hostile totalitarian governments. In the rest of Eastern Europe a similar experience goes back almost forty years. Until at least the middle 1950s they had to live within a ruthless social system derived from Lenin's all-embracing view of man and society. Since the death of Stalin in 1953 there have been significant changes, many for the better, but none of the fundamental ideological conflicts between those in power and religious believers has been in any way resolved.

A basic tenet of Marxist doctrine is that religion, whatever its limited past virtues, is one aspect of man's lack of freedom. It is one of the unfortunate consequences of a corrupt economic order which, at many different levels, binds men in chains. Although Marx was critical of the way in which the Prussian State used Protestantism as a means of controlling ordinary citizens, he was at pains to stress, particularly in his *Critique of Hegel's Philosophy of Right*, that religion is to be seen as a symptom, rather than as a cause, of a deep disorder in society and within human consciousness:

Religious distress is at the same time the expression of real distress and the protest against real distress. Religion is the sigh of the oppressed creature, the heart of a heartless world, just as it is the spirit of a spiritless situation. It is the opium of the people. The abolition of religion as the illusory happiness of the people is required for their real happiness. The demand to give up the illusions about its condition is the demand to give up a condition which needs illusions. The criticism of religion is therefore in embryo the criticism of the vale of woe, the halo of which is religion.

Here it may be noted that in his description of religion as 'opium' Marx did not see this as something offered to the people by their capitalist rulers in order to dull their revolutionary impulses;

rather, religion is a drug which people invent and accept to dull their pain and alleviate their misery, in much the same way that the ruling class of Marx's time had taken to actual opium (usually in the form of laudanum) as an analgesic. In 1844 he summed up his analysis more succinctly: 'The criticism of heaven turns into the criticism of the earth, the criticism of religion into the criticism of law, and the criticism of theology into the criticism of politics.'

This explains the stand taken by Marx at the first Congress of the First International in 1865, when he argued successfully that effort should be concentrated not on attacking religion but on bringing to an end the economic exploitation of man which had led to the creation of religion. If the decision made at this Congress had controlled the policy of the Soviet Communist Party after 1917, the history of Church-State relations in Eastern Europe would obviously have taken a somewhat different course. But there were other factors at work – some derived from Marx's analysis of history and society, others from attempts to translate this analysis into practical politics once the possibility of power was open.

Marx, the son of a nominal Christian and the grandson of a Jewish rabbi, did not engage in any serious discussion of the claims of religion. He was a man of his time, and was moulded by the early nineteenth-century German philosophical tradition which had come to take it for granted that belief in the supernatural was untenable for reasonable men. More significant and distinctive is the fact that his analysis of history was uncompromisingly atheistic. His suggestion that the determinative factors in human life and behaviour are economic, and that history is to be seen simply as a prolonged series of class struggles, leaves no room for belief in God, or indeed for anything else outside man's immediate material surroundings.

According to Marx, the only reality is matter, and the universe has come into being as the result of a dialectical process within matter. There is, therefore, no need to posit a creation *ex nihilo* by a supernatural being. Man is an integral part of the material order and at physical death individuals simply cease to exist. There is no possibility of survival for individuals, though the human race is immortal and its corporate well-being represents ultimate value. This corporate well-being requires individuals to liberate the earth from the evil of exploitation and it is in the services of liberation that individuals find purpose, happiness and satisfaction.

Given these beliefs, it was more or less inevitable that those who embraced Marxist teaching should feel moved to place serious constraints upon the activities of the churches and other religious bodies when they found themselves in positions of authority. The Christian credo inevitably appeared as a pernicious superstition which ought to be eliminated, or at least severely limited in its influence, by every means at a Communist government's disposal.

All too frequently, the actual life and activity of the churches has confirmed Communists in their conviction that religious belief is detrimental to the building of a new society in which man finds justice and freedom. Within Marxism there is an expression of the Old Testament prophetic demand for social justice, for true brotherhood and for an end to every form of exploitation and oppression. As a result of the years of conflict between religious institutions and Communist governments, it is not always recognized on the Christian side that Marxism has a humanitarian dimension. The theoretical work of Marx and Engels was a positive response to dehumanizing evils which they discerned within history and of which they were specially conscious in the social and economic orders of their own time. It was not evident to them that the Christian Church shared their concern – a point made powerfully by Nikolai Berdyaev, the great Russian philosopher who was at one time a Marxist but joined an influential group who turned to Christianity at the beginning of the twentieth century:

> It is undeniable that much of the true progress in social history is due to the open or indirect action of Christianity upon the human spirit: the abolition of slavery and serfdom, the recognition of freedom of conscience and of spiritual life are proofs of this. But instead of realizing these social reforms themselves, Christians have often left them to the hands of others; they have often even done injustice and consented to adapting higher spiritual values in the interests of the ruling class and the established order. They have succeeded in producing bourgeois Christianity, and now, since the Revolution, the most merciless judgement is being passed upon this

bourgeois Christianity, on every adaptation of Christianity to human, selfish interests ... Christian piety all too often has seemed to be the withdrawal from the world and from men, a sort of transcendent egotism, the unwillingness to share the sufferings of the world and man. It was not sufficiently infused with Christian love and mercy. It lacked human warmth. And the world has risen in protest against this form of piety, as a refined form of egotism, as indifference to the world's sorrow. Against this protest only a reborn piety can stand. Care for the life of another, even material bodily care, is spiritual in essence. Bread for myself is a material question: bread for my neighbour is a spiritual question.

It was against a background of disillusionment with the past and of prophetic hope for the future that a small group of Communists seized power in Russia in 1917 and began to create a state socialism based on Marx's analysis. In fact, Marx had predicted that the revolution would occur in advanced industrial societies when the workers were equipped to take control of their own industry. There were, therefore, serious problems involved in introducing Communism into an Eastern peasant society, but Lenin saw an opportunity in Russia and decided to force Communism on to society through a dedicated and highly organized élite.

The fact that the Bolsheviks were a small body and that they were trying to introduce an alien Western philosophy into Russia is often overlooked. The Russian people as a whole have never become Marxist. At all times there have been more convinced Marxists in Western Europe than in the East. But the Revolution was the work of a band of men possessed by immense fervour and moral passion, whose courage was matched only by their ruthlessness and lack of scruple, and who secured a power base from which, as a result of the Second World War, their influence spread throughout Eastern Europe.

In this process Lenin was a key figure. He was responsible for translating Marxist theory into practical politics through the organization of a dedicated and highly disciplined Communist Party which was able to gain power and both initiate and sustain a remarkable programme of reform. The techniques employed were unashamedly totalitarian. Lenin had earlier theorized about the totalitarian implications of Marxism, and it was his view which prevailed in Eastern Europe. It led to the emergence of governments that made absolute claims not only over the structures of society but also over truth, thus creating conditions of conflict with scientists, artists and other intellectuals, as well as with religious bodies.

Lenin appears broadly to have shared the views of Marx on religion. Where he differed slightly, but significantly, from Marx was in his belief that religion was to be seen as both a symptom and a cause of disorder within man and society inasmuch as the ruling class used religion as an instrument of oppression. Lenin also drew a distinction between the attitudes to religion appropriate for the State and those appropriate for the Communist Party. The State, he theorized, must regard religion as a private affair and everyone must be free to profess any religion or no religion. There should be complete separation of Church and State, and the State should not discriminate against citizens on account of their religious convictions. On the other hand, the Party was involved in an active struggle for the emancipation of the working class and could not therefore be indifferent to those beliefs and institutions that were engaged in the 'religious bamboozling of the workers'. Lenin's critique was sharp enough to provide an impetus for an all-out assault on religious bodies, though Lenin seems usually to have opposed such an assault on the grounds that it was likely to be counter-productive. He had perceived that religion frequently thrives on persecution.

Yet in the conflict and chaos of a revolutionary situation after 1917 the fine points of Marxist theory were often forgotten or modified to meet immediate situations or the personal needs of those holding the reins of power. The corrupting influence of power has often been noted, and it did not disappear from Russia when the Tsars were replaced by First Secretaries. The close identification of the Russian Orthodox Church with the Tsarist past also made it inevitable that this great Christian community should feel the painful blows of those who were determined to get rid of the instruments of oppression and to bring in a new order. Furthermore the Russian Orthodox Church presented the most formidable obstacle to the assumption of comprehensive power by the new rulers, since its beliefs and its organization stood in stark contrast to all that the Communists planned for the future. The Church had to be either tamed or destroyed.

This represented a departure from pure Marxist theory, but there remained throughout the early years of Soviet Communism the orthodox belief that the days of religion were numbered. The improvement of the social and economic conditions of the proletariat, combined with the undermining of the economic position of religious institutions, was sure to bring about the end of 'man-made' religion. Steps taken against the churches were to be seen as no more than the assistance of an inevitable process and the tidy despatch of doomed reactionary societies. Any suggestion that religious beliefs are not so easily disposed of was met by a naïve faith that science had proved conclusively the non-existence of God.

Marxist theory, with its philosophical and ideological basis, was offered as a substitute for the old religious beliefs which had provided society with a necessary mystique and played a powerful part in cementing social relationships. The early Communist leaders – particularly those with Orthodox Church backgrounds – saw the importance of this, and the sustained programmes of Marxist propaganda and the carefully devised school curricula have aimed to fill the space expected to be left by the disappearance of religion. Yet the results must be profoundly disappointing for the present Communist leaders. The number of people in Eastern Europe who are interested in dialectical materialism or any other ideological tenet of Marxism-Leninism remains extremely small. The basic doctrines of Communism have neither convinced the minds nor satisfied the emotions of the intelligentsia or of the proletariat. On the other hand, religious life has displayed remarkable resilience and, far from disappearing, has in many instances found new vitality and power.

The Warsaw Pact countries are Communist today because they found themselves at the end of the Second World War under Soviet military and economic domination. In no case was the national Communist Party strong enough to have secured power by normal democratic process. A form of Communism was imposed upon people who found both the doctrine and the practice unacceptable, and though many have, at least to begin with, appreciated the economic ard social changes, there have been few converts to the theory. Indeed, in certain parts of

Eastern Europe, outside the Soviet Union, Marxist theory has been modified somewhat.

If the political question has not been finally resolved, neither has the religious question. The manoeuvring for power continues, with governments sometimes closing around religious institutions and forcing them into a ghetto-like isolation, yet on other occasions and in some countries encouraging them to contribute openly to the life of the nation. It is never completely clear whether there has been a change of policy or simply a change of tactics to reach the same goal. The religious institutions, for their part, have produced no stereotyped response to Communist policies. The words which suggested the title of this book, Falstaff's declaration in the first part of *Henry IV*, give at best only one side of the picture:

> Counterfeit? I lie, I am no counterfeit: to die is to be a counterfeit; for he is but the counterfeit of a man who hath not the life of a man; but to counterfeit dying, when a man thereby liveth, is to be no counterfeit, but the true and perfect image of life indeed. The better part of valour is discretion; in the which better part I have saved my life.

In some places in some situations religious institutions have exercised the utmost discretion, even to the point of accepting or seeming to accept uncritically the pronouncements of the secular authority. Yet sometimes they have displayed remarkable valour in their opposition to what they believed to be evil, and there have been martyrs.

While neither extreme is typical, there can be no easy judgements about which is the preferable course. In Soviet Church-State relations, confrontations of life-and-death dimension, both for individuals and for the continuing visible existence of the faith of the fathers, have been a recurring theme. But the dilemma of how to serve the higher good when in the hour of trial has a poignant reality that words can never recapture nor outsiders ever really fathom, and those who stand at a safe distance are in no position to pass judgement. The Moscow Patriarchate, the All-Union Council of Baptists and the Jewish Rabbinate, for example, may have been no less heroic in shouldering the agony and burden of accommodation than Orthodox resisters, Baptist reformers and spokesmen of the new voice of Soviet Jewry have been in their refusal to yield any ground to the totalitarian claims of the State.

The main response, then, has involved a mixture of discretion and valour, with individuals and communities driven to their decisions not in libraries or comfortable armchairs but in the painful torment of violent social upheaval. It has become clear that obedience to God in a Communist-ruled society has a dynamic quality which does not leave society unaffected.

# Chapter 2

# USSR
## General Introduction

There is a common belief in the English-speaking world that the Union of Soviet Socialist Republics is one nation, and therefore comparable with the single-nation states of the West. However, though the Russian element predominates, the USSR is to a large extent what its name implies: a union of republics.

These republics – fifteen in all – occupy about eight and a half million square miles of the earth's surface and have a combined population of 265 million. Among the people are to be found at least 54 major nationalities and 91 distinct languages. About three-quarters of the population are classified as Eastern Slavs, made up of 137 million Russians, 42 million Ukrainians, and over 9 million Byelorussians. Then there are a large number of Turkic people, most of whom have a Muslim culture and religious background, and a substantial number of Yakut, Baltic and Jewish people, besides many other national minority groups. The principal languages are Russian, Ukrainian, Byelorussian, Uzbek, Georgian and Armenian. Russian, however, is given the dominant position and is taught in all Soviet schools, though the various national and ethnic groups have from time to time been encouraged to use and develop their own languages. In these circumstances, it is quite impossible to make hard and fast generalizations, and this is as true of the religious situation in the USSR as of any other aspect of life in this vast land of flat plains and rolling country. I shall confine myself to those parts of the Soviet Union which are within Europe.

Another common misunderstanding is that until 1917 Russia was an unreformed society, and that a Communist revolution was needed before the land of the Tsars could enter the twentieth century. It is certainly true that Russia did not experience the radical political and social changes which affected much of Western Europe in the late eighteenth and early nineteenth centuries, but in the latter half of the nineteenth century Russia entered a period of far-reaching change. The freeing of the masses from serfdom, the rapid spread of industry and the movement towards a more equitable sharing of wealth thus began well before 1917, and the dramatic events of that year can be seen not so much as the result of a revolutionary uprising as of the collapse of an ancient autocratic system which had been unable to cope with a disastrous war in conjunction with such swift and broad change. Yet under the Tsars efforts at reform were not entirely absent, and from 1905 onwards reforms were under discussion in both State and Church, with several actually introduced.

Change during the Soviet era has been enormous. In 1914 only 17 per cent of the Russian population lived in urban areas; now over 60 per cent do, with all the consequences this implies. Other changes could be cited, such as those in literacy and technology. On the other hand, it can be argued that the basic structure of society in the Soviet Union has shown more continuity than is commonly supposed.

Today the number of members of the ruling Communist Party is more than 17 million. Over the years, through its management of power this new class has accumulated in its own hands a disproportionate amount of power and wealth. Increasingly the leadership of the Party has shown itself concerned to defend its privileged status. Confronted by the need for flexibility and the ability to adapt, the myopia and dogmatism of the authoritarian Communist Party more and more resembles the rigidity of the Tsarist regime in its last decades; this poses a far more serious threat to its continued existence than any of the ideological deviations with which it frequently seems obsessed.

Among these deviations religion is one of the most trouble-some. Hard statistics about church attendance are unobtainable, but it does seem that the percentage of the population of the Soviet Union who attend church regularly – if a church is open within easy reach – is higher than in Britain or other parts of Western Europe. When this fact is viewed in the light of the very serious disincentives to any kind of church allegiance provided by the State, and combined with the persistence of private and clandestine religious practice, it appears that much of modern Soviet society is as close or closer to the traditions of Holy Russia than to the values of an aggressively atheistic society, which is the image often presented to the outside world by the present Communist rulers. Not surprisingly, the great movement of population from the rural areas to the towns – many of them new – has led to greater secularism, as in every other part of the world; but any discussion of the religious situation in the Soviet Union must assume a continuing heritage of belief and devotion which has been unknown in the industrialized parts of Western Europe.

An English visitor to Moscow in the 1970s described his experience in three Orthodox churches on Good Friday evening as follows:

At the first, Skorbyashchenskaya (The Joy of the Sorrowing), we found that the service would not start until 8 p.m. and so we decided to return. Nearly two hours before, people were already gathering. The next was St Nicholas. We stood at the back for a while. I do not think I have ever seen a church so full, with people standing shoulder to shoulder as at a football match. Where would one see that in England? The priest attracts the young and intellectuals as well as the faithful *babushki* (old women). The third church, St John the Warrior, we could not get into at all. A couple of good-natured policemen were standing outside, apparently in case any mocking youngsters should try to break things up. The crowded congregation was tight-packed and reverent.

We returned to the first of the three, the church of Archbishop Kyprian, who was once Bishop in Berlin. Now the service was only a quarter of an hour away. We went into a side entrance and soon found ourselves beyond the *babushki*, some of whom were sitting on the floor in the growing heat (but they would all stand up with the beginning of the service) and among the vesting priests. The chief of them was the Archbishop, white-haired, short and stocky, his eyes twinkling through rimless spectacles. Here we were in a different world from the patriarchal cathedral and its solemn order; here there was happy chaos – nobody quite knowing what to do or what would happen next.

On the Tuesday of Easter week the same visitor was in Leningrad, and reported:

In the morning liturgies were being celebrated in the churches which were open. At each one crowds of people were present, mostly *babushki*, but 'old men and maidens, young men and children' too. Rather than staying in any one church we went from one to another. As this was a day for processions outside round the buildings to follow the triumphant cross, there was coming and going within the congregations too and people outside could join in services without necessarily seeming to. This was particularly true of the church, Prince Vladimir's, where Metropolitan Nikodim himself was offering the liturgy and where a vast throng assembled who had to be carefully held in check, all wanting to be wetted in the asperging.

We went to four churches – St Nicholas Cathedral, which was in two storeys with a church and liturgy upstairs and downstairs and a crowd at both; and the church of the Transfiguration; then to St Seraphim's in a public park and cemetery, a small green wooden building which we should certainly not have gone into if we had not been able to get into the sanctuary behind the iconostasis by a private side door, and finally Prince Vladimir's. It was interesting to go from church to church and hear part of the service at each. By this time I had mentally completely absorbed the Easter Greeting and Troparion, and I was also becoming fascinated by the congregational settings of the *Our Father* and the *Creed*: how melodiously Russian congregations sing, without any musical accompaniment. Those two congregational settings sung by massed soprano voices, pure without being trained, were a foretaste of angels' voices, they are so clearly part of the life and soul of the Russian people. At each of these services we were just in time to hear the congregations in the full joy of belief in the Risen Christ.

Russian history, in which religion is inextricably intertwined, has taken such a different course from that of Western Europe and has drawn on such different cultural roots that the Western observer often finds it exceptionally difficult to enter into an adequate understanding of the Russian way of life. When all has been described, an element of mystery remains.

---

As early as the ninth century there were scattered communities of Christians in Rus' – then essentially a pagan land – but the conversion of the first rulers of Rus' did not take place until a century later. When Prince Vladimir of Kiev was baptized in about 988, many thousands of his subjects were expected and encouraged – sometimes at the point of a sword – to follow suit. At this early moment, and as was general at the time, the question of Church-State relations was thus posed to Russian Christians: the religion of the rulers was to determine the religion of their subjects. The same principle persists today.

Christianity came to Rus' from the Byzantine Empire, but it quickly took on a native character. From the beginning the services and the essential portions of scriptures were translated into Slavonic – a language close to the vernacular. Iconography, too, though imported, was quickly indigenized. Constantinople had the right to control the appointment of bishops for several hundred years, but distance, growing maturity, Muscovite ambitions and Byzantine concessions to Rome at the Council of Florence determined that by 1448 the Orthodox Church in Muscovy was no longer willing to tolerate this situation. The fall of Constantinople in 1453 furthered this process, and by the end of the sixteenth century Moscow had become an independent patriarchal see.

Until the Mongol conquest of Kievan Russia in the thirteenth century, the men of Rus' had numerous and lively contacts with the West. Even so, the schism between Rome and Constantinople of 1054 was gradually to affect these relations, and Prince Alexander Nevsky chose to combat Western 'crusaders', the teutonic knights, rather than the Mongols. The Catholic West was to be seen as an antagonistic and an alien force for centuries to come. Though hated as political predators, the Mongols proved to be exceptionally tolerant in the religious sphere. Under their rule Orthodoxy spread from the élite to become the faith of the masses, and at no other time in Russian history did the Church occupy such an independent and advantageous position *vis-à-vis* the State. Yet with the growth of the centralized Muscovite kingdom in the fifteenth and sixteenth centuries, and the identification of the Church with the cause of unification, this independence was challenged and modified. Still, in theory the 'symphony' between Church and State, developed under Constantinople, continued.

The troubles of the seventeenth century, when the very existence of the Muscovite State was seriously threatened, were followed by far-reaching changes – political, social and religious. Muscovy's subsequent expansion into the Ukraine brought the

Westernized Kievan metropoly into the orbit of the Russian Church, a move not unconnected with the traumatic schism suffered by the Russian Church when large numbers of its adherents, subsequently to be called 'Old Believers', refused to accept certain 'corrections' of the rites and liturgical books promoted with the support of the State by Patriarch Nikon. Thus weakened, the Church was in no condition to resist when, at the beginning of the eighteenth century under Peter the Great, the very principle of 'symphony' was spurned. The Patriarchate was abolished in 1721, the church administration subjected to state control, and the Westernization and secularization of Russian culture was actively encouraged by the State.

The Russian Orthodox Church – still the Church of the vast majority of the Russian people – was allowed to retain its diocesan structure, but state officials supervised the administration at every level of its hierarchy. The clergy were expected to promote state policies, and in many respects to serve as functionaries of the State. Over the next two centuries the Church as an institution became heavily compromised in the eyes of most educated Russians – Christians and non-Christians alike. Despite the confiscation of monastic lands in the reign of Catherine II, the residual wealth of the Church – unevenly and inadequately deployed in the field of social welfare – remained an obvious target for criticism and reform. Yet none of this prevented church life from having a powerful influence on the lives of most Russians. The corruption of some monastic institutions was offset by the sanctity of monastic elders (*startsy*), and the devotion of some parish clergy. The 'official piety' of the ruling classes could not overshadow the deep commitment and living spirituality of many of the uneducated masses.

This duality of the 'outer' and 'inner' Church came into stark relief at the beginning of the twentieth century, against the background and under the influence of the economic and social changes disturbing the Russian Empire. Widespread discussion on the question of church reform, including anticipation of a new Russian Church Council, took its place on the agenda of general reform everywhere. But the convocation of the Council had its opponents, and was to be delayed until the end of the Empire; when eventually it began to meet between the two revolutions of 1917 the Church hardly had time to begin reassessment of its role in the old situation before an entirely new situation with unprecedented demands was upon it.

In the old situation under the Tsars the non-Orthodox were at a disadvantage, though the degree of difficulty varied from one reign to another and whether or not the non-Orthodox citizens were ethnic Russians. Certainly this has been the case since the late seventeenth and early eighteenth centuries, years that witnessed the outbreak of schism within the Orthodox Church, the transformation of the Muscovite State into the Russian Empire by means of enormous physical expansion, and the gradual spread of a secular outlook among the ruling class.

Citizens of the Empire of Russian descent who did not adhere to Orthodoxy suffered discrimination throughout the eighteenth and nineteenth centuries, which at times reached the level of persecution. Such coercion struck the large body of Old Believers during the reigns of Peter the Great and Nicholas I, and – from time to time during the nineteenth century – the smaller but still numerous sectarian communities, both of traditional type, such as the Dukhobors, and the more modern variety, such as the 'Stundo-Baptists'. The plight of the Dukhobors in the 1890s so moved Leo Tolstoy that he donated the receipts from his novel, *Resurrection*, to aid several thousands to reach refuge in Canada.

By contrast, the Tsarist State in the eighteenth and nineteenth centuries generally tolerated the non-Orthodoxy of its non-Russian citizenry so long as no attempt was made to proselytize among the ethnic Russians. Protestantism, for instance, though regarded as a hostile foreign force by the Muscovite Tsars of old, was under Peter the Great given a certain patronage in its Lutheran forms. Later in the eighteenth century Catherine II encouraged the immigration of European settlers to the empty spaces of South Russia. Most who came were Protestants, some enticed – as the Mennonite descendants of the Anabaptist reformers – by an offer of religious toleration broad enough to include even their pacifist tenets. Toleration of Protestants reached its apogee early in the nineteenth century, when for a time Alexander I even embraced a form of Protestant mysticism. Subsequent Tsars were to be much more Orthodox in outlook and commitment, and in the latter half of the nineteenth century, when evangelical Protestants such as Baptists began to win converts among the Russian people, their reaction was sharp.

Hostility to 'Latinism' had longer and deeper roots in the Russian past than that experienced by Protestantism. Yet Roman Catholics from the time of Peter the Great were generally tolerated so long as they were confined to those nationalities for whom, in whole or in part, Catholicism was the traditional faith. This limitation was hardly significant, for by the end of the nineteenth century the Russian Empire contained large numbers of Poles and Lithuanians and small pockets of Italians and Czechs, nearly all of whom were Roman Catholics, as well as bodies of Germans, Latvians, Armenians and Georgians, in each of which a certain minority adhered to the Roman faith. As a consequence, though somewhat thinly spread in Russian Asia, there was hardly a large town in European Russia without its Catholic church or chapel. It was not, however, the same with Eastern-Rite Catholics, known also as Uniates. Here the attitude of the Tsarist State coincided with that of the Orthodox Church, considering them to be Orthodox by origin and won to Rome by means of coercion. As a result, Eastern-Rite Catholics who found themselves in the Empire with the expansion of its borders were subjected to various pressures until (in three stages, 1796, 1839 and 1875) they were 'won back' to the Orthodox communion.

The experience of the Jews was different again. Large numbers became citizens of the Russian Empire when substantial Polish territory was incorporated in the last half of the eighteenth century. Isolation was the chief Tsarist prescription for them, and a Pale of Settlement was devised outside which the majority of Jews were not allowed to live. From time to time other discriminations – legal, economic, social and educational – were levelled against them, but there was no wholesale interference in the religious and cultural life of the Jewish people, except indirectly in that they could escape the disabilities imposed on their race if they accepted Christian baptism. In spite of some persecution and much discrimination, they were generally able in the Tsarist era to develop their own distinctive way of life, and this was due, in part, to the fact that they were so isolated. However, their ghetto existence was not always acceptable to the State. Notably in the reigns of Nicholas I,

Alexander III and Nicholas II, when 'Russification' of national minorities became state policy, difficulties mounted, and in the last quarter of the nineteenth century this was combined with an outbreak of virulent anti-Semitism, often encouraged if not instigated by government officials.

Such repression was only part of a broad reactionary trend on the part of the Russian State which followed the assassination of Alexander II by revolutionaries in 1881. Though successful for a time in the re-establishment of order, the hyper-conservatism of the Russian State proved bankrupt at the turn of the century when confronted with the dynamics of massive social and economic change. The revolution of 1905 forced broad concessions from the autocracy, among them religious toleration of greater scope than at any previous period in the history of the Russian Empire. For the Old Believers, Roman Catholics and Calvinist Protestants this liberty was to remain until the end of the Empire. Others, such as the Lutherans, the Mennonites and the Baptists, lost ground and, when the First World War broke out, in some cases even encountered persecution – largely because they were suspected of pro-German sympathies. Eastern-Rite Catholics, on the other hand, were not provided for in the toleration decree of 1905, nor did the lot of the Jews improve. On the contrary, the Jews were frequently made scapegoats for the disturbances of the times, and officials were sometimes prepared to channel off popular discontent into pogroms. Large-scale Jewish emigration, which had begun in the late nineteenth century, thus continued into the twentieth century with momentous consequences for the world. British and American Jewry became significant forces, the Zionist dream of an independent state was born, and key Jewish figures were won to the cause of revolution in Russia.

---

In view of the close connection between the Russian Orthodox Church and Tsarism, it was perhaps inevitable that the leaders of the 1917 Revolution should see religion as a pernicious influence in human society and the destruction – or at least the repression – of the Church as a necessary part of the revolutionary process. Yet Lenin, who was to guide the USSR during the early years of its development, had at first no developed theory about religion and the handling of religious institutions by a

Communist government. He was, it seems, too busy with the organizing of revolution to concern himself to any great extent with what he generally regarded as a secondary issue. But Lenin's writings on religion, which are short and scattered in various polemical tracts, give some background to the policies pursued by the Bolsheviks when they were in a position of power.

An uncompromising and dogmatic atheist, Lenin accepted Marx's view of religion and was particularly concerned to stress that it was used by the ruling classes as an instrument of oppression: 'Autocracy cannot do without its twin agents: a hangman and a priest; the first to suppress popular resistance by force, the second to sweeten and embellish the lot of the oppressed by empty promises of a heavenly kingdom.' The established religions – in particular Orthodoxy – he regarded as extremely undesirable and the clergy, 'gendarmes in cassocks', as especially despicable, for they 'plundered and corrupted the people'. On the other hand, Lenin saw sectarians as the victims of oppression and, therefore, as potential allies in the revolutionary cause. During the early years of the twentieth century he made a number of statements designed to win their support in return for promises of religious freedom. Yet at the same time he argued that reformed and refined religions were more dangerous than the more conservative and crude expressions of faith:

> The crowd is much more able to see through a million *physical* sins, dirty tricks, violence and physical infections which are therefore much less dangerous than is the *subtle* spiritual idea of dear little God arrayed in the smartest of ideological costumes.

In translating his ideas into the policies to be pursued in the future Communist State Lenin made a careful yet theoretical distinction between the policy to be pursued by the State and the policy of the Communist Party. As far as the State was concerned, religion must be regarded as a private matter: 'Everyone should be absolutely free to profess whatever religion he prefers or to recognize no religion.' And, because religion is private and personal, there can be no support – financial or otherwise – of religious institutions by the State and no church involvement in state education. The State itself must remain neutral in regard to the private expression of religious belief. The position of the Communist Party was quite different. It could not regard religion as a private matter, since it was committed to fighting for the liberation of the proletariat and could not therefore 'be indifferent to lack of consciousness, ignorance or obscurantism in the shape of religious beliefs'.

Unlike some Marxists, Lenin was uncertain whether religion would wither away automatically. In order to assure – as well as hasten – the liberation of the workers and peasantry from religious deception, they must be indoctrinated in 'scientific atheism', and it was the task of the Party to lead in this process and to expose the folly and corruption of religion. Yet for all this Lenin was not prepared for the attack on religion to be the chief item on the Party's agenda. It was to be seen as part of a much broader strategy which was concerned to promote the class struggle. On some occasions and in certain circumstances anti-religious activity would have a significant contribution to make, but there would be times when it was much less important, and Marxists must be able to judge what actions were appropriate at a particular time. This pragmatic yet implacable approach characterized Lenin's religious policy. He believed that a dialectical materialism could only deal with the matter in response to concrete situations. Thus, though ideologically hostile to religion, Lenin opened the way for the apparent inconsistencies of policy which were to characterize the Communist Party's dealings with religion after 1917.

Other factors were to influence Lenin once the reins of power were in his hands. It is one thing to speak and write about revolution; quite another to be at the centre of an actual revolution in which decisions of momentous importance have to be made quickly and on the basis of incomplete information. Again, the leadership of a great nation is very different from the leadership of a revolutionary party seeking power. Lenin also found himself faced with very strong hostility from the Russian Orthodox Church which, in the early stages, made no secret of its opposition to the new regime and pronounced an anathema against it, as well as calls to resistance by the faithful. In these circumstances Lenin gave Church-State matters a good deal of personal attention and either wrote or edited the various decrees which in large part determined future relations between the State and religious bodies at the legal level.

---

On 23 January 1918, a decree was published on the separation of Church and State, and its provisions were sweeping:

1.  The Church is separate from the State.
2.  It is prohibited to enact on the territory of the Republic local laws or regulations which would put any restraint upon, or limit freedom of conscience or establish any advantages or privileges on the grounds of the religion of citizens.
3.  Each citizen may confess any religion or no religion at all. Loss of any rights as the result of the confession of a religion or the absence of a religion shall be revoked. The mention in official papers of the religion of a citizen is not allowed.
4.  The actions of the government or other organizations of public law may not be accompanied by any religious rites or ceremonies.
5.  The free performance of religious rites shall be granted so long as it does not disturb the public order and infringe the rights of the citizens of the Soviet Republic. In such cases, the local agencies are entitled to take the necessary measures to secure public order and safety.
6.  No person may evade citizen's duties on the grounds of his religion.
7.  Religious oaths shall be abolished. In cases where it is necessary only a solemn vow may be given.
8.  The acts of civil status shall be kept solely by civil agencies.
9.  The school shall be separate from the Church. The teaching of religion is prohibited in all state, municipal or private educational institutions where a general education is given. Citizens may give and receive religious instruction privately.
10. All ecclesiastical and religious associations are subject to regulations pertaining to private societies and unions, and shall not enjoy any advantages or receive any subsidies

either from the State or from local self-governing institutions.

11. The compulsory exaction of fees or impositions to benefit
ecclesiastical and religious associations as well as any kind
of coercion or infliction of punishment by these associations upon their members is prohibited.

12. No ecclesiastical or religious association shall have the
right to own property. Such associations shall not enjoy the
right of legal entity.

13. All property belonging to churches and religious associations existing in Russia shall become public property.
Buildings and objects intended especially for religious
worship shall be handed over by special decision of local
or central authorities, free of charge, for use by the
religious associations concerned.

When the Constitution of the Russian Soviet Federated Socialist
Republic was adopted a few months later, the clergy – along with
capitalists, criminals and imbeciles – were deprived of the right
to vote or to hold office in the State. In practice, this also meant
that they had no right to food rations and their children were
deprived of education. Shortly after this, with the issuing of
detailed instructions for the implementation of the new laws, it
was ordained that while the Church was to be separate from the
State as far as any support or privilege was concerned, it was not
to be separate in the sense of being free from state interference
and ultimately of state control.

For the Russian Orthodox Church these decrees were a
devastating blow. Its legal position of privilege and power,
consolidated over many centuries, was removed overnight. So
also were the rights to its chief sources of wealth. For certain of
the sectarian bodies, however, the position was different. They
had never enjoyed any privileged position in Russia and had very
little to lose. During the years of Tsarist repression they had
organized their life to meet the prevailing conditions, and little
further adjustment was needed to meet the demands of Lenin.
The new legal arrangements certainly did not represent any
erosion of Protestant rights and at this stage the leaders of these
churches were far less worried than their Orthodox brethren.

In the event, the implementation of the decrees separating

Church and State took place unevenly and at a much slower pace than originally anticipated. The outbreak of civil war gave government officials other matters to occupy their minds and, in the face of the struggle for survival, action against the churches seemed relatively unimportant. Nor did the administrative machinery exist to implement so comprehensive and far-reaching a programme of legislation. Furthermore, the conditions of civil war made it undesirable that a large section of the population should be alienated from the Bolsheviks because of contentious religious matters. By the end of 1918 the central government was warning local officials against crude and insensitive application of the new laws, and during the next two years certain laws were passed as part of a campaign to strengthen the support of certain groups such as the sectarians. Pacifists were allowed to undertake community service, as an alternative to military service, and in 1920 a law was passed transferring some farm land to religious communes.

Throughout the civil war (1918–21) the general approach of the government to religious matters proved far more cautious than during the days immediately following the 1917 October Revolution, and there was much greater emphasis on the need to undermine religion by social and economic action rather than by direct confrontation with religious institutions and believers. Lenin warned against the danger of offending religious feelings, and the programme of the Communist Party adopted in 1919 reflected this:

> The Communist Party of the Soviet Union is convinced that only a conscious and determined planning of the total social and economic activities of the masses will bring about the end of religious superstition. The Party is fighting for the complete abolition of all connections between the exploiting classes and the organization of religious propaganda and wants to facilitate the liberation of the working masses from religious superstition and wants to organize the most effective possibility for scientific educational and anti-religious propaganda. At the same time it will carefully strive to avoid all offence to the religious feelings of believers, because such offence may lead to an intensifying of religious fanaticism.

If the civil war brought a new caution to the religious policy of the Communist Party, it also laid the foundation of a regime under which repression of the severest kind could be exerted without any form of restraint. As a consequence of the war all the opposition parties in the USSR were destroyed, and from this point onwards it was, in practice, impossible to differentiate between the Communist Party and the Soviet government. Lenin's pre-1917 concept of the State as neutral as regards religion, while the Party was militantly antagonistic, was therefore finished. The Party's position on religion became entrenched in state policy and in the organs of government, though this position and its implementation through state policy was still controlled by wider considerations and determined by the requirements of a particular time.

In the period immediately following the civil war the Soviet Union was on the verge of socio-economic collapse. Widespread famine, administrative chaos and general disorder left little space for the application of radical political and economic policies. The chief task facing the government was that of securing the country's future through the revival of the sense of common purpose and the provision of adequate administrative machinery. From 1921 onwards a great effort was made to obtain from all religious groups in the USSR a commitment of loyalty to the new State. In most cases this required a fair amount of coercion, and led to the actual persecution of key religious leaders who were unwilling to meet the government's demands. Émigré church sources, with close contacts with the Soviet Union at the time, estimated that between 1917 and 1923 over 1,200 priests and 28 bishops of the Russian Orthodox Church met their death, and other leaders who refused to express loyalty to the government were eventually forced more or less underground.

Once they had expressed their loyalty, religious communities were allowed greater freedom of action. They were regarded as private bodies who might pursue their own interests, provided these did not conflict with state policy, and during the 1920s some religious groups, particularly the sectarians, took advantage of this freedom to engage in evangelism, and as a result entered upon a period of considerable growth. On Easter Day 1925, however, the foundation congress of the League of Militant Godless was held. This organization, which was led by a group of Communist intellectuals, took a hard line towards religion and the churches and was committed to the dissemination of atheism. It enjoyed government patronage and made ambitious plans, but since many of its activities did not fit in with the government's policy of appeasing the peasants, it was from 1926 onwards subjected to state control.

Lenin had died in 1924, leaving his comrades in a struggle for power. He also left a highly ambiguous legacy concerning religion: a militantly atheistic outlook tempered by the conviction that the subordination of action against religious bodies to the wider objectives of the State leaves the maximum freedom to pursue whatever policy appears to be most expedient at any particular juncture. Lenin's successor, Stalin, was in few other matters to be so faithful a disciple. The New Economic Policy (1921–28) had brought a measure of recovery to the country after the disasters of civil war and famine. It now seemed possible to return to the original radical programmes of the Communist Party and to elaborate on these in the new conditions. This took shape in the first Five Year Plan announced in 1928, and consisted of such an ambitious economic programme that it could only be implemented if the government exercised the most stringent control over every aspect of the life of the nation.

---

In this context certain critical changes in the religious legislation of the Soviet Union were introduced in 1929. A Law on Religious Associations was published on 8 April, and in October the Instructions of the People's Commissariat of the Interior were published in order to clarify and supplement the Law. Both are formidable documents, consisting of upwards of sixty articles, and, in addition to telling religious organizations the few things they may do and the many they may not, they lay down the rights and duties of individual believers. Among the more significant requirements of the Law are the following:

A religious society or group of believers may start its activities only after the registration of the society or group by the committee for religious matters at the proper city or district soviet.

In order to register a religious society at least twenty initiators must submit to the agencies mentioned in the previous Article an application in accordance with the form determined by the Permanent Council for Religious Affairs at the Council of Ministers.

The registration agencies are entitled to remove individual members from the executive body of a religious society or the representatives elected by a group of believers.

Religious associations may not organize for children, young people and women special prayer or other meetings, circles, groups, departments for biblical or literary study, sewing, working or the teaching of religion, etc., excursions, children's playgrounds, libraries, reading rooms, sanatoria or medical care. Only books necessary for the purpose of the cult may be kept in the prayer buildings and premises.

The activities of the clergymen, preachers, preceptors and the like shall be restricted to the area in which the members of the religious association reside and in the area where the prayer building or premises are situated.

Prayer buildings with objects shall be leased to believers forming religious associations by the Council for Religious Affairs at the city or district soviet.

The members of the groups of believers and religious societies may pool money in the prayer building or premises and outside it by voluntary collections and donations, but only among the members of the given religious association and only for the purpose of covering the expenses for the maintenance of the prayer building or premises and religious property, and for the salary of the clergy and activities of the executive bodies.

In the powers granted to 'registration agencies' and 'Councils for Religious Affairs' the contrast already present in the legislation of 1918, which called for separation of Church and State and at the same time set up instruments for state involvement in – and control of – church life, became more pronounced than ever.

Since 1929 this Law, slightly revised in 1932, 1962 and again in 1975, has remained the fundamental law on religious matters in the Soviet Union but its implementation has varied considerably, and it is usually possible to relate the vigour or otherwise of its implementation to the broad policy of the Soviet government at the time. From 1929 to 1941 those articles of the Law which limited, rather than guaranteed, religious life and activity were applied with very great vigour and there were many

occasions when the government's attack on religious bodies
went far beyond the restriction imposed even by this draconian
law. It was the period when Stalin's persecution of religious
institutions and believers was most intense and when the
churches suffered acutely. It was also the period when Stalin
was carrying out purges at all levels of Soviet society in an
attempt to rid himself of all his actual and potential opponents.

Between 1941 and 1959 the Law was still in force but it was
more or less disregarded. During the war years the religious
bodies displayed their loyalty to the State, and in the desperate
circumstances of the time Stalin was more than ready to promote
the unity of the nation and to make use of its total resources in
defeating the German invaders. This was the period of 'concordat' between Church and State, and it continued for more
than a decade after the end of the war – partly because the
government recognized the contribution which religious bodies
had made to the victory and could continue to make by
supporting the domestic and foreign policy objectives in the
years of post-war reconstruction and 'cold war' confrontation.
Unregistered churches were nevertheless vigorously persecuted
in this period.

In 1959, however, Khrushchev launched a vigorous anti-religious campaign which lasted five years. During this time the
government demanded that the 1929 Law should be rigidly
adhered to, and in fact went well beyond this Law in its attack
on the churches. It was already illegal for parents to compel their
children to attend church against their will. Young people under
the age of eighteen were forbidden in any case to be members
of religious organizations. Participation by them in church
services or religious ceremonies of any kind which had previously been discouraged was now illegal. Clergy who, at the
invitation of parents, had given private religious instruction to
children, without infringing the law which decreed that they
must not teach groups larger than three, were forbidden to
instruct children in any circumstances. Some of the extra-legal
pressures initiated during this period were subsequently given
legal basis. A criminal code amendment adopted in 1962 makes
it punishable to 'infringe upon the person and rights of citizens
under the appearance of performing religious rites', and this has

been interpreted to include alleged threats to personal health from religious practices such as infant baptism and fasting.

Since Khrushchev's removal in 1964 the situation seems to have stabilized. On the whole the Law on Religious Associations has been interpreted and applied more literally than in the 1930s and in the Khrushchev era, but a good deal less leniently than in the 'concordat' years of the 1940s and 1950s, when much of this Law was all but ignored.

The revision of the 1929 Law announced in July 1975 was substantial inasmuch as it affected almost half of the sixty-eight articles. Yet the overall effect of the changes has been to leave the position of religious bodies and individual believers more or less unaltered. One modification which could be significant is the provision for religious bodies 'to acquire church utensils, cult objects, means of transport; rent, construct and purchase buildings for their needs in accordance with established legal procedure' (Articles 3 and 20). This replaced the 1929 statement that religious bodies could only lease buildings and objects, and it also omitted a phrase which had previously denied churches the right of legal entity. Another change was the removal of final decisions about registration of religious associations and closure of church buildings from local soviets to the Council for Religious Affairs. All in all the power of the Council for Religious Affairs has been greatly increased at the expense of the local authorities. Lists of church members attending local, regional and national conventions no longer have to be submitted to the authorities but such conventions can only be convoked by an official, central church body and not by a local group. Religious organizations can collect voluntary donations from their members only within church buildings, and special permission is required for acts of worship held out of doors or in the apartments and homes of believers. All the other restrictive provisions of the 1929 Law are unchanged and breaches of the Law are still severely punished.

---

It is not enough, however, to cite only those laws and decrees which specifically pertain to religious organizations and believers to understand their actual legal situation. A number of laws exist which seem to be unrelated to religion, yet which can be used to coerce believers. Among these is the so-called anti-parasite law which may be applied to all citizens whose work is not deemed socially useful by the Soviet authorities. This is used not only against poets and prostitutes but also, and frequently, against priests and preachers. Again, the new Constitution for the USSR adopted in 1977 acknowledged for the first time the leading role of the Communist Party in the formulation of state policy and, since the Party is avowedly atheistic and anti-religious, this exposes to arbitrary persecution or discrimination all who are deemed to be standing in the way of the building of a classless Communist society.

The legal situation is further complicated in that the basic laws of the Soviet Union are subject to augmentation by secret instructions sent by government departments to local officials and the police. These cover a wide range of subjects, including religion, and their nature is such that they cannot be challenged, nor resisted in a court of law. It is now clear, for example, that most of the new restrictive provisions in the 1975 revision of the Law on Religious Associations were in fact promulgated as secret instructions as early as 1962. Besides the specific measures contained in the secret instructions, the mere possibility of their existence introduces a note of considerable uncertainty into the entire social order. In matters relating to religion, no one can ever be quite sure what will be permitted in a particular place at a particular time, which means that almost every area of religious activity is fraught with risk.

Two Russian Orthodox priests, Fathers N. I. Eshliman and G. P. Yakunin, called attention to this in a critical letter to Patriarch Alexii in December 1965, in which, among other things, they accused the church administration of:

> obeying the unofficial oral instructions of the Council for the Affairs of the Russian Orthodox Church, which, in violation of the clearly stated Soviet law, were used as a means of systematic and destructive intervention in ecclesiastical life. Instructions by telephone, oral demands, undocumented and unofficial agreements – such is the unhealthy, mysterious atmosphere which has enveloped as in a heavy mist the relations between the Moscow Patriarchate and the Council for the Affairs of the Russian Orthodox Church.

To all this must be added a third factor involving uncertainty over whether those who break the laws affording religious bodies a degree of protection are ever brought to book and punished. There is no doubt that officials do sometimes overstep the mark, and that it is sometimes necessary for higher officials to restrain them. But there is little evidence to suggest that the offenders are brought before the courts and sentenced.

In these highly complicated circumstances, the law books are an insufficient guide to actual conditions for religious life. The only sure evidence is provided by the living experience of those who have sought to express their religious convictions in the Soviet Union in recent years. While this evidence is far from easy to come by and evaluate, enough has been accumulated of late and subjected to scholarly scrutiny to make possible the compiling of a rough listing of the various forms of extra-legal pressure applied against religious institutions and individual believers in the post-war period. This list is not exhaustive, but it has been compiled to illustrate the variety of extra-legal or illegal pressures which have been applied in recent years to Soviet citizens because of their religious beliefs. It must be emphasized, however, that the application of any or all of these pressures has not been constant in time or place; neither have all the religious bodies nor every believer suffered them.

### Concerning Denominations or Religious Confessions

1. Outlawed or denied legalization (e.g. Jehovah's Witnesses)
2. Forced to merge with another confession (e.g. Uniates)
3. Denied a centralized body (e.g. Mennonites) or deprived of one (e.g. Adventists)
4. Denied a local or national congress (e.g. Baptist reformers)

### Concerning Local Churches or Religious Societies

(N.B. – This listing is that of the priests Eshliman and Yakunin and pertains to parishes within the Russian Orthodox Church, though it has a wider relevance.)

1. Illegal registration of the clergy as a means of interference in their placement
2. Illegal campaign for the mass closing of churches and monasteries and illegal liquidation of religious societies

3.  Illegal insistence on registration of baptisms and other religious rites
4.  Illegal restriction on the freedom to conduct burial services at cemeteries and to administer communion to sick people in their homes
5.  Violation of principle of freedom of conscience by forbidding children to participate in public worship
6.  Violation of the principle of separation of Church and State through administrative interference in the financial affairs of a church congregation
7.  Illegal limitation of the number of members of a religious society to the *dvadtsatka* (the twenty) and denial in practice to the large majority of believers of their legal right to participate in managing the administrative and economic life of the Church
8.  Illegal limiting of the number of clergy and inhibiting the performance of religious rites
9.  Economic discrimination in taxation and rent against the clergy and other workers in religious organizations

*Concerning the Faithful or Individual Believers*

(N.B. – Non-believing citizens of the USSR have for various reasons suffered all the following pressures, but the listing here is based on known instances of each form of discrimination solely on the grounds of an individual's religious belief.)

1.  Discrimination at work, such as the kind of work, promotions, holidays, pensions made available
2.  Discrimination in education, such as the kind and level of education permitted
3.  Discrimination in living conditions, such as the region and residence allowed to live in
4.  Discrimination in family life, such as the removal of children from parents who persist in religious training at home
5.  Defamation of character in the media without the right of reply or redress

The number of people held in prison or in labour camps, or consigned to exile within the USSR for religious offences is impossible to ascertain and presumably varies from time to time.

In January 1981 the obviously incomplete records of Keston College, England gave details of 307 Christian prisoners, but it is often said by well-informed and experienced observers that the number of religious prisoners in the Soviet Union is in the region of 2,000. During the 1970s there was a considerable increase in the number of religious people incarcerated against their wishes in special psychiatric hospitals, even though they had no history of mental illness prior to their arrest. In some instances (though the decisions appear to be quite arbitrary) it is apparently convenient to the authorities to attribute religious fervour to mental instability, and numerous cases were reported in 1979 and 1980 of forcible administration of psychiatric drugs. Courtroom confessions of guilt and recantations have also become more common.

---

In seeking to analyse and explain the religious policies of the government of the Soviet Union during the past sixty years it is necessary to take account of several interrelated factors. There are strong political reasons for keeping religious institutions in subjection: the concept of a pluralist society occupies little or no place in the Soviet consciousness. From the earliest days, Russian society was monolithic, and today's rulers are maintaining an ancient tradition. The system required a single cultural pattern and the concentration of political, social and economic power in the hands of a central government. Neither the culture nor the organs of government can, under such a system, be challenged without threatening the stability of the entire social edifice. Nonconformity – in whatever form – is therefore tantamount to treason and must be treated as a major evil in the body politic.

This being so, every Soviet government is bound to work for the elimination of all institutions and groups which cannot be integrated in the system established during the years immediately following 1917. Religion and the institutions which support and express religious belief are now almost the only legalized bodies not dedicated to the creation of a single Soviet ideology and culture. They naturally appear as troublesome obstacles since they are deeply rooted, demand of their adherents a supernatural allegiance and simply cannot be reconciled with or absorbed by the present Soviet system. Hence the need for policies aimed at the ultimate destruction of religious institutions and of the beliefs which keep them in being.

At this point, however, successive Soviet governments have found themselves with two interrelated problems. It is one thing to destroy religious institutions; it is quite another to destroy religious beliefs. And, as Lenin clearly recognized, it is dangerous to suppress religious institutions while large numbers of believers remain, for this will only drive them to a more tenacious attachment to their convictions. The solution of such problems obviously calls for a good deal of sensitivity and more social and psychological skill than has so far been shown by the Soviet leaders. None the less, the present government appears to have settled for a long-term pragmatic policy.

The first element in this policy is the propagation of materialist ideology, or what is called 'scientific atheism', on a mass scale and by every means available to a powerful modern government – radio, television, cinema, at school, office, factory, on the farm, in the army. In what is now traditional fashion, such propagation depicts atheism as the most advanced of world-views, scientifically verifiable and humane. Religious faith, in contrast, is at best primitive and unreasoning, at worst fanatical and dogmatic. To propagate a counter-view in any public forum other than the registered religious sanctuaries is a violation of the Law and Constitution. This suggests the second major element of present Soviet religious policy, namely the containment of all religious institutions and the minimizing of the influence of religion in society as a whole. A great deal of the legislation which restricts the activities of the churches has this as its chief aim and, given the assumptions of the Soviet government, it would be unreasonable to expect much relaxation here. Closely related to the containment activity is the government's effort to prevent or discourage young people from becoming involved in the life of religious bodies. The previous investment of the churches in schools and youth work suggests an awareness of the need to nurture the Church of the future; if the recruitment and nurture of the young by the churches can be prevented it is at least possible that there may be no future. And, since negative policies often fall short of what is needed, the government has continued the effort launched by Khrushchev to provide secular substitutes for traditional religious rites and ceremonies. Communists, it seems, have discovered that most human beings need to mark the significant moments in their life with some form of ritual or celebration. The monopoly of religious institutions in this area must be broken if they are eventually to be left without any accepted role in society, and so starved of life.

Having settled upon a long-term policy which involves these elements, the Soviet government is next obliged to consider how it is to present the policy to the people, the majority of whom need to be kept reasonably happy and co-operative. In view of the persistence of religious belief, the government is hardly in a position to make an open declaration of its aims. Instead, it produces a number of different reasons to justify its persecution of individual believers and its repression of religious institutions.

One of the reasons most commonly alleged is the need to maintain the internal and external security of the country. Christians and others who are brought before the courts or punished summarily are frequently accused of anti-Soviet activities. Broad accusations of this kind offer the state authorities considerable scope. Another explanation of action against religious bodies is that their activities are having a deleterious effect on the economy of the country. It is argued that priests and ministers and other officials are parasites on the community and would be more profitably employed on the production lines. Church buildings are said to be using scarce resources in their upkeep, heating and lighting. People are absent from work on religious festivals, sometimes travelling long distances to the nearest open church. A government concerned for improving the economic position of the Soviet Union and raising the living standards of its people must husband the country's resources and discourage all forms of luxury and waste – of which religion is considered a prime example. Once again, the government pleads the national interest and seeks to escape the charge of discrimination against religious believers. The churches are also said to encourage 'reactionary' attitudes of mind and hinder the development of a truly Communist society based on science by diverting the attention of large numbers of people to mythologies which previously held the proletariat in bondage. There are, therefore, good political reasons for keeping a close watch on the churches and for restricting their influence. Again, the scope for repression is virtually unlimited and difficult to counteract.

It should not be supposed, however, that the attitude and actions of the Soviet government in respect of religion form part of a carefully worked out and coherent strategy. There is general agreement among Communist leaders that life would be easier for them, and for the country, if religion could be got out of the way. But, when this general hostility to religion is translated into specific policy decisions, certain disagreements and inconsistencies become evident. Hence the periods of intense repression, followed by periods of relaxation, which have characterized government action throughout the entire Soviet era.

Undoubtedly there is a division in government circles, and particularly in the Party, over the pace at which religion should be repressed. Hardline ideologists, or fundamentalists, plead for an all-out assault on the churches, believing that their existence should no more be tolerated than any other subversive organization. They argue for a 'quick kill'. But pragmatists in the Party point out that it is impossible to destroy religious beliefs. Better, therefore, to allow them to be expressed within institutions which can be kept under strict control and, on certain occasions, used to further the interests of the State. They see this as a positive interim arrangement for the lengthy period during which religious beliefs and institutions are fading away. There is probably a third element in the Party who consider that a 'Romanian solution' should be tried. By this they mean that the existence of religion should be accepted as a fact of life, and that the co-operation of believers and of religious bodies should be accepted – up to a point – as a factor that makes for national solidarity and social concern. So far there is no hard evidence of any group in the Party leadership holding such views.

An unexpected consequence of the government's generally pragmatic approach is its concern for church unions. When a division occurred in the Baptist Church in the 1960s the government soon recognized that its control would now have to be extended to two Baptist groups, one of which, by reason of its dissidence, would be far less amenable to state control. Steps were therefore taken to facilitate the reconciliation of the two groups, even though this involved turning a blind eye to certain government instructions which had caused the schism. In the

1970s, some dissident Baptist congregations were encouraged to register with the Council for Religious Affairs without formally acknowledging their subservience to the State. This did not of course change the intention of the authorities to bring them under state control.

The pragmatists, who have in fact been in power for almost all the Soviet era, also take into account other considerations. If, for example, they are pursuing a policy of *détente* with the West, or wish to win concessions from countries where religious freedom is highly valued, they will not mount – or at least they will be careful to mask – a campaign against religious bodies which might lead to unfavourable international publicity. Or if they are seeking to avoid division within the fifteen republics, they will lessen action against churches in Armenia, Georgia and other places where religion and nationalism are inextricably intertwined.

These appear to be the main elements that make up the present government's religious policy. How successfully can they be pursued? Much is in the government's favour, but there are complicating factors. The huge size of the Soviet Union and the concentration of power in its central government organs combine to make it virtually impossible for effective control to be maintained over every aspect of Soviet life. The government's Council for Religious Affairs has enormous power, and tries to implement the current policy of the Party; but as instructions are passed from the Kremlin to remote towns and villages there is the ever-present possibility of local officials either going beyond or neglecting the directives which apply to the churches. The inefficiency of the Soviet system, and the cynicism of many of those who are called upon to administer it, add greatly to the dimension of uncertainty and inconsistency in the State's relations with religious bodies and individual believers. In such a situation the police find it possible to assume not only considerable powers, including the opportunity to arrest, intimidate and suppress, but also control over many of the channels of communication, between local communities and the central government.

The frustrations which such a situation creates for the policy-makers may once again make the hardline approach of the dogmatists tempting, but this way also holds its problems. Even if the giant bureaucratic machine were an efficient and pliable instrument of the ruling Party, it is unlikely that a Stalinist form of totalitarian rule could again root itself in the land as a whole – or even in the religious realm alone. Neither ideological utopianism nor wholesale terror, having once been experienced, retains its paralysing force. Harbingers of a new spirit are the dissident groups now springing up within both church and secular society and finding common ground in their demands for basic human rights and for the rule of law, and for a more open society. These groups are not strong enough to provide any prospects of immediate change in the arbitrary and authoritarian order now established. But their very existence at this moment in the history of the Soviet Union may well be a pointer to future changes in the structure of Soviet society. A breach in the barrier that separates the Soviet Union from some other East European countries where there is greater religious freedom could bring those changes much nearer.

Chapter 3

# USSR
# The Russian Orthodox Church

An Anglican visitor to Russia once asked Patriarch Alexii for a definition of the Russian Orthodox Church. The answer – a church which celebrates the divine liturgy – disappointed him. No doubt he understood the remark to mean, 'A church which only celebrates the divine liturgy'. Had he emphasized *celebrates* and even more, *divine*, he would have come closer to an understanding of the Patriarch's (and the Russian Church's) attitude. For the new and enforced concentration on worship has once more revealed to Russian Christians that liturgy can act as Jacob's Ladder, can be a meeting place between heaven and earth, an area of life in which man communes with God.

Hence their willing acceptance of elaborate and (by Western standards) excessively lengthy services – services throughout which, often in crowded and under-ventilated churches, young and old alike will stand (and stand attentively and devoutly) for several hours on end. Abbreviation of the services is barely tolerated. On the contrary, as Metropolitan Nikodim once remarked, 'faithfulness to our ways of worship – in this lies our salvation'. For it is in the traditional forms that the Church's teaching is most adequately expressed and (as the Old Believers once argued also) to tamper with any aspect of tradition could mean tampering with the faith itself. In any case, however well motivated a reform might be, the simple Christians of Russia would immediately suspect it as a secular attempt to infiltrate and undermine church life.

So the old ways are cherished and retained. The argument that the new circumstances demand new forms of worship meets with little or no response. And yet the new circumstances have given the old forms a new significance and a new vitality. There can be few countries in the world where such fervour – uninhibited, yet unhysterical – may be observed and shared.

This is not to say that the services are intellectually understood. The average Russian has neither the theological nor the
linguistic training to understand Byzantine formulae in Slavonic
translation (and Slavonic remains the principal liturgical language to this day). But the latter is not the whole. And the image
(*obraz*) of God is powerfully communicated by a synthesis of
poetry, painting, drama and music which has served throughout
the centuries as the medium through which Russians were
converted and taught their faith.

It is a synthesis that makes its impact also on outsiders. For
Soviet society and its institutions can offer no comparable calm
and beauty – nor can they provide so easy and so unalloyed a
contact with the Russian past (something that attracts a certain
category of visitor).

The Church has its twelve major feasts, as well as Easter, and
a calendar replete with saints' days and red letter days. Some of
these are celebrated nationally, others are patronal feasts with
local application. Local feasts may affect a given rural area (and,
complain the state authorities, disrupt production there for
several days). Others may provide the focal point for distant
pilgrimage. The summer festivals of St Iov at Pochaev or of St
Sergii at Zagorsk, for example, will attract thousands (in the case
of Zagorsk, hundreds of thousands) of pilgrims from all parts of
the USSR.

Nor are pilgrimages limited to particular feasts or seasons. At
the relics of St Sergii, humble daily services are conducted –
largely by the pilgrims – throughout the year, from dawn to dusk.
Elsewhere, relics may not even be exposed for veneration and
yet still attract the pilgrims. Thus the Caves Monastery in Kiev
is closed and the relics of the monastery's saints are exposed for
scientific comment and ridicule. Yet there are pilgrims still, who
make the rounds and cross themselves and venerate the relics
surreptitiously. Holy springs, no less than icons, are held to
mediate divine grace. The Russian Christian is often vividly
aware that the material world was not merely the setting for the
Incarnation: it has organically participated in it.

Sacraments, *materia sacra* and sacramental actions thus
occupy an all-important place in the devotional life. Despite all
impediments baptism is sought even by families whose overt
links with the Church are tenuous; at the other end of the

life-span, the Church's participation in funeral rites (if only, sometimes, to the extent of blessing a handful of the earth intended for the grave) is widely appreciated. The impressive quantity of modern crosses in Soviet cemeteries, not to mention the occasional *lampadki*, is evidence of more than a residual faith. The same may be said of the commemorative foods that are shared by relatives at the graveside (and left also for passers-by to share). From baptism to burial, the sacramental system offers comfort and support.

At the same time, the awe which it generates has its negative aspect. Communion is a comparatively rare (albeit therefore extremely important) event in the life of most believers. Four times a year is still considered a desirable norm. Georgi Fedotov wrote of Russian people in the Middle Ages, who 'loved the Church with all the beauty and richness of its ritual and all the spiritual comfort they found in it', and in which 'so many sacred things – icons, crosses, relics, holy water, blessed bread – surrounded them and nourished them that they did not miss the sacrament which had once been the core of liturgical life but had gradually become practically inaccessible or irrelevant to them'. These strictures, only lightly modified, might still be addressed to their descendants.

Since the four penitential seasons are considered particularly appropriate for communion, and since confession is considered a necessary preliminary to it, there is excessive pressure on confessors at such times. Private confession has given way in many parishes to a mixture of public preparation, common expression of penitence and a brief moment of individual absolution, a moment at which the penitent may speak privately of particular sins that burden him. Those who feel the need for more sophisticated spiritual direction may still occasionally establish a relationship with some *starets*, though he may be far to seek.

The Lenten periods and the period of preparation for communion (*govenie*) are periods of abstinence, as are Wednesdays and Fridays of each week. Many of the faithful – the less sophisticated in particular – will keep the fasts with some rigour, fasts that require abstinence from all foods of animal origin (including eggs and dairy products), as well as from frivolity. Their faith thus has an everyday dimension; it is rooted and expressed in Lenten frugality or, at the appropriate time, in festal foods and joy.

Much less frequently does it have an intellectual dimension or expression. Partly this is because aids to thought, rather than devotion, are rarely available. Texts are difficult to obtain, whether scriptural, liturgical, devotional or apologetic – though a limited production of church *samizdat* is undertaken. At the same time, the rarity of texts increases the receptivity of readers to an extraordinary degree. The occasional, fragmentary type-script has greater impact than the idle rows of religious paperbacks on many a Western Christian's shelves.

Something similar could be said of sermons. Sermons are preached at most services. Their subject matter is based on the day's readings or commemorations: most are unambitious and largely devotional in tone, but whatever their limitations they are listened to with intense seriousness and gratitude.

Contacts between clergy and laity tend to be cordial, though irregular. There is certainly not the regular or extensive visiting of parishioners that clergy in most parts of the Western world might wish to practise. At the same time, pastoral visits are not out of the question, especially at times of need. Furthermore, some of the clergy will themselves be visited. In the larger cities some, circumspectly, convene discussion groups or take part in them. A zealous clergyman is highly prized. As one parishioner wrote to her priest:

> Your stature, pastor, is known to God; and we can only observe with wonder how he trusts you and grants you souls that are torn by prayer out of the clutches of death and hell. God can say to you, Go; and you go. And according to the fullness of your obedience there is no barrier on earth that can impede your approach to the unique lost soul that God has found for you. And when you have found it, pastor, you serve it in all its lowliness as you would serve Christ himself.

According to provincial standards, a pastor's stature is particu-larly enhanced, not only by his zeal, but also by his devout appearance, his *blagoobrazie*. A bearded, long-haired and – most important – booted cleric conforms to simple people's expec-tations and to some distant (nineteenth-century-cum-iconic) prototype. But a venerable beard is not enough by itself. A cleric's lassitude can lead to low attendance, low parish revenue, poverty-line emoluments for the clergy and, consequently, further lassitude or else withdrawal from the situation.

---

Ordination to the priesthood of the Russian Orthodox Church does not depend upon academic attainment; holiness of life and genuine vocation are considered more important. It is therefore quite common for men to be ordained without any formal theological training, and during the 1930s it was of course impossible for anyone to attend an academy or a seminary. Soon after the Church-State accommodation of 1943 the Russian Orthodox Church was given permission to reopen theological schools. Two academies, offering education at university level, were reopened, together with as many as eight seminaries. During the Khrushchev era five of the seminaries were closed, but the remainder are still open. These academies and seminaries have recently been permitted to increase their intakes of students quite substantially, thus compensating for some of the earlier closures. Four years of training is provided by the seminaries, and a further four-year course in the academies of Moscow (at Zagorsk) and Leningrad is offered to the more academically gifted students. Candidates for the seminaries must be at least eighteen years of age, but more demanding is the government requirement that they receive permission from their employer to leave their present secular job, and that they obtain the necessary health certificates and residence permits. These requirements lead to the exclusion of many suitable candidates. Even so, the number of candidates far exceeds the eight hundred or so available places, and their social backgrounds are as wide as their geographical origins. The Orthodox clergy no longer constitute a caste in which a son automatically followed his father into the priesthood.

Those who cannot be given a place in a seminary are now finding their way into the priesthood by other routes, and at the end of 1980 about 1,100 students were studying by correspondence. During the course of a visit to London in November 1980, Metropolitan Philaret of Minsk and Byelorussia reported:

In Byelorussia it has become a common practice to draw new priests from the congregations themselves. Men who have been active in parish life, and have proved their devotion and piety, are taken into training by rural deans, who subsequently recommend them as candidates for the priesthood to the bishop of their diocese. Subject to the bishop's approval, these candidates are then required to pass an examination, after which they are ordained deacon. Thereafter they are advised to enrol for a correspondence course in theology. Because the number of applicants is far in excess of the places available, a quota system is in operation and as a result only five out of the fifteen who applied from Byelorussia in 1980 were accepted. When these men reach the required standard they will be ordained as priests.

Monasticism was an outstanding feature of the Russian Orthodox Church's life before the Revolution, and in 1917 there were 1,025 monasteries and convents in Russia and the territories of her empire. Today, as a result of the work of Stalin and Khrushchev, there are six to ten monasteries and ten to fifteen convents in the entire Soviet Union. The most famous of these religious houses is the Trinity Monastery of St Sergii at Zagorsk which has about ninety monks (half of them priests) and includes the largest of the seminaries. Because of its proximity to Moscow, this monastery draws many Russian pilgrims and visitors from other parts of the world, so it is generally a hive of activity and is in a sense a privileged showplace. The largest of the women's communities is the Pokrovsky Convent at Kiev, in the Ukraine, where there are just over two hundred nuns. At one time there was a long waiting list for entry to the noviciate of this convent, which is famous for its icon-painting workshop, but during the last twenty years the authorities have allowed only a few novices to be accepted. The Pskov Monastery of the Caves is over five hundred years old and has about a hundred monks who maintain the discipline and life-style of the pre-revolutionary monasteries. The only surviving religious house to have been founded during the Communist era is the Rozhdestvensky Convent near Odessa which began as a monastery in 1924 and became a convent in 1934. Here there are about forty Russian, Ukrainian, Moldavian, Gagauz and Bulgarian nuns, the most active of whom work on a collective farm nearby. There are occasional reports of new monastic communities which figure on no list. In recent years the number of young people making pilgrimages to monasteries and convents, as well as to other holy places, has greatly increased, and there have been reports of pilgrims being harassed by the police and militia at the Pochaev Monastery, in the Ternopol region, and also at Zagorsk.

No precise figures are available for the number of Orthodox Christians who now attend church – or would do so if they were within reach of one that is open. In recent years, however, a certain amount of research has been carried out by Soviet sociologists and others, and by putting together the various pieces of evidence it is now possible to form some estimate of the scale of religious commitment in the Soviet Union. In 1976 a booklet containing the results of research by two professional sociologists said that 41 per cent of those questioned in Leningrad admitted to celebrating religious festivals in their homes, or in the homes of friends. The authors came to the conclusion that one in five of the adult population of the Soviet Union would call themselves believers. This conclusion confirmed the opinion of three specialists in 'scientific atheism' from Kiev, the results of whose research into religious practice (published in 1970) indicated that 15 to 20 per cent of the entire population were believers. A sociological study of religious belief and practice published in London in 1978, and based on Soviet material, indicated that in rural areas about 50 per cent of the children are baptized into the Russian Orthodox Church, and about the same proportion of the dead have church funerals. In the same year an article in a Moldavian newspaper complained about the ineffectiveness of atheist education and pointed out that in the village of Bachoi, of 206 babies born in 1977, 185 were baptized and most of these were the children of young graduates. It is commonly stated that one in three Russians is buried with a church ceremony, and a visitor to Leningrad in 1979 carried out some research in the Southern Cemetery of that city, discovering that of 222 graves dug between 1974 and 1979, 132 were marked with a cross, 73 had no marking, and 17 had a red star. Although the presence of a cross does not necessarily mean that the funeral was conducted by a priest, it would seem to imply religious beliefs in the deceased person or in the relatives. The late 1970s also saw a considerable increase in the number of requests from Orthodox Christians for the reopening of church buildings closed in the Khrushchev era, or earlier, and from time to time articles and letters in Soviet newspapers complain about the increasing number of young people who are wearing crosses or have icons in their homes. Taking the evidence as a whole, it seems reasonable to suppose that the number of Orthodox believers in the Soviet Union is not much less than fifty million.

Other statistics, culled from official sources and relating mainly to the past, help to illustrate the broad pattern of the Russian Orthodox Church's experience under Communism. The detailed accuracy of these figures cannot be guaranteed but, once again, they may be used as an indication of general trends.

TABLE 1

*The Russian Orthodox Church under Communism*

|  | *1914* | *1939* | *1947–57* | *1962* | *1980* |
|---|---|---|---|---|---|
| Dioceses | 73 | ? | 73 | 73 | 73 |
| Bishops in diocesan service | 163 | about 4 | 74 | 63 | 64 |
| Parish clergy | 51,105 | some 100s | about 20,000 | 14,000 | 6,000 |
| Churches | 54,174 | some 100s | about 18,000 | 11,500 | 7,500 |
| Monasteries and convents | 1,025 | nil | 67 | 32 | 16–20 |
| Monks and nuns | 94,629 | ? | about 10,000 | 5,000 | ? |
| Church academies | 4 | nil | 2 | 2 | 2 |
| Theological seminaries | 57 | nil | 8 | 5 | 3 |
| Pre-theological schools | 185 | | | | |
| Parochial schools | 37,528 | | | | |
| Hospitals | 291 | Forbidden by Law | | | |
| Homes for the aged | 1,113 | | | | |
| Parish libraries | 34,497 | | | | |

Behind these figures is the story (still largely undocumented) of a half century in which a national Christian community has lived within a militantly atheistic State. It has been a chequered experience, most of which could be characterized as cold war. The Church has known periods of relaxation or peace – in the 1940s and 1950s – but it has also encountered a dozen years of severe persecution carried out on such a scale and with such severity as the Christian community has not experienced in Europe since the third century. This Communist attack has come in five brief but bitter waves, with one of the longest as recently as the early 1960s. Here no more than an outline of the chief events and significant turning points can be attempted in an agonizing historical experience that for many believers brought a cruel martyrdom.

Immediately after the 1917 October Revolution the new State and the old Church found themselves locked in combat. Under Lenin's leadership, the Bolshevik rulers at once set out to secularize the State by placing all schools under government control and recognizing only civic marriage and divorce. As part of the move towards socialism, all land was nationalized, including that owned by the churches and monasteries. The Orthodox Church, under Tikhon (who had just been elected to the newly restored Patriarchate), responded by issuing firm instructions that all Communist attempts to seize church property should be strongly resisted. Most of the Russian church leaders, in common with many others, believed that the new government would not last long, and an anathema was pronounced against all politicians and officials who were using their position to attack the Church.

The government countered with further, tougher legislation which separated the Church from the State and the school from the Church, deprived religious organizations of the rights of juridical persons and the clergy of electoral franchise. The church leadership rallied the faithful to defence of the Church, and in the bitter struggle between those who sought to implement the new decrees and those who resisted there was violence and bloodshed. This went on for almost a whole year, but as the country became more and more caught up in the brutal civil war between Reds and Whites the conflict between Church and State tended to recede. The government lacked the machinery to implement its far-reaching decrees, and in any case could not afford to alienate the masses for whose allegiance the civil war was being waged. So orders were given to slow the implementation of the Church-State decrees and to avoid offending religious believers. In response to this amelioration, and partly out of the conviction that wholesale opposition to the new regime was helpful to neither Church nor country, Tikhon began to urge his clergy to stand aloof from the political arena.

Following their victory in the civil war in 1921, the Bolsheviks were able to turn their attention to other matters, among them the still strong loyalty to the Orthodox Church in the nation. The disastrous famine which followed the war offered the necessary pretext for discrediting and attacking the Church. To aid the distressed, the Patriarch had offered to the government many of the Church's precious possessions as security for a foreign loan. Consecrated articles were excluded from this offer on the grounds that their disposal would be contrary to the Church's canons, but congregations were asked to give cash to the equivalent of their value. The government publicly scorned the distinction between consecrated and unconsecrated articles, and sent agents to the cathedrals and parishes to seize any valuables they could lay their hands on. As a result there was a great deal of bloodshed in local churches and a large number of the clergy, including bishops, together with monks and nuns, were killed, imprisoned or deported to remote places. Icons, sacred relics and other religious objects suffered destruction or abuse and many churches were closed or converted to secular use. In 1922, as the conflict between the Church and the authorities intensified, Tikhon was arrested and imprisoned.

In the Patriarch's absence a chancery was opened to provide continuing leadership for the Church, and a number of radical church leaders – most of them associated with the so-called 'Living Church' movement – took control of this. They called a dissident council which decided to abolish the Patriarchate and declared itself ready to work with the Communist government 'for the realization of the Kingdom of God on earth'. It also proposed a number of ecclesiastical reforms, including the appointment of married bishops, liturgical changes, and the adoption of the Gregorian calendar. Popularly known as the 'Renovationist Church', this new body enjoyed the regime's backing and, for a time, attracted a good deal of support from the parish clergy. So much so that in 1923, while still in prison, Tikhon feared that the Church might fall prey to an entirely new leadership detrimental to its welfare in so critical a time: hence his decision to adopt a policy of co-operation with the government instead of the outright opposition which had characterized the years immediately following the Revolution. He was then freed from prison and in a famous statement issued on his release he said, 'Raised in a monarchical society and until my imprisonment exposed to the influence of anti-Soviet circles, I succumbed to a negative attitude towards Soviet power. I disavow definitely and clearly any connection with the counter-revolution abroad and the machinations of the monarchists and White Guardists in this country.' There seems little doubt that the government accepted Tikhon's *volte-face*, released him from prison and reduced its active aid to the Renovationists primarily because this movement was opposed by the Orthodox hierarchy and also by the overwhelming majority of the laity. The representations of Western church leaders were also influential in effecting Tikhon's release.

Tikhon followed his disavowal of opposition to the Soviet regime with another declaration along similar lines, and on the day of his death in 1925 a statement over his signature was published calling on the Church 'to permit no activity directed against the government, to nourish no hopes for the return of the monarchy, and to be convinced that the Soviet government actually is the power of the workers and peasants and that for this reason it is unshaken'. Though seemingly satisfied with Tikhon's latter-day position, the government does not appear to have had equal confidence in his likely successors, and it refused to allow the election of a new Patriarch.

Metropolitan Peter of Krutitsy succeeded to the leadership of the Orthodox Church as Patriarch-Vicar and declared his loyalty to the State, but was soon imprisoned. His responsibilities were eventually taken over by Metropolitan Sergii, who was himself arrested a few months later. Without leadership the Church found itself in a perilous position, but in the spring of 1927 Sergii was rather surprisingly released from prison and acknowledged by the government as Administrator of the Russian Orthodox Church. The explanation of this came some four months later, for on 29 July he issued an important pastoral letter in which he said that the reason for the government's mistrust of the Church was to be found in the activities of bishops who had emigrated to foreign countries and were betraying their fatherland. He added:

> We want to remain Orthodox believers and also want to recognize the Soviet Union as our earthly fatherland whose joys and successes will also be our joys and successes, and whose misfortunes will also be our misfortunes. Every blow against the Soviet Union, through war, boycott, natural catastrophe, or assassination on the streets – as recently at Warsaw – we shall consider a blow against ourselves.

This letter, and the statements made earlier by Tikhon and Peter, caused a sharp division within the Orthodox Church. There were those – to be found not least among the many bishops and priests who were still in prison for their resistance to the government – who believed that the hierarchy had 'sold out' to an atheistic State. Some of those who were still free rallied round such alternative centres of authority as Metropolitan Joseph of Leningrad, who had declared his opposition to Sergii's letter, but the government quickly went into action and, in addition to imprisoning Joseph and many of his followers, executed some of the more prominent dissenters. By this time, also, the government had further reduced its involvement with the 'Living Church' movement which had already suffered further schism and decline. It managed to survive, albeit in a very weak form, until the end of the Second World War when most of its few remaining members were received back into communion with the Moscow Patriarchate. Some of the leaders of the movement were undoubtedly trying to curry favour with the government to serve their own ends, although others were seriously concerned that the Church should not appear to be defending its position by clinging to the reactionary past, but should rather show itself ready to co-operate with any government which had the true interests of the Russian people at heart.

Thus was raised in a most dramatic form the question which in more than one age has haunted Christian people: what is the appropriate response of the Church to a hostile government? When the government concerned is as ruthless as from time to time that of the Soviet Union has been, certain questions about personal behaviour have to be tackled first. What value, for example, is to be given to the statements made by Patriarch Tikhon and Metropolitan Sergii either during or immediately following their time in prison? There is ample evidence of what the techniques of persuasion can achieve in such circumstances, and there is no doubt that in both these instances the release of the men from prison was closely related to their making of 'confessions'. Again, it is apparent that some individuals can cope with more physical and mental strain than others – for reasons not immediately related to their religious convictions – and this affects their reactions to threats and to actual punishment. How far any or all of the leaders of the Russian Orthodox Church were influenced by these considerations at this crucial moment is, of course, impossible to tell, though there was – and still is – no shortage of people who believed them to have made wrong decisions and to have allowed considerations of personal safety or destiny too much weight.

Yet, allowing the highest and best motives among the Russian church leaders, the question must still be asked: was the decision of Tikhon or Sergii to yield to the government the correct one? Had they chosen otherwise and pursued a policy of direct confrontation there seems little doubt that the Church's institutional life might have been essentially destroyed. Ruthless governments can destroy ecclesiastical institutions if they so decide, as the experience of religious bodies in Communist Albania demonstrates. Obviously the destruction of the institutional Church is not the same as the destruction of the Christian faith, and there is plenty of evidence in Christian history to show that suffering and death have a powerful capacity for edifying and strengthening the community of faith. Equally, however, there is a long Christian tradition that martyrdom must be the last choice – not the first, or even the second. And among the decisions which have to be weighed by church leaders who find themselves faced with devastating choices of this kind one of the most important concerns is their responsibility for those to whom they act as shepherds and pastors.

While the Christian community can continue in some form without the structures of an institutional Church, the fact remains that a very large number of Christians – perhaps the overwhelming majority – do require the support of a recognizable and living institution if they are to grow to maturity of faith. Pious ideas about martyrdom should not be allowed to conceal the disastrous element in the destruction of Christian institutions and individuals. From the personal point of view some at least of the Russian church leaders might well have found martyrdom the more desirable course in the 1920s – and since. Their decisions to bend to secular authority were certainly not easy ones, for they were likely to be faced not only with the continuing assaults of the State from without, but also with the accusations and scorn of those within the Church who believed them to have betrayed the Gospel. Yet the result of their anguish is now to be seen in the existence in the Soviet Union of a Church which, though shackled and handicapped in many ways, is still alive and unswervingly Orthodox.

---

The period during which Sergii was released from prison, reached some kind of agreement with the State and took over the administration of the Patriarchate proved to be only a short lull before another storm of severe persecution. A new frontal attack on the Orthodox Church, indeed on all religion, proved to be more severe than any which had gone before. No doubt the intensity was increased because the attack was an integral part of the first Five Year Plan – a dramatic and radical programme by which Stalin, who was now firmly fixed at the pinnacle of power, sought to transform at breakneck speed the whole of Russian society. The direct attack on religion lasted almost the life-span of this plan.

Of enormous significance to religious bodies, then and now, was the comprehensive legal revision adopted in 1929 under the title of the Law on Religious Associations. This was deliberately intended to tighten the State's control over religion and to facilitate its destruction. Looking back on that period, one Russian churchman who worked in the Patriarchate has written: 'We compared our position with that of chickens in a shed, from which the cook seizes victims in turn – one today and one tomorrow, but not all the chickens at once.' It seems that this particular wave of violence against the Church was closely related to the problems which the government was experiencing with the peasant population of the Soviet Union over its policy of collectivization. The Orthodox Church retained a certain amount of strength in the rural areas and, since many of the peasants continued to share in the Church's sacraments and ceremonies, it was quite easy for Communist officials to blame the bishops and priests for the reluctance of the people to submit to collectivization. The punishments meted out by the State followed the familiar pattern, and even in 1934, when religious persecution was no longer at its peak, four bishops were shot. By this date most religious communities had ceased to exist: some because they were deprived of leadership, some because their place of worship had been destroyed or boarded up, some because they were ordered to discontinue under dire physical threat.

The persecution of the Church was accompanied by a highly organized campaign to promote atheism and to destroy Russia's religious culture. The League of Militant Atheists was formed in 1925 and by 1930 had recruited three million members. Five years later there were 50,000 local groups affiliated to the League and the nominal membership had risen to five million. Children from eight to fourteen years of age were enrolled in Groups of Godless Youth, and the League of Communist Youth (*Komsomol*) took a vigorous anti-religious line. Several anti-religious museums were opened in former churches and a number of Chairs of Atheism were established in Soviet universities. Prizes were offered for the best 'Godless hymns' and for alternative versions of the Bible from which the concept of God had been removed. Anti-religious caravans were sent on missionary tours of the villages, films and radio programmes were produced to demonstrate the foolishness of religion and the wickedness of the Church, and there was an extensive publications programme of books and pamphlets. Much of this anti-religious propaganda was extremely crude – embarrassingly so for some Party intellectuals – and probably did not greatly harm the Church, though the long-term programme of indoctrinating children and young people in atheism has clearly helped to produce two generations of adults who are largely alienated from the Church and from Russia's traditional culture and piety.

One effect of the savage persecutions of the 1920s and early 1930s which was not foreseen by the Communists, but came as no surprise to Christian historians, was the beginning and rapid growth of an underground Church. The hermits and wandering monks who had been a feature of the Russian religious scene for three centuries or more became highly significant figures. They were joined by a large number of bishops and priests who had either been expelled from their posts or forced to flee for their lives. A moving contemporary report of their activities has been preserved and bears comparison with the earliest days of Christian persecution:

> When the last church building has been closed in a town, then they take their staff and go from place to place. They teach everywhere, in the villages, in the houses and in the stables, in the forests and under the open sky in the field. They look pale and miserable, and often their clothing is torn. A few crumbs of bread are their only nourishment. In their little sack they carry a Bible, their most precious belonging. They are warmly received by the people, but woe to them if they fall into the hands of the stool-pigeons of the police.

Bishops and priests were secretly ordained, acts of worship were held in the houses of the faithful, and in every Christian home the icons took on new significance, with the father of the family often assuming the traditional role of the priest. The size of the underground Church then cannot even be estimated, but it was large enough in the 1930s to call for public statements on the subject by Party leaders. Speaking at a conference of trade unions held in Moscow in April 1939, the leader of the League of Militant Atheists (Yemelian Yaroslavskii) said:

> When a priest is deprived of his congregation, that does not mean that he stops being a priest. He changes into an itinerant priest. He travels around with his primitive tools in the villages, performs religious rites, reads prayers, baptizes children. Such wandering priests are at times more dangerous than those who carry on their work at a designated place of residence.

The twentieth anniversary of the October Revolution was marked by the beginning of yet another onslaught on religion and, once again, the campaign formed part of a wider political policy. On this occasion it was the final phase of a series of mass purges which affected the whole of Soviet society during the second half of the 1930s – the so-called Great Terror of 1936–38. These were the years when Stalin purged the country of all whom he deemed to be his enemies or potential enemies. He made no distinction between Communists and non-Communists, and though no official figures are available it is widely believed that the number of people murdered ran into millions.

The Church was inevitably caught up in this reign of terror. The followers of Metropolitan Joseph, who had opposed Sergii's compromise with the State in 1927, disappeared from the Russian picture and, though it is difficult to ascertain what happened, the probabilities are that all its leaders and the majority of its members were killed. As much from human destruction as from anything else, there was another drastic inhibition of the functioning of the churches and religious communities so that, as the statistics given earlier in this chapter indicate, by 1939 the entire Russian Orthodox Church organization had been reduced to a tiny proportion of its massive strength in 1914. This was the point at which the institutional life of the Church reached its lowest ebb, and although the faithful remained loyal to Sergii it seemed to some observers that in spite of his concessions to the State the Christian community was still moving towards extinction, though perhaps at a slower pace.

---

But it is an ill wind . . . The Nazi-Soviet Pact of 1939, followed by the Soviet annexation of the Western Ukraine, Western Byelorussia, Bessarabia and Bukovina, with their numerous Orthodox parishes, gave the Moscow Patriarchate a new lease of life. Moreover, the German invasion of Russia in 1941, which devastated the country on an unprecedented scale and is still deeply burned into the Soviet consciousness, led to the further restoration of the fortunes of the Orthodox Church. The Orthodox Church for its part immediately gave spiritual and moral authority to those who were fighting for the fatherland. Military units were blessed, the Church even raised enough money to equip an armoured division for the Red Army, and priests took an active part in the propaganda war against the Nazi invaders.

Stalin, recognizing that a vast number of Soviet citizens were still believers, and that he needed to mobilize the united efforts of the entire population if the country was to survive the war, embarked on an entirely new religious policy. In 1943 Sergii and two other bishops were called to the Kremlin and received by Stalin. Feeling sure of their loyalty to the State and the willingness of the Church to support the war effort, Stalin promised them new freedom and immediately began to relax many of the oppressive restrictions. A month later the government set up a Council for the Affairs of the Orthodox Church and the Church moved into an atmosphere of freedom which many had believed to have gone for ever. In this context 'freedom' is of course a comparative term, for the Church was still hedged about with many restrictions, and the government never relaxed its overall control. Even so, a large number of churches and monasteries were reopened, bishops and priests came out of prison or hiding, relics were returned to the old shrines, anti-religious propaganda ceased, and the State even provided money and scarce material resources to assist the Church to find its feet again. All in all it was an astonishing *volte-face*, though it was easily explicable in the circumstances. It was a political move made necessary by a desperate situation, but it was also a response to deep personal need at a time of great crisis.

The war years were a time of religious revival, with crowded churches. The revival was no less marked in those areas of the Soviet Union that were occupied by the Germans. Many of those in the armed forces were said to be believers. By the end of the war the number of bishops, parish priests and local churches was not much less than half the number in service before the Communists seized power in 1917. It was an amazing revival which took less than four years to accomplish, and this in a time of great disruption.

In 1943 when the war was at its height Metropolitan Sergii was elected Patriarch of Moscow by a synod of bishops. This was a few days after his reception at the Kremlin by Stalin. The Patriarchate, which had occupied a log cabin in an unpaved street on the outskirts of Moscow, was moved to the impressive surroundings of the former German embassy. Unfortunately, Sergii was able to enjoy his new status and improved conditions for only a short time, as he died in April 1944. A Council was convened, with the assistance of the government, in the early part of 1945, and Metropolitan Alexii of Leningrad was elected as the new Patriarch. At his enthronement the Communist chairman of the Council for the Affairs of the Orthodox Church expressed the gratitude of the government for the great contribution which the Church had made to the war effort, and the new Patriarch responded by thanking the government for the assistance it had given the Church.

---

The decade immediately following the end of the Second World War continued to be a time of *détente* between the Communist State and the Orthodox Church. The government blessed, if not inspired, the forcible conversion of Ukrainian Uniates to Orthodoxy and permitted Orthodox believers to practise such religious observances as did not encroach upon the established social and political order. Needless to say, the Church remained under the close surveillance of the State, and all senior appointments and significant decisions required the approval of the government. In return for the modest degree of freedom it was experiencing, the Church found itself able to render certain services to the government, chiefly beyond the borders of the Soviet Union.

Having secured the dominant position in Eastern Europe at the end of the war, the Soviet government contrived – by a variety of methods – to secure the emergence of Communist regimes in every other East European country. In the aftermath of war it proved not too difficult for determined Communist minorities to seize power, and where the political situation was unfavourable to Communist take-overs the presence of the Soviet army was a powerful means of persuasion. Before long the Soviet Union had achieved its aim, and was supported on its western borders by a large group of satellite states. But not all the inhabitants of countries like Romania, Bulgaria and Yugoslavia were convinced Communists, and many of them were far from happy with their position, in what was, in effect, an extended Soviet empire. It was at this point that the Soviet leaders saw the Russian Orthodox Church as a useful integrating force. In those satellite countries where there was a large Orthodox community, the Moscow Patriarchate began to exercise a powerful influence. Thus at a time when church leaders in Eastern Europe were unable to move outside the 'Iron Curtain', the ecclesiastical traffic between Moscow and the Balkan capitals became significant for both Church and State.

The Russian Orthodox Church also proved to be a useful instrument of Soviet propaganda during the years of the cold war. Selected church leaders were permitted to visit Western countries where they testified to the positive features of life in the Communist world and to the religious freedom they enjoyed. Church leaders became deeply involved in the peace movement, and their presence at international conferences and assemblies guaranteed that the wickedness of Western capitalist imperialism and the evils of the American foreign policy would not be publicly ignored. Within the Soviet Union itself, the speeches of church leaders also provided backing for the government's claim that it was defending the Russian people against the Western imperialists who were striving to overthrow Soviet socialist society.

The significance of the speeches of Russian Orthodox Church leaders, both at home and abroad, is, however, difficult to assess. In situations of oppression or potential oppression, public utterances do not necessarily fully accord with private opinions. Anyone wishing to travel abroad certainly must demonstrate his loyalty to the Soviet Union. East Europeans generally understand this well and interpret speeches accordingly. What a church leader does not say is often more important than the actual content of his speech.

Even so, it seemed to many that the Russian Orthodox Church had allowed itself to become a tool of Soviet foreign policy. Yet the benefits were not all on one side. There were positive ecclesiastical gains in the Moscow Patriarchate's relations with other Orthodox churches, who would otherwise have been without experienced counsel as to how to survive under hostile and aggressive governments flushed with recently acquired power. On more than one occasion the influence of the Patriarchate secured some amelioration of conditions for a heavily pressed national church. The opportunity for travel and contact with the churches of the West also became of considerable importance for the Russian church leaders. After more than two decades of life under conditions akin to those of an isolation ward, the opening of the doors, albeit very slightly, to the influence of the wider Church, and eventually to involvement in the ecumenical movement, offered advantages which are not always appreciated by Christians who live in open societies where there is no restriction on movement and communication. The fact that they are now active in the World Council of

Churches, along with representatives of almost every Christian tradition from every part of the world, may well appear to some Russian churchmen to be a fair reward for their modest contribution to Soviet foreign policy since the war.

---

The stresses and strains implicit in so close an alignment with the policies of the State were destined to increase dramatically once Khrushchev had consolidated his position as head of the Soviet government in the late 1950s, and launched his anti-religious campaign. The onslaught of 1959–64 was fierce and more concerted than the attacks which followed the 1917 Revolution and the civil war, but it came nowhere near the savagery of the persecutions of 1928–32 and 1937–39. That Khrushchev could be so hostile to religion and the churches was not apparent during his rise to power, but it is now clear that during 1959 he devoted a good deal of his attention to a Seven Year Plan that would also seek to stamp out the 'survivals of capitalism', among them religion.

In January 1960 the Central Committee of the Communist Party called for an increase in anti-religious propaganda, and government ministers began to make accusations against the churches in their speeches. In February G. G. Karpov, who had been chairman of the Council for the Affairs of the Russian Orthodox Church since its beginning in 1943, was replaced by V. Kuroyedov, and his counterpart in the Church, Metropolitan Nikolai, was replaced by the youthful Bishop Nikodim. This was a highly significant development, for the two deposed men had worked closely together during the extended period of Church-State *détente*, and had come to symbolize the more tolerant relationship which had grown out of the wartime experience but which was now at an end.

The anti-religious campaign of the next four years consisted of two elements: a massive increase in atheistic propaganda and very severe repression of religious institutions. In the field of propaganda the schools were required to increase and improve their teaching of atheism, and the government spent large sums of money in providing new educational material for this purpose. A similar development took place in the *Komsomol* youth organization. A new attempt was made to encourage the people to abandon the Church for occasions such as baptism, marriage and burial and to make use of the secular ceremonies and settings. Wide publicity was given to such occurrences as the death of an infant – which was alleged to have been caused by the customary immersion in water at an Orthodox baptism – and then when the atmosphere was judged to be favourable a law was passed making it a crime for anyone to threaten the health of an individual through the administration of religious rites and ceremonies. It was also decreed in these years that a child could only be baptized if both parents had given written permission, which could be made available to the authorities. The State also attempted to provide secular substitutes for the traditional religious festivals, and a special propaganda campaign was directed towards women, who were believed to be the prime obstacles to the elimination of religious belief and practice. As on previous occasions, much of the propaganda was crude and ineffective, and in some instances was counter-productive since it aroused new interest in that which it was trying to defeat. The propaganda is, however, to be seen as a planned and necessary complement to the physical persecution of the Church during these same years.

The change of leadership in the Council for the Affairs of the Russian Orthodox Church coincided with a change in its function. For some years previously it had served as a liaison body between the government and the Church, but from 1960 onwards it became the instrument of stricter government control over the Church and its policies were in the main directed towards the restriction of Christian activity and the undermining of the Church's life. The Council assumed covert control over church appointments and did not hesitate to use its powers to dismiss bishops and priests, thereby weakening the Church's leadership by the removal of able pastors and the substitution of men who, in some instances, were appointed to be the eyes and ears of government agencies.

An early development in the campaign was the publication in 1961 of a decree by the Holy Synod, the effect of which was to drive a wedge between the parish priest and his local congregation by forbidding the priest to serve on the parish council, of which he now became an employee subject to dismissal. It was laid down that his activities must be confined to spiritual matters. This decree, which was forced upon the Holy Synod by the government, was accepted by a meeting of bishops which was convened at impossibly short notice and without any prior indication that this controversial proposal was to be discussed. However, in 1971 it was accepted by a Council of the Church in accordance with the wishes of the government. The effects of the implementation of the decree were – and still are – very serious. Parish councils became extremely vulnerable to penetration by outsiders – often Party members – whose sole aim was to impede the work of the priest and finally secure the closure of the local parish church. Between 1960 and 1964 there was wholesale closure of churches, sometimes by administrative fiat on the part of the government, sometimes by the initiative of corrupt parish councils. The precise number of churches closed is unknown, but it is generally believed to be in the region of ten thousand, or about half the number in use in the immediate post-war period.

The religious houses and seminaries were also severely hit. It was reported in 1964 that the number of monasteries and convents had been reduced from sixty-seven to about thirty, and that many of those that remained were on the way to liquidation. When the religious houses were closed the monks or nuns were normally directed into industry or sent home, though it is known that some continued their vocations in the outside world. Five of the eight Orthodox theological seminaries were closed and the number of students in those that remained open was heavily reduced, chiefly by calling up for military service young men who had indicated their intention of training for the priesthood and by the application of a variety of other pressures.

Within the local churches various obstacles were placed in the way of an open and developing community life. Government agents attended services of worship and reported to the authorities anything in the sermon which could be construed as subversive. Some priests were sentenced to imprisonment on trumped-up charges or even obliged to enter mental hospitals, and in a number of cases were simply dismissed and reduced to living like beggars. The records of some clergy who had been in prison during the 1930s but had been amnestied during the war were opened for re-examination so as to obtain excuses for their further persecution. At least three bishops were sent to prison, and many hold that Metropolitan Nikolai of Krutitsy, the chief counsellor of the Patriarch and president of the Council of the Church for Foreign Relations, was not only dismissed from office but died in untimely and mysterious circumstances. Lay people were also subject to considerable pressures. Believers were purged from the Party and its organizations, and frequently Christians who held responsible posts in their places of work were given the choice of renouncing their church allegiance or losing their jobs.

An integral part of the campaign was the placing of very serious restrictions on the Church's work among children and young people. After a number of public warnings about the illegality of attracting children into churches and providing them with religious instruction, it was decreed (but not openly published) that children under eighteen years of age were forbidden to attend worship, and must not take part in religious ceremonies of any kind or receive formal religious instruction. During the early 1920s it had been decreed that priests should not give religious instruction in groups of more than three, but they could give individual instruction at the request of parents, so the secret dictates of the Khrushchev regime represented a severe setback for the future of the churches. Steps were also taken to discourage and sometimes to prevent parents themselves from giving religious instruction to their own children. Though difficult to detect, a careless word to a neighbour or an innocent reply to a schoolteacher's query could prove their undoing, and there are a number of shocking cases on record of children (chiefly of sectarians and Baptists) being forcibly removed from their parents' care and taken to atheistic boarding schools. It was claimed that parents had no right to cripple a child spiritually, and that the State which granted parental rights also had the power to withdraw them.

At the beginning of the Khrushchev campaign the Orthodox bishops seemed to accept the State's new religious policy. Why the bishops should have put up so little visible resistance is far from clear. It may be that in the early stages of the campaign the bishops could not foresee all the likely consequences of the government's actions, or that the memory of the brutalities of earlier decades may have paralysed them. Or again, it may be that they adopted the classic Orthodox posture of passive compliance in the hope that at least some elements of church life and spirituality might survive the onslaught. It was in fact while the campaign was at its height that the government gave the Russian Orthodox Church permission to join the World Council of Churches. Given the Orthodox concepts of time and history it can never be out of character if immediate tactics are controlled by long-term aims calculated on a much wider time scale than is usually applied in the West.

------

Nevertheless, there are signs in the address which he gave at Bishop Nikodim's consecration in 1961 that Patriarch Alexii was fully aware of the extent to which the Orthodox Church was by then being penetrated by government agents and others who were concerned only to promote their own interests even if this meant the destruction of the Church. From 1965 onwards the voice of protest began to be heard in certain quarters. Archbishop Yermogen of Kaluga and seven other bishops went to the Moscow Patriarchate to protest against the attempted closure of churches in their dioceses and to challenge the validity of the regulations concerning parish councils which the hastily convened council of bishops had accepted in 1961. This was a courageous act in the circumstances, and Archbishop Yermogen was rewarded by dismissal from his diocese and forced retirement to a remote monastery. He died in 1978.

The action of the Patriarchate in dismissing Yermogen virtually coincided with a highly significant open letter to Patriarch Alexii from two Moscow priests – Fathers Nikolai Eshliman and Gleb Yakunin. This letter listed the main areas of persecution stimulated by the Khrushchev campaign and, after calling attention to the sufferings of the Church, pointed out that the activities of the Council for the Affairs of the Orthodox Church had in the main been contrary to the laws of the Soviet Union. They also lamented the extent to which the Patriarchate had failed to protect the Church against the government's onslaught:

> Today the bitter truth is obvious to everyone who loves Christ and his Church. It is clear that the Russian Church is seriously and dangerously ill, and that her sickness has come about entirely because the ecclesiastical authorities have shirked from fulfilling their duties . . . The Orthodox Church has always recognized the absolute right of the State to leadership

in the civil life of society, and for this reason has always instilled in her members the obligation to submit themselves, according to their conscience, to the State ... However, during the period 1957–64 the Council for the Affairs of the Russian Orthodox Church radically changed its function, becoming instead of a department of arbitration an organ of unofficial and illegal control over the Moscow Patriarchate. We stand with respect before the mystery and grandeur of the episcopal rank, we have the fear of God in our hearts, we recognize our own human unworthiness. Nevertheless, moved by the intractable demands of Christian conscience, we feel that it is our duty to say that such a situation in the Church could occur only with the connivance of the supreme ecclesiastical authorities, who have deviated from their sacred duty before Christ and the Church and have already violated the apostolic command by 'compromising with the world'.

After pointing out that certain bishops and priests were actively supporting the destructive activities of the State, the two priests said that the submission of the Patriarchate to state demands in 1961, including the separation of parish priests and parish council, was a greater assault on the life of the Russian Church than had been experienced even during the reign of Tsar Peter I. But the time had come for the process to end:

There is a growing desire in the Russian Church for purification from the disease which has been growing in her through the fault of the church authorities; there is an ever-increasing desire in the Church for true conciliar communion; and finally there is an ever-increasing feeling of responsibility for those souls who, through the fault of the pastors of the Church, have not been enlightened by the light of the Gospel and who, despite their awakened religious thirst, remain outside the frontiers of the Church ... The supreme ecclesiastical authorities are now confronted with an unavoidable choice: they must either redeem their serious guilt before the Russian Church by definite actions or else completely join the enemy camp, for 'no man can serve two masters ...'

A month later, on 15 December 1965, Eshliman and Yakunin wrote to N. V. Podgorny, Chairman of the Presidium of the Supreme Soviet. Copies of their open letter to the Patriarch were sent to all the diocesan bishops of the Russian Orthodox Church, and this prompted the Patriarch – without publicly discussing its contents – to pronounce the circulation of such open letters to be contrary to canon law. On 12 May 1966 the two priests were summoned to the Patriarchate to explain various points in the open letter and a day later Alexii announced that they were relieved of their appointments and forbidden to exercise the priesthood until they fully repented. They were also warned that if they continued their 'evil activity' it would be necessary to resort to more severe action. Reference to the treatment accorded to Eshliman and Yakunin was made by the Russian novelist and Nobel Prizewinner, Alexander Solzhenitsyn, in a 'Lenten Letter' to Patriarch Alexii's successor, Pimen, in 1972. He pointed out that seven years had passed since the two priests called attention to the 'internal enslavement' of the Russian Church, and during this time the leaders of the Church had made no attempt to refute their allegations, neither had the priests been allowed to celebrate the liturgy. Solzhenitsyn also expressed his own concern and sadness at the Church's plight:

A study of Russian history over the last few centuries convinces me that it would have followed an incomparably more humane and harmonious course if the Church had not renounced its independence and the people had listened to its voice, in the same way as in Poland, for example. Alas, for us it has long since been a different story. We have lost the radiant ethical atmosphere of Christianity in which for a millennium our morals were grounded; we have forfeited our way of life, our outlook on the world, our folklore, even the very name by which the Russian peasant was known. We are losing the last features and marks of a Christian people – can this really not be the *principal* concern of the Russian Patriarch? The Russian Church expresses its concern about any evil in distant Asia or Africa, while it never has anything at all to say about things which are wrong here at home . . . The Church is ruled dictatorially by atheists – a sight never before seen in two millennia! . . . By what reasoning is it possible to convince oneself that the planned *destruction* of the spirit and body of the Church under the guidance of atheists is the best way of *preserving* it? Preserving it for whom? Certainly not for Christ. Preserving it by what means? *By falsehood.* But after the falsehood by whose hands are the holy mysteries to be celebrated?

Once again, the Patriarchate remained silent, but a Russian priest, Sergii Zheludkov, offered a personal reply to Solzhenitsyn in which he accused him of betraying his own moral principles by directing a charge towards 'a man who finds himself unable to reply to you'. Father Zheludkov went on to defend the policy of the Orthodox bishops:

> There exists a system of government, strictly monolithic, at the heart of which there subsists, quite extraordinarily, a body which is a stranger to it: the Russian Church. She maintains herself under conditions which are rigorously determined . . . One thing alone is conceded to us: religious services in the churches. And yet one knows that this is a concession made to a generation which is disappearing. What can we do in such a situation? Say: all or nothing? Attempt to go underground, something unthinkable under a regime of this kind? Or again, subscribe in some way to the system and exploit the possibilities which are still permitted? The Russian hierarchy has chosen this second solution. From this, today flows all the evil which with justice you have described and also all the evil which you have left unmentioned. But it has no other choice . . . never has one seen human conditions as peculiar as ours.

---

It is apparent from the events of the 1960s that the quality of the Orthodox hierarchy was uneven, and so it remained throughout the 1970s. Among the bishops there were, and are, men who could well be described as saints. One of them, Archbishop Methodius of Omsk, in Western Siberia, is widely believed to have been murdered as recently as 1974. Others yielded so far that their motives can only be regarded as suspect. Most were men struggling to make the best of what was, and remains, a near-impossible situation. In the West, the best-known of the Russian church leaders for more than a decade was Metropolitan Nikodim of Leningrad, who was head of the Foreign Department of the Moscow Patriarchate until 1972 and one of the outstanding figures in the Orthodox world until his death, after a long period of failing health, in 1978.

Nikodim was born in 1929, and although his father was a

Communist and his mother an atheist, he was drawn to the Church at an early age. When he was fifteen he came under the influence of Bishop Dmitri of Ryazan and it was decided, against strong family pressure, that he should become a monk. Three years later he received the tonsure. Although his theological education was somewhat modest – he graduated from the Leningrad Theological Academy as a correspondence course student – his outstanding talent was quickly recognized and his rise to a position of authority in the Orthodox Church was meteoric. After becoming a monk in 1947, he served as a secretary to Bishop Dmitri, who had by this time become Archbishop of Yaroslavl, but soon Nikodim was transferred to the Patriarchate in Moscow. At the age of twenty-eight he was sent to Jerusalem as an archimandrite and as head of the Russian Orthodox mission. After two years he returned to Moscow to become head of the Patriarchate office. In the following year he was made Bishop of Podolsk and head of the Foreign Department of the Patriarchate. A year later he succeeded his old patron, Bishop Dmitri, as Archbishop of Yaroslavl, and in 1963 – when he was still only thirty-four – he became Metropolitan of Minsk. Only two more years were to pass before he was elevated to one of the great Orthodox sees: Leningrad and Ladoga. All his bishoprics were held in conjunction with the leadership of the Foreign Department, and for almost twenty years he also exerted very considerable influence within the internal life of the Russian Orthodox Church, so much so that it was sometimes asserted that no bishop could be appointed or any piece of church legislation accepted without Nikodim's approval. He travelled widely and was deeply involved in the work of the World Council of Churches where he exercised considerable influence, being elected to the Presidium in 1975.

The manner of Nikodim's death in 1978 was dramatic. After the Second Vatican Council he enjoyed a most cordial relationship with the Roman Catholic Church, and it was on his initiative that the Russian Church shocked the Orthodox world in 1969 by issuing unilaterally an encyclical allowing Roman Catholics to receive Absolution and Holy Communion from Orthodox priests. It was natural, therefore, that he should have represented his church at the funeral of Pope Paul VI and remained in Rome to greet his friend's successor. And it was during an audience with Pope John Paul I, himself to die within a month, that Nikodim died of a heart attack. He was an enigmatic figure. There are some Russian Christians who believe that he never managed to break out of the Stalinist atmosphere in which he was brought up, and that in the end his close, albeit careful, collaboration with the government alienated him from a new generation of intellectuals and students who believe that the Church, rather than the government, is the more authentic organ of national life and ought never to be subordinated to Russia's present rulers. How far Nikodim managed to achieve complete integration of his roles as a servant of God and as a servant of Caesar is impossible to tell, and any attempt to understand him outside the Byzantine tradition of 'harmony' between Church and State is bound to be misleading. But the Russian Orthodox Church is stronger today than it was when Nikodim became a bishop and no one who knew him ever doubted the depth of his spirituality or the immense difficulty of his position as a church leader.

Of the present leadership of the Russian Orthodox Church it has to be acknowledged that the government would not have permitted the election of Patriarch Pimen had he been renowned for his outspoken views and opposition to current state policies. In contrast to the late Metropolitan Nikodim, Pimen is a quiet and somewhat introverted character, lacking in sparkle. In public he is a strong supporter of the government and told a West German newspaper correspondent in 1978 that Orthodox Christians, in their social and labour activities, were keeping to the ideals declared sixty years earlier when Soviet power was established. On the occasion of his seventieth birthday, in June 1980, he was awarded the government's Order of Friendship of the Peoples.

Like many of his contemporaries, Pimen had no formal theological education, since all the seminaries were closed when he was a young man. He first appeared on the church scene as a singer, and then as a choirmaster, and he continued his work as a musician after his profession as a monk in 1927 and his ordination to the priesthood in 1932. Soon after his ordination, however, Pimen was conscripted for army service for two or three years, and on his discharge from the army was evidently in trouble with the authorities for he was arrested in either 1935 or 1936 and obliged to work on the Moscow River Volga canal until 1938. What happened to him then is not clear but he was back in the wartime army in 1941 and reached the rank of major. Towards the end of the war, however, he was charged with desertion and sentenced to ten years' imprisonment. He served one year of this sentence before being amnestied in 1946. From then onwards his career was uninterrupted. In 1949 he was put in charge of the ancient Pskov Monastery of the Caves, and in 1954 became Abbot of the monastery at Zagorsk. In both places a great deal of restoration work on the fabric was required, owing to war damage, misuse and general neglect. Pimen was conse-crated Assistant Bishop of Balta in 1957, and at the beginning of the Khrushchev persecutions was moved to an unenviable post as Chancellor to the Moscow Patriarchate, where he remained until his appointment as Metropolitan of Leningrad in 1961. Two years later he was back in Moscow as Metropolitan of Krutitsy and Kolomna, and in 1971 he was elected Patriarch of Moscow and All Russia.

Pimen is very conscious of his lack of formal training, and is said to be a good example of someone who has received his theological education through the Church's liturgy. When he became Metropolitan of Leningrad he told the priests and people of the diocese, 'Coming on to you, my new flock, I have brought no brilliant gifts of intellect, nor splendour of thought, nor oratory, nor beautiful preaching: I have brought you only one thing as a gift, something most precious and necessary. I have brought you God's peace . . . I hope you will help me with your prayers.' This was typical of Pimen's humility. In church affairs he is essentially a traditionalist, and sees the maintenance of the Church's ancient forms as the strongest bastion against the assaults of a hostile State. He is sometimes criticized for his conservatism and unwillingness to confront the government, but his policy has not yet been proved wrong.

---

Criticism of the policies of the Soviet Union's present rulers is by no means confined to those who live in the safety of the West, and the 1970s saw the emergence within the Soviet Union itself of a number of dissident movements, some of which had a religious base and a specifically religious concern. Earlier, in 1964, a clandestine All-Russian Social-Christian Union for the

Liberation of the People had been founded in Leningrad, and although it was doomed to failure this movement can now be seen as a first attempt to respond to the sense of dissatisfaction with Soviet life felt by many Russian people after the fall of Khrushchev. Igor Ogurtsov and three other intellectuals who founded the All-Russian Union were committed to Neo-slavophilism, an approach to life which sees Russia as having a distinctive destiny, of which Orthodoxy is an essential element. The Union was also apparently committed to overthrowing the Communist government of the Soviet Union by means of a coup d'état and by 1967 had recruited twenty-four other like-minded members, together with thirty candidates for membership. But the movement was betrayed to the KGB by one of its members, and during 1967 there were two trials at which more than twenty of the Neo-slavophils were found guilty of treason and given long prison sentences. Igor Ogurtsov was still in confinement in 1981 and said to be broken in health.

This unrealistic attempt to overthrow the Soviet government having failed, another Christian intellectual, Vladimir Osipov, who had been converted during a period of imprisonment in the early 1960s, tried to float the idea of a 'loyal opposition' to the government. The main forum for this idea was a journal, *Veche*, which although self-published was circulated openly. Its articles were concerned with religious and moral issues, rather than political ones, for Osipov believed that Russia needed a moral and spiritual regeneration before it could advance politically. Even so, after nine issues of *Veche* had appeared between 1971 and 1974, Osipov was arrested, charged with 'anti-Soviet agitation and propaganda' and sentenced to eight years in a strict regime camp. His naïve attempt to question aspects of government policy while remaining within the letter of the law had been quite unsuccessful, though it had demonstrated once again the paranoia of the Soviet leaders and the hypocrisy of their claims concerning freedom of speech and of the press.

Meanwhile a group of young Orthodox Christians had begun to hold informal meetings on religious and philosophical issues in Moscow. Led by Alexander Ogorodnikov, who had been educated at Moscow State University and the Urals University, and was then in his mid-twenties, the members of the group said that attendance at the Sunday Liturgy provided them with neither the Christian education nor the Christian fellowship they needed. They also wished to meet with non-Orthodox Christians and to have serious discussions with atheists. Regular meetings were held in the homes of members, sometimes with visiting speakers, and in 1978 the group started to call itself 'The Christian Seminar on Problems of Religious Renaissance' – a reflection of the increasing number of young people joining the Orthodox Church. Already the Seminar had attracted the attention of the KGB and from 1976 onwards its members were subjected to harassment and sometimes to physical assault. A *samizdat* journal *Obschina* (Community) appeared in 1978, but the first issue was confiscated by the police and the second seems to have been the last. Ogorodnikov was arrested in November 1978 and his closest colleague, Vladimir Poresh, in August 1979. The best-known member of the Seminar, Lev Regelson, who had joined Father Gleb Yakunin in appealing to the World Council of Churches' Nairobi Assembly in 1975, and is the author of an important book, *The Tragedy of the Russian Church 1917–45,* was taken into custody in December 1979. Altogether nine members of the Christian Seminar were arrested between the end of 1978 and the early part of 1980, although informal discussion groups are not actually forbidden by Soviet law. Those arrested were all charged with other crimes and after serving a one-year prison sentence for 'parasitism' Ogorodnikov was sentenced to six years in a strict regime camp to be followed by five years of internal exile for 'anti-Soviet agitation and propaganda'. Regelson was eventually given a five-year suspended sentence after confessing his guilt to the court and repenting of his actions – a turn of events which caused considerable surprise to his friends. Five other members of the Seminar have been committed to psychiatric hospitals, though none has any previous record of mental illness. The size of the Christian Seminar's membership is unknown but, in spite of continuing KGB pressure, it continues to meet and has members in Leningrad and Smolensk, besides the main group who live in Moscow. Another group founded by, but not confined to, Orthodox Christians is the '37' group which meets in Leningrad and consists of writers, poets, artists and other creative people who are concerned with the spiritual dimension of culture.

Working parallel to, though not connected with, the Christian

Seminar is the Christian Committee for the Defence of Believers' Rights in the USSR, which came into being at the end
of 1976 in the wake of the Helsinki Declaration on Human
Rights. Founded by Father Gleb Yakunin, Hierodeacon Varson-
ofi Khaibulin, and a layman, Viktor Kapitanchuk, the Committee is basically Orthodox in its composition, but it has the
support of friends in other churches and is equally concerned for
the rights of non-Orthodox believers. At the launching of the
Committee, which took place at an unofficial press conference,
it was pointed out that although the Soviet Constitution provides
for freedom of individual conscience there is inevitably a
conflict between religious believers and a government committed to atheism and the building of an atheistic state. The
Committee insisted that its sole aim was to uphold the
constitutional rights of Soviet citizens and to work within Soviet
law. To this end it proposed action in five areas:

1.  To collect, study and distribute information on the
    situation of religious believers in the USSR.
2.  To give legal advice to believers when their civil rights are
    infringed.
3.  To appeal to state institutions concerning the defence of
    believers' rights.
4.  To conduct research, as far as this is possible, to clarify
    the legal and factual position of religion in the USSR.
5.  To assist in putting Soviet legislation on religion into
    practice.

A declaration which preceded this action programme said, 'At
present, the bishops of the Russian Orthodox Church and the
leaders of other religious organizations do not concern themselves with the defence of believers' rights, for a variety of
reasons. In such circumstances, the Christian community has to
make the legal defence of believers its own concern.'

During the first three years of its life the Committee was
extremely active in sending information to the West about the
problems facing believers in the USSR, and by mid-1980 over
four hundred documents had reached various centres in Western
Europe and North America. Some of these documents gave facts
about the general position of the churches, while others called
attention to specific problems and disabilities. In April 1978 the
Committee wrote to the Ecumenical Patriarch in Con-

stantinople, appealing to him to come to the aid of the Russian Orthodox Church, since the Russian bishops were not fulfilling their responsibility towards oppressed believers. Later in 1978 three letters were sent to the Pope and other Christian leaders calling attention to the position of the Russian Orthodox Church and also urging the adoption of an international 'Pact on religious rights'. A detailed report by Father Yakunin on the state of the Russian Orthodox Church in 1979 expressed the view that the Moscow Patriarchate was unable to respond to the religious renaissance now taking place in Russia, especially among young people, and went on to suggest that the Orthodox Church should follow the example of Protestants and Catholics who had established unregistered communities free from state domination. Another document consisted of an appeal, signed jointly by the Christian Committee and the Christian Seminar, asking Christians in other parts of the world to send Christian literature to the Soviet Union.

To what extent the Christian Committee has been able to assist individual believers in the Soviet Union is unknown but, in spite of its avowed non-political aims, it was inevitable that the Committee should fall foul of the state authorities. After a number of warnings from the KGB, the two founder members, Father Gleb Yakunin and Viktor Kapitanchuk, were arrested at the end of 1979 and early 1980 respectively. (Hierodeacon Khaibulin had left the Committee some time earlier by mutual agreement.) Father Yakunin was tried in August 1980, found guilty of 'anti-Soviet agitation and propaganda', and sentenced to five years' imprisonment, to be followed by five years of internal exile. Viktor Kapitanchuk, like Regelson of the Christian Seminar, 'repented of his anti-Soviet activities and renounced further such activities' and escaped with a five-year suspended sentence. Long before their arrests the two men had arranged that in the event of their being removed from the active scene their places on the Christian Committee would be taken by others. So the work continues under the direction of three known and ten unknown members of the Committee. Over two hundred and fifty other Russian Christians have applied to join the Committee or offered to help.

---

Father Gleb Yakunin is one of the most courageous priests of the

Russian Orthodox Church to have emerged in the post-war era. Born in 1934, and now married with three children, he had been ordained only three years when, in company with Father Nikolai Eshliman, he addressed the now famous open letter to Patriarch Alexii, complaining of the hierarchy's subservience to the government. This led to the suspension of the two priests from any official ministry, and Father Yakunin has not exercised his priestly office since 1966. He found employment in a number of menial jobs and was for a time a night-watchman in a Moscow church. Not much was heard of him until 1975 when he and Lev Regelson wrote to the Fifth Assembly of the World Council of Churches describing the pressures on religious believers in the Soviet Union and asking for support from Christians in other parts of the world. For the next four years, and under the constant threat of arrest, Yakunin worked tirelessly to explain to the world Church what is happening to those of its members who live in the USSR. It was obviously important to the Soviet government that he should be silenced for a long time. His final words to the court were, 'I thank God for this test that he has sent me. I consider it a great honour and, as a Christian, accept it gladly.'

A close friend of Father Yakunin is Father Dimitri Dudko who was born into a peasant family in 1922 and served in the Russian army towards the end of the Second World War. On demobilization he entered a theological seminary but was arrested in 1948 for, allegedly, publishing a poem lamenting the destruction of holy places in Russia. Eight and a half years later he was released and on completion of his training was ordained to the priesthood in 1960. After a time he was made a parish priest at St Nicholas Church in Moscow and during the early 1970s became very well known for his striking and fearless sermons in which he often criticized the atheist programme and Communist world outlook. In July 1972 Father Dudko was officially warned about the content of his sermons and, following pressure by the authorities to have him dismissed, he appealed to his parishioners for support. Towards the end of 1973 he began a series of question-and-answer sessions after Saturday Vespers, and these attracted very large audiences, including many young people. After nine of these sessions, Patriarch Pimen ordered them to be stopped and a few months later, in September 1974, Father

Dudko was transferred to a village parish about fifty miles from Moscow. Once again congregations increased – people travelled from Moscow to hear the sermons – and after fifteen months Father Dudko was dismissed, even though his parishioners signed numerous appeals supporting him. Early in 1976 he was appointed second priest in the village of Grebnevo, just over twenty miles from Moscow, but he soon came under pressure again and was warned about his sermons by Metropolitan Yuvenaly. Throughout 1979 he was subjected to harassment by the police, and on 15 January 1980 he was arrested by the KGB after conducting worship in the village church. Before leaving he blessed the congregation, asked them to pray for him and to remain united. After spending five months in prison, Father Dudko unexpectedly appeared on television where he read a statement admitting to 'systematic fabrication and dissemination abroad of anti-Soviet materials'. It was noticed that he read this serious statement quite happily and without any hesitation, and on the following day he was allowed to go home. Three weeks later the news bulletin of the Moscow Patriarchate published a letter to Patriarch Pimen which Father Dudko had written a fortnight before his televised 'confession'. In this letter he said, 'Forgive me for all my folly, all my insults, for the sorrow I have caused you as well as my spiritual children and all believers – not to mention the shame I have brought on my Fatherland because of my selfish ambition, of which I myself am now ashamed.'

This letter and the television appearance surprised Father Dudko's many friends and admirers every bit as much as did the recantation of the much respected Lev Regelson a few months later. They commented on his strained appearance after his release and read with considerable interest a letter which he had sent to a friend in the West shortly before his arrest:

It seems that 1980 will be a very difficult year for all of us. Some have already been seized. I have been summoned to interrogation as a witness, and maybe yet as an accused . . . If anything happens to me, let this letter be my message from behind prison walls. At present there is a wave of transfers of priests in Moscow churches. Some congregations are shocked and horrified by the kinds of priests arriving to take up duties in their churches. It is quite clear now why the authorities put away Father Gleb Yakunin – they want to silence dissenting voices as far as possible. Their aim is to stifle any remaining dissident forces in the Church and they do this – grievous as it may be to say so – by the hands of the church leadership . . . Sound the alarm! Silence and compromise are not tactical steps, they are betrayal. This is now being understood by many who have some love for the Church, but who have been unable to understand in the past. May God be with you!

The sentiments expressed in this letter and the courageous witness of an increasing number of Orthodox priests and laity are attracting into Orthodoxy, though not necessarily in its established form, enough young people to enable well-informed observers to speak of a religious renaissance in Russia. How quickly this renaissance will develop in the remaining years of the twentieth century, and what effect it will have upon the ancient Russian Orthodox Church and upon Soviet society, is impossible to tell. One thing seems clear: the government is in no mood to relax its grip on the Church, and those Orthodox Christians who choose the path of valour in preference to that of discretion will, for some time to come, pay a heavy price for their choice. The Church as an institution is unable to pay this price, having already suffered within the last half century to the edge of extinction. But its witness continues and its condition resembles that of the Rublev icon of Christ, found in the autumn of 1918 under a pile of firewood, ready for destruction. Four-fifths of its paintwork has vanished. Yet the steadfast features of a humble Saviour remain. His gaze ignores the barren wood around, renders it insignificant and, simultaneously, provides it with new dignity.

# Chapter 4

# USSR
# Churches and Religions
# other than Orthodox

Among the industrial countries of the world, only the United
States can rival the Soviet Union in the number and variety of
religious groups. The communities discussed in this chapter
represent only the main ones. The way in which they are
classified is somewhat arbitrary since, as will be seen, clear
demarcation is often impossible. This in itself is a commentary
on religious conditions in the USSR.

OLD BELIEVERS
One of the oldest religious groups in the Soviet Union is the Old
Believer community. It is also the most intriguing, though more
is known of its history than of its present life. At the beginning
of the seventeenth century Russia was faced with a double
threat. The long and despotic reign of Ivan the Terrible (1533–84)
had torn and weakened the country. When his successor died
without issue a dynastic crisis arose which further promoted a
mounting social and economic crisis marked by massive peasant
rebellions. Thus enfeebled, the country was vulnerable to the
aggression of its neighbours, and for a time Moscow was in the
hands of an invading Polish army. There was good reason to call
this the Time of Troubles.

As the nation emerged from this period and sought to renew
its life, there were some in the Russian Orthodox Church who
believed the time had come for ecclesiastical renewal. Among
them was the Patriarch Nikon who – among other things –
embarked upon certain liturgical changes. To the twentieth-century Western mind, Nikon's proposals appear to have been
exceedingly modest, but for many Russians at the time they
created a major problem. For one thing, any interference with
the Orthodox liturgy was to be regarded with suspicion since it
touched the heart of the Church's life and faith. For another,

Nikon had sought the assistance of the Greek Orthodox Church in the matter, which implied foreign influence at work, and this from a church which the Russians regarded as apostate. Together they represented a root-and-branch threat to the sacredness of the Russian realm, long expressed in the popular parlance as 'Moscow – the Third Rome' and, more recently, 'Holy Russia'. Immediately there were protests and resistance to the changes. But with the help of the State Nikon forced his proposals upon the Church, and in the end this led to the Great Russian Schism of 1666.

The best-known among the leaders of the schism was an archpriest named Avvakum, whose regularly republished auto-biography – now a classic of Russian literature – gives a vivid account of his beliefs and sufferings. He was a man of great piety, and when he was executed in 1682 the Old Believers – as the schismatics came to call themselves – regarded him as a martyr and a saint. The day of his death – 14 April – is now a saint's day in the Old Believers' calendar. The fact that Nikon's reforms had the backing of the State meant that all opponents of them were breaking the law of the land, and for much of the next century the Old Believers were the victims of severe persecution. Moreover, they were quickly faced with a division in their own ranks over the place and future of the ordained ministry. In the absence of any bishops to ordain new priests, one group (the priestless) came to the conclusion that the church of the future was called to dispense with the ministry and all the sacraments, apart from baptism which can be administered by lay people. The other group (the priested) decided to retain the traditional elements of the church's life, relying on a supply of rebel or dismissed priests from the continuing Orthodox Church until such time as they could persuade a bishop to join them. Subsequently these two groups split into a large number of smaller bodies, so the Old Believers do not form a single, united body but now consist of a multitude of groups, all of which trace their ancestry back to the schism of 1666 and all of which belong to the traditions either of the priestless or the priested. A movement to reintegrate the Old Believers into the Orthodox Church, by permitting the once-forbidden old ritual in selected parishes, has met with scant success since it was initiated at the end of the eighteenth century, though at least one parish of this kind still exists in Moscow.

In the nineteenth century the Old Believers experienced persecution but not uniformly, since some of the Tsars were relatively tolerant. After the 1905 Edict of Toleration they had a good deal of freedom. Great uncertainty has always surrounded their numerical strength, partly because they are so fragmented, partly because they have for much of their history been driven to a clandestine existence, and partly because the various calculators have often had reason to exaggerate or diminish the number. At the official census of 1897 there were said to be about two and a quarter million Old Believers, constituting 1.8 per cent of the entire population of the Russian Empire, but scholars believe the true figure was closer to fifteen million. In 1917 there was talk of twenty million. Recent estimates of Soviet scholars have acknowledged the existence of at least one million Old Believers in 1973, but no one really knows, nor does there seem to be any satisfactory way of finding out.

During the Soviet era the Old Believers appear to have been treated generally in the same chequered fashion as the bulk of non-Orthodox religious bodies. In the 1920s they were allowed a measure of freedom, possibly because their long years of conflict with Tsarism led some Communists to believe that they were 'of the people' and less committed to the old political order. Most Old Believers, it seems, had no particular criticisms to make of Communism *per se*, virtually all the State's activities since 1666 were equally under the sign of the anti-Christ. Further centuries of persecution had not only scattered many of them to the remoter parts of the Russian Empire but also taught them to live quietly and unobtrusively. As recently as the 1950s two monasteries and four convents of Old Believers were discovered – for the first time in the present century – in the forests of Siberia. In the 1930s they suffered in company with members of other religious bodies, but they shared in the reliefs afforded by Stalin's wartime concordat. At the end of the war the number of Old Believers in the Soviet Union increased considerably with the annexation of the Baltic States, where from the beginning many of them had found refuge from Tsarist oppression. Under Khrushchev they were, in company with other religious bodies, persecuted once again. The most recent reports suggest that some of their number are still subject to harassment, though the full extent of this is not known.

Of the many Old Believer groups in the Soviet Union today, easily the largest is the Church of the Byelo-Krinitsa Concord, which some scholars believe to be larger than all the others put together. In 1846 this church managed to establish a hierarchy when a deposed Orthodox metropolitan joined them, and in the mid-1920s it had as many as twenty-one bishops. At the present time it is recognized by the State as a religious body, and has about three hundred parishes in five dioceses. Its present archbishop was enthroned in 1979. The main cathedral is in the Rogozhsky Cemetery in Moscow, and this building, which accommodates ten thousand people, is said to be often full. Like many Old Believer churches, it houses a magnificent collection of ancient icons and also has a fine array of old vestments.

Also in Moscow is the centre of the Old Believers of the Transfiguration, one of the main groups of priestless Old Believers. How strange their life seems to the outsider, and how jealous they are of their separation, may be seen in a description of a visit to the Moscow centre in 1968 by Professor P. Hendrix, of the University of Leiden, who wrote in the American magazine *Diakonia*:

The worshippers at divine service were very aloof, despite my rapport with their elder. At an evening service a nun asked me if I ought not to be in an Orthodox church. I replied that I was a curious stranger who wanted to attend services with the group and get a glimpse of their life. 'The last you can do, but not the first', she replied severely. I could sit in the corner and watch, but I was not to make the sign of the cross or sing – and, most important of all, I was not to pray. I tried to point out that a fellow baptized Christian was welcome to pray with the Orthodox in their churches. This clearly annoyed her: 'Yes, that *is* the Nikonian way', she retorted. '*Here* it is different.'

From my solitary corner I watched the congregation. They were all elderly people. The men were bearded and their clothing seemed to be from another era. The women were veiled; some wore black and seemed to be nuns of a sort, others had white veils and made up the two choir groups which sang antiphonally. The walls were completely covered with icons. At the eastern end of the church, in front of a wall hung with lamps, stood a small table wrapped in brocade. On the table lay a large Gospel, over which towered an enormous cross decorated with paper flowers. The service began when several men in long black robes stepped forward to the sound of a high, shrill female voice intoning, 'Heavenly King, Comforter, Spirit of Truth...' The liturgy – in comparison with that of the Orthodox – has been considerably augmented; also, everything is much slower and throughout is character-ized by an indescribably melancholy undertone. As it became darker outside and more and more candles were lighted, the flickering light from the icon corner cast an eerie glow over the wide-eyed icons and the robed figures. The sight of the congregation bowing their heads to the floor time and time again and the buzz of their private prayers was somehow reminiscent of a mosque.

It has to be remembered, of course, that what seems strange to the outsider can be replete with meaning for the insider and, as might be expected, the customs of Old Believer groups vary enormously. Some are quiet, old-fashioned people. Some insist on celibacy. Others will not give their names to the state authorities. Instances have been reported of an Old Believer smashing a cup or plate which has been used by someone of another faith, to ensure that there is no contaminating contact with him. On the other hand, some groups are beginning to make cautious contact with the Orthodox. Common ground occupied by all Old Believers is rejection of the secular present in favour of the now distant, and ever-receding, sacred past. Whether a religious faith of this kind can survive in a country which becomes increasingly modernized and secularized is far from clear. But the Old Believers have for three centuries shown remarkable tenacity. The once widespread feeling that they, and they alone, represent the authentic Russia is still alive and exerts a fascination which is not simply romantic or antiquarian. Nor is their membership entirely elderly – in 1960 a young student was dismissed from Moscow State University for serving as an acolyte in the Old Believer cathedral.

THE SECTS

There is some evidence of sectarianism in medieval Russia, but the growth and spread of sects has taken place chiefly since the seventeenth-century schism of the Old Believers, and may be seen as one of the consequences of Russia's emergence from its medieval past and its gradual integration in the main stream of European history. After the emancipation of the serfs in 1861, the move towards sectarianism quickened. Official efforts to maintain the centralized control of Church and State, which left little room for spontaneity or individualism, furthered the process and gave to sectarianism the character of a protest movement. That the sects have continued during the Soviet era, and some new ones been formed, again points to the fact that repressive authoritarian regimes provide good breeding and nurturing ground for this often eccentric religious phenomenon.

The many sects now to be found in the Soviet Union can be divided into three groups – traditional, foreign and Soviet – and each group illustrates a different origin. It is possible here to discuss only key illustrations of each type.

*Traditional Russian Sects*

Two representatives of traditional Russian sects are the Dukhobors and the Molokans. The Dukhobors originated in about 1750. Their name means 'Those who fight for the Spirit', and in order to pursue the battle unhindered they have rejected the Church and much of the Bible. They believe in the pre-existence and transmigration of souls, and have taken from Orthodoxy the cult of the saints and of the Mother of God. They are committed to social work and, in theory at least, to pacifism and sharing of possessions. During the early part of the nineteenth century the Dukhobors were allowed to settle on the banks of the Molochnaya river, but when they refused to accept military service and various other laws in 1837 they were deported to Transcaucasia. This eventually provoked a large proportion of them to emigrate to Canada and other parts of the world, where they have sometimes caused problems even for tolerant democratic governments. Those who remained in Russia when the Communists came to power were mainly in villages on the Soviet-Turkish border, and the government found them somewhat difficult to handle since they did not read newspapers or official communications and refused to take part in any educational or cultural activity. During the 1930s they suffered severe persecution and most of their leaders were in prison or labour camps. Today the Dukhobors are few in number and live in isolated villages; the government appears to be making no serious effort to interfere with them.

The Molokans developed out of the Dukhobors in 1765, and at the beginning of the twentieth century they had well over a million adherents in Russia. Their name means 'Milk drinkers', and was given to them because at one time they drank milk during the Lenten fast, but they prefer to be known as 'Spiritual Christians'. Like the Dukhobors, they reject the Church and the sacraments and favour pacifism, but they have a fundamentalist approach to the Bible and will only use scriptural prayers. Soon after the Communist regime was established they tried to set up an All-Russian Union of Molokans, but this lasted only a few years and the 1930s were a time of serious decline. During and immediately after the Second World War nothing was heard of the Molokans, but at a church peace conference held in Zagorsk in 1952 there were two Molokan representatives who reported that there were tens of thousands of Molokans in Transcaucasia, as well as some in Asia. They are, it seems, gathered in small village communities which have managed to retain their own simple way of life in spite of the threats and distractions of the twentieth century. They do not appear to be seriously harassed, and in recent years their decline has been mainly due to secularization and the movement of adherents to the mainstream evangelical churches. Some of the strongest Baptist churches have been built on the Molokan tradition, and the present President and many members of the All-Union Council of Evangelical Christians-Baptists have Molokan family backgrounds.

## Sects of Foreign Origin

In Russian terminology, religious communities made up mostly of ethnic Russians that are neither Orthodox nor Old Believers are called sects. Hence the Seventh Day Adventists and the Jehovah's Witnesses, though originating abroad, are considered to be sectarian bodies in Russia.

The Seventh Day Adventists arrived in 1883 with Philipp Reiswig, a German who normally lived in Russia and became an Adventist while visiting the United States. Early missionary work was confined to the German settlers in the Crimea and spread to Siberia when their leaders were deported by the Tsars. By the early part of the twentieth century they had attracted some Russian adherents, though in 1911 their total strength was no more than four thousand. During the decade following the Revolution they took advantage of the relative freedom enjoyed by most of the sects and in 1928 there were just over thirteen thousand Adventists in six hundred congregations. Growth was accompanied, however, by a serious disagreement over collaboration with the State, and also over military service and Sabbath observance. This led to schism resulting in the formation of a reformist group of 'True and Free Adventists', sometimes known as 'True Remnant Adventists', committed to a strict, uncompromising position. During the 1930s almost all the Adventist communities were disbanded and most of their leaders were imprisoned, but the movement reappeared during the Second World War and continued to grow in the immediate post-war period.

In the 1950s official figures listed twenty-six thousand Adventists in three hundred congregations, but it was sometimes suggested that the actual size of the movement was very much larger. Their main stronghold remained in the Ukraine, where they had more than a hundred registered congregations, and there were large Adventist communities in the Baltic capitals of Riga and Tallinn. To what extent the anti-religious campaign of the Khrushchev era diminished their strength is unknown, but it was probably considerable. It was during this time that the Adventists were again divided: this time over the issue of registered congregations. In 1965 another reformist group was founded by a hundred and eighty Adventist leaders who rejected the official leadership and refused to have any dealings with the State. This group appears to have merged with the True and Free Adventists who had somehow managed to survive since the 1920s. For twenty-five years these strict Adventists were led by a remarkable, heroic figure, Vladimir Shelkov, who was ordained as a preacher in 1929, was a prolific writer, and spent a total of twenty-three years in prisons and labour camps. His fourth prison sentence – five years in a strict regime camp – was imposed in March 1979 when he was eighty-three, and he died in the camp in January 1980. The True and Free Adventists now have close links with the Soviet secular human rights movement and are subject to constant persecution and harsh punishment. Fifty-nine of their members were known to be in prison in early 1981. The other Adventists have generally sought to avoid conflict with the State, and on some occasions have published statements supporting government policies. Their congregations register with the authorities and usually share Baptist churches. They are reported to be attracting large numbers of young people and an Adventist congregation of about five hundred meets for worship in the Baptist church in Moscow.

The Jehovah's Witnesses did not arrive in the Soviet Union until 1940, though a movement with similar beliefs (the Jehovists) came into being a hundred years earlier. They received reinforcements at the end of the Second World War with the return of Russian prisoners of war who had come under the influence of Witnesses in German prison camps, and also through groups which had been established in countries annexed by the Soviet Union. Since 1945 the Soviet government has regarded them as having special associations with Fascism or, alternatively, with American capitalism. Unlike the Adventists, as far as the law is concerned the Jehovah's Witnesses are an illegal organization, and consequently not just under Khrushchev but for more than a quarter of a century they have been subjected to intense persecution. Between 1948 and 1951 there were mass arrests and a letter was sent to the Soviet government in 1956 by the world organization of Jehovah's Witnesses, in which it was alleged that at the beginning of 1951 about seven thousand Witnesses had been arrested and sent to camps in remote parts of Siberia and other Arctic regions where many of them died of cold and hunger. A request that conversations might be held between representatives of the Jehovah's Witnesses and the government was ignored. None the less this sect has weathered persecution. When its members are imprisoned they make converts among the desperate and often disillusioned people who are sharing prison life with them. On their release these prison converts join the ranks of active Witnesses at work in the wider society. Those who are deported to remote regions of the Soviet Union often create new cells which sometimes become very strong. Persecution seems not to curb the activities of the Witnesses. Astonishingly, in the circumstances, they still engage in door-to-door visiting and even publish and distribute literature containing criticism of the government. Recent reports indicate that the trial and imprisonment of Witnesses is continuing, and the frequency of such reports suggests that this movement is still very active and remarkably resilient. Some well-informed observers believe that the Soviet Union branch of the Jehovah's Witnesses is one of the strongest in the world.

### Sects of Soviet Origin

Of the new sects that have sprung up during the Soviet era, perhaps the most revealing are the True Orthodox Church and the True Orthodox Christians. There is a curious irony in the fact that, although Marx and Lenin forecast the disappearance of religion and religious institutions from the Russian scene, one of the consequences of the implementation of their teaching in the Soviet Union has been the emergence of a number of new religious sects. As religious institutions have come under the control of the Communist government and made accommodations with the authorities, there have been those who disagreed with the policies of their leaders and in the end expressed their disagreement by forming separate bodies. Within the Russian Orthodox Church there have been a number of such breakaway movements, with their names often indicating that they consider themselves to represent the 'true' Church, in distinction from the body which accepts so much State interference in its affairs. Strictly speaking, they are probably more accurately described as schismatic, rather than sectarian, but classifications have always been difficult in the realm of religious belief in Russia, and the present is no exception.

The True Orthodox Church and the True Orthodox Christians first came to light in the West in 1948 when it was revealed in the journal of the Moscow Patriarchate that in the Tambov region there were some Orthodox Christians who not only refused to accept the authority of Patriarch Alexii but also called themselves the only 'True Orthodox Christians'. Later it was discovered that these Christians were part of a fairly widespread movement with two wings. The True Orthodox Church is to be found mainly in Central Russia, where its line of descent can be traced back to 1927 when Metropolitan Sergii made major concessions to the government and thus provoked a minor schism. Since the government is strongly opposed to the existence of clandestine religious bodies, the True Orthodox Church can have only a perilous existence. Its members meet secretly in one another's homes and with never more than twenty present. The total number of members is, for obvious reasons, unknown but, though this church has an attraction for certain young people, it is thought to be in serious decline. Many of its leaders were arrested and sent to prison or labour camps in 1950.

The True Orthodox Christians sprang from the True Orthodox Church during the Second World War and they have no institutional life, preferring to hold open-air meetings at places which they consider to be sacred. These meetings sometimes attract large numbers of young people, but admission to the sect is restricted to those who will dissociate themselves completely from the State – even to the extent of giving up their employment and withdrawing their children from school at an early age. They are particularly concerned for the healing of the sick and their meetings are often characterized by ecstasy and prophecy. In 1955 a split was reported: some of their number abandoned their extreme opposition to the government, while others became even more extreme and formed groups ('Silent Ones') which now live in isolation and in total silence. Once again, it is impossible to know the size of this movement, for those of its members who are discovered by the police are severely punished, but groups of True Orthodox Christians and 'Silent Ones' are said to exist in several regions of the Soviet Union. In 1977 ten women described as True Orthodox Christians were reported to be serving seven- to ten-year sentences in a labour camp in Barashevo; three years later four of them were still there and others were in exile.

At the end of this brief survey, it is necessary to emphasize again that the six sects discussed here represent only a small proportion of the multitude of sects now to be found in the Soviet Union. Many of them are small, and some have beliefs and practices which are as bizarre as those of their counterparts in the West, but they exhibit remarkable staying power in a situation where their existence is illegal and the authorities are committed to their eradication. Thus the sectarians as a whole powerfully illustrate a dictum of the first chairman of the Godless League (Yaroslavskii): 'Religion is like a nail; the harder you strike it the deeper it goes.'

ALL-UNION COUNCIL OF EVANGELICAL
CHRISTIANS-BAPTISTS

One of the largest Christian bodies in the Soviet Union is the All-Union Council of Evangelical Christians-Baptists. This consists of four evangelical communities: the Baptists and the Evangelical Christians, who founded the Union in 1944 and whose influence, if only from size, still dominates; the Pentecostals who joined in 1945; and some of the Mennonites who formally joined in 1963.

*Baptists and Evangelical Christians*

The Baptists and the Evangelical Christians both go back to the third quarter of the nineteenth century when evangelical movements arose almost simultaneously in three different parts of the Russian Empire. This suggests that the ground was well prepared. In the Caucasus adherents took the name Baptist, and their converts came chiefly from Russian nationals, most of whom were artisans and smaller merchants who belonged to the sect of Molokans. In the Ukraine the evangelical movement began when native peasants began to attend, and then adopt, the *Bibelstunden* of German settlers who had been there since the time of Catherine II; hence the name 'Stundists'. In St Petersburg the movement began as a result of the revivalist preaching of the English Lord Radstock, who was himself an evangelical with Plymouth Brethren connections. His followers first tried to work inside the Russian Orthodox Church but this proved impossible and later they came to be called Pashkovites after Colonel V. A. Pashkov, their chief local activist. In the early stages the movement was confined to the aristocracy but it spread rapidly to all classes.

At the instigation of Colonel Pashkov, a conference was arranged in St Petersburg in 1884 with the aim of merging these three evangelical streams into a single movement. The police intervened, and nothing came of it. In fact, the next two decades were a time of severe repression. Pashkovite activity was halted and the leaders exiled abroad. Pressure was applied to the Baptists and Stundists, and in 1894 the latter were declared illegal; their meeting houses were boarded up and those deemed responsible for their growth were confined.

Not until the revolution of 1905 did the government change its attitude. Legal reforms included religious toleration, so the disorganized and scattered evangelicals began to redevelop their life. In the south, a Russian Baptist Union was formed from the remnants of the Caucasus Baptists and the Ukrainian Stundists. In the north, I. S. Prokhanov, who had for a time been a student at Bristol Baptist College, England, founded the Evangelical Christian Union with the assistance of some former Pashkovites. Prokhanov was a very remarkable man and in some ways a genius. An engineer by training, his evangelical zeal was matched by a deep social concern. At St Petersburg the Dom Yevangeliya, with two thousand seats, was built for William Fettler, a famous Latvian Baptist preacher, in 1911. Efforts to bring together the two Unions failed, but each developed extensive missionary work and both Unions were represented at the Second Baptist World Congress held in Philadelphia in 1911.

In the same years, however, the Tsarist government's policy of toleration towards religious sectarians was changed and a number of severely restricting laws were reintroduced. This was part of a general reaction against the 1905 revolution, but the fact that the evangelicals had made remarkable growth during the brief years of toleration also caused disquiet in government circles. With the outbreak of war in 1914 the situation became even worse because the Protestant bodies were identified with German influence, while nationalist fervour was expressed through Orthodoxy. So once again most of their religious life was curtailed, many of their churches were closed and the key leaders sent into exile.

The Revolution of February 1917 was not therefore unwelcome to the evangelicals, and soon they were able to resume their activities. The chief obstacles they faced were caused by the general disorder in the country, and this remained so even after the Bolsheviks had seized power. When the civil war came to an end in 1921 and the first atheist government in Russian history was firmly established, there began – paradoxically – what is sometimes known as 'the golden decade' in the life of the Russian evangelical movement.

Lenin's decree separating Church from State and school from Church broadly coincided with evangelical convictions. Its implementation struck severe blows at the Orthodox Church and sometimes the evangelicals benefited from the changes. Once again the Russian Baptist Union and the Evangelical Christian Union tried to unite and once again they failed, but this failure seemed hardly important when seen in the light of the missionary successes of the two bodies. Their memberships grew rapidly, often at the expense of the Orthodox Church, and their members would have been even more numerous had not the rise of Pentecostalism drawn away some of their adherents. In 1924 a theological school for the training of future leaders was opened in Leningrad by the Evangelical Christians and another was opened in Moscow by the Baptists in 1927. Prokhanov developed an enthusiasm for Christian 'collectives' and planned an evangelical 'City of the Sun' – a bold but impracticable scheme for building a Christian community. The Russian evangelical leaders who attended the Fourth Baptist World Congress in Toronto in 1928 were able to report exciting developments, but a year later most of them were either in prison or in exile. During 1928 the Dom Yevangeliya was confiscated and this was soon followed by the closure of the Bible Schools in Leningrad and Moscow.

Stalin's rise to power led to the adoption by the Soviet government of a policy of rapid industrialization which was to be financed by the collectivization of agriculture. This could be carried out only by means of massive coercion at all levels of society, and religious bodies suffered along with the rest. If the 1920s had been the brightest years for the Russian evangelicals, the 1930s were the darkest. There was large-scale closure of churches, leaders were sent to labour camps, the theological schools were shut down, and religious publications ceased. In 1935 the Russian Baptist Union stopped functioning and a year later the Moscow church in which it had been housed was forced to close its doors. Left without a church in the capital, the Baptist members were welcomed by the one remaining Evangelical

Christian church in Moscow, and the years of darkness were a time of growing co-operation.

Relief came with the entry of the Soviet Union into the Second World War when the interests of patriotism and national unity led Stalin to withdraw – in public policy but not in published law – many of the restrictions that had crippled religious institutions. As a result of the so-called Stalin concordat between Church and State of 1943, the evangelicals were able to reorganize their forces, but only within the structure of a joint body. As a result, the All-Union Council of Evangelical Christians-Baptists (AUCECB) was formed in October 1944. In August of the following year it was joined by some of the Pentecostals.

In the post-war period the new body was intended to co-ordinate and administer the activities of all religious communities of a generally evangelical character. But this goal has never been fully realized. From the outset some groups of Baptists and Evangelical Christians, and an even larger number of Pentecostals, refused to be involved in the All-Union Council. During the first years of its life many of the Pentecostals who had joined decided to withdraw. Doctrinal and personal differences played their part here, but another factor was the uncomfortably close relationship between the new All-Union Council and the body set up by the State to oversee the activities of all non-Orthodox religious bodies – the Council for the Affairs of Religious Cults. Faced with potential or actual fragmentation, the work of unification has remained one of the chief concerns of the leadership of the All-Union Council to the present day.

While there were problems and disappointments in the realm of Christian unity, the All-Union Council had considerable success in directing the religious life and activities of the many congregations and individuals who acknowledged its leadership. Under the experienced leadership of Ya. I. Zhidkov, the President, who was a disciple of Prokhanov, and of A. V. Karev, the General Secretary, reconstruction and growth on a broad front took place among the churches of the Union during the fifteen years of the Stalin concordat. In the aftermath of war, and following the years of repression, there was much to be done. Churches had to be repaired and new ones opened and legalized. A journal was launched, and negotiations begun for the printing of the Bible and hymns, though approval was not

actually given until after Stalin's death. The Council assisted
with the choice of local leaders and a network of supervisory
presbyters was set up on a regional basis. Congregations were
helped and encouraged to develop a variety of activities,
including musical evenings, youth clubs and mutual aid societies. According to the law of 1929 all such activities were
illegal, but in the new atmosphere the government rarely
intervened. As a result of the new and vigorous life of local
churches, and the personal witness of individual believers, the
evangelical movement grew very rapidly. Brakes were applied
during the last years of Stalin's life, when social controls were
reimposed throughout the country, but after his death in 1953 the
strong forward movement was resumed and by the end of the
1950s the Baptists and Evangelical Christians were on the way
to recovering the position they had reached by the end of the
1920s. A large body of Pentecostals had returned to the Union
in 1957, following failure to get permission for their own Union,
and, although some internal tensions and external obstacles
remained, the general health of the evangelical movement as
expressed in the All-Union Council seemed sound and its future
promising.

It was not to remain so. In 1959 Khrushchev unleashed a brutal
anti-religious campaign. Old techniques were employed and the
restrictive provisions of the law were strictly enforced. But there
was a new feature which proved to be a critical one for the
evangelicals, as indeed it did for the Orthodox. The leadership
of the two bodies felt it necessary to alter the statutes by which
they governed themselves and impose new rules on their own
members. In effect, the churches were made instruments of their
own containment and restriction.

In the case of the Baptists, the All-Union Council sent out to
its member churches in 1960 a set of New Statutes to replace
those issued in 1944. Regional senior presbyters also received a
Letter of Instructions to guide them in the implementation of the
statutes. Together these documents laid down, among other
things, that children were to be excluded from acts of public
worship, baptism of people between the ages of eighteen and
thirty was to be discouraged and reduced to a minimum, and
evangelistic activities curtailed. The Letter of Instructions
justified the new policy on the grounds that 'the main purpose

of religious service at the present time is not the attraction of new members but the satisfaction of the necessary spiritual needs of the believers'. This was a novel approach for evangelicals and it became apparent that aspects of the church's life traditionally deemed imperative were to be reduced or even halted – and this at the behest of the church's own leadership.

There can be no doubt that the leaders of the All-Union Council, as well as those directing the affairs of the Orthodox Church, were at this time responding to severe government pressure. Once again they had been faced with the painful problem which has haunted the Christian communities in Eastern Europe since the advent of Communism: what does it mean to be the Church in a society ruled by a hostile government? As far as the Baptists were concerned, the drastic policy changes accepted in 1960 provoked widespread opposition within their membership. Under the leadership of three determined men, Alexii Prokofiev, Gennadi Kryuchkov and later Georgi Vins, this opposition crystallized in a so-called 'Action Group' (*Initsiativnya gruppa*) which challenged the All-Union Council to recant its decisions or face expulsion from the Union. At the same time the Action Group sought to win as many congregations as possible to its side and organized a number of activities – for example, unauthorized meetings and duplicated publications, which violated the laws of the State. Arrests, trials and imprisonments followed. By the end of 1962 more than a hundred of these Baptist reformers had been imprisoned.

This attack by the government was met by vigorous protest from adherents of the Baptist opposition, usually in the form of signed appeals to high government officials. These appeals probably moved the government to allow the All-Union Council to call a congress in 1963, the first since the founding congress of 1944. During the course of this an important section of the Mennonites were admitted into the Union. There was also some softening of the dictates of the New Statutes and the Letter of Instructions, but these did not approach the demands of the Reform Baptists (as they came to be called), who were not represented at the congress and were still under attack. By mid-1964 some one hundred and seventy of their number were in prison and four more were under investigation.

The fall of Khrushchev in October 1964 then introduced a period of uncertainty in the country, and the Reform Baptists, having declined an invitation to talk with the All-Union Council, took advantage of the respite to found their own Council of Churches of Evangelical Christians-Baptists (CCECB). They also stepped up their appeals to the government to change its policy, and in 1965 something of a new policy did emerge. Three new laws governing religious life were published, and all Church-State affairs were consolidated in a single government body: the Council for Religious Affairs (CRA). In theory the new body was supposed to protect the interests of religious believers and institutions; in practice it has never ceased to be an instrument of control and frequently of harsh repression. The subsequent history of the two groups of Baptists demonstrates clearly what this has meant for the Christians concerned.

For the All-Union Council and its member churches there has since 1966 been more room in which to operate. Another congress was held in 1969 at which the New Statutes were further liberalized. In default of a seminary for the training of ministers, permission was given for a correspondence course to be organized, and in 1979 it was reported that over the previous ten years four groups, totalling two hundred and seventy students, had successfully completed this course. A seminary, associated with a projected second Moscow church, is planned for the 1980s. Some of the closed churches have been reopened, but only a tiny proportion of the thousand or more closed between 1960 and 1964. Modest increases in the amount of religious literature printed and imported have been allowed, and in 1976 one of the All-Union leaders said, 'Things have never been better.' In some areas the state authorities are turning a blind eye to the presence of children at Baptist worship services and to the organization of youth choirs and special meetings for young people. The General Secretary, Alexii Bichkov, reported ten thousand baptisms in 1978 and a net gain of eleven thousand members during the period 1974–79. A major reorganization of the All-Union Council was carried out in 1979, as a result of which there has been some decentralization of church administration, and a special administrative organ has been set up for the Council's work in the Russian republics.

The showpiece of the All-Union Council is the Moscow

Baptist Church which has a membership of over five thousand and, since there are several acts of worship on weekdays as well as on Sunday, the average weekly attendance is in excess of ten thousand. It has a large staff and certainly does not give the impression of being a church under persecution. Here, as in other Baptist communities, the people who make up the congregation are predominantly working-class. They are warm-hearted, genuine and hardworking, and resemble in some ways the early Methodists. One English visitor with long experience of the Soviet Union has described their worship:

A Baptist service lasts two hours or a bit more and it has a definite beginning and a definite end . . . so you can always find a Baptist church at any time within an hour of service by the stream of people walking towards it. They come early to meet their friends and they think nothing of coming to a long service three or four times a week. It is like something from Hogarth, only transfigured. The service begins with a hymn, perhaps Moody and Sankey sung like a Russian folk song, perhaps a hymn from the Orthodox liturgy or perhaps something home grown. The Russian Baptists pour out new music every day . . . Then a few verses of the Bible are read and the preacher expounds them in a sermon. After this one of the preachers leads in prayer and you notice a strong, subdued sound. There is none of the exhortation which sometimes spoils free prayer . . . But the preacher puts a petition and each person turns it into his or her own words in a whisper. The whole church is filled with this scarcely audible whispering prayer and it binds everyone together. After this there are more hymns and the cycle starts again, scripture, sermon, prayer, hymns. Three sermons is the norm but there can be more. However, they are short and they are always worth hearing.

Once I was with the Moscow Baptists for the Breaking of Bread. They have Communion once a month and I have known Orthodox turn Baptist because the Baptist Church gives them Communion more often. At the service I attended large loaves were broken into pieces by the deacons and passed round on twelve very large patens to the two and a half thousand people in church; then good strong alcoholic wine was passed round in twelve chalices. You stand for a moment as you make your communion and then pass the elements on to your neighbour and sit down.

Another time I was at the baptism of forty-three men and women. A largish pool at the foot of the pulpit was filled with water and the Presbyter stood in the water above his waist while the candidates, robed in white, descended one by one, men from one side and women from the other, to be baptized by total immersion in the name of the Trinity. As each man came forward he made his profession of faith in his own words.

Young people are to be found in all Baptist congregations and their number is increasing. At the 1979 congress of the All-Union Council there was a call for the setting up of a Baptist youth department, but it was quickly pointed out that this would require government permission. Most Baptist congregations have a high proportion of women. The general approach to the Bible is conservative and the ministers, most of whom come from humble backgrounds and have very little academic training, are not well equipped to deal with the relationship between the Christian faith and many current issues in the realms of philosophy and ethics. This seems likely to become a serious problem, for some congregations already have a handful of young graduates in them and, as educational standards rise throughout the Soviet Union, the need for an ordained ministry with a better education and wider cultural life will become crucial if the Baptists are to be part of the main stream of Russian life.

For the Reform Baptists the chief problem is simply that of survival. Initially, the Reform Baptist Council, although unwilling to join the officially approved All-Union Council and to have its churches registered on government terms, sought to work with the approval of the State Council for Religious Affairs. Permission was sought for the Chairman of the Reform Council, Gennadi Kryuchkov, and the General Secretary, Georgi Vins, to be freed from secular work in order to serve the Council in a full-time capacity. But the government was not prepared to co-operate and in 1970 both Kryuchkov and Vins went underground to direct Reform Baptist affairs. Before long most of the members of the Reform Council were in prison and Vins was on the run until his capture in 1974, when he was sentenced to five years in a Siberian labour camp to be followed by five years of internal exile. Vins served the five years in the labour camp before being released to the United States in exchange for a Soviet spy in 1979. He was succeeded as General Secretary by Nikolai Baturin who had already spent sixteen years of his life in labour camps. Baturin was once again arrested in November 1979 and in August 1980 sentenced to five years in a strict labour camp and the confiscation of his private property. The Vice-Chairman of the Council, Pyotr Rumachik, has spent twelve of the last twenty years in labour camps and prisons, and was sentenced again in 1981. Gennadi Kryuchkob is still Chairman, and for the last ten years he has exercised his ministry in conditions of strict secrecy, visiting and encouraging Reform Baptist pastors and, so far, eluding arrest.

The suffering of the Reform Baptist leadership since 1965 is a vivid illustration of the persecution experienced by this particular Christian community as a whole as a result of its unwillingness to comply with the requirements of the State. Harassments, beatings, the breaking up of meetings for worship, arrests, fines, and imprisonment have been, and are, common-place. In 1976 the Reform Baptists listed fourteen different ways in which they were being persecuted. In that year just under one hundred of their number were in prison, and although this figure had fallen to forty-five in 1979 it had risen to ninety-five by the beginning of 1981.

In 1975, however, the government changed its tactics slightly but significantly. Without reducing its pressure on dissident Christians, the Council for Religious Affairs began to offer registration to more religious groups, including Reform Baptist congregations, though it insisted that they should register as autonomous local churches and not as members of the Reform Baptist Council. At the same time a few small concessions were offered to the registered churches. This new policy was, it seems, designed to weaken the dissident Christian movement by bringing some elements in it under the control implicit in registration, and also by enticing others back into the fold of the All-Union Council whose member churches were by this time beginning to enjoy a little more freedom. The Reform Baptist Council responded with a leaflet of advice to its member churches in which it said that it was ready for congregations to be registered but only on condition that there should be complete separation of Church from State and that there should be freedom to observe 'the principles of our evangelical Baptist faith'. The leaflet also advised that dealings with the State should be on the basis of 'open relations and closed membership', i.e. that negotiations with the Council for Religious Affairs should always be conducted by two or preferably three people, who would subsequently report to the whole membership, and decisions relating to the internal life of the church should be made only by those who have been baptized on their confession of faith. In the event, few Reform Baptist congregations registered and some of those that did soon de-registered when they discovered how much of their freedom had been lost.

In spite of the fierce government pressure, and some internal dissension, the Reform Baptist Council has survived and has developed an impressive life. The size of its constituency is variously estimated, and some Soviet sources have suggested that it reached a peak of 155,000 members in 1966, but it is impossible to obtain reliable figures. Within a few years of its coming into being there were regional Reform unions in the Caucasus, the Ukraine, the Leningrad area, Siberia, Northern Kazakhstan, and the Baltic region. The Council also has a department for evangelism and an underground publishing house, *Khristianin*, which published its first Bibles in 1978 and ten thousand copies of a song book in 1979. One of the most remarkable achievements of the movement is its Council of Relatives of Prisoners which, in addition to supporting prisoners and their families, accumulates information about the government's repressive activities, and about the experience of Christians in prison; it publishes this ten times a year in bulletins of 40–80 pages. Copies of these bulletins reach the West where they provide material for prayer and sometimes for protest. During the 1970s the Reform Baptists gradually lost some of their original impetus. The strain of maintaining a witness under unrelenting state pressure, and with many of their leaders in prison, took its toll. A large number of local leaders who were of German extraction emigrated to West Germany. A new generation of young people is less conscious of the powerful beliefs that drove the pioneers of the Reform movement to break away from the All-Union Council. Yet the Reform Baptists in the

Soviet Union continue to witness to their conviction that the Church should not render unto Caesar the things that belong to God alone.

Hard data concerning the number of Baptists – All-Union and Reform – in the Soviet Union is non-existent and published estimates show enormous variations. Rough calculations for the total number of Baptists and others of similar belief – in registered and unregistered communities, baptized and unbaptized, adults and children – range from one million to at least three million. All these figures must, however, be treated with reserve. Quite apart from the fact that both Church and State claim that no overall membership figures are calculated or kept, the conditions under which the Baptists work encourage church leaders and state officials to inflate or deflate the size of the Baptist community according to circumstances. It is none the less significant that the size and vigour of both the registered and the unregistered Baptist communities throughout the Soviet Union has been sufficient to provoke the unremitting concern of the government.

## The Pentecostals

Ever since the Pentecostal movement came to Russia in the early years of the twentieth century it has had some kind of relationship with the Evangelicals and Baptists. Many of its adherents were drawn from churches of an evangelical tradition, and during the wartime occupation of the Ukraine the Nazis compelled some of them to unite with the Evangelicals and Baptists.

During the years immediately following its arrival in Russia – through the work of an American missionary working in Finland – the Pentecostal movement made little progress. It was not until the 1920s, after the Communists had come to power, that there was any real growth, but by 1926 there were said to be three hundred and fifty Pentecostal congregations with seventeen thousand believers. At this time there was immense hostility between Pentecostals and other Evangelicals. They suffered greatly during the Stalinist persecutions of the 1930s and were driven more or less underground, so that nothing was heard of them until they surfaced during the changed conditions of the Second World War. To the great surprise of many, both inside and outside the Soviet Union, about four hundred of about a thousand Pentecostal congregations joined the new All-Union Council of Evangelical Christians-Baptists in 1945, and these included some from the Polish territory annexed by the Soviet Union. One of the conditions of their joining was that they would not use 'tongues' in public worship or spread the doctrine of Baptism in the Holy Spirit in united congregations.

After the Pentecostals had joined forces with the Evangelical Christians and Baptists they grew considerably in size and influence throughout the Soviet Union. Some of them had been in labour camps and during their time there had made converts who became active missionaries once they were released. The movement also spread as a result of the deliberate migration of Pentecostal groups to various parts of the country. Individual families often travelled from place to place, and wherever they went they displayed their characteristic missionary zeal. This may partly explain why Pentecostalist relations with the All-Union Council have never been very stable, and there has been much coming and going, joining and leaving, involvement and withdrawal. Added to the inner character of the movement this was probably inevitable, since in one respect it represents a protest against formal organization and anything suggestive of uniformity.

About five hundred and fifty Pentecostal congregations or groups, with an official membership of thirty-three thousand, now belong to the All-Union Council. But there are known to be several hundred groups outside the Council, and it has been estimated that there are actually 100,000–150,000 adult baptized Pentecostals who, with their children and unbaptized adherents, constitute a community of some 400,000–500,000 meeting in more than a thousand congregations. Until the 1970s the Soviet authorities were only prepared to tolerate Pentecostals insofar as they were within the All-Union Council. All others were illegal and subjected to severe penalties if they were discovered practising their faith. Since 1974, however, the government has allowed autonomous Pentecostal congregations to register and thereby acquire legal status. Pressure has been brought to bear on some Pentecostal groups to register, but by the end of 1979 only about ninety had done so – the rest believing that registration involves an unacceptable involvement of the State in Church life and a serious risk of limitations on religious freedom. Most of the Pentecostal leaders have been in prison at some time and, having paid this price for freedom of worship and conscience, are not prepared to surrender either for the sake of legality.

So the great majority of Pentecostals remain outside Soviet law and continue to suffer severe harassment, and their leaders, when arrested, are given long prison sentences (in January 1981, thirty-five Pentecostals were known to be in prison). They tend to meet in out of the way places or secretly in private houses, and although they try to avoid direct confrontation with the State most of them are unwilling to undertake military service and they keep away from all state ceremonies and celebrations. The second volume of an anti-religious book *Questions of Scientific Atheism*, published in the mid-1960s, gave a revealing picture of Pentecostal devotion:

> The first thing that strikes you on acquaintance with the life of sectarian communities is the number and length of their prayer meetings. With the majority of Pentecostals, these are held daily or at least three times a week, in the evenings. In many congregations meetings are held twice daily: before work, usually 5–6 a.m., and after work, 8–10 p.m. Meetings last two, three or more hours. On Sundays and holidays Pentecostal meetings are held two or three times during the day, the total length reaching 8–12 hours.

Requests to the authorities that an independent Pentecostal Union might be formed have always been refused, though there is an unofficial, and of course illegal, Council of Pentecostal Churches which links some unregistered congregations. In 1979 this Council appointed thirty men to work on the strengthening of weak churches and to discuss unity proposals with Baptist and Adventist groups. During the last few years there has been a growing movement among Pentecostals to leave the Soviet Union and emigrate to Western countries where there is greater freedom, especially for the religious upbringing of children. At the beginning of 1981 there were said to be about thirty thousand Pentecostals wishing to emigrate, and the United States Congress Commission on Security and Co-operation in Europe had details of ten thousand of them. The Soviet authorities are unwilling for them to leave and one of the leaders of the emigration movement, Nikolai Goretoi, was sentenced to seven years' strict regime labour camp and five years' internal exile in August 1980.

As in other parts of the world, the Pentecostal movement in the Soviet Union is much wider than the churches and groups which exist to express its particular insights and experiences. They seem to have obtained a foothold in the long-established churches, and there is evidence of the existence of a growing number of Pentecostals in Russian Baptist churches. Without wishing to quench the Spirit, the Baptist leaders are naturally anxious to avoid the possibility of further division within the ranks of the All-Union Council. They can hardly be unaware that the government is equally concerned for church discipline at this point.

*The Mennonites*

Although some of the Mennonites now comprise the smallest community within the All-Union Council of Evangelical Christians-Baptists, they have been in Russia much the longest. It was in 1789 that some ten thousand Prussian Mennonites – part of the Anabaptist movement – decided to respond to Catherine II's general invitation to Europeans to settle in territory which Russia had acquired from the Turks. During the first twenty years two large Mennonite colonies were established in the Ukraine, and about the middle of the nineteenth century two smaller colonies were established along the middle Volga. By 1900 the number of colonies had expanded to about fifty, with a total population of a hundred thousand. Here the Mennonites led their own distinctive form of Christian life, with its emphasis on a believers' Church, personal discipleship, separation of Church and State, pacifism and the sole authority of the Bible.

Under Catherine II and her successors in the early part of the nineteenth century, the Mennonites enjoyed a number of privileges. Thus they developed a particular Mennonite culture, and the fact that they retained the German language also marked them out as a quite separate community. From the 1860s, however, they saw their position threatened by reform and Russification. When a law requiring Russian citizens to undertake military training was passed in 1874 about eighteen thousand Mennonites immediately left for Canada and the

United States. For those who remained various compromises were reached which allowed Mennonites to undertake alternative forestry service when conscripted and also to continue to use German for religious purposes. In spite of emigration, Mennonite growth continued, chiefly the result of a high birth rate, but also as a consequence of continuing missionary activity.

Over the years, the Russian Mennonites produced numerous splinter groups with special emphases, but the majority aligned themselves into two main groups. Perhaps representing more closely mainstream Mennonite tradition, and at first the larger group, were the Church Mennonites. A more fundamentalist group, the Mennonite Brethren, separated from the former in 1860 and, as a result of Baptist influence, adopted the practice of baptism by immersion. Financially the Mennonites flourished. By 1917 they lived in over three hundred and fifty villages, owned about four million acres of land and are counted among those who developed the Ukraine as the 'granary' of Russia. They also had an extensive network of schools, colleges and hospitals.

The civil war which followed the 1917 Revolution devastated much Mennonite territory in the Ukraine, and the Mennonite communities not only felt the effects of famine but were also subjected to violent assaults from anarchic bands who took advantage of their commitment to non-resistance. At one point some of them formed an armed defence league – a compromise they are sometimes reminded of by the Soviet government today. Once the Communist government was established, new tensions began and, although the Mennonites had experienced relatively less privation than other peasants, about twenty thousand of them emigrated to Canada during the 1920s. In 1925 the General Conference produced an eight-point memorandum indicating what it regarded as the minimum requirements for religious freedom for those who remained. The main points of this memorandum were:

1. Undisturbed religious meetings and discussions in churches and private homes for adults and children
2. Unrestricted religious societies, choirs
3. Unrestricted erection of new church buildings, and tax exemption for churches and ministers

4.  Unrestricted creation of Christian orphanages
5.  Undisturbed acquisition of Bibles and other Christian literature, including periodicals
6.  Undisturbed Bible courses for the training of ministers
7.  Recognition of schools as a place for neither religious nor anti-religious propaganda
8.  Exemption from military service and training, and granting of useful alternative service

The memorandum was immediately rejected by the Soviet government.

When Stalin's first Five Year Plan called for the collectivization of agriculture in 1928 more Mennonites attempted to emigrate, but the government severely restricted the number allowed to leave the country. Many of those who applied for emigration permits ended up in prison and labour camps in Siberia. The 1930s were a dark period for the Mennonites, as for every other religious community in the Soviet Union, with the systematic destruction of their community life and culture only adding to the devastation of their religious practice. The majority of their church buildings were closed and the leadership was decimated. The fact that they maintained correspondence with their brethren abroad was also held against them.

The final break-up of the Mennonite community came with the German invasion in 1941. Many Mennonites were part of the forced resettlement in the East of all German-speaking people in the Ukraine lest they collaborate with the enemy. Before the evacuation was complete the Nazis arrived and some thirty-five thousand went with them when they retreated three years later. Of these, about six thousand eventually emigrated to South America and another twenty thousand were later repatriated by the Soviet authorities. The old Mennonite communities in the Ukraine had now been liquidated.

Nothing further was heard of the Mennonites in any part of Russia until an American and a Canadian Mennonite visited the Soviet Union in 1956 and discovered small groups in Siberia, Central Asia and the Urals. Others have since been discovered and, although the statistics are most imprecise, a conservative estimate suggests a minimum of fifty thousand, most of whom still use the German language. In the absence of ministers and leaders – so many of whom were killed or simply disappeared in the dark past – church services were often conducted by women, and in visits and letters to relatives abroad they complained of a great shortage of Bibles and hymn books. Reports also reached the West of a new religious revival in which the Mennonite Brethren were particularly active.

From 1963 onwards Mennonite Brethren congregations and individuals formally joined the All-Union Council of Evangelical Christians-Baptists. Initially, about sixteen thousand were said to have joined and by 1980 the total had risen to thirty thousand. Mennonite representatives were elected to the Council in 1966, and over the years their number has gradually increased. Several Mennonites are now serving as Senior Presbyters or as assistants to Senior Presbyters of larger regions. The Church Mennonites, who have an adult membership of about fifteen thousand, were unable to join the All-Union Council because they practise baptism by pouring rather than by immersion. After 1967, however, the first independent Mennonite congregations were registered by the state authorities, and in 1981 there were four independently registered Mennonite Brethren congregations and nine Church Mennonite congregations, plus another six Church Mennonite congregations with semi-legal status.

Towards the end of the 1970s Soviet atheistic writers began to devote increased attention to the Mennonites because of their unusually strong emphasis on teaching the faith to children within the family. It was also noted that historic Mennonite ideas had influenced such nonconforming groups as the Reform Baptists and that there were a disproportionate number of ex-Mennonites active in Reform Baptist circles. The independent Mennonite congregations have now been weakened by the emigration of numerous preachers to West Germany, and unless they adopt the Russian language and extend their missionary vision beyond their own ethnic boundaries their prospects for survival are poor. However, a major religious revival swept through the Mennonite communities in 1980 and this could mean new growth.

OTHER PROTESTANTS

Although the Tsars were generally well-disposed towards their Protestant subjects of non-Russian nationality, believing them to be far less dangerous than Roman Catholics, Protestantism –

apart from its Baptist and Evangelical expressions – never took root among the Russians. In 1917 there were over a million Lutherans in Russia, but 70 per cent of these were Germans, while the remainder were Finns, Swedes, Latvians, Estonians and other national minorities. The small Calvinist community consisted almost exclusively of Germans and Swiss.

During the decade following the 1917 Revolution the Lutheran and Reformed churches enjoyed far greater freedom than the Russian Orthodox Church. Their ministers suffered various disabilities, and local churches were subject to a number of restrictions, but the Lutheran General Synod of 1924 was optimistic enough to appoint two new bishops and make plans for the future. After 1929, however, both churches were subject to severe persecution. By the early 1930s all the Reformed churches had been closed, and by 1937 the institutional life of the Lutheran Church was completely destroyed. This violent assault on the two Protestant communities was closely related to Stalin's policy of rural collectivization, for many of the Lutherans were prosperous farmers who needed to be dispossessed of their land and were therefore subjected to comprehensive terror.

Many of the Germans living in the Volga region were deported to Central Asia and Siberia during the Second World War, and here the Lutheran faith survived mainly under lay leadership, since most of the clergy had either died or fled or been deported. The post-war years have seen the gradual revival of Lutheran life, and in 1956 it was reported from Kazakhstan that a pastor named Eugen Bachmann had established a Lutheran church in Tselinograd which was attracting six to seven hundred people. A year later it was registered by the authorities and for the next decade was the only official Lutheran congregation in the Russian FSR. Pastor Bachmann, who retired and went to Germany in 1972, estimates that during his time in Tselinograd some three thousand people were confirmed. Since 1968 other German Lutheran congregations have been registered in Kazakhstan and there are more in Siberia, the Urals and on the Volga – at least ten in all. These are visited by two Lutheran pastors from Riga, in Latvia. In 1977 a Finnish Lutheran congregation in Leningrad, with a membership of three thousand, was registered with the authorities, and a strong

Finnish-speaking congregation has also been established in the city of Petrozavodsk, near the Soviet-Finnish border.

In Transcarpathian Ukraine, the Hungarian Calvinists have so far survived the Soviet era. No information is available about their experience since they came under Communist rule, but they are now said to number about 100,000 in about a hundred parishes and are served by sixty pastors.

BALTIC PROTESTANTS

Another consequence of the Second World War was the acquisition by the Soviet Union of some territories with sizeable Protestant populations. The Baltic States of Latvia and Estonia, independent since 1917, had been under German and Scandinavian influence for seven centuries and many of their people (56 per cent in Latvia and 78 per cent in Estonia) were Lutherans. Even Lithuania had a small Protestant community.

The Baltic Protestant churches had first felt the pain of Bolshevik persecution when the Soviet army briefly occupied their territory in 1918. When the Red Army returned in 1940 a very large number of people were arrested and deported to the Soviet Union, thus weakening all the churches by the removal of key leaders. Many church buildings were destroyed during the war and others had to be abandoned by congregations which lacked the resources to maintain them. Ruined and abandoned churches are now a noticeable feature in country districts.

Soviet rule was re-established in 1945, and in the immediate post-war years the government was mainly concerned to pacify two nations which, not surprisingly, resented foreign invasions. During this time the churches were encouraged to elect new leaders who would assist the pacification process. But persecution began on a large scale in 1949 and was directed particularly against the Lutheran Church which, because of its German associations and its identification with pre-war national independence, was regarded as a potential expression of nationalism and thus a hostile influence.

As in other parts of the Soviet Union, however, state pressure has not been consistent. The latter years of the Stalin era and the last five years of Khrushchev's rule were times of special hardship, with the intervening and subsequent years more hopeful. Though the harassment of the churches has been uneven there has been little let-up in the sustained anti-religious propaganda campaign directed particularly towards young people, and the apparent success of this campaign may not be unrelated to the fact that the Baltic States have also been exposed to the secularism now common to many parts of Western Europe.

The Lutheran Church is, therefore, very much weaker than it was in the pre-Soviet period. In 1941 there were about one million Lutherans in Latvia and these were served by 288 pastors. Some twenty-one years later, when the Latvian Lutheran Church joined the World Council of Churches, the membership was reduced to half a million and the number of pastors to below a hundred. The membership figure for 1980 was 350,000 in 214 congregations. Since the end of the Second World War there has been an acute shortage of clergy – there were about a hundred in 1978 – but there is a Theological Institute in Riga which enrols about forty students and it is also possible to train for the pastorate by means of a four-year correspondence course. A few congregations are served by deaconesses.

In pre-war Estonia there were also about one million Lutherans served by two hundred pastors. In 1963 the membership was down to 250,000 served by a hundred and ten pastors. Today there are still about 250,000 members but only eighty pastors. There have been Lutherans in Lithuania since the Reformation, and during the 1920s there were some 200,000 of them, of whom 135,000 (mostly German-speaking) were concentrated in what was then the Lithuanian city of Memel. This golden age of Lithuanian Lutheranism came to an end during the Second World War when Memel was reincorporated into Germany and many of the Lutherans were resettled there. Today there are about 20,000 Lutherans in Lithuania, living in twenty-seven parishes, served by seven pastors and six deacons.

As might be expected, the Protestant churches have little or no opportunity for religious work outside their acts of worship in church buildings. Their leaders have moved from a militant anti-Communist stance to some sort of accommodation with the government. The Lutheran archbishops receive their salaries from the State, and Archbishop Edgar Hark of Estonia was awarded the Order of Friendship of Peoples by the Supreme

Soviet of the USSR on the occasion of his seventieth birthday. About 10 per cent of the Lutheran membership are said to be regular communicants, but it is noticeable that the churches are crowded at Christmas and Easter and it is reliably reported that from one-third to two-thirds of former church members still attend church occasionally. There is some evidence of people seeking the ministry of the Church when they can do so anonymously in the cities and large towns. All of which suggests that, although the institutional life of the Lutheran churches has taken a very severe beating, and there are still serious problems, the religious beliefs of the Baltic people are far from destroyed. In a somewhat fragmented situation the churches' links with the wider Christian world, through the World Council of Churches, the Conference of European Churches and the Lutheran World Federation, are likely to become increasingly important.

There have been small, but significant, Baptist communities in the Baltic States since the middle of the nineteenth century. They began as a consequence of missionary work by Germans and Swedes and, although they have had a chequered history, suffering losses through persecution and emigration, they are now well-established. Indeed, in Estonia they are becoming a folk church; the Lutheran cathedral in Tallinn, which has the tallest medieval spire in the world, has been given by the authorities to the Baptists and the congregations there are usually crowded. Dr Alan Walker, the Australian evangelist, was there in 1980 and became the first foreign preacher to be allowed to lead evangelistic meetings in Estonia. Over two thousand five hundred people packed the former cathedral for these meetings and it was reported that many young people, including some of Estonia's pop singers, had responded to Dr Walker's call for commitment.

In Latvia there are about sixty Baptist churches served by some fifty ministers and lay preachers, but the Baptist community is experiencing considerable difficulties. The movement of population from rural areas to the towns is leading to a loss of members, particularly young people, and since 1945 thousands of Latvians have been deported to Siberia. Some Baptist lay preachers have spent ten years in Siberian labour camps and returned home broken in health. Police harassment of both registered and unregistered Baptist congregations is reported from time to time. In general, Baptist churches are faring better in the towns than in the countryside, though there are now only three churches in Riga, compared with nine in 1939. Bibles and hymn books are very scarce and, since there is no seminary, ministers are trained by means of correspondence courses organized by the Moscow Baptists.

The Baltic Baptists form part of the All-Union Council of Evangelical Christians-Baptists, but they are mostly not involved in the Reform Baptist schism.

The only Methodist church in the USSR, apart from a small community in Transcarpathia, is in Estonia where the church has grown from about seven hundred and fifty members in 1945 to about two thousand two hundred members in 1980. There are twenty-one ministers, of whom seven are retired, and over eighty associate and lay ministers, serving fourteen congregations. The largest of these congregations is in Tallinn, where the membership is over a thousand and much use is made of choirs and orchestras in the worship. There is also a strong emphasis on work among young people.

ROMAN CATHOLICS

A German living in Russia in the second half of the seventeenth century wrote, 'The hatred of the Russians towards the Latin Church is primordial and somehow inborn; their ancestors took it over from the Greeks and passed it on as a heritage to their offspring.' This was a sweeping statement, but there appears to be at least an element of truth in it inasmuch as the number of Russians who have become Roman Catholics has always been minuscule. During the latter part of the Tsarist era a handful of the more Westernized elements in the Russian aristocracy joined the Roman Catholic Church, but prior to the edict of toleration in 1905 no Russian could leave the Orthodox Church – either to join another church or even to become an atheist – without being subject to loss of political and civil rights.

This is not to say that Roman Catholics have always been absent from the Russian picture. They have not, but they are to be identified in the main with the inhabitants of non-Russian nationality. The number of Roman Catholics in Russia, and later in the Soviet Union, has therefore been closely related to two factors: the frontiers of the Russian Empire and the presence of national minorities. Before 1917 there were just over 1,600,000 Roman Catholics living in the territory of the old Russian Empire. Those who adhered to the Latin Rite were Polish, Lithuanian, Byelorussian, German and French, while those who adhered to the Eastern Rite were mainly Ukrainian, Georgian and Byelorussian.

*Latin-Rite Catholics*
In Russia, as in Ireland, non-believers take on the religious folk prejudices of their community. So the Communists have continued and intensified the old Tsarist antipathy to Roman Catholicism, mainly because the Roman Catholic hierarchy have never been ready to accommodate themselves to the atheistic regime, but also because this church is still felt to owe an allegiance to a foreign centre in the West and can be – indeed is – often influenced by papal decisions. What this antipathy meant in practice within the pre-war borders of the Soviet Union is illustrated by the following statistics:

TABLE 2

*The Roman Catholic Church in the Soviet Union*

|  | *1917* | *1934* |
|---|---|---|
| Archdioceses and dioceses | 7 | nil |
| Bishops and apostolic administrators | 21 | nil |
| Churches and chapels | 980 | 3 |
| Priests and monks | 912 | 10 |
| Religious institutions and monasteries | 200 | nil |
| Schools and social institutions | 300 | nil |
| Seminaries | 4 | nil |
| Publications | 10 | nil |

This annihilation of the Roman Catholic Church took place in two extended waves of persecution. One began immediately after the 1917 October Revolution and the other after a brave but disastrous attempt to create a new Catholic hierarchy in 1926. Bishops and parish priests were arrested, usually charged with anti-Soviet or counter-revolutionary activities, which in the eyes of the authorities covered virtually all their ecclesiastical functions, then given long prison sentences or deported to remote labour camps, and in some instances executed. Nor did real relief come to the Roman Catholic Church within the original terrains of Soviet Russia during the years of Church-State 'symphony' beginning in 1943. Apart from the three churches in Moscow, Leningrad and Odessa, which were kept open to cater for foreign nationals, it was obliged to function underground. Following the death of Stalin, the majority of the priests in prison were amnestied, but today there are still only a handful of Latin-Rite churches open in the whole of Russia proper, and it is significant that the priest of the Moscow church is a Lithuanian. At Leningrad, where there are six masses on Sunday and one each weekday, most of the prayer books are in Lithuanian and there are also services in Polish.

Circumstances are somewhat different in the various other territories of the former Russian Empire with Roman Catholic populations which were incorporated into the Soviet Union as a result of the Ribbentrop-Molotov Pact in 1939. In the former Polish territory, now part of the Byelorussian republic, there were in 1939 about two hundred Catholic parishes and two hundred and forty-six priests; these have now been reduced to sixty-five parishes and about the same number of priests. The 30,000 Lithuanian Catholics living in Byelorussia are not permitted to have their own churches or services in their own language. In the Moldavian Soviet Socialist Republic there are about 15,000 Roman Catholics but there are only two legally registered churches – one a cemetery chapel in Kishinev – and only one recognized priest who travels to Catholic communities in outlying towns and villages. These communities and their priest are constantly harassed by the authorities, and in 1978 they appealed to the Pope to intervene on their behalf. In December 1979 it was reported that the priest, Father Vladislav Zavalnyuk, had had his government licence withdrawn because many young people were sharing in worship. Shortly after this he was replaced by another priest.

The greatest concentration of Latin-Rite Catholics in the

Soviet Union is to be found in Lithuania which, in the few months between the fall of Poland and the Soviet invasion of the Baltic States in 1940, was described by Pope Pius XII as the 'northernmost outpost of Catholicism in Europe'. The history of Catholicism in Lithuania goes back to the thirteenth century, and the place of religion in the life and culture of the nation has close affinities with that of Poland. Indeed from 1385 to 1794 the Grand Duchy of Lithuania was united with Poland, and when Lithuania was incorporated into the Russian Empire in the nineteenth century Catholicism was an important factor in the preservation of national identity. It still is, and the famous Hill of Crosses at Meskuiciai – a national shrine commemorating the murder of Lithuanian revolutionaries in 1863 – has taken on a new significance for the oppressed Lithuanians of the twentieth century.

In 1940 the Catholic Church (which had come into its own again after Lithuanian independence in 1918) was strong and flourishing. It claimed the allegiance of 85 per cent of the population, had ten bishops and just under fifteen hundred priests, four seminaries and a hundred and fifty-eight monasteries and convents. Soviet plans to destroy the Church were interrupted by the German invasion in 1941, but when the war was over Lithuania was incorporated into the USSR and given a Constitution and legal code virtually the same as that of the other Soviet republics. Throughout the post-war period the pattern of religious repression in the annexed lands has generally been that of the Soviet Union as a whole. In Lithuania, however, between 1944 and the death of Stalin in 1953, Catholics were singled out for especially severe persecution and terror. Three of the diocesan bishops and one auxiliary bishop were sent to labour camps, and one of them, Bishop V. Borisevicius of Telsiai, was shot in 1947. After 1953 there were a few years of thaw in which it proved possible to repair some of the damage, followed by a serious setback in the Khrushchev era. From 1964 onwards the persecution eased somewhat, though life remains exceedingly difficult for the Church and the position is still very serious. Many Catholics are not prepared to accept the limitations on freedom imposed by the State, and the government is aware of the importance of the Church for Lithuanian culture and national aspirations.

At the present time Lithuania has six Catholic dioceses and about six hundred parishes. There are no residential bishops and all six dioceses have apostolic administrators, two of whom are in episcopal orders. Two former diocesan bishops have been in internal exile since the Khrushchev era, and one of them, Bishop Steponavicius, is believed to be the secret cardinal created by Pope John Paul II in 1980. There are about seven hundred priests, more than one-third of whom are over sixty years of age. Only three hundred and fifty priests have been ordained since 1945, and government restrictions on the number of students entering the one remaining seminary mean that only six to ten new priests are ordained every year. All the monasteries and convents are closed (some of them are now operating secretly), and some important churches have been turned to secular use. In the face of these severe restrictions, the Church is struggling to maintain its traditional life and, in spite of the continuous anti-religious propaganda, still holds the loyalty of a large proportion of Lithuanians. They still attend mass in considerable, even if reduced, numbers and still go to church for their baptisms, weddings and funerals. As many as 10,000 people attend the cathedral at Kaunas at Christmas. When the foundations of a new church at Klaipeda (Memel) were dedicated in 1957, more than 20,000 people assembled. This church was completed in 1960, as a result of much work and sacrificial giving by the Catholic community, but it was immediately confiscated by the government and turned into a concert hall. Several petitions asking for the building to be returned to the Church, have been lodged with the authorities, and the latest of these (July 1979) was supported by 148,149 signatures. Lithuania has its places of pilgrimage, besides the Hill of Crosses, which attract thousands of believers, and at the traditional seasons there is fervent devotion to the Virgin Mary and the Sacred Heart. The parish priest retains his social, as well as his religious, role, especially in village communities where he is still a powerful figure.

One aspect of the Church's life in Lithuania which has caused considerable uneasiness in recent years concerns the appointment of bishops. These have been made by the Vatican, but the government's Council for Religious Affairs has been deeply involved in the selection process and many Catholics believe that readiness to co-operate with the government is now the prime qualification for the episcopate. In December 1971, for instance, 17,059 Catholics took the extraordinary step of signing a petition asking for religious freedom. This was addressed to the Secretary-General of the United Nations and a copy was also sent to the Kremlin. As news of this petition became known, the Soviet authorities became anxious, and in April 1972 all the bishops and apostolic administrators of the Catholic dioceses were summoned to a meeting where they were presented with a 'Pastoral Letter' which they were ordered to sign and have read in all their parishes. This letter told the faithful that they had been misled by the petition and that activities of protest were a threat to the unity of the Church. Two state officials were sent to every church to measure the response to the reading of the letter. A number of priests were so incensed by the hierarchy's action that they wrote a letter of reply to the 'Pastoral Letter', and this revealed their wider concern about the bishops' readiness to collaborate with the government:

> We have had enough of these Monsignors who spread the 'truth' about the Lithuanian Catholic Church by means of the atheist radio and press. We have also had enough of the kind of bishops who publish such 'pastoral' letters ... Help us with your prayers and tell the world that we want at the present time only as much freedom of conscience as is permitted by the Constitution of the Soviet Union. We are full of determination, for God is with us.

The signing of petitions asking for the freedom of the law, and the seeking of assistance from the Vatican and other international institutions, has been one of the marked features of Lithuanian Catholicism in recent years. In 1978, for example, fifty-six priests of Kaunas archdiocese and twenty priests of Telsiai diocese signed a document criticizing a new draft Constitution. This was followed by two more critical documents on the same subject signed by 780 laity from Telsiai and 975 laity from Kybartai parish. A year later 522 of Lithuania's 700 priests signed documents protesting against the law which gives local authorities extensive rights to close churches, to restrict the work of priests and to force agreements on parish committees which are unrepresentative of priests and believers. The protests against repression are largely centred on the *Lithuanian*

*Chronicle of Current Events* – a remarkable *samizdat* journal which began publication in 1971 and has appeared regularly ever since. It contains reports of individual cases of persecution, protests against the policies of the Council for Religious Affairs, and emphasizes the close links between Catholicism and Lithuanian nationality. In 1978 the *Chronicle* was even used by the Catholic hierarchy for the voicing of their criticisms of the draft Constitution. The government makes determined efforts to suppress this widely-read journal, and some of those who produce and distribute it have received heavy prison sentences, but others have taken their places and it has never failed to appear.

November 1978 saw the foundation of the Catholic Committee for the Defence of Believers' Rights. This works closely with the Christian Committee for Believers' Rights and, although it is concerned for all Catholics in the Soviet Union, its attention is concentrated mainly on Lithuania and it was founded by five Lithuanian priests. Its stated object is 'to attain equality of rights for believers with atheists in law and in practice' and to operate legally, without political aims. Besides general criticisms of state policy and publicity for particular cases of discrimination against Catholics, the Committee has written to members of the Catholic hierarchy urging them to uphold believers' rights and not to compromise with the Council for Religious Affairs. Among the many Lithuanian Catholics who have shown themselves unwilling to compromise was Romas Kalanta, a young layman who in May 1972 immolated himself in Kaunas, the second largest city in Lithuania. On the day following his funeral troops were needed to deal with some thousands of young people who rioted in the streets and chanted 'Freedom for Lithuania'. Kalanta is now regarded as a national hero by Lithuanians who long for the recovery of their political and religious freedom.

Although much less is heard of them, there are about 300,000 Catholics in Latvia and they have conserved their numbers well in spite of difficulties with the State. There are two dioceses, 178 churches, one bishop, 150 priests and a seminary at Riga which takes twenty to twenty-four students and prepares priests for work in other parts of the Soviet Union, as well as in Latvia. The shrine of Aglona is famous and much frequented. Latvian Catholics are nothing like as vocal in protest as are their fellow

Christians in Lithuania, and the reason for this seems to be that most of them are concentrated in the rural area of Latgale, leaving them without a broad national base from which to challenge repression openly. In the 1970s, however, a petition to the government asking for greater freedom was signed by over five thousand Catholics. In Estonia there are about three thousand Catholics, served by one priest, who is a Latvian.

*Eastern-Rite Catholics (Uniates)*
Catholics of the Eastern Rite have always been unwelcome in Russian territory. Their story goes back to 1596 when the Metropolitan of Kiev and the majority of the Orthodox bishops of the Ukraine, under strong pressure from their Polish rulers, signed an act of union with Rome at Brest-Litovsk. Under the terms of this agreement they accepted the jurisdiction of the Pope, but their dioceses were permitted to retain the Eastern liturgy and its language, communion under both kinds, local canon law and a married priesthood. This arrangement was bitterly resented by the rest of the Orthodox world and by many of the Ukrainian Orthodox whose consent had not been sought. But, in spite of this unpromising start, the Uniate Church was well served by its priests and over the next three centuries came to have strong support from the people.

After the Uniates first appeared in the Russian Empire, following the partitions of Poland and the annexation of the former Polish Ukraine and Byelorussia, the Tsars progressively arranged for them to be 're-united' with the Orthodox Church. A small incipient 'Russian Greek Catholic Church' held its first synod in Moscow in 1917, but it became one of the earliest victims of Communist repression and was destroyed in 1923. More recently it has been the turn of the Uniate Church of the Ukraine.

Western Ukraine was lost to the Soviet Union during the Revolutionary years and did not return to its control until 1939. When the Soviet army occupied the Western Ukraine in 1939 it found there a Uniate Church of nearly four million believers, served by a metropolitan, seven bishops, 2,500 priests and 1,600 monks and nuns. There were 2,772 parishes with 4,119 churches and chapels, a theological academy and four seminaries. Between 1939 and the German occupation of the Ukraine in 1941 little action was taken against the Church, apart from the arrest and deportation of a few priests. But when a Communist regime was re-established after the German army had been driven out in 1944 it soon became clear, after an initial period of caution, that the Uniate Church was to be liquidated.

The first stage in this process consisted of a violent propaganda campaign against the Church. Bishops and other leaders were accused of supporting nationalism and indulging in espionage and subversion; they were forbidden to communicate with their parishes. This led, in April 1945, to the arrest of Metropolitan, later Cardinal, Josyf Slipyj of Lvov and the rest of the Uniate bishops, who were charged with collaborating with the German army of occupation and given long sentences of forced labour. A few weeks later there emerged the 'Sponsoring Group for the Re-union of the Greek Catholic Church with the Russian Orthodox Church' – a self-appointed body which was strongly opposed by the Uniate Church as a whole, but was none the less recognized by the government as the Church's sole administrative organ and charged with the task of promoting the union of the Uniates with the Russian Orthodox Church.

At this point Patriarch Alexii of Moscow went into action with a special message to the clergy and people of the Uniate Church. This message began by accusing the Vatican and the Uniate hierarchy of pro-Fascist sympathies, and concluded with an appeal to the Uniates to break with the Vatican and to return quickly to the Russian Orthodox Church. The Patriarch also appointed a new Orthodox bishop for Western Ukraine who was charged with the task of assisting the 'Sponsoring Group' in its campaign for re-union; this bishop in fact assumed leadership of the campaign. The parish clergy and monks were then subjected to threats and propaganda in an attempt to win them over to the Orthodox Church, and by March 1946 nearly half of them (986) were said to have accepted Orthodoxy. Since only 281 other priests were exercising their ministry at this time, it must be presumed that the rest (740) were either in prison or in hiding. All that was needed now was an official Church Sobor (or synod) to indicate that the re-union was quite voluntary and fully canonical. A difficulty arose over this, since a Sobor required the involvement of the Uniate bishops who were in prison and unwilling to participate in the proceedings. However, the

Moscow Patriarchate solved the problem by consecrating two members of the 'Sponsoring Group' as Orthodox bishops, and at the 'Re-union Sobor' held in Lvov in March 1946 the specially invited participants voted 'to annul the Union with Rome, to break off the ties with the Vatican, and to return to the Orthodox faith and to the Russian Orthodox Church'. In Transcarpathian Ukraine the end of the union with Rome was announced at a church council in 1949.

It now remained for the government to make these decisions legally binding and to deal with those who were unwilling to accept the jurisdiction of the Moscow Patriarchate. The number of recalcitrants turned out to be very large, and during the reign of terror which followed the Sobor the priests among them either fled abroad or went underground. Many lay people refused to attend their parish churches, all of which had been handed over to the Orthodox Church, and since 1946 the Uniates have been forbidden to organize any religious activity. With the passage of time, some Uniates have accepted Orthodoxy as the only expression of Christianity now open to them. A number of priests are using Orthodoxy as the framework for a continuing Uniate life. Others have made their home in the few Catholic churches of the Latin Rite now open. But the rest are obliged to meet secretly and have to beware not only of the police but of Orthodox priests who are sometimes ready to report them to the authorities. This is a 'Catacomb Church', with severe penalties awaiting those who are caught, and in 1980 Cardinal Slipyj stated that since 1941 ten of his fellow bishops, more than 1,400 priests, 800 nuns and 'tens of thousands' of Uniate believers had laid down their lives. For obvious reasons it is impossible to discover how many Uniate clergy and laity are keeping their church alive underground, but an estimate in 1980 suggested that there are some 300–350 priests and three or more secret bishops. Several of the monastic orders are also said to be maintaining some form of the religious life, with their monks and nuns dispersed and employed in a variety of jobs. In 1973 three Uniate priests working within Orthodoxy and three laymen were put on trial for secretly printing over 2,000 Uniate prayer books on state printing presses. A year later a Ukrainian priest from Lithuania took to the Council for Religious Affairs in Moscow a petition asking for the legalization of the Uniate Church and signed by 12,000

believers in the Lvov area. The result of this was an intensification of measures against Ukrainian Uniates, and the government
frequently makes use in its propaganda of the views of a minority
of Uniates who have fiercely nationalistic aims and openly
repudiate Soviet rule.

Sadly, a conflict has arisen recently between the leaders of the
exiled Uniates and the Vatican. For some years now the Vatican
has been silent about the Ukrainian problem, evidently believing
that public complaints or denunciations might make the position
of the Uniates even worse. This is displeasing to Cardinal Slipyj,
who has been in Rome since his release from prison in 1963 and
who believes the silence of the Vatican and the *Ostpolitik* of the
Holy See represent a betrayal of the suffering Uniates of the
Ukraine. The Uniate Primate, who maintained silence on the
subject until 1971, would now like the Vatican to take positive
steps to uphold the continuing existence and integrity of his
church, but so far he has met with little response and this has
provoked him to angry outbursts against the Roman authorities.
Successive Popes have also resisted frequent requests that
Cardinal Slipyj should be appointed Patriarch of the Ukrainian
Catholic Church in diaspora. His title remains Archbishop-major
of Lvov and the Pope announced in 1980 that when the
eighty-eight-year-old Cardinal dies he will be succeeded as head
of the Ukrainian Catholic Church by Archbishop Myroslav Ivan
Lubachivsky, who was born and ordained to the priesthood in
Lvov and is now Archbishop of Philadelphia, in the USA.

### THE JEWS

The existence of a large Jewish population in the USSR is due
almost entirely to the acquisition of Polish territory by the Tsars
in the seventeenth and eighteenth centuries. For a long time the
Jews who lived in former Polish territory were forbidden to
move into Orthodox Russia, but though towards the end of the
Empire these restrictions ended, and with the Revolution of 1917
were abolished, the overwhelming majority have remained
within the European republics of the Soviet Union. The Jews are
still regarded as a distinct nationality, and this is entered in their
passports and identity documents. According to a census carried
out in 1979, some 1.8 million Soviet citizens registered as Jews,
and if it is assumed that a sizeable number of people of Jewish

origin registered as members of other nationalities a total of 2.25 million Jews seems reasonable. Moscow itself has almost a quarter of a million registered Jews – after New York the largest number in any city of the world outside Israel. Jews constitute 15 per cent of all Soviet medical doctors and a similar proportion of economists, musicians and other professional occupations. In 1976 almost 300,000 of the sixteen million members of the Communist Party identified themselves as Jews, and during the 1950s Khrushchev sometimes complained about the large number of Jews in important Soviet institutions. Today no Jew occupies a top position in the Party, the State or the army apart from the veteran Veniamin Dymshitz, who is Deputy Prime Minister – a mainly administrative post.

In discussing the religious situation as it affects Jews in the Soviet Union it is necessary to recognize at the outset that factors of unusual complexity are involved, and that the interlocking of these factors creates a territory in which it is essential to walk circumspectly. First, and most important of all, the Jews are both a religious community and a national minority. Bearing in mind that of the 2.25 million Jews now living in the Soviet Union probably 250,000 adult Jews practise their religion, it is tempting to try to separate questions of religion and nationality. Such a division would certainly make for easier analysis, but it simply cannot be done. The identity of the Jewish people is built on foundations which are deeply religious and, notwithstanding the fact that many other elements have helped to mould the outlook of the twentieth-century Jew, religious and national questions are inextricably intertwined. If, therefore, in the Soviet context religious Jews are subject to persecution because of their religious practices, this is felt by the overwhelming majority of the Jewish people to represent an assault on the Jewish community as a whole because it touches something crucial in their identity. Equally, if the State seeks to suppress the Jewish national culture and, for a time, concentrates its attention on Jewish organizations, authors and publications, this has its repercussions on religious Jews who regard such attacks as highly significant and a threat to their own future. In this book it is possible to discuss only the attitude of the Soviet government to those aspects of Jewish life which find expression in religious practice, but it must not be supposed that the government's attitude to the wider Jewish question is lacking in religious implications.

Secondly, it is necessary to view the persecution of the Jews in the Soviet era against the background of a long history of anti-Semitism in Russia. According to Professor Leonard Schapiro, 'It would not be far wrong to regard Russia as the classical home of anti-Semitism.' It is sometimes debated whether the Jews have suffered more under the Soviets than they did under the Tsars, and scholars are divided on the matter. The early years of Soviet rule were a time when Jewish secular culture, and Yiddish literature in particular, flourished, and anti-Semitism was discouraged as a matter of official policy. There can be no doubt, however, that ever since the Jews came under Russian hegemony they have been treated barbarously. During the Tsarist era anti-Semitism was explicable partly in terms of the intrusion of the Jewish faith into an arena marked out for Russian Orthodox Christianity and the threat to national unity which this was thought to pose. Whatever the explanation, by the time the Communists came to power there was plenty of fertile soil in which anti-Semitic propaganda could grow – as it did under Stalin after the Second World War.

Another complicating factor in recent years has been the Soviet government's attitude to Zionism. Soon after the 1917 Revolution, the Zionist movement was declared to be illegal and all Zionist activity a criminal offence. This has been the official line ever since, despite the Soviet Union's support in the United Nations of the creation of the State of Israel, and it has been developed further since 1950 as a result of the alignment of the Soviet Union and the Arab states. During the 1960s there was an increase in repressive action against Soviet Jews, and the Six-Day War in 1967 led to a great increase of violent anti-Zionist propaganda by the government which, in turn, stimulated anti-Semitic activity by certain elements in the population at large.

It is also necessary to recognize certain divisions and differences of attitude within the Soviet Jewish community. While the deeply-rooted unity of the Jewish people remains, it is possible to discern within their ranks three different approaches. There are those who would be quite happy with their life in the Soviet Union provided they were free to observe their own customs and openly express their distinctive culture, which for many includes religious observances. But there are others who are ready to be assimilated into Russian culture and have generally abandoned all those Jewish beliefs and practices which mark them out from Russian people as a whole. At the time of the 1917 Revolution there were a considerable number of Jews among the Bolsheviks, and during the 1920s and 1930s the Sovietization of the Jewish community and the persecution which accompanied this process, was in the main entrusted to Jewish Communists. A third group consists of deeply committed Zionists who, for religious or other reasons, or simply to escape from an unbearable situation, wish to get away from the Soviet Union as quickly as possible and help to build and defend the new Israel. To these may perhaps be added a fourth group who are not Zionists but wish to leave the Soviet Union simply to be free, and are ready to settle in any country where there is real liberty.

Among the other factors at work in the situation, the effects of the traumatic experience of the Jews under the Nazis are still being felt in the Soviet Union by those Jews who were alive at the time, and also by many of their children who are aware of what happened. During the Second World War some two and a half million Jews in the Soviet Union were killed by the Germans or died as refugees, thus reducing their percentage of the population as a whole from two and a half to one; these losses were proportionately four times as great as those of the entire population. In addition to this, millions of Jews were slaughtered in neighbouring European countries and, naturally, the Russian Jews bore some of the corporate pain. Against this background of recent experience, further Communist persecution inevitably appears to be extremely sinister and is more difficult to bear.

An assessment of Jewish religious conditions must also take account of the growth of secularization. Although many Jews cling most tenaciously to their religious beliefs and practices, the Jewish people are not specially protected against those winds of change that have affected the other religious bodies of the industrialized Western world during the twentieth century. A census carried out in 1970 indicated that less than 50,000 Jews now live in rural areas. The years of Communist rule in the Soviet Union have been a time of enormous social change and even if the government had adopted a benevolent attitude to the Jews and encouraged them to pursue their own way of life, it would have been surprising if the Jewish community had not experienced some decline in religious practice. It cannot be assumed, therefore, that the falling away from the synagogue and the reduction in the number of those observing the key religious festivals is entirely due to the policies of the Soviet government.

In view of the Tsarist treatment of the Jews, it is no surprise to discover that a significant number of Jews were active in the revolutionary movement which led to the events of 1917. Indeed, in the early days of the Soviet regime the Foreign Ministry was jokingly known as 'the Synagogue'. There were several Jewish socialist parties, most of which were anti-religious, and within the Communist Party there was a Jewish section, or *Yevsekt-siya*, which was strongly anti-religious. After the Revolution the *Yevsektsiya* was made responsible for the repression of the Jewish religion – a move that had the advantage of presenting the conflict as internecine warfare within the Jewish community, rather than as the result of deliberate government policy.

When the decree 'On separation of Church and State and School from Church' was promulgated in January 1918, the Jewish community was immediately affected by the requirement that religious education in schools should cease, but a more serious blow came in June of the following year when it was decreed that all Kehilahs should be dissolved. These were the Jewish community councils which were responsible for the organizing of social welfare and educational work among the Jews, and it is interesting to note that the dissolution decree was signed by Stalin – at the time Commissar for Nationality Affairs. For the first three years these decrees were not seriously enforced, partly because of the disorder caused by the civil war and partly because the government was unable to provide alternative facilities in education and social welfare. Once the civil war was ended, however, the assault on these Jewish councils began in earnest. Over a thousand schools were closed in 1922 and 1923 as part of a campaign to liquidate all Jewish primary and secondary schools, and, although the 1918 separation decree made no provision for the closing of places of worship, a large number of synagogues were closed on the pretext that the buildings were required for urgent community needs in a time of crisis. Much of the anti-religious propaganda was crude and had little direct effect, but it helped to create a climate in which it was recognized that the Jewish religious and cultural institutions could not rely on state protection and were, therefore, open to attack from any quarter and for any reason. The propaganda was always increased before and during the Jewish festivals, and in some towns parades designed to ridicule Jewish beliefs were held outside synagogues on the Day of the Atonement and Passover. During the 1920s an attempt was made to organize a schismatic 'Living Synagogue' movement on the lines of the 'Living Church' movement, but this secured virtually no support and soon had to be abandoned.

After 1929 the Jews, in common with all religious bodies in the Soviet Union, were faced with even stiffer persecution as a result of Stalin's tough policy. Many more synagogues were closed, rabbis were charged with anti-Soviet activities and despatched to labour camps, and in most of the smaller Jewish communities they were forced to resign. During the 1930s the Jews found themselves faced with certain other problems. Securing *matzos* (unleavened bread, described by the Communists as 'counter-revolutionary bread') became extremely difficult because of government restrictions. It also became increasingly difficult for Jews to observe the Sabbath as they were required to be at work on Saturdays and were liable to incur severe penalties for 'disrupting production' if they stayed away from the factory or the farm. Most serious of all, the social and economic changes introduced by the government, and its repression of religious institutions, began to have a marked effect on the life of the Jewish community. Intermarriage became more frequent, the closure of synagogues made formal religious observance difficult and as young people moved from rural areas to the large industrial towns they often became absorbed in the mainstream of Soviet life. Many of these young people were also inspired, through their membership of Communist youth organizations, by the vision of a new and greater Soviet society in which all distinctions of race, nationality, culture and religion were abolished.

All in all, the attack on the Jewish religion (as indeed on all religious faiths and institutions) during this period was near

overwhelming, as Dr Zvi Gitelman, Professor of Political
Science at the University of Michigan, has pointed out:

> The twin hammers of forced-draft industrialization and
> extremely rapid modernization, on the one hand, and persuas-
> ive terror, on the other, combined to exert enormously
> powerful pressures on the remnants of religious Jewry in the
> USSR. The Jewish religion fought a rearguard action against
> the forces which would destroy it; but fresh reserves were not
> forthcoming, and the army of the faithful dwindled into an
> ageing and exhausted band of believers. (*Aspects of Religion
> in the Soviet Union 1917–67*, p. 339f)

The rearguard action fought by the religious Jews in the 1930s
was an heroic one. Rabbis who were forced out of office by
government officials often went underground, where they were
maintained by the faithful, and continued to minister. A network
of illegal educational establishments was kept going until 1936,
and Dr Joshua Rothenberg writes:

> There was hardly a town or hamlet in which a group of
> religious Jews, large or small, would not keep their faith alive.
> The places of worship of these groups, overt or clandestine,
> were sometimes the only quarter where a needy Jew could find
> sympathy and assistance, and an itinerant Jew refuge. For
> religious Jews the house of prayer remained the only 'Jewish
> address' in a Soviet town. (*The Jews in Soviet Russia since
> 1917*, p. 171)

The war years brought relief from Soviet government pressure,
but the advance of the German army into the Soviet Union
brought disaster to the Jews. Special units of the Nazi forces
were employed on the mass execution of more than a million
Jewish men, women and children, and those who fled before the
invaders arrived became unwanted refugees who often died of
starvation or other privations.

Stalin's policy of relative toleration of religious bodies,
introduced during the war, did not apply to the national identity
any religious group might have, and 1948 saw the beginning of
the so-called 'Black Years' of Soviet Jewry which were to last
until 1953, culminating in the 'Doctors' Plot'. During these five
years most religious aspects of Jewish life were not seriously
attacked, but a massive assault was made on Jewish culture and
few prominent leaders in the intellectual and artistic life of

Soviet Jewry escaped arrest or even execution. All secular Jewish organizations and practically all Yiddish publications were closed down, and anti-Semitism reached a new peak of intensity. Although the religious Jews escaped direct persecution, they were deeply affected by the government's action against the Jewish community as a whole and became even more insecure and fearful.

Soon it was to be the turn of the Jewish religion again. In 1957 Khrushchev began an anti-religious campaign directed against all religious bodies. Many of the remaining synagogues were closed, and by 1964 only ninety-two were open in the entire Soviet Union. The usual method employed in securing their closure involved a local press campaign in which it was alleged that illegal or pro-Israeli activities were taking place in a certain synagogue; letters from readers, some of whom were said to be Jewish believers, were then published. These invariably asked for the 'corrupt' synagogue to be closed. Finally came an official announcement from the authorities to the effect that they had closed the synagogue in response to local demand. The buildings were then generally converted into warehouses or secular meeting places. At this time the building of new synagogues was forbidden and any Jews who applied for permission to build were likely to be interrogated by the police and threatened. Meetings for prayer in private houses were also forbidden by the authorities.

It was after the Suez episode that the Soviet government launched a new campaign against the State of Israel, which it pilloried as the representative of Western imperialism in the Middle East. Yet on the whole it seems improbable that the attack on religious Jews during the late 1950s and early 1960s was connected with Soviet foreign policy, since it took place within the context of a much wider oppression of religious bodies. But the attack on Israel complicated matters for the religious Jews and helped to create a more generally hostile climate. This climate became even worse after the Six-Day War in 1967, and the sustained anti-Zionist campaign, which includes denunciation of both Jewish religion and national culture, has continued ever since, with clear signs of intensification since 1977.

In 1980 the World Conference on Soviet Jewry produced a comprehensive report on the position of Jews in the Soviet

Union, in the context of the Helsinki Accords of 1975 and follow-up meeting of the Conference on Security and Co-operation in Europe held at Belgrade in 1978. This report listed eleven areas in which, in addition to their general disabilities *vis-à-vis* the Soviet State, the Jews experienced repression of their religion:

1. The Jewish religious community is denied the right to form an all-Soviet or regional organization.

2. Judaism is the only recognized religious body unable to maintain organized links with co-religionists outside the USSR.

3. No Jewish religious periodical or bulletin is permitted.

4. Apart from a calendar, no religious literature can be published.

5. The importing of religious literature is fraught with difficulty and, even when permitted, there are problems over its distribution.

6. Jewish ritual objects cannot be manufactured and it is generally forbidden to receive them from abroad.

7. The supply of *matzos* is totally insufficient, and since 1977 there has been a ban on the receiving of *matzos* from abroad.

8. Rabbinical training in the USSR is virtually non-existent, and although three students have recently been permitted to study at the Rabbinical Seminary in Budapest, a promise that two others would be allowed to study in the United States has not been fulfilled.

9. Only fifty-seven synagogues are known to be open, and twenty of these are in Georgia where, according to the 1979 census, there are only 28,000 Jews. Leningrad, Kiev and Odessa, with Jewish populations ranging from 120,000 to 160,000, have only one synagogue; Moscow, with its quarter of a million Jews, has only one; Kharkov with a Jewish population of 75,000 has none. Meetings for religious services in private houses (*minyanim*), of which there are said to be about two hundred, are subject to interference by the authorities.

10. Leaders of the Jewish religious community can only hold office at the pleasure of the state authorities, and since 1978 the Moscow Jewish Religious Community has lost two chairmen.

11. There are almost no Jewish cemeteries, and the old

cemeteries can be turned into public gardens twenty or thirty years after the last burial in them.

Moshe Davis, Director of the Office of the Chief Rabbi of Great Britain, was in Moscow in 1976 and described the ordinary worship and life of the Moscow synagogue in the Winter 1976 number of *Religion in Communist Lands*:

The only synagogue in Moscow is the Great Choral Synagogue, nearly a hundred years old. It is situated in Arkhipova Street, quite close to the Kremlin and the centre of town. Three services are held each morning at seven, eight and nine o'clock, attended by some two hundred old men. During the day a Yeshiva [Talmudic College] is in session. It has about six students and its standards are low. There are also late afternoon and evening services, less well attended than in the morning. There are, of course, no religious classes for children and youths. This is forbidden by Soviet law.

On the Sabbath morning the main service of the week is held. It starts at ten o'clock and lasts until approximately two o'clock. Generally the synagogue is almost full – with a congregation of some 600–800 – but there are very few women and no children. The congregation is made up of people of sixty and over. The form of service is the same as in orthodox synagogues in Great Britain. During the Reading of the Law, which lasts between three-quarters of an hour and an hour, most Jews simply turn to their neighbour and exchange gossip. Others stroll in the foyer and there meet acquaintances and relations. The foyer becomes a bourse, trading in information. So the synagogue, as a whole, serves the purpose of a meeting place as well as a House of Prayer. The main language of conversation is Yiddish.

At two o'clock every Saturday afternoon, on the pavement opposite the synagogue, some 100 *refuseniks* (i.e. those refused emigration visas) gather in the open air and hold their 'club'. Frequently they are joined by non-Jewish dissidents, who wish to support their assertion on human rights. In order to overcome the law relating to public meetings, the crowd splits up into some twenty or thirty groups, each numbering three to four people. Individuals move from group to group and so there is continuous circulation. Here again information is exchanged, about the latest position of families in need, about the replies received from the OVIR (the visa department), about news from Israel and so forth. Visitors from abroad frequently participate. I noticed an increase in traffic along the road whilst the 'club' was meeting, and many of the vehicles carried uniformed men.

Whereas the synagogue attracts the elderly, the 'club' consists of young people, teenagers and young professionals. It is significant that these young people do not go into the synagogue. They find no message with a meaning in the synagogue services. Yiddish is not their language. Many speak English and an appreciable number speak Hebrew. The synagogue, for its part, is disturbed by the 'club' and finds it a source of potential danger. 'They are hooligans', I was told by elders of the community. Quite obviously, many ordinary members of the synagogue did not agree. They chatted with the *refuseniks* on their way home.

Other visitors to the Soviet Union have commented on the sad atmosphere that seems to pervade the synagogues where ageing congregations struggle, against formidable odds, to keep the torch of religious faith alight. The overwhelming majority of Soviet Jews are, of course, living a considerable distance from their nearest synagogue and few of them can make the necessary long journey. The synagogues do, however, come alive on the important Jewish festivals, especially for the celebration of *Simhat Torah* (Rejoicing in the Law) which marks the annual completion of the synagogue reading of the Pentateuch. A young Jewish writer, Eli Wiesel, who was in Moscow for this festival in 1966, described what he experienced in *Le Figaro Littéraire* on 9 February 1967:

Some hours earlier, I had attended the service taking place within the synagogue. More than 3,000 people were packed in. The atmosphere was at the same time festive and solemn. Like the year before. More so than the year before. Men, women and children mingling. Faces bathed in sweat, languishing, devoured with yearning, with intoxication. One would have said they were conscious of the fact that their presence together in that place, that evening, revealed a meaning which perhaps transcended them: they represented three or four generations of Jews in search of each other, finding each other, aware that what they had in common must be transmitted . . . Someone pointed out to me an old captain of the Red Army, holding a Torah in his arms, and refusing to part with it. He was quite close to the microphone, his voice rising above the others. He was singing, 'Praised be the Lord who created us for his glory.' Behind him the great rabbi assented, 'Yes, yes, for his Glory' . . . The number of young people was impressive. Before, they hardly ever crossed the threshold of the sanctuary. The separating line could be neatly drawn; the old prayed in the synagogue, the young rejoiced outside. Now they were beginning to join those inside. Not many of them. But they were there.

Wiesel also reported on the scene outside the synagogue:

Feverish faces, burning, cheerful expressions. More people than the year before. Thirty thousand? Forty thousand? The police, fearing an accident, had set up first-aid posts, with ambulances and male nurses. It was a superfluous precaution. No one even fainted . . . They danced the *hora* exuberantly, and the earth trembled under their feet. Their shouts rang out, tearing through the night into the distance. They sang in Hebrew, in Yiddish, in Russian and, without its being realized, they were re-living the traditions of Israel, keeping them alive, to be hurled back as if in defiance at the face of the world around them.

After many years of silence a growing number of Soviet Jews are feeling strong enough to address petitions to the West asking for assistance in their struggle for survival, and seeking support for those of their number who are trying to emigrate to Israel and other parts of the world. In the West there are a considerable number of Jewish support groups which seek to bring pressure to bear on the Soviet government, and also maintain contact with Soviet Jews. The 'exodus' to Israel is now taking place on a considerable scale, though only about a quarter of those wishing to emigrate have been allowed to do so, and there continues to be severe harassment, often amounting to persecution, of Jews who have applied for emigration permits. (It is of course virtually impossible for other citizens of the USSR to leave the country.) The 'exodus' is primarily an expression of nationalism but it has many religious facets, some of which are reflected in the slogans,

'Let my people go', 'Next year in Jerusalem' and 'If I forget you, O Jerusalem'.

Notwithstanding the emigration, the vast majority of Jews remain in the Soviet Union where a growing number of them believe that the development of their religious life in the country that for so long has been their home is of the first importance. (The devotion to Russia traditionally felt by many Jews was brought home to the West in the 1960s through the successful musical *Fiddler on the Roof*.) This is proving to be exceedingly difficult as the Jews are deprived of much that they regard as important for the practice of their faith. In 1977 the government allowed the American Appeal of Conscience Foundation to send Soviet Jews ten thousand Torahs (the first five books of the Old Testament), and in the same year the Jews of Romania sent three hundred prayer shawls. But concessions of this sort are extremely rare and the position of religious Jews is generally worse than that of other believers who belong to recognized religious bodies. It seems that the Soviet government aims to solve its Jewish 'problem' by traditional methods: enforced assimilation, to which has been added recently emigration for the most recalcitrant minority. Numerically, the Soviet Jewish community is still large, but it is now in serious decline and the main hopes for its survival, assuming no significant change in government policy, can lie only in the remarkable resilience of the Jewish people under persecution.

THE MUSLIMS
The main Muslim communities in the USSR are in Central Asia and therefore beyond the concern of this book. There are, however, a substantial number of Muslims in the Checheno-Ingush autonomous republic, in the North Caucasus, and news of them appeared in an article by Marie Broxup in the Spring 1981 number of *Religion in Communist Lands*. When two small tribes in this republic rebelled against Soviet rule during 1940–41, the revolt was crushed, the entire Muslim population (over half a million people) were accused of treason and deported to Siberia and Kazakhstan, and the republic itself was liquidated. In 1944 all the mosques in this territory (there had been 2,675 of them in 1920) were destroyed. It was not until after the death of Stalin that the surviving Chechens and Ingushes were allowed to return

home; in 1957 the republic was restored. Another twenty years were to pass before any mosques were built, but in 1978 it was announced that two mosques had been opened, one in a suburban area of the capital, Grozny, the other in Ingush territory.

As it happens, the Muslims of Checheno-Ingush seem to have managed quite well without mosques, chiefly because of the work of two Sufi brotherhoods, the Naqshbandiya and the Qadiriya, who first appeared in the area in the eighteenth and nineteenth centuries. A number of surveys carried out in the late 1960s and the 1970s, and published by a government institute, indicate a considerable amount of religious faith and practice, especially among young people. Of 746 young people interviewed in two villages, 38.8 per cent observed the fast during Ramadan, 23.4 per cent of them actually fasting the whole month. Thirty-five point two per cent of the young men working on a state farm in 1976 maintained the *namaz* (five prayers every day), 56.1 per cent celebrated the *Mawlud* (the Prophet's birthday). Of Chechen and Ingush marriages 92.7 per cent are with a religious ceremony, most young parents have their male children circumcised, all burials, including those of Communist Party members, are with religious rites. Of the population of one million in the republic, something like 280,000 are thought to be Muslim believers, and Marie Broxup is of the opinion that Checheno-Ingush society is more attached to Islam and its traditions than it was sixty years ago.

RELIGIOUS LITERATURE
In the Soviet Union the propagation of religious beliefs is prohibited. Although the 1918 Constitution made provisions for freedom of religious expression, a significant change was made in the Constitution of 1929 and continued in the Constitutions of 1936 and 1977. Article 52 of the 1977 Constitution reads: 'Freedom of conscience, that is, the right to profess any religion and perform religious rites, or not to profess religion and conduct atheist propaganda, shall be recognized for all citizens of the USSR.' Although this does not mention religious propaganda, the absence of any reference to it has always been interpreted to mean that the publication of religious materials, apart from works essential to the formal functioning of religious bodies, e.g.

liturgical texts, is not allowed, and there may well be secret laws or instructions which are more specific on this point.

In practice, some of the recognized churches have been permitted to publish a limited amount of literature, and this seems to have increased since 1968, possibly as part of a government attempt to reduce the circulation of unauthorized and illegal material. All literature is subject to censorship, and approval would not be given for anything which directly challenged Communist doctrine or Party practice. At various times, particularly during the periods of most severe repression, the churches have not been allowed to publish at all. Paper shortage is sometimes offered as the reason for prohibition or restriction of the number of items printed. Problems also arise over the distribution of printed material, which is very uneven, and public display of religious literature is forbidden.

The Russian Orthodox Church publishes a monthly magazine *Zhurnal Moskovskoy Patriarkhii* (Journal of the Moscow Patriarchate). This is a well-produced magazine, with photographs in colour as well as black and white, and in addition to the Russian version there is an English one which is usually, though not always, a complete translation of the Russian. In its eighty pages there is a mixture of official statements and news from the Patriarchate, news of church events – mainly important acts of worship and peace conferences – articles and reviews, obituaries and devotional material. Never is there any suggestion that the Russian Orthodox Church has problems in its relations with the State, or indeed problems of any kind. The size of the circulation is not stated. Each diocese gets a few copies and parish priests can receive the journal on a subscription basis. It is sometimes alleged, however, that it is easier to obtain a copy if you live in London or New York than if you live in Moscow or Leningrad. Another official magazine is published in Ukrainian. The Russian Orthodox Church also publishes books of prayers for use by the laity, but though a collection published in the early 1970s had an edition of 250,000 copies this did not meet the need, and copies are now difficult to obtain. There are no copies of the text of the Orthodox liturgy available for use by lay people, and publication of liturgical texts is confined to the large copies needed for use by the priest at the altar. In 1976, however, an Orthodox hymn book, containing prayers to be sung and read, the sequence of the hours, and music scores for the Sunday canticles, was published. Church calendars, listing saints' days and other important occasions in the life of the Church, are also published by the Patriarchate, and papers on academic theology are published occasionally under the title *Bogoslovskiye Trudy* (Theological Works).

The All-Union Council of Evangelical Christians-Baptists publishes *Bratsky Vestnik* (Fraternal Messenger), a magazine which appears six times a year in an eighty-page edition and contains mainly devotional articles. A calendar or yearbook is also published by the Council, and there have been small editions of a hymn book.

The Old Believers publish calendars, or church yearbooks, and there has been a book of icons. The other churches and religious bodies may be publishing their own magazines and literature and, although this short survey has mentioned the main publications, it cannot claim to be exhaustive. It may be assumed, however, that the circulations of other religious literature are extremely small and that the contents are some-what mild.

It was not until 1876 that the first translation of the Bible from Old Slavonic into Russian was completed, and even then only 20,000 copies of the first edition were printed in 1889. Small reprints followed in 1889 and 1905, but these tended to be large-format Bibles for use in public worship, rather than for private reading. During the 1920s some 45,000 Bibles and 30,000 New Testaments were published, and in 1957 the Baptists were allowed to print 10,000 Bibles. The Baptists also obtained permission to print 20,000 Bibles in 1979, and a further 20,000 in 1980. Since 1945 there have been four Orthodox editions of the Bible with references and three editions of the New Testament with the Psalms. The importing of Bibles into the Soviet Union is extremely difficult. The American Bible Society delivered 10,000 Bibles, 5,000 New Testaments, 100,000 Gospels, and 1,000 Greek Testaments to the Russian Orthodox Church in 1947, but almost thirty years were to pass before in 1976 the United Bible Societies were permitted by the authorities to send any more, namely 3,000 Bibles in German for the All-Union Council of Evangelical Christians-Baptists. The All-Union Council was allowed to receive a further 25,000 Bibles in December 1978. In Estonia, Latvia and Lithuania there have been new translations of the New Testament and the Psalms, but these have appeared only in small editions of about 10,000. Throughout the Soviet Union copies of the Bible are extremely scarce.

A considerable black market for books now exists in the Soviet Union and a report from a reliable source in the 1970s stated categorically that, 'in the last decade the demand for all kinds of religious literature has moved into first place on the black market'. A second-hand Bible may cost up to a month's salary on the black market. The price of books by Berdyaev and other leading writers on the philosophy of religion has gone up by eight or ten times the already high price they had reached in the 1960s. Among modern writers there is a particularly strong demand for Russian translations of Bernanos, Graham Greene, C. S. Lewis and G. K. Chesterton. Books on theological and philosophical subjects are sometimes printed abroad in Russian, occasionally with a Moscow imprint, and then taken back into the Soviet Union by individuals, though Customs procedures have recently become much stiffer and books are often confiscated.

Quite a different matter is the *samizdat*, or self-published literature. The general restrictions on freedom of expression in the Soviet Union have led to the creation of a very considerable literature of articles, statements, documents, petitions and full-scale books which are produced in typescript or duplicated form, and sometimes on illegal printing presses, and circulated secretly. Among this literature is a good deal of religious material. Keston College, Kent, England holds extensive archives of *samizdat*, and in the year 1980, for example, over four hundred items of religious *samizdat* were registered at the College. It is reasonable to suppose that the *samizdat* reaching the West represents only a small proportion of that which is actually circulating in the Soviet Union.

The Reform Baptists provide one of the chief sources of religious *samizdat*. They produce *Bratsky Listok* (Fraternal Leaflet), which comes out every two months, and a quarterly magazine in three colours *Vestnik Istiny* (Herald of Truth) was developed from a less ambitious journal in 1976. There are also leaflets for children, and these are produced by a printing press which has so far escaped detection by the authorities, although two illegal Baptist printing presses were seized on different occasions in 1980. In addition to this regular material, the Reform Baptists publish accounts of the effects of their persecution by the State and make appeals to the Soviet government and to outside bodies such as the United Nations, that the persecution should cease. *Samizdat* relating to Church-State issues is also produced by most of the other religious bodies and there is a very considerable output in Lithuania where the *Lietuvos Katoliku Baznycios Kronika* (Chronicle of the Lithuanian Catholic Church), which first appeared in 1972, is now one of the outstanding examples in the whole field.

Besides the literature of protest, which inevitably appears in *samizdat* and for which severe penalties await those writers and distributors who are located by the authorities, there is a considerable range of religious material which appears in this form simply because there are no journals and newspapers in which it could otherwise appear. This material, which is often of great spiritual depth, includes sermons, articles on the liturgy, the Bible, theological topics, ecumenism, icons and so forth. Some of the secular *samizdat* also occasionally includes items of religious interest, either because a writer is handling religious themes or the experience of a religious body is used as an example of repression. Two Jewish *samizdat* journals, dealing with the history, culture and problems of Soviet Jews, often contain articles on religious themes.

One very important consequence of the Soviet government's restrictive policy regarding literature is that such items as do appear, whether in officially published or *samizdat* form, are greatly valued and very closely examined by those who are able to obtain them. Many of them are regarded as precious possessions and they are handed from person to person with the utmost care and seriousness. Their influence is, therefore, quite out of proportion to their circulation.

SURVIVAL AND FAITH

It is not necessary to be imperialist, capitalist, anti-Marxist, or anti-Russian in order to discern that the years since the 1917 Revolution have for the religious peoples in the Soviet Union been a time of great trial and deep tragedy. Although in theory

Lenin's position left open the possibility of mutual respect and co-existence between Church and State, the policy of successive regimes in the USSR has included the destruction of religious institutions and the elimination of religious belief. It has been, and is, the intention of the Soviet government that religious bodies shall wither away and die. This is a fact which cannot be ignored in any examination of the religious situation in the USSR.

The policy on religion has achieved only limited success. The territories which comprise the Soviet Union have rarely been attracted to the idea of compiling and publishing statistics about religious belief and church commitment, so quantitative comparisons are impossible. However, there can be no doubt that since 1917 all the Christian churches and Jewish synagogues of European Russia have been very seriously reduced in number and seriously disabled. Moreover, the combination of atheistic teaching and creeping secularism has had a significant effect upon the incidence of religious faith and practice. There are fewer churchgoers than there were fifty years ago, for oppression and propaganda do have their results.

Yet, in spite of all the Communist efforts, the religious communities are still very much a part of the Soviet scene. Not only are they still there; if we look at the situation as a whole, they are there in considerable strength. The number of Russian Orthodox believers is generally estimated to be of the order of fifty million – hardly a figure to be overlooked or dismissed as unimportant. The various religious sects are of course smaller, but there are signs here and there that they are very much alive, with some even growing and attracting significant numbers of young people, particularly among the educated. The persistence of personal belief obviously cannot be quantified, but it is at least interesting that icons are still to be found in a large number of Soviet homes, and sociological surveys carried out over the last two decades show that many people still have their children baptized and still have religious burials. And if the retention of icons and traditional ceremonies can be dismissed as indicating no more than a cultural lag, similar treatment is hardly appropriate for the firm evidence of intellectuals in the Church, especially in the last decade, or for the fact that a number of the great writers of the Soviet era have been Christian believers.

Indeed, for the last few years there has been more interest in religion, and probably more religious belief, among the Soviet intelligentsia than there was among the Tsarist intelligentsia for most of its history.

The persistence of religious belief and the survival of the churches in the Soviet Union is a plain fact. But serious difficulties are encountered as soon as any attempt is made to offer an explanation for this phenomenon. For one thing, precise sociological data are almost entirely lacking. For another, the factors which influence religious belief and practice are extremely complicated and, in any situation, rarely permit the luxury of scientific analysis and confident assessment. None the less, study of the continuing life of religious communities in the Soviet Union leaves certain impressions.

Chief among these is the fact that the culture and traditions of a people cannot be destroyed and replaced overnight. The Marxist-Leninist revolutionaries of 1917 were firmly convinced that religion would disappear as soon as man ceased to be alienated from the fruits of his labours, and they did not foresee any undue delay in the completion of this process. But they made a serious miscalculation in the significance and likely speed of economic progress, and erred in their supposition that religion would only survive for as long as it was able to feed on poverty and exploitation. Russian Orthodox culture, for example, with its intricate intertwining of the sacred and the secular, the mystical and the ethical, the personal and the institutional, had been evolving for almost a thousand years and was not ready to collapse at the wave of a red flag. The evidence of history from other parts of the world confirms that when religious belief has become an integral part of a cultural tradition it is exceedingly difficult to destroy.

A second element in the persistence of religious belief and the survival of the churches is to be found, perhaps paradoxically, in the nature of Soviet society itself. For more than half a century the main organs of corporate life and expression have been held in the suffocating grips of a government even more authoritarian than its predecessor. Rigorous control, censorship, elaborate systems of espionage, propaganda and much else have been developed to maintain the power of the Communist Party over almost every part of life. It is not surprising that since Stalin's

death a growing number of Soviet citizens have become more
and more unhappy about this arrangement, and have begun to
look for areas in which they can breathe a different air. The
churches and the synagogues provide one of the few places –
perhaps the only place – where such air exists. Hence their
attraction to those who are seeking an alternative to the shifting
orthodoxy of the Soviet Communist Party or who believe that
life has dimensions not yet acknowledged by the Kremlin.
Significantly, some of those in search of an 'alternative society'
or a 'counter culture' often turn to the nonconforming sects
rather than to the major churches which have State agreements.

Institutional durability is yet another factor which has worked
to promote the survival of religion. The historic churches have
developed a quite remarkable facility for adjusting their life to
meet new challenges. Like those parts of the natural order which
are obliged to change in order to survive, the churches seem to
have been able to move through every disaster, if not actually
unscathed at least with their essential life intact. The adjust-
ments, though, have been far from easy, and the demand for
courage and self-sacrifice has been enormous – perhaps especially so for the responsible leadership. More than anything else,
it seems, the creative tension which has arisen between
courageous leaders and their courageous critics, between the
forces of conscientious accommodation and conscientious
resistance, has nurtured the durability of religious institutions,
which are themselves so important in the nurture of the life of
faith.

There is one more survival factor, if reasons given by the
Russian religious people themselves are accepted. Many
Christians there believe that the promise to the apostolic
community, 'The gates of hell shall not prevail against it', was
not an empty one. They, therefore, have deep theological
reasons for supposing the Church will survive all the onslaughts
of unbelievers. As for the Jewish faithful, they rest the survival
and destiny of their community in the loving succour of the God
of Abraham, Isaac and Jacob. Such matters are rooted in faith,
which in the nature of things cannot be confirmed in advance of
unfolding life experience, and they offer no acceptable guide to
the future of any local religious community for those who

confine themselves to external evidence. But there can be no disputing that many millions of religious believers in the Soviet Union today are sustained by their belief in the ultimate indestructibility of the community of faith and, by their deep devotion and heroic courage, they are turning this belief into reality.

# Chapter 5

# POLAND

There were – to Western eyes at least – some strange pictures on television screens and in newspapers during August 1980. The striking shipyard workers in the Polish port of Gdansk were shown kneeling in corporate prayer. Other photographs showed priests moving among the crowds of workers, hearing confessions and distributing Holy Communion. The strikers were concerned mainly with the right to establish their own, independent trade unions and with the problems of Poland's ailing economy, but also on their 'shopping list' was a demand that mass should be broadcast every Sunday on radio and television. It is hard to believe that any of this could have taken place in any other country in the world, and the fact that it occurred in Communist Eastern Europe made it all the more poignant, and significant.

The Polish People's Democracy has Communist rulers and about two million of the thirty-five million population are members of the Communist Party. The Soviet Union is so dominant a neighbour that, while she remains unchanged, there will be no possibility of Poland's Communist order being replaced by another. But there the similarities with the rest of Eastern Europe end. Eighty-two per cent of Poland's agricultural land is privately owned and almost 40 per cent of the population are private landowners. In the rapidly developing industrial areas, unrest and strikes have become fairly common. Unemployment is a serious problem and 37 per cent of the population are under the age of nineteen. Moreover, Poland is Catholic, tenaciously so. *Polonia semper fidelis* was the motto of the old Polish gentry and bourgeoisie, and neither passage of time nor radical political change requires this motto to be modified.

It was in 966 that Poland's first ruler – Mieszko I – became a Christian and, following the custom of the time, the rest of the new nation was baptized soon afterwards. This brought Poland into a close relationship with the other countries of medieval Europe and during the Middle Ages the foundation was laid of an intense devotion to the Blessed Virgin Mary which remains a major characteristic of Polish Catholicism. At the same hour every evening Polish villagers can still be heard singing the simple, lullaby melody of the hymn 'Queen of Heaven'. Over the centuries a special relationship has existed between the Catholic Church and the Polish people, and whenever Poland has been occupied by foreign powers – as it has been for so much of its modern history – the Church has been the guardian of the nation's language, history and culture. The Byzantine icon of the Black Virgin at Czestochowa, which is visited by as many as half a million people in August, on the Feast of the Assumption, is not only a religious symbol, but also a symbol of Poland's resistance to foreign tyranny, and few Poles would wish to draw any distinction between the two, for they are a very romantic as well as a deeply religious people, and interpret their long history of suffering as martyrdom in the religious sense.

Herein is the significance of the beatification of Maximilian Kolbe by the Church in 1971. Father Kolbe's example of self-sacrifice stands as an inspiration to Christians in every part of the world. But for the Polish people the suffering and sacrifice of this priest, who called himself 'knight of the Immaculate Lady', focuses in one man the vocation to which they feel called as a nation and which they have experienced within their own lifetime. During the Second World War Father Kolbe was imprisoned in the Nazi concentration camp at Auschwitz, where he became an inspiration to many of those incarcerated with him. One day a group of prisoners were ordered to parade, and ten were picked out for execution. One of them cried out that he was a married man with children, and on hearing this Father Kolbe stepped forward and asked if he could take the condemned man's place. His offer was accepted by the authorities, and he was placed in an underground cell, where he was left to die of starvation. During his final days those who passed by the cell heard him praying and singing hymns. Father Kolbe's place in the history books of Poland, as well as in the Church's calendar, is assured. During the Second World War, in which one-fifth of the entire population of Poland was killed, 3,646 Catholic priests were sent to concentration camps, and 2,647 of them were killed. Almost a thousand church buildings were destroyed.

This close identification of the Church and the Polish people, especially in times of danger and suffering, gives the leadership of the Catholic Church a unique authority in Poland today. The overwhelming majority of the people have no time for Communism, which they regard as an alien creed imposed upon them by the hated Russians and as an affront to the Christian conscience. But they recognize the realities of their present situation, and so look to the Church to safeguard the Catholic culture and Christian values which are so precious a part of their national inheritance. The Church is an expression of their true identity and a mouthpiece of protest against attempts to dehumanize them. The Catholic hierarchy, and not least the new Primate, Archbishop Josef Glemp, are also aware of present realities. They have enormous influence over their 32.5 million members (well over 90 per cent of the population), but they recognize that an all-out confrontation with the government will achieve nothing. Thus no attempt is made to challenge the government in its own sphere: in fact, in times of economic and industrial crisis, even after the declaration of martial law by General Wojiciech Jaruzelski, the bishops have counselled moderation. But they have stubbornly insisted on the Church's right, and duty, to lead the Christian mission in Poland and to defend Christian moral values in Polish society. The denial of human rights during the period of martial law brought swift and courageous responses from Archbishop Glemp and his fellow bishops, and the teaching of the Catholic Church, especially as expounded by Pope John Paul II, constitutes a powerful challenge to the Communist government, which the leaders of the State fully recognize.

---

In examining the numerical strength of Catholicism allowance must be made for considerable changes in the population of Poland since 1939. During the twenty years immediately following the end of the Second World War, the population increased by more than eight million to just over thirty-three million. The overwhelming majority of these were Catholics, for the Jews had been annihilated during the war, the Germans had subsequently been expelled, while the Ukrainians and Byelorussians had been ceded to the USSR. In 1939 nearly 40 per cent of Poland's population were non-Catholics; in 1971 they amounted to only 3 per cent. Some 95 per cent of all Polish children are now baptized in the Catholic Church. The large increase in church buildings is directly related to the acquisition of property in the territory gained by Poland from Germany in 1945.

Today the Catholic Church is stronger in Poland than at any time during the past hundred and fifty years, and statistics indicate very considerable growth in recent years:

TABLE 3

*Recent Growth of the Roman Catholic Church in Poland*

|  | 1937 | 1980 |
| --- | --- | --- |
| Number of dioceses | 20 | 27 |
| Number of parishes | 5,170 | 7,240 |
| Number of priests | 11,239 | 20,234 |
| Number of churches and chapels | 7,257 | 14,000 |
| Number of lay monks and nuns | 24,000 | 26,745 |

While churches in almost every part of the world bewail the decline in the number of men offering themselves for the priesthood, ordinations in Poland have for some time been double, or even three times, the pre-war figure. Ordinands are trained in twenty-seven higher diocesan seminaries and seven monastic seminaries, where in 1980 there were 6,285 students in residence. There is one priest for every 1,750 people in the country.

Although the Roman Catholic Church now dominates the Christian scene, there are about 700,000 non-Catholic believers in the country, of whom the largest number are members of the autonomous Orthodox Church which has approximately 450,000 members, four dioceses, 233 parishes, 301 church buildings, two small monasteries, 256 priests and five bishops. These Orthodox

Christians are Polish citizens but are not of Polish nationality –
their numbers being determined by the shifting frontier between
Poland and the Soviet Union. On the whole they have benefited
from the Communist regime and gained greater freedom than
they enjoyed prior to 1945. The Polish National Catholic Church
is Old Catholic – it identifies with those Catholics who at various
times and in several places have separated from Rome – and has
about 29,000 members, three dioceses, 87 parishes, 102 priests
and three bishops. The Old Catholic Church of Mariae Vitae has
about 25,000 members, three dioceses, 42 parishes, 30 priests,
three bishops, a seminary, three convents and about a hundred
nuns.

Among the Protestant churches, the Lutherans are easily the
largest with about 80,000 members, six dioceses, 122 parishes,
305 churches and chapels, 99 pastors, 37 deaconesses and eight
religious teachers. This church has declined somewhat in recent
years owing to the emigration of members to Germany. The
Baptist Church, which was about 10,000 strong in 1939, lost a lot
of ground owing to frontier changes and emigration after 1945,
but it has attracted new support recently and now has about 2,500
baptized members and about 7,000 adherents. There are
fifty-four Baptist churches and seventy-three other centres of
Baptist work served by twenty-four ordained pastors and
thirty-five lay preachers and leaders. A new Baptist headquar
ters was opened in Warsaw in the early 1970s. The Reformed
Church, which was almost completely destroyed during the
Second World War, has about 4,500 members, fourteen
churches and chapels, seven ministers and twenty-five lay
workers, while the United Evangelical Church has just over
8,000 members and 222 churches and prayer houses. In 1971 the
Methodist Church in Poland celebrated the fiftieth anniversary
of its foundation. It now has a membership of just over 4,000 and
a total community of about 6,000 in sixty-six congregations and
preaching stations. These are served by twenty-nine ministers,
four of whom are retired, and a number of local preachers and
deacons. An English-language school organized by the Methodists in Warsaw is very popular. The Seventh Day Adventists
have about 8,000 members and sixty ministers in 124 centres.

The only significant religious minority which, for political
reasons, has been denied legal status in post-war Poland is the

Eastern-Rite Catholic (Uniate) Church embracing the majority of Poland's estimated 200,000 Ukrainians who now live dispersed among the Polish population in the former German territories in which they were forcibly resettled in the late 1940s. After October 1956 the authorities granted a *de facto* recognition to an arrangement worked out during the previous decade, whereby some fifty Uniate priests have been installed as assistants to Polish Roman Catholic parish priests in the localities with larger concentrations of Ukrainians. Despite repeated Ukrainian requests, the government has refused to allow the establishment of Eastern-Rite parishes. The Uniate diocese of Przemysl and the Uniate Apostolic Administrature of Lemkowszczyzna remain without bishops, with the Primate of Poland temporarily accorded by the Holy See the rights of the *ordinarius* for the Uniates.

The treatment of the Jewish community in Poland during the twentieth century constitutes one of the most shameful episodes in human history. At the outbreak of the Second World War there were 3.25 million Jews in Poland. During the next six years some 2.9 million of these were killed by the Nazis, and of those who survived the war a large proportion have now emigrated to Israel. They have been encouraged to go – some by their own Zionist aspirations, others by a series of anti-Semitic or anti-Zionist campaigns supported by the government. In 1967 First Secretary Wladyslaw Gomulka referred to the Jews as a possible 'Fifth Column'. A year later Jews were purged from all responsible positions in Polish society, and at the same time Gomulka 'invited' them to leave the country with the aid of the special emigration facilities provided by the government.

Now there are only 6,000 (mainly elderly) Jews in the whole of Poland, and the Union of Religious Congregations, which has eighteen affiliated local Jewish congregations, can arrange only limited activities owing to a shortage of leaders. There is no religious education for children and there have been no rabbis since 1965. The Yiddish-Polish newspaper *Folks-Sztyme* (The People's Voice), which appeared four times a week until 1968, is now published weekly and has a circulation of about three thousand. The well-equipped Yiddish State Theatre in Warsaw gives performances three times a week, and these attract large audiences which are supplied with Polish translations. The

Institute of Jewish Affairs in New York has forecast the ultimate
extinction of the Jewish community in Poland and the end of its
900-year-long history, and in 1980 the religious life of the
community was said to be deteriorating quickly.

All the non-Roman Catholic churches have their own periodicals, mainly small-circulation magazines for church members.
The Catholic press consists of about twenty newspapers and
magazines, ranging from small journals published by monasteries to the daily newspaper *Slowo Powzeche* (Universal Word)
which has a circulation of about 80,000, rising to 170,000 on
Sundays. (This newspaper is published by the Pax Association,
which lacks the support of the hierarchy and generally favours
the government.) *Tygodnik Powszechny* (Universal Weekly) is
a social and cultural weekly of the highest standard, published
by Znak, a movement of Catholic intellectuals concerned with
both political and ecclesiastical renewal. This newspaper often
falls foul of the government censor, and for many years its
circulation was restricted to 40,000, though it could have sold
many times this number had it been allowed to purchase
sufficient paper. (Towards the end of 1980 the government,
under pressure, allowed the circulation to rise to 50,000, but
copies of the newspaper remain extremely difficult to obtain.)
Znak also publishes two monthly magazines, *Znak* and *Wiez*,
while Pax publishes in several languages a monthly magazine
entitled *Catholic Life in Poland*. In April 1980 the official
Vatican newspaper *L'Osservatore Romano* started a Polish
edition for the benefit of Polish Catholics in all parts of the
world. About six thousand copies of the first number were
allowed into Poland but immediately there were problems with
the government's censors over material relating directly to
Church-State issues in the country. Several months of negotiation followed and at the end of 1980 it was agreed that the
newspaper would be allowed back, provided it confined its
contents to papal speeches, Vatican instructions and other
material originating in Rome. Documents of the Polish episcopate can also be included, and of the 95,000 now printed, some
90,000 are circulated in Poland free of charge. Attempts by the
Church to launch its own daily newspaper in Poland have always
been frustrated by the government. In addition to their newspaper and magazines, Pax and Znak both have thriving book

publishing houses, and the Pax list includes many of the best-known writers on theological subjects in the West. Again, Pax is given more favoured treatment over the supply of paper and printing facilities, while Znak battles against petty restrictions and has difficulties with State-owned bookshops which often refuse to stock its titles.

The British and Foreign Bible Society opened an agency in Warsaw in 1816 and began publishing the scriptures for both Catholics and Protestants. Its building was destroyed during the Second World War but a new headquarters was opened, with government support, in 1947. Since then the production of Polish scriptures has taken place in Poland, and in 1975 a new translation of the Bible – 'The Millennium Bible' – was published in Catholic and Protestant editions. By the end of 1980 the Polish Bible Society had published more than 130,000 copies of the new Protestant edition, and the government had given permission for a second edition to be printed. A Polish New Testament with full-colour illustrations has proved to be extremely popular, and 20,000 copies of its third edition were sold within a week in June 1980. The Bible Society's shop, located in one of Warsaw's main streets, stocks the Bible in sixty-seven languages and has a large mail-order business. Visitors from other East European countries often purchase copies to take home with them. The Catholic Church prints about the same number of scriptures as does the Bible Society, but there is a serious paper shortage and the demand for Bibles by Catholics is much greater than the supply.

---

Like all the other constitutions of Eastern Europe, that of the Polish People's Republic speaks grandly of 'freedom of conscience and religion' and of the freedom of churches to 'exercise their religious functions'. But Poland is different from the rest in that its constitution is, in this respect at least, fairly close to reality. The churches, in particular the Catholic Church, have a fair amount of freedom: not as much as they would wish, of course, but a lot more than the Communist government of the country would allow them to have if it had the power to bring them to heel.

Poland's 15,000 or so church buildings are open and well used. They are generally packed with worshippers on Sundays and feast days, and the Catholic churches are rarely empty during the week. Outdoor processions are allowed on certain feast days, and the parish priest is an important figure in the local community, as indeed the bishop is an important person in the region and in the nation as a whole. In the rural areas, where just under half the population still live, the integration of Church and society is more or less complete. Successive governments have found it impossible to modify an approach to life which has hardly changed since the Middle Ages. Officially, it is impossible to belong both to the Church and to the Communist Party, but low-ranking members of the Party are frequently seen at mass, and many of them have their children baptized. Until the latter part of 1980 the bishops frequently complained that miners and some other workers had to work on Sundays to facilitate continuous production processes – which was bad for their bodies as well as their souls, said the bishops – but the hours of work have now been modified and the miners are back in church again.

Religious observances for Polish Christians tend to be of a decidedly traditional character. Poland is not a country where liturgical innovation is encouraged, and at the Second Vatican Council Cardinal Wyszynski was among those who opposed the introduction of vernacular liturgy, going so far as to suggest that medieval Latin was part of the tradition of the Polish people. The number of people who receive Holy Communion when attending mass is still quite small, though it has risen in recent years. Catholics are well accustomed to hearing letters from their bishops read from the pulpit during the course of mass. Indeed, this is the chief, and most reliable, means of communication between the hierarchy and the people. Bishops' meetings usually end with a message to the faithful, and the most important statements are always signed by each of the bishops in an impressive display of solidarity. Some of these statements are highly critical of the government, especially when the Church's freedom or human rights are threatened.

One constant complaint of the bishops concerns the difficulty they experience in obtaining sufficient government licences for the building of new churches in the expanding urban areas. A notable case of government obduracy involved the new town of Nowa Huta, a huge project, planned to house 100,000 people, and intended to be the showplace of the Polish society of the future. No provision was made for any churches to be built in the town, but after much protest by the Catholic hierarchy and by the Catholics who had moved into Nowa Huta, the authorities eventually gave in. This town now has a very fine, exceedingly large church which includes a Chapel of Reconciliation in which thousands of people pray every day for personal reconciliation with God, for ecumenical reconciliation and for the reconciliation of Poland with her traditional enemies. In some parts of the country, especially in recent years, local congregations have gone ahead and erected new buildings without government permission or under the pretext of building something other than a church, and sometimes bishops have consecrated the completed structure secretly by night. The authorities have tended to turn a blind eye to this, not wishing to have a confrontation with a large section of the local population, but sometimes priests are heavily fined for breaking the regulations and in some instances unauthorized buildings have been demolished.

Access to the mass media has long been a bone of contention between Church and State, and the Church's demands have been only partially met by the 1980 decision to allow a mass to be broadcast on radio every Sunday. The Church believes that it should be allowed much more broadcasting time and that important church events should be adequately reported in news bulletins and in the national press. The censorship of the Church's own publications and the limitation of paper supplies for books and journals is another sore point. The weekly newspaper *Tygodnik Powszechny* is often required to remove particular items or parts of bishops' statements, though its courageous editor, Jerzy Turowicz, is now refusing to publish censored material and on a few occasions the paper has failed to appear because of unresolved conflict with the censor. In 1977 the bishops complained that only 300,000 copies of the catechism had been published in that year – an output of teaching material that would have seemed manna from heaven in any other East European country but which in Poland, as the bishops pointed out, represented only one copy for every twenty-six children.

The Catholic Church lost the right to teach the catechism in Poland's schools in 1955, at the end of the Stalinist era, and although the right was restored in December 1956 it was removed for good in July 1961. The government then decreed that all religious instruction should be given on church, rather than school, premises but with some financial support from the State. The bishops were unhappy about this but eventually conceded defeat and concentrated on the establishing of catechetical centres free from government interference. There are now almost 20,000 of these centres. Parents are required to give written consent for their children to receive instruction in them, and the overwhelming majority do so. University chaplaincies are very active, and in addition to celebrations of mass for the students there are extensive programmes of lectures and study groups on a wide variety of topics. The level of student participation is high. The Catholic University of Lublin, founded in 1918, is unique in Eastern Europe. It offers courses in the humanities and theology to over three thousand students, and is financed by the Church, with some assistance from the Church in the West. The university is now a most important centre of Catholic intellectual life for both clergy and laity. Parish clergy are invited to attend four- to five-day courses on theology and pastoral work at Lublin and also at the Catholic Academy of Theology in Warsaw, which receives financial support from the State. The academy has about 1,100 full-time students, of whom about one-third are priests, and about 500 part-time students, most of whom are priests. The bishops complain from time to time that university chaplains are prevented from carrying out pastoral work in university halls of residence, and that priests sometimes have difficulty in obtaining access to residential schools and youth camps. They also denounce those who put pressure on young people to join Communist organizations, and during the International Year of the Child (1979) the bishops had a letter read in all churches denouncing the 'systematic atheism' to which children were subjected in public educational institutions.

Well-organized and imaginative pastoral programmes, arranged on a national basis, are a feature of church life in Poland, and a remarkable programme extending over a novena (nine years) was carried out immediately prior to the celebrations of the millenary of the Polish Church and Nation in 1966. This programme brought a new strength and sense of solidarity to the whole life of the Church, and the arrangements give a fascinating picture of the spirituality of Polish Catholicism. It seems that when Cardinal Wyszynski was in exile in a monastery in East Poland (1953–56) he re-read Henryk Sienkiewicz's powerful novel *Potop* (The Flood), based on Poland's famous victory over the Swedish invaders in 1655. The prelude to this victory was the taking of an oath by the then king of Poland, John Casimir, who pledged himself on behalf of the nation to serve God and the Virgin Mary, to free the country of the foreign invaders, and to improve the social conditions of the Polish people. This gave the Cardinal the idea of getting the Polish people to renew King John Casimir's oath as a way of preparing for the millennium. The hierarchy adapted the oath to meet contemporary needs and produced a programme based on it for use in their dioceses and parishes. The bishops themselves took the oath at Czestochowa in August 1956, while the priests and people in the parishes pledged themselves on the Feast of Our Lady, Queen of Poland, in the following year.

The first year of the programme (1957–58) was called 'The Year of Faith', and its theme came from a section of the oath: 'We swear fidelity to God, the Cross and the Gospel.' Sermon outlines were provided for every Sunday and Holy Day for the whole year, together with study outlines for use in catechetical groups. The provision on a national scale of outline preaching and teaching material was one of the main features of the nine-year programme, and has continued in the years following the great celebrations of 1966.

The second year (1958–59) was called 'The Year of Grace', and described as a year of encouragement to do penance. Its central theme was 'Mother of God's grace, we promise you to guard in each Polish soul the gift of grace as the source of godly life'. The social implications were not neglected, and attention was directed to the importance of family life, the education of children, the evils of abortion and the need for Christians to be thrifty and industrious. Besides the Sunday sermons and catechetical teaching, various other activities were arranged. The first Friday of every month was set aside for the cult of the Heart of Jesus, with lessons on how to live in grace. An annual Week of Mercy was devoted to the mystery of the Mystic Body and life in grace. Monthly meetings were held for particular groups of men and women, and special conferences were held during Lent and Advent in the larger cities. Certain Saturdays were dedicated to the Queen of Poland, and submission to the Virgin Mary was presented as integral to the carrying out of the oath.

The icon of the Black Virgin, from the Jasna Gora monastery at Czestochowa, is carried to the towns and villages of Poland from time to time and is regarded with great awe, becoming both a focus of devotion and a source of renewal, as well as a considerable irritant to the government. At a different level, 'Sacrosong' (a religious songs festival) attracts a great deal of support from the young, and the Light and Life Movement is supported by Catholics of all ages. Characteristically, the national pastoral programme for 1980–81 was entitled 'Evangelizing through the Family'.

---

Officially, all Church appointments require State approval, but only in the case of appointments to bishoprics is there any kind of tug-of-war. How many priests have actually been refused episcopal consecration because of opposition from the government is impossible to ascertain, but it is plain from the composition of the hierarchy during the Communist era that the Church has never consecrated anyone of whom it did not approve. In cases of serious conflict, dioceses are left vacant until the matter is resolved to the Church's satisfaction. The only point at which the government has ever been able to subvert the unity of the Catholic Church has been through the Pax Association. Founded in 1946 by a former Fascist, Boleslaw Piasecki, this association was designed to provide a rallying point for Catholics who were prepared to support the Communist Party. There is strong evidence, however, that Pax was set up by the Soviet and Polish security services to perform a special task inside the Catholic community. During the Stalinist era, i.e. until October 1956, the association was more Stalinist even than the Communist Party, and in the 1960s it formed the spearhead of a campaign against writers and students who were demanding a relaxation of censorship. Pax has never been recognized by the Catholic hierarchy and priests are forbidden to join it, though some in fact have done so, arguing that the association arranges good literary events and has sometimes mediated creatively between Church and State. The size of Pax is variously estimated: in the mid-1970s it was said to have about 4,000 members, but it is now very much smaller and its chief activities are in the field of religious publishing, where its work is greatly valued. Since the death of Piasecki in 1979, the Catholic hierarchy has been a little more open to the association, although still disapproving of it: Pax is represented in the *sejm* (parliament) by five deputies.

Another organization which priests are forbidden to join is the Catholic Association 'Caritas'. This was formed in 1950 when the government seized about a thousand charitable and educational institutions which were at that time being administered by an association of the Catholic Church also known as 'Caritas'. These institutions were all placed in the hands of the new body, which was under State control, and gradually the most significant of them were handed over to the government. At the same time the organization became increasingly involved in political activity, and recruited into its membership a number of priests who were ostensibly engaged in charitable work, but devoted most of their time to pro-government propaganda at home and abroad. The retention of the name 'Caritas' has caused some confusion outside Poland, where it is often thought to be a part of the worldwide Catholic charitable movement of the same name, but it has on several occasions been disowned and condemned by the Polish bishops. Even so, it was reported to have fifty-one priests' 'circles' and nine laymen's 'circles' in 1976, all of them involved in political work.

The Znak group originated in 1956 when, with the approval of the hierarchy, a number of Catholic intellectuals launched the monthly magazine *Znak*. This was more or less suppressed during the Stalinist era, but when the Gomulka regime came to power in 1956 the group was allowed to take over from Pax the weekly newspaper *Tygodnik Powszechny* and also to establish 'Catholic Intellectual Clubs' in Warsaw, Krakow, Wroclaw, Torun and Poznan. These have flourished and, together with the publications, make up the Znak movement, which until 1976 had five deputies in the *sejm*, who constituted the nearest thing to an opposition party in the whole of Eastern Europe. The movement has sometimes been critical of the Catholic hierarchy for its tardiness in accepting the need for ecclesiastical reform, but it has always enjoyed the support of Cardinal Wyszynski and

Karol Wojtyla (the present Pope) when he was Archbishop of Krakow. In 1976, however, there was a disagreement within Znak over the movement's attitude towards certain government proposals for the reform of Poland's constitution. This reflected a wider unhappiness about these proposals in the Church at large. As a result, a minority group within Znak, calling itself ODISS (Centre for Documentation and Social Study), secured the support of the National Unity Front at the next election, and the five deputies who were elected do not have the confidence of the majority of Znak members in the intellectual clubs. The government has sought to exploit this split by transferring Znak's main financial assets to the ODISS group, though the larger group retains its newspaper and magazines.

---

Poland's small non-Catholic churches are generally experiencing as much freedom as is the huge Catholic Church, and from time to time Protestant leaders have commented that their churches now have greater freedom under the Communists than anything they ever experienced before the Second World War. When the foundation stone of a new Baptist church was laid at Bialystok in 1972 the President of the Baptist Union in Poland said he thanked God that every denomination was now on an equal basis. In these circumstances, and since neither the State nor the Protestant churches regard one another as a threat, relations between them are quite relaxed. So also are relations between the non-Catholic churches. Pulpit and altar fellowship between the Lutheran and Reformed Churches was introduced in 1970. The Polish Ecumenical Council was formed in 1945 and eight churches, including the Polish Orthodox Church, are members. This Council provides the basis for a limited amount of co-operation between the churches and also offers an important link with the World Council of Churches. It is in theological education that the co-operation has been most effective. One united seminary serves all the member churches of the Ecumenical Council. Warsaw's Theological Academy trains students for the ministry of all member churches in a five-year course. The Academy is part of the state educational system; professors are paid and appointed by the government, and students study on state scholarships. In 1972 there were twenty-five lecturers and 125 students. The Ecumenical Council's greatest significance lies in its wide international contacts, and through it the very small Polish member churches are represented at many international gatherings. It has also been used by West German Protestantism as a stepping-stone to German-Polish reconciliation. So close are the links now between the Ecumenical Council and the Protestant Christians of West Germany that it is almost possible to describe the relationship as going beyond reconciliation to mutual adoption. Whether the Council has the resources to develop and maintain comparable contacts with other countries and churches is rather doubtful. Even so, the international significance of the Council is out of all proportion to the size of its constituency.

Relations between the Roman Catholic Church and the other churches have improved slightly in recent years but, even though a joint commission of the Polish Ecumenical Council and the Commission of the Episcopate for Ecumenical Work was established in 1974, the ecumenical spirit is not much in evidence. The conservatism of the Catholic hierarchy is matched by that of the Lutheran leadership, and the Lutherans still remember that a good deal of Lutheran church property in the territory ceded by the Germans at the end of the war was seized by the government and handed over to the Catholic Church. The occupation of a number of Lutheran churches by Catholic congregations in 1980 and 1981 led to a strong protest by the Secretary of the Ecumenical Council, who accused the Catholic authorities of behaving 'positively arrogantly'. The Catholics, for their part, complain that tiny Lutheran congregations are housed in large buildings in areas where the mission of the Catholic Church is hampered by the lack of adequate meeting places for worship. In some local situations, however, there is good collaboration between Catholics and Protestants, and in 1976 Cardinal Wyszynski urged Catholics to collaborate with Orthodox and Protestants in order to 'make a common front against an individualistic ideology which imprisons man in the cocoon of his egoism'. On the other hand, the non-Catholic churches are unhappy about Catholic intransigence over mixed marriages, and during the early part of 1981 the Ecumenical Council, while expressing its approval of recent evidence of democratization in the apparatus of the State, went on to voice its unhappiness about what it called 'recent tendencies to

Catholicize society in Poland'. It pointed to the close relationship between the Roman Catholic Church and the independent
trade union movement Solidarity as evidence of 'the Roman
Catholic Church's exclusive claim to represent the identity of the
Polish people'. Disappointment was also expressed that the
Protestant churches had not been allowed access to the
broadcasting media at Christmas, whereas the Catholic Church
had been allowed to broadcast a mass.

---

The history of Church-State relations in Poland since the end of
the Second World War can be divided into five phases. The
country was liberated from German rule by the armies of the
Soviet Union in 1945 and a Communist-dominated provisional
government of national unity was set up. The next two years
were, as far as the Church was concerned, a time of relative
toleration, chiefly, as it now appears, because the new government had many things to attend to and was, in any case, too weak
to risk a major confrontation with an institution which had so
firm a hold on the allegiance of the overwhelming majority of the
ordinary people. A certain amount of State money was provided
for the rebuilding of churches destroyed in the war, the Catholic
University of Lublin and a number of seminaries were reopened,
the Church was permitted to retain its pre-war land holdings, and
religious education remained compulsory in all schools. Communist leaders were sometimes seen walking in religious
processions, and great occasions in the life of the State began
with mass in the cathedral at Warsaw. Already, however, there
were clear signs of an impending conflict. The government
quickly suspended the concordat which had governed relations
between Warsaw and the Holy See since 1925. Ostensibly this
was because the Vatican refused to recognize Poland's post-war
frontiers by appointing diocesan bishops to the territory taken
from Germany, but it is doubtful whether the Soviet-dominated
leadership would in any case have continued an official
relationship with a Church which was so closely identified with
the country's 'old guard' establishment. Civil marriage was also
decreed to be the only form recognized by the State, and the Pax
Association was formed in order to promote collaboration
between Catholics and Communists and, it was hoped, to
undermine the authority of the Catholic bishops.

The bishops, for their part, were not inactive, and when an election was announced at the beginning of 1947 the hierarchy caused a letter to be read in every church in the country stating that Catholics must not vote for, or be associated with, systems of government which were against Christian ethics and the teaching of the Church. The then Primate of Poland, Cardinal Hlond, also expressed the hope that Poland, 'ahead of other nations, will find in its warm and Christian patriotism the possibility of reconciling the healthy revolutionary contents of our times and the faith of the people'. The electorate had, however, little choice in the matter and the Communists were voted into government by an overwhelming majority. Once again the new government had many urgent matters to deal with, but by 1948 it was ready to launch an all-out attack on the Church which lasted until 1956. This was the height of the Stalinist era, and events in Poland cannot be seen in isolation from attempts to suppress religion in all parts of Eastern Europe between 1948 and 1956. The main difference in Poland was that there was a good deal more of it to suppress. 1948 also saw the translation of Mgr Stefan Wyszynski from the bishopric of Lublin to the primatial see of Gniezno and Warsaw, and the beginning of his leadership of the Catholic Church.

The government's first move against the Church was to declare illegal Catholic Action and other church organizations. A decree published in 1949 purported to guarantee freedom of conscience and of religious confession but, as with similar decrees and constitutions in Soviet bloc countries, it also provided a place for atheism and gave the state authorities wide powers for dealing with alleged abuses of religious freedom, especially when these were deemed to conflict with the interests of the State. A year later the government took over all the educational and charitable institutions administered by 'Caritas', and placed them under the control of its own organization, which was given the same name. The Church's lands were also nationalized, though parish priests were allowed to retain small amounts of land for their own use. In the same year, however, three bishops, representing the Catholic hierarchy, and three Communists, representing the government, signed a nineteen-point Accord which was intended to provide a new definition of Church-State relations. The supremacy of the Pope in matters of faith, morals and ecclesiastical jurisdiction was recognized, and the freedom of the Church to arrange acts of worship, carry out pastoral work, give religious instruction in schools, publish newspapers and magazines, maintain the Catholic University of Lublin, minister in hospitals, prisons and the armed services, and organize charitable institutions, was acknowledged. But the Church was required to undertake to urge the faithful to work harder for the reconstruction of the country, to oppose 'activities hostile to Poland', not to oppose the development of agricultural co-operatives, to condemn any act against the State and punish any ecclesiastics guilty of having taken part in any clandestine action against the State, and 'to support all efforts for the consolidation of peace'. The Accord also included an acknowledgement by the Church that the German territory allocated to Poland after the war should belong to Poland 'for all time', and an undertaking to ask the Pope to appoint residential bishops to the dioceses within that territory.

At the Potsdam meeting of the victorious Allied powers in 1945 it was agreed that Poland should, in compensation for territory ceded to the Soviet Union in the east, be given some former Slav territory on the Oder and Neisse rivers which had been part of Germany for a long time, and that a new State frontier should be drawn between Poland and Germany. Although Poland assumed immediate control of this territory and the great majority of the German population were expelled from it and replaced by people from East Poland, the West German government withheld recognition of the new frontier until May 1972. This irritated the Polish government, and the request to the Vatican for residential bishops to be appointed to the dioceses in this territory was an attempt to obtain further international recognition of the Potsdam agreement. The Vatican was not prepared, however, to get entangled in the political controversy surrounding the frontier, and although titular bishops were appointed to the territory in 1967, in an attempt to placate Polish opinion, the dioceses were regarded as apostolic administrations until West Germany finally acknowledged Poland's frontiers. Only then were residential bishops appointed and the five dioceses fully integrated in the Church of Poland.

After the signing of the 1950 Accord, Cardinal Sapieha of Krakow made a special journey to Rome to seek papal support for the appointment of residential bishops, but he returned disappointed, and from that point onwards relations between Church and State steadily deteriorated. Whether the government was ever prepared to concede to the Church the freedoms outlined in the Accord is very doubtful. In the event, the unwillingness of the Vatican to meet Poland's requirements over the bishoprics provided the government with an excuse for its persecution of the Church, but the views of the Polish bishops on the matter were well known, and the reasons for the reneging on the 1950 Accord are perhaps to be sought in Moscow, rather than in Rome. From the point of view of Archbishop Wyszynski and his colleagues, the signing of the Accord was a difficult decision. They had been accustomed to more or less untrammelled freedom and considerable influence for the Church. Moreover it went against the grain to have dealings with an atheistic government. But now the bishops were facing a battle for survival, and the Accord was seen as part of a 'buying time' strategy.

In 1952 a new constitution declared the separation of Church and State and at the same time made the Church subservient to the State. In the same year Wyszynski was appointed a Cardinal, but he decided not to go to Rome to receive his hat from Pope Pius XII as it seemed most unlikely that he would be allowed back into Poland. In September 1953 Wyszynski, having strongly objected to the nomination of new bishops by the government, was arrested and confined to a convent outside Warsaw, where he remained until June 1956. By 1953 eight other bishops and 900 priests were imprisoned, and towards the end of that year the rest of the hierarchy were pressured into taking an oath of loyalty to the State. All Church appointments were now made subject to State approval, the number of seminaries was reduced from ninety to twenty, the theological faculties of the universities were closed, the Catholic University of Lublin was curtailed, the church press was seriously restricted and heavily censored, punitive taxes were levied on church property and church collections, and in 1955 religious teaching was forbidden in schools. Throughout this period the Church and the Vatican were constantly attacked by government spokesmen, and by 1955 there were about two thousand bishops, priests and lay Catholics in Polish prisons.

There was no sign of a thaw in Church-State relations until Wladyslaw Gomulka, who had himself spent several years in prison for 'Titoist deviation', returned to power as First Secretary of the Party in 1956. One of his first actions was to release Cardinal Wyszynski and reinstate him as Primate. All the other imprisoned bishops and priests were released soon afterwards, and representatives of the government and the hierarchy concluded a new agreement on 7 December 1956. The communiqué issued afterwards said:

> The Joint Commission of representatives of the government and the episcopate discussed a number of unresolved questions concerning relations between the State and the Church. In the course of the conversations, the representatives of the government emphasized their readiness to remove the remaining obstacles to the realization of the principle of full freedom for religious life.
>
> The representatives of the episcopate stated that as a result of changes in public life aimed at the consolidation of legality, justice, peaceful co-existence, the raising of social morality and the righting of wrongs, the government and the state authorities would find in the church hierarchy and clergy full understanding for these aims.
>
> The representatives of the episcopate expressed full support for the work undertaken by the government aiming at the strengthening and development of People's Poland, at concentrating the efforts of citizens in harmonious work for the good of the country, for the conscientious observance of the laws of People's Poland and for the implementation by the citizens of their responsibilities towards the State.

The communiqué went on to outline the agreement which had been reached on a number of practical matters, in particular, the appointment of bishops, and religious education in schools. On the question of episcopal appointments, it said:

> The new legal act regulating these matters will guarantee the influence of the State in the appointment of archbishops, diocesan bishops and co-adjutors with right of succession, as well as parish priests, preserving at the same time the requirements of church jurisdiction.

This meant in effect the continuation of the long-established Polish tradition that the Church consults the State when appointments are made. On the question of education, the agreement said:

Full freedom is assured and the voluntary character guaranteed of religious instruction in elementary and secondary schools for children whose parents express such a wish. Religious instruction will be conducted in schools as an extra-curricular subject. The school authorities are to make it possible for religious instruction to be followed through a properly drafted syllabus of lessons. Teachers of religion will be appointed by the school authorities in agreement with the church authorities. The teachers of religion will be paid from the budget of the Ministry of Education. The programme of religious instruction as well as the religious instruction manuals must be approved by the Church and the educational authorities. The school authorities will endeavour to enable the children and youth to participate freely in religious practices outside the school. The school authorities and the clergy will ensure complete freedom and tolerance both to believers and to non-believers and will firmly counteract all manifestations of violation of freedom of conscience.

In addition to this considerable concession over religious education, the Church was permitted to reopen many of its seminaries, bringing the total number to seventy, the punitive taxation of church property was reduced, the Pax Association was required to hand over *Tygodnik Powszechny* to Znak, and the Znak movement was promised eleven (in the event it was given only five) seats in parliament. Gomulka needed all the support he could get and was at this stage wooing the Church. Wyszynski was anxious to ease the pressure on the Church and, although his concessions to the government were not trifling, he was generally thought to have struck an excellent bargain. Partnership between Church and State was out of the question, but a form of *détente* seemed a real possibility.

Unfortunately, this lasted for only two years. From 1958 onwards the recently signed agreement was laid on one side, and for the next twelve years the government pursued hardline repressive policies against the Church. These policies were not as savage as those of the Stalinist era, and their main aim seems to have been to reduce the influence of the Church in Polish society and to restrict its activities to its own buildings. Religious education was banned in most schools and transferred to church-based catechism centres. The religious orders were forbidden to teach, and Cardinal Wyszynski was not allowed to leave Poland (this ban was lifted in time for him to attend the Second Vatican Council). The heavy taxation of church property was restored. Many church publications were banned and no children's religious books were allowed. Difficulties were put in the way of the observance of religious holidays, pilgrimages and processions, and the government tried to offer counter-attractions in the form of secular festivals and school outings. Attempts were made to interfere in ecclesiastical appointments and in the running of the seminaries, and the government tried to undermine the bishops' authority by giving increased support to Pax. The creation of new parishes in the expanding industrial areas was forbidden, and licences for new church buildings were severely restricted.

It is still far from clear why the Gomulka regime so quickly went back on the 1956 agreement, and neither research nor speculation is assisted by the fact that there were some slight, probably tactical, variations in the hardline policy between 1958 and 1970. The unwillingness of the Vatican to give official recognition to Poland's new frontiers obviously caused the Warsaw government great irritation. The government itself became more secure and possibly felt less need to treat with the Church. A Communist regime, looking forward to the gradual decline of religious institutions and the secularization of society, was bound to react against the presence of a Church which was undoubtedly increasing in strength and in its influence among the great mass of the population. The ambitious, and highly successful, pastoral programme launched in 1957, and designed to provide a nine-year preparation for the millennium in 1966, indicated clearly that this historic year for the Polish nation was to have a powerful religious dimension, and that the Church, rather than the Communist Party, would have the leading role in the celebrations. Whatever the reason, or reasons, confrontation was once again the order of the day. Cardinal Wyszynski and the other bishops protested against the government's repressive policies, and in 1964 the Cardinal denounced Pax as a Communist-front organization. The government responded to the hierarchy's attacks by accusing the bishops of interfering in political matters and in the country's foreign relations.

Towards the end of 1965 the government eagerly seized what seemed to be ready-made ammunition against the Church, in the form of a letter from the Polish bishops to the German episcopate. From 1945 onwards, Polish governments – expressing much Polish popular opinion – had declared that the Nazi war crimes would never be forgotten or forgiven. The Polish bishops decided, however, that it would be appropriate to end the preparations for the millennium by sending a letter to the German bishops offering forgiveness and asking the German people to forgive the Poles for any wrongs which they had done, especially in the savage retribution exacted immediately after the German defeat: 'The hour of pardon and dialogue has come: we forgive you.' The government at once accused the bishops of political action and questioned their loyalty to Poland and its post-war political order. A sustained propaganda campaign against the Catholic Church was mounted, a proposal that Pope Paul VI should visit Poland for the millennium celebrations was blocked, and Cardinal Wyszynski was forbidden to travel to Rome. On the other hand, throughout 1966 there were many public demonstrations in support of the Cardinal and protests against the victimization of him by the government.

---

In Cardinal Wyszynski the Polish government faced one of the most formidable figures in the entire Catholic world. Born in a small village in north-east Poland in 1901, he studied canon law and social science at the Catholic University of Lublin and was ordained in 1924. Later he became professor of social science at the seminary of Wloclawek and earned the reputation of a progressive social reformer. During the Second World War he taught secretly in Lublin University, which was functioning 'underground', and in 1944 was appointed Bishop of Lublin. Four years later he was translated to the Archbishopric of Gniezno and Warsaw.

Soon after his consecration as Bishop of Lublin, Wyszynski issued a pastoral letter in which he said of himself: 'I am no politician, no diplomatist, and no reformer.' This proved to be a very accurate description of the man who led the Polish Church during one of the most difficult periods in its long history. Yet he displayed many of the attributes of a great statesman. In his dealings with the Communist government he was often very shrewd, and normally fought battles only on ground of his own choosing. He never ceased to be conscious of the immense power of Polish Catholicism and the unique claims of the Church. Although Church and State in Poland co-exist under a massive compromise the Cardinal was a man of very strong principles. He always sought the maximum freedom and greatest advantage for the Church and was never satisfied with anything less than he asked for. But the fact that he outstayed four Party secretaries increased his standing in the nation, and his battles on behalf of the Church were seen by most Poles as battles for the freedom of the entire people of Poland.

During the early years of his primacy Wyszynski's tough independence created a number of problems, not only for the Polish government but also for the Vatican. (Relations between the Cardinal and Pope Pius XII were always ambivalent.) The unwillingness of the Pope to create the residential bishoprics displeased Wyszynski, partly because it made life difficult for the Church in Poland but chiefly because it was an affront to the nationalism which, like Catholicism, is an integral part of Polish life. For its part, the Vatican often had serious reservations about agreements reached between the Polish hierarchy and the government. When Wyszynski visited Rome to report on an agreement signed at the time of Gomulka's return to power in 1956, Pius XII showed his displeasure by keeping him waiting several days for an audience. The Polish bishops seem to have conducted most of their negotiations with the government without reference to Rome, for when, in 1961, Gomulka accused the Church of looking for trouble, on Vatican instructions and to serve Vatican ends, Wyszynski promptly declared that during his thirteen years of office no Pope or Secretary of State had ever attempted to give the Polish hierarchy instructions on the ordering of the Church's life.

It was not until John XXIII became Pope that the Polish Primate received cordial recognition and co-operation in Rome. There was a moving occasion when, at one of the midday blessings in the early days of his reign, Pope John presented

Cardinal Wyszynski to the crowds gathered in St Peter's Square. Further, although there were still no concessions over the bishoprics, the Pope made it known privately that he fully approved the policy which the Polish Church was pursuing. In fact the bishops were given a wider measure of freedom to negotiate with the government, and when Pope John received them during the Second Vatican Council he referred to 'the Western territories which have now been recovered after centuries'. This was music to the ears of the Church, and the sound reverberated throughout Poland.

Wyszynski's reluctance to treat with the Communists was matched by his reluctance to become involved in church reform. While he was ready to make a progressive approach to social affairs – he is on record as advocating the nationalization of industry, and at Christmas 1972 wrote a strong letter to the American bishops about their country's involvement in the Vietnam war – in theological and ecclesiastical matters he was a thorough conservative. At Vatican II it was the Polish Primate and his colleagues who asked the Church to proclaim the Motherhood of Mary as embracing the whole of humanity, and in the important debates on the Constitution of the Church he emphasized frequently the need for the Church to be seen primarily as an instrument of personal sanctification.

There was, in fact, a strong mystical element in Wyszynski which also showed itself in his introspective temperament and in a certain unpredictability. In other words, he was Polish through and through, and embodied the traditional ethos of his country. It was a great disappointment to him, as it was also to Pope Paul, when the Polish government refused permission for the Pope to visit Czestochowa in 1966 for the celebration of the millennium. But there was more than adequate compensation twelve years later when Poland provided the first non-Italian Pope for 455 years. At John Paul II's inauguration mass in St Peter's Square in October 1978 there was no more moving sight than that of the new Pope embracing Cardinal Wyszynski, at great length and with tears in his eyes. Wyszynski was different from Wojtyla in certain ways – less intellectual and more inflexible – yet there can be no doubt that without the outstanding ministry of 'the Iron Cardinal' over almost three decades there would have been no Polish Pope. In 1976, when

Wyszynski reached the age of seventy-five, he submitted his resignation to Pope Paul VI, in accordance with canonical requirement. But he was immediately reconfirmed in office – with, it is said, the support of the First Secretary of the Party, Edward Gierek, who sent him a bouquet of seventy-five roses on his birthday. His death in May 1981 was marked by three days of national mourning and tributes from leaders of the State and the Communist Party. After an open-air mass, celebrated by Cardinal Casaroli in Victory Square, Wyszynski's body was buried in Warsaw Cathedral, though the independent trade union Solidarity had suggested the traditional burial place of Polish kings in Krakow.

---

Gierek had come to power at the end of 1970, when the Gomulka regime collapsed under the pressure of strikes and food riots in the Baltic ports and popular revulsion against the violence of the police when attempting to deal with the strikers. In a Christmas sermon, given a few days after Gierek had taken office, Wyszynski said that this was a time for forgiveness, rather than mutual recrimination, and he called on Catholics and Communists to work together for economic and social reconstruction. A pastoral letter issued by the hierarchy on New Year's Day 1971 asked that the fundamental rights of the human person be guaranteed as a condition for living together peacefully within the same nation:

1.   Freedom of conscience and of religious practice on the basis of a full normalization of the relationships between Church and State.
2.   Free access of the people to the Christian culture of the nation.
3.   Social justice to meet and satisfy the legitimate demands of the people.
4.   Right to freedom of expression and truthful information.
5.   Right to decent living conditions for all the families of the nation.

These five demands constituted the ground on which the tug-of-war between Church and State was to take place throughout the 1970s, and they approximated closely to what were to become the demands of the great majority of the Polish people by the end of the decade.

The new First Secretary proved to be much more flexible than his predecessor. In March 1971 the government told Cardinal Wyszynski that it looked forward to the 'normalization' of relations with the Church, and as a mark of goodwill it formally recognized the Church's ownership of some thousands of church buildings, and handed over about two thousand acres of land which it had been holding, in the Oder-Neisse territories. In the following year the Church was told that it need no longer submit to the government annual accounts and inventories of its possessions. For a space of about two years relations between Church and State were relatively relaxed. During this time the Oder-Neisse dioceses were given residential bishops, and the embassy of the 'Polish government-in-exile' at the Holy See was closed.

The Gierek government's view of 'normal' was outlined by the Director of the Office for Religious Affairs, Vice-Minister A. Skarzynski, in a speech to Pax on 3 October 1971:

Our State will consistently aim at fully satisfying the religious needs of believers, to allow the Church to conduct in good conditions its pastoral and educational activity, including teaching of religion to children and Catholic youth. We are of the opinion that in the field of social morality there are problems of basic importance for the future of the nation as to which Marxists and Catholics, though basing themselves on different ideological and philosophical assumptions but guided by common patriotism, have convergent views . . .

We expect all practices and trends which were hostile or antagonistic towards People's Poland, which in the past were often the cause of serious tensions and conflicts between the State and the Church, to be gone never to return.

We expect the episcopate and the whole clergy to understand and respect the patriotic and political interests of our Socialist state. This does not mean in the least that we expect bishops and other church authorities to use their religious prestige directly to influence clergymen or lay Catholics with a view to making them assume progressively socialist attitudes. However, we have the right to expect that the episcopate will not show partiality to people with a hostile attitude towards the People's State or towards socialism . . .

The durability of this understanding can be guaranteed by two fundamental principles:

(a)   The church authorities, the episcopate – in agreement with the suprapolitical character of the religious mission – must consistently recognize the socialist political order of our country, the political orientation of People's Poland as an invincible and patriotically supreme reality.

(b)   The People's State will respect the durable character of the Church's religious activity, will show recognition for the social value of its educational functions in relation to believers.

The Church's view had been stated earlier in a document dated 21 June 1971, and entitled 'How Normalization should be understood'. It was of course the work of the hierarchy, and took its stand on three theses:

1.   *The Church in Poland is part of the universal Church.* Here the bishops made the point that the Catholic Church is different from all the other Christian communities in that it has a centre outside the country: 'the Catholic Church cannot be a national Church, otherwise it would cease to belong to the universal Church'. It follows from this that the Catholic Church cannot be dependent upon or subordinate to the State.

2.   *The Church in Poland has served the nation for a thousand years.* Appealing to history, the bishops portrayed the Church as an integrating factor in the life of the Polish people, especially during the 124 years of partition when the country disappeared from the maps, and again during the Nazi occupation when 'the Church together with the nation went through a most terrible agony'. The document also mentioned that: 'Through its educational influence and the cultivation of national values, the Church defended the nation from Germanization and Russification.'

3.   *The Polish nation is Catholic.* Hence, said the bishops, 'All efforts to isolate the Church in the nation and to curtail its tasks and its mission lead to the disintegration of society and bring the faithful into opposition with the rulers, a situation which is harmful both to the nation and to the State.'

Having outlined the Church's basic position, the document went on to summarize the Vatican II teaching on Church-State

relations. It then recognized that social, political and economic
conditions had changed in Poland after the war and continued:

> The Church in Poland, which is served by the episcopate, does
> not want to create a political opposition, nor does it mobilize
> social forces to fight against the system established in the
> constitution. The episcopate has not assumed and does not
> wish to assume the role of political leadership.

Yet the Church can only serve the nation under these new
conditions if it has freedom to uphold moral values in public
life:

> The Church cannot be said to be fighting against the political
> system or with the state authority when, according to its
> mission, it strives for freedom of action or when it defends
> basic civil rights as moral values deriving from human natural
> law and the Gospels, especially when these rights are curtailed
> or even violated by individual governments.

The document concluded with a number of practical proposals
to give substance to its general concept of normalization. These
included recognition of the Church as a legal person, ruled by its
own laws; freedom for the Church to meet, to appoint its leaders
and to communicate both within Poland and with Rome; and
freedom for the Church to manage its own property.

Yet, as far as the Church was concerned, the situation was still
quite a long way from normal. In the spring of 1972, a makeshift
chapel erected illegally in the village of Zbroza Wielka, near
Warsaw, was dismantled by 150 policemen, and the tabernacle
containing consecrated hosts was carried in a lorry to a nearby
church. A government spokesman explained that since the
chapel had been built without a licence it was necessary for the
local authority to remove it, and the police had returned the
property to the local priest. But in a sermon in Warsaw cathedral,
Cardinal Wyszynski accused the authorities of an 'irresponsible
act' and of 'unprecedented sacrilege', both of which were
regrettable in view of the government's declared intention of
improving Church-State relations. Furthermore, he warned the
First Secretary in a private letter that if such policies continued
he would suffer the same fate as his predecessor, Mr Gomulka.
He went on to accuse the government of attempting to 'atheize'
the people and of frightening those who wanted to follow Christ.

A year later – May 1973 – a pastoral letter issued by the bishops repeated this accusation:

> We must defend ourselves, our families and the whole nation against the secularism and atheism that are being imposed upon us . . . If some have the right to atheize the nation against its will, against the will of Catholic parents and of young people themselves, against the constitution which guarantees everyone freedom of conscience and of confession, then Catholics have all the more right to defend themselves against this abuse of law.

By this time a considerable storm was brewing over the future of religious education for children. The government adopted a policy of closing small village schools and transporting children to much larger schools serving a wider area. As in other parts of the world, this policy was designed to provide better educational facilities, and the bishops accepted this point, though they were very unhappy about what they regarded as the 'Sovietization' of Poland's educational system. The bishops were also aware that the 'busing' of children had a disruptive effect on the village communities in which the Church had prospered for centuries. What is more, it made religious instruction much more difficult, since the children were required to spend much longer hours either in school or travelling to and from school, and there were far fewer opportunities for parish priests to give instruction in their catechetical centres during the normal educational day. Classes in the evening or at the weekend were obviously much less attractive to a child. So the bishops opposed the new policy on the grounds that making religious instruction difficult and undermining the stability of communities could not be regarded as good education; neither was it good for Poland. The conflict over this issue between Church and government raged for some years and, although the policy of closing village schools has continued, provision has now been made for most of the children to receive religious education during the afternoon.

---

Soon the government was to have a much more serious conflict on its hands. From 1973 onwards there were signs of unrest in the universities, not least in the Catholic University of Lublin where, for the first time, an informal, independent student body was formed. The government's proposed amendments to the constitution in 1975–76, which formalized the principle of 'the leading role of the Party', provoked protests from many Polish intellectuals and from the Church. These protests prevented the proposals from being adopted in their original form, and it thus became clear that strong, united opposition could in some circumstances compel the government to make concessions. By this time the Helsinki Declaration on Human Rights was being widely discussed in Poland. In June 1976 a government announcement of increases in food prices led to serious strikes in three towns and, though the strikers were treated harshly by the authorities – many of them were beaten up, imprisoned and dismissed from their jobs – the government was obliged within twenty-four hours to withdraw the price increases. From now on Poland had a dissident movement. The Social Self-Defence Committee was founded in September 1976 to defend workers and their families who had been victimized in the strikes. In March 1977 the Movement for Human and Civil Rights was started and many *samizdat* publications began to circulate, including *Spotkania* (Encounters), a journal edited by a group of young Catholics and particularly concerned with the Catholic approach to social and political change in Poland. 1977 saw also the formation of the 'Flying University' (The Society for Academic Courses), an educational project organized by dissident intellectuals who are trying to break the State monopoly on education and give courses of lectures in private apartments throughout Poland.

The Church was, from the outset, deeply involved in the protests which followed the 1976 strikes. In September of that year Cardinal Wyszynski, speaking of strikes, demonstrations and repression, said, 'Such difficulties cannot be solved by the police, by beating people or by sticks or gas or dogs. Only one thing will solve them: open your hearts and show yourselves to your brothers, show yourselves to the citizens ... Stop the repression, start to serve your brothers ... whoever would want to govern here must learn to govern through our hearts and not through police and prison ... We desire so much that the whole style of government change ... this is what we ask for, what we pray for, what we demand.' The hierarchy as a whole protested against the harsh sentences passed on those who had taken part in the strikes and demonstrations, and in November 1976 the

Bishops' Conference appealed for an amnesty for all who had been imprisoned after the strikes, at the same time reminding priests and parish councils of their duty to help those who had lost their jobs. In June of the following year a number of Catholics, including Bohdan Cywinski, editor of the journal *Znak*, staged a hunger strike in St Martin's Church, Warsaw, as a protest against the imprisonment of five particular workers who had taken part in the demonstrations.

Surrounded by rising dissent, Gierek apparently decided to work for better relations with the Church. Concessions were made over educational reforms, and more licences for church buildings were granted. In December 1977 Gierek visited Pope Paul VI in Rome and later in the same month had his first-ever meeting with Cardinal Wyszynski, during which he sought to assure the Cardinal that the government was anxious to preserve religious freedom. The Church took the First Secretary at his word and immediately began to ask for much greater freedom, including provision for religious broadcasts on radio and television and an end to censorship. Then, on 16 October 1978, came the election of Cardinal Karol Wojtyla of Krakow to the papacy.

The election, and subsequent nine-day visit of Pope John Paul II to his homeland in 1979, had an impact upon Poland of such a magnitude that the consequences cannot yet be fully evaluated, and are indeed still in process of unfolding. The immediate reaction in Poland to the news of the election was of disbelief, turning to intense joy. The government was placed in the impossible position of trying to maintain its anti-religious stance without turning its back on the deep religious and patriotic feelings of the great majority of the people. Within days, permission had to be given for the broadcasting of the new Pope's inaugural mass from Rome, and for the first time in the experience of millions of people religious worship was seen and heard on television and radio. Pope Paul VI had been denied entry to Poland for the millenary celebrations in 1966, but clearly a Polish pope could not be kept away. The government asserted its authority by refusing permission for him to return for the feast day of St Stanislaus, a Polish bishop who was martyred in the eleventh century after reproving the then king for scandalous conduct. In the event Pope John Paul's visit took place in June, about one month after the festival. It was described as a pastoral visit, and was limited to a certain number of places, but inevitably it became a great national event and, Poland being Poland, there was no possibility of separating the pastoral from the political. In no sense, however, was there a direct confrontation between the power of the government and of the Church. Party leaders met the Pope, exchanging civilities and gifts, and the behaviour of the huge crowds was impeccable. For an unforgettable forty-eight hours a large red cross was mounted in Warsaw's Victory Square where the Pope celebrated an open-air mass in the presence of some 300,000 people. In the cathedral at Krakow he told the congregation, 'The future of Poland will depend on how many people are mature enough to be nonconformists.' Bishops gathered at the shrine at Czestochowa were urged to continue the dialogue between Church and State, always remembering that normalization of relations must involve respect for human rights, 'among which the right of religious freedom has undoubted, central importance'. In an address to an open-air gathering of students in Warsaw, he commented on the way in which his audiences had shared in all the meetings with their applause and interruptions, and added, 'This society has become some sort of theological society.' And there could be little doubt that the theology expounded by the Pope and embraced by the Polish people, with its strong emphasis on human dignity derived from a unique relationship with God, presented a formidable challenge to the rather tired Marxism of Poland's rulers. At the end of the visit the Polish authorities were warmly thanked by the Pope for making it possible, and for their co-operation with the Church in the various arrangements.

These events clearly had a considerable effect on the morale of Poland's Catholics. After many years in which their governments have treated them as second-class citizens, and in which anything relating to the Church has been excluded from the press and broadcasting, they now take pride in their identification with a pope who is recognized as an outstanding world leader, and some of whose activities have required recognition of the Church as an integral part of Poland's public life. Moreover, Polish Catholics – and indeed the Polish people as a whole – are aware that they now have a powerful friend on the international scene. And a friend who does not keep silent about his homeland, especially when its people are in trouble.

By the middle of 1980 Poland's leaders had a great deal to be worried about. The country's economic crisis had deepened, there were food shortages, and signs of serious unrest among the workers as well as dissent among the intellectuals. A rise in the price of meat in July provoked a number of unco-ordinated strikes in various parts of the country, but these were quickly settled. On 14 August, however, the traditionally militant shipyard workers of Gdansk went on strike, shutting themselves in the Lenin shipyard and deputing their leader, Lech Walesa, to present the government with a twenty-one-point list of demands. These demands, compiled by representatives of the workers and the intellectuals, went far beyond the price of meat and wage levels. They included the right to free speech, the right to establish independent trade unions, a monument to the workers killed during the repression of the Baltic coast strikes in 1970, and access of the Church to the mass media. The government appointed a negotiator, the Prime Minister was dismissed, and by the end of the month the strikers had won most of their points, in principle at least, and were back at work. In mid-September First Secretary Gierek was himself dismissed by his colleagues and succeeded by Stanislaw Kania. A confederation of independent trade unions – Solidarity – was formed under the leadership of Lech Walesa and by the early part of 1981 claimed to have a membership of ten million: two-thirds of Poland's blue- and white-collar workers. In April 1981 they were joined by three million peasant farmers, and for a few months this powerful body, unique in Eastern Europe, was engaged in constant dialogue with the government. Solidarity claimed that Polish problems required Polish solutions, and that a new Polish society was needed.

The Church was deeply involved in this extraordinary development, and many observers believe that it stemmed directly from Christian teaching and from the new confidence given to the Polish people by the election of a Polish pope and his subsequent visit to Poland. Lech Walesa is a devout Catholic who normally attends mass daily, carries a rosary about with him, wears a miniature of the Black Virgin of Czestochowa, and says openly that the Catholic faith is a vital inspiration for himself and his fellow trade unionists. During the August 1980 strike the Catholic hierarchy, while identifying the Church with the cause of the strikers, counselled caution, fearing – in company with many others both inside and outside Poland – that signs of serious instability in the political order might provoke a Russian invasion. In an address given during the early days of the strike, Cardinal Wyszynski said, 'It is right for us to demand this bread, so that no one will be without it. But let us do this in a worthy and noble way.' A major part of this address was broadcast on television, the first time for thirty-six years that a church leader had been allowed to broadcast. In October the new First Secretary of the Party, Mr Kania, met Cardinal Wyszynski, and a communiqué issued after their meeting stated: 'A unanimous view was expressed that the constructive co-oper-ation of the Church with the State serves well the interests of the nation and therefore will be continued.' A month later a leading, though somewhat discredited, Catholic layman, Jerzy Ozdow-ski, who is a member of the ODISS group that broke away from Znak, was appointed a Deputy Prime Minister, with special responsibility for family and social affairs. In December eight Catholic bishops joined Party and trade union leaders at the unveiling of a memorial in Gdansk to those who had been killed by security forces during the 1970 strikes, and towards the end of the year a joint commission of representatives of Church and State declared, 'Poland is capable of resolving all its problems through its own efforts.' This joint commission continued to hold meetings to discuss and negotiate matters of mutual concern, and in March 1981 it recommended that priests should be allowed access to hospitals, old people's homes and prisons, from which they were excluded in the 1950s.

As the demands by Solidarity for more and faster change become more insistent, the Catholic bishops became more and more fearful of Russian intervention. Thus in a statement issued after their meeting in March 1981 they said: 'The preservation of internal freedom and national sovereignty is the highest priority at the moment . . . It is necessary, therefore, to remain calm and patient in the face of any provocation. Great self-discipline and patience are required, not only from the trade unions but also from the government.' The need for self-discipline and prudence within the Church itself was also emphasized by the bishops in a pastoral letter to the clergy issued after the same meeting. The letter asked the clergy:

> to be particularly sensitive to preserving peace in society and to practise prudence in order to achieve further progress in the aspiration of society to justice . . . and to leave to the hierarchy the right to issue declarations and pose demands of a public nature. It comes within the duty of the episcopate and its legitimate representatives to speak in the name of the Church to the authorities. The episcopate in Poland has been engaging in this task for a number of years and has gained much experience in how to act in periods of tensions and changes (which are not over by any means). The Church has much to contribute to the process of ensuring the implementation of healthy principles of co-operation in society. The episcopate expects the clergy to trust the bishops and leave public declarations to the main council of the Polish episcopate and to the Conference of the Polish Episcopate. This will enable the Church to maintain a united line of conduct and observe the fundamental principles of public life, morals and activity. Because of these emotional times, there have been many initiatives towards renewal, some of them shortlived; the priests who have wider, more essential religious tasks should not mix their pastoral work with political pronouncements. The Church in Poland has never been subordinated to emerging pseudo-political or political groups and has never been their servant. Similarly, the clergy, who are called to the service of the people of God, should not give their affiliation to any – even the most noble – initiatives of political renewal, but confine themselves to offering religious, moral and charitable help to all, giving their strength and time to suitable pastoral service to the country's believers. Priests should not sign declarations of a political or public nature or issue protests of this kind. Instead, they should inform their bishops of any violations of the moral and civil rights of their parishioners. Only in this way do we believe that we will be acting in accordance with the instructions of the Holy Father for the sake of peace in our country, in the spirit of prudence and in the interests of further progress.

Four months later Pope John Paul II announced that Bishop

Jozef Glemp was to be the new Primate of Poland. Glemp had been Cardinal Wyszynski's personal secretary from 1967 until his consecration as Bishop of Warmia in 1979, and he was known to be the late Primate's nominee. Born in 1928 into the family of a miner, the new Primate is a tough character who worked as a farm labourer during the Nazi occupation of Poland and was trained for the priesthood during the worst years of repression in the 1950s. Although lacking the authority of Wyszynski, he shares his predecessor's faith and patriotism, and has continued his policy. In an interview published in *Tygodnik Powszechny* shortly before his appointment as Primate, he said:

> The precarious survival of the nation is crucial but it must not be pursued at the price of moral capitulation. The defence of Solidarity and of human rights is vital, but the Church must not become directly involved in the new trade union. The role of the priests is primarily spiritual, in an active sense; they must learn to grasp the new problems of the changing situation and so they need a detachment which precludes loyalty to any political faction. A different danger facing the priests now is that they might fall prey to consumerism or get too involved in the material concerns of the Church now that the building of churches and parish halls is possible. Only detachment brings spiritual freedom.

Soon the new Primate and his church found their freedom challenged from an unexpected quarter. A rapidly deteriorating economic situation and increasing social unrest led to the downfall of Stanislaw Kania and his replacement by General Wojiciech Jaruzelski, who became First Secretary of the Party, Prime Minister and Defence Minister. In mid-December martial law was declared and in what was obviously a carefully and skilfully prepared operation the Polish army seized control of the country's communications network, arrested many of Solidarity's leaders, drove striking workers back to the factories and mines, killing a large number of them in the process, and imposed a tough, repressive regime. General Jaruzelski said that he had taken this action 'with a heavy heart' but it was necessary since the country was 'on the edge of the abyss'.

It is too early to discern what lay behind this sudden crackdown. Whether the old guard in the Polish Communist Party were reasserting their authority, or whether Jaruzelski was faced with a secret ultimatum from the Soviet government and obliged to take action, is not yet clear. The Russians have disclaimed all responsibility, yet it is hard to believe that they were unaware of what was proposed and disapproved of the steps actually taken by Jaruzelski and the army. Solidarity has, for the time being at any rate, paid the price for its concentration on social reform at the expense of solving Poland's critical economic problems. General Jaruzelski has promised that, once these problems become less serious, martial law will be removed and the basic reforms demanded by Solidarity will be implemented. But economic recovery is a distant prospect, and the Polish churches are back on familiar ground, with considerable freedom to order their own affairs but little opportunity for furthering the freedom of the Polish people as a whole.

# Chapter 6

# THE GERMAN
# DEMOCRATIC REPUBLIC

A British or American churchman travelling to East Germany in search of an 'underground church' would doubtless be astonished if on his arrival in, say, Leipzig, he was stopped in the street and invited by a student or a nun in her habit, collecting tin in hand, to support one of the Church's social projects. His astonishment would increase even more if he enquired about these projects and was supplied with the facts. The Protestant and Catholic churches of East Germany have, between them, fifty-two hospitals, eighty-seven homes for the mentally and physically handicapped, eleven mother and baby homes, 280 homes for the elderly and nursing homes, twenty-three children's homes, six hospices for the dying, 328 day-care centres for children, and 419 rural nursing stations. Social work on this scale obviously implies churches which are strong and have a degree of freedom to express their faith in action. And, since most of this work is carried out in partnership with the State, it also implies that the government is prepared for the churches to play a significant part in the life of a socialist society.

None the less, the image of the German Democratic Republic (GDR) in the Western world is still far from good. The Berlin Wall suggests a harsh regime, Soviet divisions and hardline Stalinist rulers – a bleak life in which grey is the predominant colour and people are isolated from their natural neighbours in the West. This image is almost as distorted as the one in which the GDR presents itself in glowing colours as the first German workers' and peasants' state where peace is pursued and all men live in harmony and prosperity. Because the German Democratic Republic is the frontier outpost of the Warsaw Pact – and very German in its thoroughness – Marxist-Leninist dogma was and is preached there more assiduously than perhaps anywhere outside the USSR. On the whole the West remains ignorant of what life in East Germany is really like. Western journalists are still treated with considerable suspicion and are sometimes refused entry. So Eastern Europe's most prosperous state, which is also the land of Bach, Handel, Luther and Goethe, has yet to be opened up. Of this and its effects the Communist rulers are afraid. Abroad the policy is one of *détente* and of peaceful co-existence. The more that policy succeeds the more vigilance is thought to be needed at home to keep the nation free of ideological ferment. The effect is a widespread feeling of claustrophobia.

The key to a proper understanding of the East German situation is that it is a German situation. The GDR is Western in its culture, outlook and ethos – and this is not just because most of its citizens spend their evenings eavesdropping on one of the West German television networks. The GDR today still has a good deal more in common with the Federal Republic than with any of its partners in the Warsaw Pact. This is never publicly admitted. Official adulation (in massive doses) is reserved for the Soviet Union. Yet privately 'drawing level' with West Germany is part of the GDR's constant dream. Looking eastwards, current East German humour proves that the day when Germans cease to look down on Poles and Czechs is still some way off. Inevitably, ignorance about the GDR has extended to the churches and, although there have been frequent contacts between East German church leaders and the leaders of the other churches, there remains an impression of Christian communities struggling to retain their identity and to continue their witness in the face of bitter hostility. The true picture is somewhat different. There are certainly social and political pressures but they are a far cry from the sort of persecution that has not been unknown elsewhere in Eastern Europe.

The churches of the GDR are affected by their country's uniqueness in three important ways. First, the GDR is a heavily industrialized nation. Germany's history accounts for much of this, but the 'economic miracle' of the GDR's post-war years has been the result of phenomenal growth in industry which has enabled the GDR not only to move from utter ruin to become the most prosperous country in Eastern Europe, but also to become the source of considerable wealth to the Soviet Union and other less developed members of Comecon, the East European counterpart of the Common Market. For the churches, industrialization also spells secularization and with it some erosion of Christian faith and practice. Here is common ground occupied by the churches of the GDR and those of Western Europe. Their generally small congregations are the consequence not so much of Marxist-Leninist pressures, but of the secularist outlook which characterizes almost every industrial society. The most discerning church leaders in the GDR now see quite clearly that Leninist ideology is not the Church's chief enemy.

The second important difference for the churches is to be found in the historical and cultural strength of Protestantism. East Germany has been described as the heartland of the Lutheran Reformation and the fact that Martin Luther lived and worked here is of great significance. Just under half the population of the GDR are inscribed members of the eight predominantly Lutheran church provinces which make up the Federation of Protestant Churches. Church boundaries are still those of the states which pre-dated Bismarck's Reich. Although Christians in the Lutheran tradition have often found it all too easy to accommodate themselves to the powers that be, their social position in post-Reformation Germany meant that they were, and remain, an influence which no secular ruler can afford to ignore.

The third, and perhaps most important, factor in post-Second World War Germany is the influence of the Church's traumatic theological encounter with Nazi tyranny. Under Hitler the Church split in three directions. A minority embraced the Nazi ideology and perverted the Church into an instrument of the State. The traditions of Prussian Protestantism which had merged Church and State (no less than Tsarism) made that an easy option for some. The Confessing Church, also a minority, followed their prophet Martin Niemöller in costly resistance to Hitler. They were driven underground, and Dietrich Bonhoeffer was only the best-known of their many martyrs. The great majority joined neither group, kept out of politics and waited to see in which direction the wind would blow.

---

The *Evangelische Kirche*, embracing the Lutheran and Reformed traditions, is by far the largest of the churches of the GDR. Almost half of the country's 17.3 million people regard themselves as belonging to it and most of them continue voluntarily to pay church tax. Far, far fewer are regular worshippers and since the end of the Second World War even the nominal membership has declined from over sixteen million to under eight million. Less than one-fifth of the infants of the GDR are now baptized. The *Evangelische Kirche* is made up of two major blocs: the United Lutheran Church with three *Landeskirchen* (church provinces) and the Evangelical Church of the Union with five *Landeskirchen*. Since 1969 these eight provinces have come together in the Federation of Evangelical Churches in the GDR, which is an umbrella organization and leaves its constituent bodies with a considerable degree of autonomy. Within the Federation there were, in 1979, 7,433 parishes, served by 3,996 pastors (of whom just over 200 are women), 5,000 trained catechists and 5,000 social workers, who are usually deacons or deaconesses. Each of the eight *Landeskirchen* has an elected bishop and a synod with extensive powers and a carefully drafted constitution. Ecclesiastical lawyers are far from being redundant in the GDR. Pastors are trained in the theological faculties ('sections') of the universities of Berlin, Leipzig, Halle, Jena, Rostock and Greifswald, where academic standards are high. Just over 400 students were reading theology at these universities in 1979, which was slightly more than the number in 1976 but a lot less than the 642 who were there in 1965. Besides the university students, another 500 are training to be pastors at the Church's own seminaries, which have become more popular in recent years since, unlike the university faculties, they are not subject to State control and their professors are not so obviously supporters of the government. No one knows how long this dual system will continue.

The census figures for the Roman Catholic Church showed in 1980 a declared allegiance of nearly 1.3 million people which is about 8 per cent of the GDR's population. They live in 920 parishes and are served by nine bishops, 1,520 priests (diocesan and religious) and twenty-six permanent deacons. There are 3,244 nuns and fifty-six lay monks in twenty religious orders. Within the GDR there are only two recognized dioceses (Berlin and Meissen) as the Vatican has not formally acknowledged the frontier between East and West Germany, and the ecclesiastical areas which abut West Germany have been designated apostolic administrations. The bishops work closely together through the Berlin Conference of Ordinaries. Catholic priests are trained mainly in the major seminary at Erfurt, and there are minor seminaries in other parts of the country. Some 270 students were in training in 1980. Training centres for catechists have been established in various parts of the country, and at Magdeburg there is a training centre for women pastoral assistants.

The Methodist Church in the German Democratic Republic is larger than in any other part of Eastern Europe. It began in 1850 when Erhard Wunderlich returned home from the USA and now has a total community of about 35,000, of whom over 27,000 are full members. There are 270 local Methodist churches and another sixty worship centres. These are served by about 150 ministers (30 of them retired) and over 300 lay preachers, with a bishop residing in Dresden. The church runs four hospitals, four old people's homes, a nursing school, a home for handicapped children and three other centres of social work. Most of the Methodist deaconesses, who number about 125, are trained nurses. A theological seminary at Bad Klosterlausnitz has ten to twenty students.

The Baptists have about 22,000 baptized members in just over two hundred local congregations which are affiliated to the Federation of Evangelical Free Church Congregations. There are about 130 Baptist pastors who are trained in a small theological seminary, and lay workers are trained in a Bible school. The church has a number of homes for the aged, and a care centre for the handicapped. There are several very small Protestant communities and a handful of Orthodox, Old Catholics and Quakers. Among the sects, the New Apostolic Church is the largest, with a membership of about 80,000, and the Seventh Day Adventists have just over 11,000 members. The largest of the eight Jewish communities is in East Berlin, but of its 360 members only 120 are under sixty years of age. Altogether there are fewer than 800 Jews in the GDR.

More than thirty theological journals, magazines and newspapers are published in the GDR. The main Protestant Church has five weekly regional newspapers, with circulations of up to 40,000, and the Catholic Church has two weeklies as well as two other church magazines and an information service. The Methodists and Baptists each have their own magazines, and so do a number of the other smaller communities. Although there is no pre-censorship, a whole edition can be lost if the State forbids its distribution; editors have learnt to judge how far they can go. The three main religious publishing houses produce about 12 per cent of the total number of books published in the GDR, and the largest of them – the Protestant *Evangelische Verlagsanstalt* – produces over two hundred titles a year, covering a wide range of subjects, including scientific works and novels. All books are subject to government censorship.

The Berlin Bible Society is allocated sixty-nine tons of paper a year for the production of scriptures, and with this, plus further supplies from the United Bible Societies, publishes about 200,000 Bibles and scripture portions a year, including illustrated editions, modern language versions, and copies in Braille. They are distributed through church, commercial and State-owned bookshops, as well as through local congregations, and in general there is no shortage of Bibles.

Radio GDR has always broadcast a religious service, Protestant or Catholic, every Sunday at 7.30 a.m. The music is provided by well-known choirs, and a sermon is preached by one of a panel of preachers agreed by Church and State. Scripts are vetted and sometimes rejected. On the whole, the more narrowly religious the sermon the more likely it is to be approved: a sermon based on Christ's temptation to misuse power, which went on to praise non-violence, was rejected. The act of worship is followed by a Christian commentary on some topical subject, given by a speaker chosen by Radio GDR. Since 1979 there has been an additional monthly radio programme of news and reports about church life, and six television programmes a year. These are scripted by the Protestant churches and there is an advisory board elected from the eight provinces.

---

When, in 1945, British and Russian troops met on the Elbe and Germany lay in ruins, a new Protestantism constituted itself, based on a policy of renewal through penitence. Its leaders almost to a man were the Christians of the anti-Nazi resistance. There was little danger that they would bow down to some new idol; but neither would they readily fall for the anti-Communist ideology which Hitler had successfully used to bid for a wide measure of Christian support. These Christians had shared prison cells and concentration camp experience with many of the Communists who were now taking over in East Germany. Nor could these Communists tar the Church with a Fascist brush. When it was tried in the GDR the tar would not stick.

In the light of the Reformation and of recent German history, it is therefore no surprise to discover that Christians in the GDR have a deep concern for the social and ethical issues that arise in their form of socialist society. In some respects this offers the possibility of close collaboration with the State; in others the possibility of sharp conflict. This position *vis-à-vis* the new society, sometimes described as critical solidarity, and, more recently, as the Church within socialism, is unique in Eastern Europe. And this uniqueness finds expression through an impressive body of theological writing, some of which is published in the GDR, some abroad, and quite a lot is circulated from hand to hand.

However great the tension, there is some genuine, but grudging, respect at top level between Church and State in the GDR. Even when, in the 1950s, relations were at their very worst, and some pastors and laymen were imprisoned, no German church leader (of any denomination) was ever arrested or forced out of office. This has no parallel elsewhere in Eastern Europe. Nor does this point to a supine Church. The position of the Church was powerfully enunciated at a meeting of the General Synod of the Federation of Evangelical Churches held in Dresden in June 1972, and also at the triennial conference of the Baptist Union of the GDR held in Leipzig a month earlier. In an important speech to the Synod, Dr Heino Falcke, then Principal of Gnadau Theological College, spoke of the State's claim that socialism is in fact primitive Christianity put into practice, and that specifically religious activity is something for private life and leisure hours. He commented:

To this we must say 'No' ... We cannot accept withdrawal into sacred isolation from the secular world ... Were we to settle for that we would be falsifying the Gospel of freedom into a spare-time Gospel. We would ourselves be victims of the misunderstanding that declares the Gospel to be an instrument of man's alienation rather than of his social liberation. We would be conceding that man's political maturity depends on his liberation from Christ rather than on his being liberated by Christ.

Dr Falcke then considered what it means for Christians to live in and co-operate with a socialist society:

> We mean this above all: we can accept in faith that in a socialist society, too, the lordship of the liberating Christ is a reality . . . So we are set free to reject socialism's rigid view of itself, a view which would face us with the need either to reject or accept it totally. We are set free from the paralysing alternatives between outright opposition and uncritically allowing ourselves to be taken over. Thus we are set free to offer practical and discerning co-operation.

One area of 'practical and discerning co-operation' is concerned with the struggle against the things that oppress mankind:

> The liberating Person of Christ in his identification with those who suffer and in his promise of freedom forces us to make our own the socialist protest against man's misery, and to co-operate in putting an end to inhumanity and in achieving greater justice and more freedom . . . The love inspired by the promises of Christ becomes creative as it leads to the changing of social conditions. That is not the least we have learned from our encounter with socialism . . . Christians then will commit themselves to involvement at all these points where the construction of socialism is likely to lead to greater social or economic justice.

Yet Dr Falcke was equally clear that suffering and lack of freedom is not confined to capitalist societies:

> The need to struggle against injustice and lack of freedom also applies to our own society, for all of history is subject to the judgement of the Cross. But this is a worthwhile task, for history is also subject to the promises of the liberating Christ. These promises remain valid even when a socialist society proves to be a disappointment or where the socialist ideal is distorted or becomes unrecognizable. Because through Christian eyes socialism cannot be expected to lead directly to the reign of freedom, our disappointments at its performance will not lead us to reject it totally. Nor will we compare the ideal and the reality and lapse into cynical disapproval . . . rather we shall resolutely continue to believe in a socialism that is capable of improvement.

The final section of Dr Falcke's speech consisted of a plea for greater freedom of discussion in the GDR:

To facilitate our responsible co-operation with society would it not be well to extend the scope for free discussion?... Would the leading role of the Party not be enhanced, its authority strengthened, if that authority were seen to be the source of liberty which helped men to stand on their own feet?... A common purpose will only emerge when men trust each other, respect each other in genuine partnership and allow all points of view to be put in free discussion, argument pitted against argument. Does not the very life of socialism depend for its survival on striving for and attaining such maturity?... If citizens are to co-operate responsibly they must possess the information on which valid judgements depend. Only thus can the State's slogan 'Work with us, Plan with us, Govern with us' be put into effect.

Dr Falcke's outspokenness was a challenge the State would rather have done without; but it did not fall entirely on deaf ears. Fortunately for those in power, few church leaders were in any mood to echo this kind of analysis in public, and indeed Dr Falcke's speech could be circulated only in duplicated form. An open society was not in prospect. Yet during the 1970s the Church's self-confidence grew. Its leadership had a clear vision and was preparing for a future in which the Church would be even slimmer but better equipped to stand its ground. There was to be no retreat from social commitment into an introverted pietism. Bishop Albrecht Schönherr, then Bishop of Berlin-Brandenburg, and Chairman of the Federation of Evangelical Churches, propounded the concept of 'a Church within social-ism' that was neither bent on opposition to the State nor willing to become subservient to the State.

The government itself evidently decided that a process of trying to integrate the Church into the GDR's socialist society was the only way forward. Walter Ulbricht, then First Secretary of the Party and Head of State, had erratically set out on this path from 1960 onwards, and his successor, Erich Honecker, ratified this approach when he took over in 1976. The Church, according to a policy statement made by Paul Verner, a member of the ruling Politburo, was to be accorded a positive place in society. It was to be allowed to develop an independent identity and serve in a socialist society on its own terms. But none of this was ever closely defined; nor was it ever established what was meant by 'the separation of Church and State'. Strains and stresses continued, and the question of the right to higher education for Christian young people remained a matter of dispute. Relatively good relationships at leadership level were often not reflected locally. Then Church and State were both shaken by the suicides, by immolation, of two pastors. The two men concerned were in no way typical of the clergy as a whole, and both were unstable characters, yet one of them vividly expressed his opposition to continuing State harassment of the local churches, while the other pointed to the inability of the Church to resolve theological differences, in this instance between traditional Protestants and charismatic renewers.

---

6 March 1978 is now recognized by both Church and State as a date of great significance. On that day, and with a blaze of publicity in all the Communist media, Erich Honecker and other State leaders received the leadership of the Federation of Evangelical Churches almost as though two bodies of comparable significance were meeting. No concordat was signed, but the establishment of a king of *entente cordiale* was clearly intended by the State, and accepted – albeit cautiously – by the Church. The concept of religion as a harmful remnant of bourgeois society was in effect being abandoned in return for the hoped for co-operation of the Church in nation-building. Ideologically, the Church appeared to emerge intact and the Communist Party badly mauled, though it was of course Church and State meeting, not Church and Party. But that fine distinction was lost on most people, and probably meant to be lost. All the concessions again seemed to be on one side – always assuming that the Church was not allowing itself to be used for State ends by agreeing to such a meeting at all. Such a possibility was not overlooked by many members of local churches, but three years later the concessions seem to be real.

What was conceded? First and foremost a place in public life for the Church, even when it is critical of the State. In 1979, for example, the Synod of the Church in Saxony called for a more open debate on national problems, and in the same year the Synod of Mecklenburg, inspired by the World Council of

Churches conference at Boston, USA, on 'Faith, Science and the Future', called for a public debate on the use of nuclear energy. The State also re-affirmed equality for all citizens, regardless of their ideology, and Bishop Schönherr's response, 'The proof of the pudding will be in the eating', was actually published. Then came a number of concrete agreements, hammered out in preparatory sessions. The Church was promised increased radio time, and access, for the first time, to television: the promise has been kept. The right to more prison chaplaincies was acknowledged: these now exist. The right to build new churches where they are needed was agreed: a building programme is under way. The Communist assumption that in a socialist society religion will rapidly wither away has apparently been buried.

So the churches of the GDR have a degree of freedom and a place in society not to be found elsewhere in Eastern Europe except, perhaps, in the very different circumstances of Poland. There is no State interference in episcopal appointments. Synods have never elected a bishop from the small minority of clergy who give unqualified support to the policies of the ruling (Communist) Socialist Unity Party. There is no totally conformist bishop in the GDR; on the other hand, a GDR Synod has never elected a bishop who is totally hostile to the government, for the Church is no more eager than the State to have a showdown.

---

Among the Protestant bishops there have been – and are – men of outstanding ability. Dr Moritz Mitzenheim, the first post-war Bishop of Thuringia, did become to some extent the darling of the authorities because he felt sincerely that he could go nearly all the way with the prevailing policies of the State. He was on good personal terms with the Party Secretary, Walter Ulbricht. Nevertheless even he retained his critical faculties and never lost the respect of the parish clergy or his fellow bishops. At the other end of the political scale, Bishop Fränkel of Görlitz frequently and fervently lambasted the authorities, never minced his words, and was not liked by the politicians. Yet he always spoke from a clear position of loyalty to the State, the principles of which he often invoked. He too retained the full respect of his colleagues. In any other part of Eastern Europe, apart from Poland, a bishop who spoke as Fränkel did would soon be in serious trouble. He chose to retire to West Germany where he became, paradoxically, a frequent defender of the East German State. Presiding Bishop Albrecht Schönherr of Berlin, who retired in October 1981, was a pupil of Dietrich Bonhoeffer, and during the important period when he was leader of the Protestant Church showed himself to be a sophisticated theologian, a man of independent mind, able to compromise in non-essentials but fully able to stand up to the pressures of the State, and always to be trusted.

Much less trusted by many churchmen is the Christian Democratic Union (CDU) – one of the GDR's five political parties which make up, with certain mass organizations, the National Front of the GDR. All parties accept the leadership of the 'Party of the workers and peasants', the Socialist Unity Party (SED), or the Communist Party, as it would be known in most other parts of the world. All power lies with the Communists. But it is recognized that other sections of the people also want to be represented. The CDU's task is to speak for 'socialist citizens of Christian faith', i.e. those Christians who fully accept the moral and historical necessity for the 'dictatorship of the proletariat' expressed through the SED. In large part, the CDU's job is to 'sell' the policies of the SED to those believers who accept them reluctantly. A distinction is made by the establishment between reactionary and progressive Christians; that is, between those who do and those who do not accept Communist policy.

At the national level, very few prominent churchmen identify themselves with the CDU, and many of its activities are viewed with suspicion in the corridors of ecclesiastical power. None the less, of the five hundred deputies in the People's Chamber, the CDU has fifty-four, of whom four are clergymen or church officials. Several CDU members hold positions of some influence in the government. Gerald Götting was for many years Vice-Chairman of the Council of State and President of the People's Chamber. Friedrich Kind is a member of the Council of State. Others serve as senior and junior ministers in various government departments. In local government the CDU also has its place – 281 of its members are in county assemblies and 1,399 in district assemblies. Over 10,000 are said to be working on town and community representative bodies. Relations between the

CDU and local churches vary considerably; in some places leading laymen hold positions of responsibility in the party; elsewhere there is an open or veiled hostility. At the thirteenth Party Congress held in 1972 the local bishop, representing the Federation of Evangelical Churches, was on the platform at the opening ceremony – an action which would displease the great majority of church members. Yet the existence of the CDU offers no consolation to those who believe that true democracy requires official 'opposition' parties, to give the electorate a real choice. It simply introduces a little variety into what would otherwise be a monolithic political system, and its representatives in the People's Chamber have at least some limited freedom; for example, a number of CDU deputies voted against the Communist bill which legalized abortion.

The CDU is not popular. Communists tend to look down on it, and so do most Christians. Nevertheless, in the context of Eastern Europe, its existence is not to be despised, neither should the sincerity of many of its leaders be underestimated.

---

The finances of the East German churches are provided mainly by their members, chiefly in the form of a voluntary tax on personal income, collections at church worship services, and donations. The Evangelical Church still owns about 500,000 acres of agricultural land and runs fifty agricultural enterprises. It is in fact the only non-State landowner in the GDR. The government also provides the churches with 12 million marks (about $6 million or £3 million) a year for clergy salaries and general administration. This payment, which has remained constant for more than twenty years, is an obligation taken over from the old Reich which in the nineteenth century confiscated the greater part of the Church's wealth and promised to pay compensation in perpetuity. In addition, the State contributes just over two million marks a year towards the upkeep and restoration of church buildings which are considered to be of historical or architectural interest. About four million marks a year go to the theological faculties of the State universities. Somewhere around 40 per cent of the Evangelical Church's overall costs are met by its sister churches in West Germany which, because of the West German system of taxation, are probably the richest churches in the world. Building restoration is largely financed by Western money; the clergy drive GDR-made cars paid for by the West; and in this way the Church manages to maintain its buildings, pay its clergy and finance its fairly elaborate administrative structure. The State is happy for the Church to receive this assistance from the West, because it provides the national economy with much-needed hard currency, and the Church, conscious of its good fortune, gives generously to appeals for help from Vietnam, El Salvador and other places for which gifts in kind can be organized. It also contributes to the World Council of Churches Programme to Combat Racism.

Although the churches are not permitted to advertise the times of their worship services on secular notice boards, they are allowed to engage in evangelistic activity. In June 1980, for example, a week-long evangelistic crusade was held in Görlitz. This was advertised by 500 posters and 20,000 invitation cards which went to about three-quarters of the town's population. Attendance at the meetings in St Peter's Church varied between 1,700 and 2,500, more than a third of whom were young people. A choir of 160 members and 40 trumpeters took part, and the guest speakers were two evangelists from West Germany. In Thuringia a Youth Sunday is held every three years, and in June 1979 about 10,000 young people took part in the day's events, which included a question and answer session with the bishop and came to a climax with the celebration of the Eucharist. There are proportionately more church musicians in the GDR than in any other country in the world. The great musical tradition of Germany is still very much alive. St Thomas – Bach's church in Leipzig – and the Kreuzkirche in Dresden have choirs which are probably rivalled only by that of King's College, Cambridge. The Protestant Church supports ten church music training centres, and in addition to the choirs and organists of international reputation there are few towns which do not have choirs and musicians devoted to the traditional music of the Church. Concerts of sacred music are increasingly popular, especially among the young.

The position of the Roman Catholic Church in the GDR is not fundamentally different from that of any other church, but it is a relatively small community and this, combined with an unwillingness to collaborate with the State, has taken it into an isolation which is not entirely approved of by the Vatican, nor even by every East German Catholic. The 1.3 million Catholics are spread rather thinly over the whole country, with greater concentrations in the regions around Erfurt and Dresden. Cardinal Alfred Bengsch, who was Bishop of Berlin from 1961 until his early death in 1979, was theologically and pastorally conservative. He continued the policy of his predecessor, Cardinal Döpfner, which was to maintain the cohesion of the Catholic community and not to become involved in political matters in any way. The political passivity of the Catholic hierarchy is almost complete, and its public utterances on social matters have been confined to expressions of disapproval about abortion and military training in schools. Cardinal Bengsch never met the former Head of State, Walter Ulbricht, or his successor, Erich Honecker. A few Catholic laymen are, however, members of CDU – which is not approved of by the hierarchy – and one of them, Herr Otto Fuchs, is a member of the presidium of the party. But the priests have maintained a solid front and not a single one of them has joined the 'Berlin Conference of European Catholics', a State-sponsored body which invites Catholics from all parts of Europe to Soviet-style meetings which invariably support Warsaw Pact foreign policy positions. The leadership of this body is entirely lay and untypical of rank and file church members.

Since 1945 the question of diocesan boundaries and the status of bishops has been a bone of contention between the Catholic Church and the State. Although the government of the GDR has always loudly proclaimed its independent identity as a nation, the major churches maintained for more than a quarter of a century the concept of a united Germany, and saw the organizational unity of the Church as an expression of something that transcended political lines of demarcation. So neither the Protestant nor the Catholic churches changed their territorial jurisdictions or their overall organizations. Not surprisingly, the government of the GDR interpreted this as a sign of the Church's lack of commitment to the life of the new socialist state in East Germany, though in the end it was the German churches which helped to prepare the people of West Germany for a change of political policy which acknowledged the existence of the GDR, entered into diplomatic relations with its government, and opened the way to relief of tension at every level. In 1969 the Protestant church provinces of the GDR formed their own national federation, and three years later the division of Berlin was recognized when Bishop Schönherr ceased to be the deputy of Bishop Scharf (whose jurisdiction had officially included the entire city), and was formally installed in East Berlin's cathedral, the Marienkirche. But although the Catholic Church has in recent years carried out some administrative reorganization to enable it to function more efficiently in the GDR, it has not changed any of its diocesan boundaries, and the diocese of Meissen, which was recreated in 1921 and relates directly to the Holy See, is the only Catholic diocese whose boundaries are wholly within the GDR. The government of the GDR continues to be irritated by this but, leaving the political issue on one side, the financial benefits to the Catholic Church of the present arrangement are considerable. Their parishes and all their structures are magnificently maintained by the Catholic Church in West Germany. Catholic institutions, administrative buildings, churches and bishops' residences are quite palatial.

Like the other churches of the GDR, the Catholic Church has a considerable involvement in social work. This work is co-ordinated by Caritas which maintains over thirty hospitals, about a hundred homes for the aged, two sanatoria, thirty-four children's homes, over eighty kindergartens, fourteen rest homes, fifteen nursing homes, and two rest homes for mothers. The State provides a great deal of money for all these institutions. There are training centres for social work in Magdeburg and Karl Marx Stadt, and an institute for training boy choristers in Dresden.

---

In spite of the very considerable degree of freedom enjoyed by all the Christian communities in the GDR, some problems and tensions remain. Individual Christians are still subject to penalties, which are not less severe because they are more subtle than those imposed during the Stalinist era of the 1950s. It is, for instance, very difficult for anyone who is not a card-carrying member of one of the National Front parties to obtain a leading post in East Germany. Promotion in industry and the great state corporations is limited for Christians, and they cannot expect to be given university posts or positions of influence in schools.

There are no official regulations about this, but Christians tend simply not to be appointed to vacant positions and, despite some exceptions, this has now happened frequently enough, and over a long enough period, for the undeclared policy to be understood.

The area in which the greatest tension is experienced concerns education and work among young people. Christians have often found it extremely difficult, if not actually impossible, to gain access to higher – and especially university – education, even though their intellectual gifts may be more than adequate for the education offered at this level. It is clear that the government aims to have the next generation of state leaders thoroughly versed in, and committed to, the Marxist-Leninist line undiluted. Once again, there is no declared policy that Christians shall not be admitted to universities, but some are undoubtedly excluded. At meetings of the Synods of the Protestant Church held in Saxony, Mecklenburg, Greifswald and Anhalt in the autumn of 1971, it was reported that in the previous spring there had been an increase in the number of children and young people excluded from high schools and colleges, and that the exclusion of Christians from higher education now appeared to be the rule.

When challenged on this point university and state officials (between whom it is anyway difficult to distinguish) sometimes explain that, while the intellectual capacity of a Christian applicant may be adequate, it is also necessary to take social factors into account, with priority accorded to those of working-class origins. More recently it has been suggested that the number of university graduates needs to be reduced and the supply of skilled workers improved, thus requiring the rejection of candidates who are intellectually qualified for higher education. This policy, it is fair to say, is not directed exclusively against Christians but against all young people who show signs of rejecting the official government line or even of not promoting it with sufficient vigour.

In July 1971, the Synod of the Federation of Churches gave this matter careful attention and, while recognizing that selection for higher education should not solely depend on intellectual capacity, felt moved to declare:

There are many Christian and non-Christian pupils who do not need to fear comparison with those who fully go along with

Marxism/Leninism in the degree of their social commitment. Would it not be better to judge young people, apart from their intellectual ability, according to their readiness to be useful members of society?

Interesting and significant here is the Synod's general line of approach, which does not regard Christian young people in isolation but sees them as members of a particular generation, all of whom, irrespective of their ideologies, should be judged according to the same criteria – in this instance, readiness to be useful members of society.

In June 1972 the Catholic bishops of the GDR issued a pastoral letter on the subject of the *Jugendweihe*. This is an official state dedication ceremony for boys and girls who wish to declare their readiness to accept responsibilities in the life of the nation. Before the ceremony there is a certain amount of training in Communist doctrine and practice, often including a somewhat crude atheism. It is estimated that about a quarter of a million young people go through the ceremony every year. In their pastoral letter the bishops confirmed their statements of September 1967 and February 1969, in which they had declared the *Jugendweihe* to be essentially a non-Christian and atheistic substitute for confirmation. They called on all Catholics to boycott the ceremony, and added that any Catholic who voluntarily took part in it while aware of its atheistic implications committed a sin against faith. According to the bishops, pressure to take part in the *Jugendweihe* had increased in recent years, and their letter concluded with a reminder of the GDR constitution's guarantee of freedom of conscience and faith: according to these constitutional provisions, a citizen who refuses on conscientious grounds to take part in the *Jugendweihe* should experience no disadvantage. We would like to think that practice always accorded with these norms.

The Catholic bishops are quite clear as to what the young people of the Church should do. Protestant leaders are much less certain and in fact most young Protestant Christians do now take part in the *Jugendweihe*, even those who subsequently get confirmed. Some feel that an all-out assault on the *Jugendweihe*, including refusal to participate, would make life even more difficult for those young Christians who are remaining loyal to their faith in spite of all the disadvantages that accrue. It is pointed out that the preparation course for the ceremony is exceedingly tedious and that the ceremony itself is quite dull; better, therefore, to go through it all rather than face accusations of refusal of social commitment. On the other hand, those Christians who have been through the ceremony have not found it any easier to secure university places, so it is not unreasonable to ask whether a compromise at this point has any tangible benefit either to individuals or to the Church.

Another area of tension, again concerning young people, developed in the late 1970s when the government introduced compulsory military education into the curricula of all high schools. Both Protestant and Catholic leaders protested against this and, although the Secretary of State for Church Affairs assured the churches that 'those refusing to participate and those who criticize the programme will not be discriminated against', the matter is one of continuing concern in church circles. This concern was not eased when, in 1978, a young man was arrested and sentenced to two years and nine months in prison for distributing leaflets protesting against the introduction of military education into schools. It is in fact in their differing understanding of peace that Church and State have found their new relationship most vulnerable. 'Peace', interpreted as current Communist Party policy, is a key concept in a Communist State and the Church is expected to support the 'peace policies' of the State. When therefore the Church launches a peace education programme of its own – as the Protestant Federation in the GDR has done – and when peace in this Christian context evidently has a somewhat different meaning, serious tension is inevitable.

Even here, however, Church and State occupy some common ground. Uniquely among Warsaw Pact States – and largely as a result of Christian influence – the GDR recognizes a form of legal conscientious objection to military service. All young men have to serve, but Christians and others who object to serving in a combatant capacity can choose to be *Bausoldaten*, i.e. soldiers on construction work who are not trained to use weapons. To choose to be a *Bausoldat* will not make a young man popular, and will block his way to higher education or a responsible post. But it is legal, whereas Jehovah's Witnesses and other Christians who refuse to be soldiers of any kind have no alternative to prison.

---

In view of Germany's experience of Nazism and the nation's disastrous involvement in the Second World War, it is hardly a matter for surprise that issues related to war and peace have played a significant part in relations between Church and State in the GDR. The Republic itself came into existence as a result of war, and from 1945 to 1949 East Germany was under Soviet occupation. During these four years the various social and political institutions were brought under Communist control, and when the German Democratic Republic was declared on 7 October 1949, power was concentrated in the hands of the Socialist Unity Party of Germany (SED), which was simply another name for the Communist Party. The churches had fared not too badly during the Soviet occupation, and the constitution of the new Republic 'guaranteed' freedom of conscience and religious belief, freedom for religious institutions to function, religious education in schools, and freedom for the churches to express their views on social issues. (Other parts of the constitution implied, however, that the churches' expressed views must coincide with those of the government.) The *Evangelische Kirche* was, as anticipated, to lose its privileged position in East German society, but there was to be plenty of space for religious belief and practice.

Less than twelve months later the Third Party Congress of the SED launched a vitriolic attack on the leaders of the churches, accusing them of having approved Nazi terror and blessed Hitler's weapons, and of continuing their warmongering under the Anglo-American imperialists. At the same time the Congress praised the handful of clergy who had aligned themselves with the National Front of Democratic Germany, and during 1950 a peace movement was started, in the hope of bringing more clergy and laity into active support of the government. The 'guarantees' of the constitution were quickly forgotten. Police permission was required for all church meetings, apart from routine acts of worship and administration. Church papers and periodicals were subjected to censorship. Difficulties were placed in the way of religious education in schools. Communist youth organizations were set in competition with the Church's youth work, and the

*Jugendweihe* was introduced as an atheist initiation ceremony. By 1953 forty-nine pastors and priests were in prison, and their number eventually rose to seventy-two.

All this took place during the Stalinist era, when religious institutions throughout Eastern Europe were subjected to repression, generally of a more severe form than that experienced in the GDR. How far the government of the GDR was influenced by external pressure at this time is impossible to tell. In any case it was committed to two tasks that were bound to bring it sooner or later into conflict with the major churches. The first of these was related to the consolidation of its own position and the establishing of the Marxist-Leninist ideology as the main driving force of the State. Hence the desire to remove, or at least minimize, the influence of all other institutions, and to make ideological inroads into the educational system. The second task was to affirm and protect the national integrity of the new Republic. The division of Germany had been imposed by the victors of war, themselves sharply divided, and was bitterly resented by the leaders and people of West Germany, who encouraged the belief that the division was only a temporary matter and that Germany would soon be reunited. The leaders of the GDR, faced with this problem and struggling to obtain international recognition, found themselves dealing with Protestant and Catholic churches which, in their own organizations, took no account of the existence of the two Germanys and showed no sign of doing so. At best, therefore, the commitment of the churches to the new order was suspect; at worst, they might be the cover for political forces determined to destroy the GDR in order to bring the German people together again. Either way, there was, from the point of view of the then leader of the GDR, Walter Ulbricht, good reason for keeping the churches on a firm rein.

The churches resisted the State pressure as well as they could, and in April 1953, when the pressure was at its heaviest, the Catholic bishops of the GDR addressed a letter to all Catholic young people in which they declared, 'As all of us, you have the inalienable right to freedom of conscience and of faith. No one should dare to persecute you on account of this. You have the right to be Christians and to remain Christians.' In the same month, after the Prime Minister had said in a speech in Erfurt that there was no 'church struggle' in the GDR, Bishop Otto Dibelius, at that time President of the Evangelical Church, replied by telling him:

> You cannot constantly arrest pastors and expel members of the Young Congregation [a church youth movement] and student congregations; you cannot forbid the printing of church publications; you cannot close one institution of the Church after another and then declare that there is no church struggle . . . The Church has not looked for this struggle which you have forced upon her, but she also has not tried to run away from it. A Church which is afraid of a struggle and of suffering would not be a Christian Church.

By this time Stalin was dead, and on 5 June 1953 the Protestant leaders wrote to the Prime Minister asking for a meeting between the leadership of Church and State so that an understanding between the two might be reached through joint discussion. Five days later a meeting took place, in the course of which the State representatives declared their readiness to 'guarantee the life of the Church in accordance with the stipulations of the constitution of the GDR'. The pressure on the churches eased quite quickly, but the concessions made by the government proved to be quite limited and it was not until the late 1950s that much progress was made towards a reasonable accommodation between Church and State.

The initiative this time came from Ulbricht, who seized what appeared to him to be a golden opportunity to separate the Protestant churches of the GDR from those in the German Federal Republic. In 1957 the *Evangelische Kirche*, which was still united across the whole of Germany, concluded with the West German government an agreement under which Protestant pastors could serve as chaplains to the armed forces. Ulbricht interpreted this agreement as evidence that the Church approved of the North Atlantic Treaty Organization, the re-armament of West Germany, and nuclear warfare. But instead of a further crackdown on the church in the GDR, he held up the church of his own country as an example of authentic humanist Christianity in contrast with the militarist, NATO church of the West. Thus, at a meeting with church leaders in February 1961, he said:

> It appears to me that capitalism and basic Christianity are

really irreconcilably opposed to each other. Socialism, on the other hand, despite all the imperfections it may still have, will bring about the implementation of the Christian humanist and social ideals . . . I am coming increasingly to the conclusion that Socialists, Communists and Christians, despite the differences in their philosophies, simply must work together in shaping life and society and in ensuring peace.

Throughout the early 1960s Ulbricht made statements of this kind and sought to win the support of the churches, both for his internal policies and for his efforts on behalf of the GDR's national integrity. Without displaying much consistency of policy, he allowed the churches greater freedom, and gradually the way was prepared for the separation of the organization of the East and West German Protestants. In 1968 Bishop Mitzenheim declared, 'State boundaries must be considered as Church boundaries', and the following year saw the founding of the Federation of Evangelical Churches in the GDR. The State had gained its reward. Another ten years were to pass before the Church was to feel any real benefit from the commitment to the GDR symbolized by its formal separation from the West. By that time Ulbricht was dead and the leadership of the State was in different hands.

---

The rapprochement between Church and State achieved in 1978, though obviously beneficial to the Church, has at the same time highlighted some deep tensions within both the Church and the Communist Party. Old Party stalwarts, brought up to believe that religion is no more than an opiate and the churches the remains of reactionary bourgeois capitalism, were required, almost overnight, to treat Christians and churchmen as privileged equals. Not all have been converted to this new outlook, and some have been unwilling, or at least reluctant, to co-operate. Equally, many traditional Christians are highly suspicious of the current top-level hobnobbing of church leaders and the Communist bosses. Traditional anti-Communism is a long way from dead. Again, some of the younger, more radical Christians are just as disturbed: does the new Church-State relationship mean a creeping (or maybe not so creeping) return to the Prussian tradition of 'throne and altar' in unholy alliance?

Manfred Stolpe, an able lawyer-diplomat and at that time chief lay administrator of the Federation of Evangelical Churches, joined Bishop Schönherr in ushering in the new era and has no qualms about the Church's position in it:

> The Church today is an independent entity which has been formally granted a social role of its own and the right to comment in its own way. Its share in responsibility for the future is not open to question. That being so, the Church no longer appears as an agent of the enemies of the working class but as a social force in its own right.

Just how strong a social force the Church will be in the future is much less certain. In the GDR, as in almost all the countries of Western Europe, the post-war years have witnessed the rapid advance of secularization, and this is far more of a problem for the East German churches than the doctrines of Marx and Lenin. At the end of 1980 Herr Stolpe, reporting on the state of the Protestant churches, said that since 1950 the number of baptisms had fallen by 75 per cent, confirmations by 80 per cent, religious marriages by 85 per cent, religious funerals by 33 per cent, and church attendance by 50 per cent. On the other hand, participation in the Holy Communion had increased, and church members had doubled their contributions to the Church's finances.

The Evangelical Church has also assumed a major role in international ecumenism. After its traumatic separation from the West, this church felt hurt, isolated and often caged-in, but now it is one of the most ecumenically active and effective churches in the world. Hardly any Christian leader anywhere now fails to put the GDR on his or her itinerary. There is much to be learnt in this country, and the church offices in Berlin sometimes find it difficult to cope with all their guests. The Central Committee of the World Council of Churches met in Dresden in the summer of 1981. Even more significantly, Christians from the GDR are to be found at almost every important international church meeting. Christians nominated by the Church are, almost without exception, given exit visas for foreign travel – all a result of the new privileged status of the Church. There is a sour joke in the Communist Party that you have to join the Church if you want a holiday in Hawaii. But it is not lost on the State that even though very many Christians have gone abroad, they have all returned. In bi-lateral relationships with other churches, there have been important conversations with the Russian churches and also with the American churches. On contentious issues such as human rights, GDR Christians, being politically in the East yet with Western traditions, have an important contribution to make, and it is significant that the Human Rights Commission of the European Conference of Churches and the American and Canadian Council of Churches (set up to monitor progress after the Helsinki Declaration) is chaired by Frau Christa Lewek, a senior staff member of the Federation of Evangelical Churches in Berlin.

Symbolic of many things in GDR Church-State relations during the last three decades is the slow but steady reconstruction of Berlin's imperial cathedral. Kaiser Wilhelm II had it built in 1905 as a monument to Prussia's greatness and the new German imperialism, linked with the Lutheran Church. Since 1945 it has stood in the heart of Berlin, a burnt-out shell. The Communists demolished the ruins of the Kaiser's palace next door, but did not extend their demolition work to the cathedral lest the world should call them barbarians. Instead, they decided in the early 1970s to build a modern 'palace of the republic' on the site of the old palace and to carry out a complete restoration of the cathedral. The Church did not need this, or even want it, for the Marienkirche, the medieval parish church of Berlin, is only a few hundred metres away and serves very well as a cathedral. But the State has insisted, and so with Western money ($20 million on the exterior alone) the cathedral is being reborn in all its former imperial glory, mirrored in the glass side of the Communist parliament building nearby. The interior is to become a great living church centre in socialist Berlin – housing a theological seminary, a religious art centre, a communications centre, a publishing house, a place of worship and, perhaps most ironical of all, a museum with the graves of the Hohenzollern dynasty in the crypt.

An even greater irony, however, is the government's decision to elevate Martin Luther to the company of the heroes of the revolution. In the Communist textbooks of not so long ago, Luther was portrayed as the scourge of the peasants, the ally of the princes in putting down the common people. But the textbooks were wrong, history was different, Luther was a great German and, however indirectly, helped to pave the way for the first German workers' and peasants' State. So 1983 – the five hundredth birthday of the Reformer – is to be Luther Year in the GDR. A State commission, with Erich Honecker in the chair, is now preparing the celebrations, and all buildings in the GDR that have any association with Luther are being restored at State expense. Politely the Church has said: 'We already have our own commission – you celebrate Luther your way and allow us to celebrate him in ours.' But the front pages of the Communist press showed the Party Secretary and the bishops seated together at a great banquet held to launch the preparations, and the message to the little man in the church pew or the Party office was, 'We are all one in celebrating our national heritage.' The world is to be reminded, therefore, that it was on the territory of the German Democratic Republic that Martin Luther translated the Bible into German and nailed his Reformation theses to a church door in Wittenberg. Thus he changed the face of Europe in the sixteenth century, and four centuries later Luther has come nearer to supplanting Marx than anyone in the GDR would, even fifthteen years ago, have thought possible.

# Chapter 7

# CZECHOSLOVAKIA

In the course of over three hundred years the talented Central European peoples who now constitute the population of the State of Czechoslovakia have experienced no more than twenty years of real independence. Their history constitutes a major example of the struggle between freedom and oppression in human experience. For the greater part of this history the Bohemians, Moravians and Slovaks have been dominated by their powerful neighbours, and as recently as 1938 were regarded by the West European leaders who met at Munich as expendable pawns on the chessboard of European power politics. Again in 1968, an attempt to exercise a degree of freedom within the constraints of Communism was ruthlessly crushed by the tanks of the Soviet Union and other Warsaw Pact armies. The Russian army is still there, and Czechoslovakia is a police state of the most repressive kind. But religion, and religious conflict, has also played a crucial part in the shaping of their national life and there can be no proper understanding of twentieth-century events in Czechoslovakia without reference to the creative – and destructive – religious movements which dominated the lives of the Czech and Slovak people from the emergence of Jan Hus in 1400 to the Battle of the White Mountain in 1620.

The Bohemians, who with the Moravians are known as the Czechs, came under Western influence from the twelfth century onwards, and were among the pioneers of the Reformation. The movement led by Jan Hus in the early years of the fifteenth century was a rebellion against the social as well as the religious corruption of the medieval Church, and after the martyrdom of Hus in 1415 virtually the whole population of Bohemia and Moravia were identified with the Hussites. Attempts to create a new social order based on Protestant insights were, however, finally thwarted in 1620 when the Catholic Habsburgs defeated the army of King Friedrich von der Pfalz on the White Mountain, near Prague, and set in motion the Counter-Reformation. This was carried through with ruthless efficiency. The entire nobility and many Protestant leaders were put to death, the practice of evangelical religion became a crime, and the people had to choose between fleeing from the country or accepting the disciplines of the Catholic Church. A small number continued to meet in out of the way places and were known as 'Still Ones in the Land' or 'Hidden Seed'. The period from 1620 to the Edict of Toleration (1781) is often known as 'the era of darkness', and is still regarded by Protestants and Czech nationalists in Bohemia as a national disaster. One result of the slaughter was that Czech Protestantism, unlike its German neighbour, had no princes in which to put its trust. The Church of the Czech Brethren became a people's church, looking to professors for guidance rather than to princes for protection and leadership, and the Czech Protestant experience played an important part in preparing the nation for the concept of democracy, both in the period between the two world wars and in the Dubcek era.

The events of the post-Reformation period led to widespread disillusion with religious belief and particularly with religious institutions. Thus Bohemia became one of the most secularized territories in Europe. The effects are still evident in modern Czechoslovakia, but the Reformation and its consequences also established the pattern of Czech Protestantism and, in due course, influenced the responses of the Protestant Church to the dramatic events of the twentieth century.

This pattern has five elements. There is in Czech Protestantism a marked emphasis on personal discipleship, based on a concept of the Kingdom of God which demands that the Christian believer shall express his faith in a recognizably Christian life-style. Some of the Hussites experimented with forms of Christian communism. There is also the recognition that suffering is an integral part of Christian experience, involving for some actual martyrdom and for all acceptance of a servant role in the world. The Hussite movement was basically a movement of the oppressed and, in contrast with other parts of Europe, the Czech Protestant communities consisted mainly of the underprivileged. Another element is the historic concern for ecumenism. The Protestant pioneers of Bohemia and Moravia became deeply conscious of their affinities with reformers in other parts of Europe, and took a great deal of trouble to maintain contact with them; they also stretched out a hand of friendship to the Orthodox in the East. Last, but not least, there is a strong concern for reconciliation and peace. Although the Hussites were, owing to the circumstances of their time, nearly always involved in conflict, they never ceased to regard themselves as disciples of the Prince of Peace, and this particular emphasis was taken up and developed in the seventeenth century by another great Protestant reformer, Johannes Amos Comenius, who was obliged to spend most of his life in exile but left a lasting mark on Czech religion and culture.

In Slovakia the position was somewhat different in that the country was dominated by Hungary. During the sixteenth century the Magyar rulers of Slovakia were greatly influenced by Lutheranism, and the people also welcomed the Lutheran preachers. But after the Thirty Years War Slovakia was driven to Counter-Reformation and, although the repression of Protestantism was less severe than in the Czech lands, it left no room for open practice of evangelical faith. Slovakia remains predominantly Roman Catholic.

Czechoslovakia came into existence in 1918 as a succession state created from the ruins of the Austro-Hungarian Empire. Under the successive presidencies of T. G. Masaryk and Eduard Benes it soon became the great manufacturing centre of Central Europe, noted for its fine craftsmanship, and a model social democracy with a living culture which produced fine films and writers (notably Franz Kafka and Karel Capek) while rejoicing in its ancient universities and towns. But the presence of a large number of discontented Germans in Sudetenland, who were stimulated by the rise of Hitler's Germany in the 1930s, undermined the precarious freedom and prosperity of the country and led to the occupation of 1939–45. During the Second World War the Czechoslovak Republic disintegrated. The Czech lands were joined to Germany, as a protectorate, while Slovakia became an independent state – strictly subject to Hitler, of course, but enjoying a degree of autonomy under the energetic leadership of President Josef Tiso, who was also a Roman Catholic priest. When the war was over Tiso was executed as a traitor.

Following the liberation of Czechoslovakia in 1945 a provisional coalition government was set up and pledged itself to carry out a democratic socialist programme. Prior to the war friendly relations had been established with the USSR, and in 1943 the Benes government in exile signed a twenty-year treaty with the Soviet Union. The first post-war elections were held in May 1946 and the result, again, was a coalition government, but with the Communists as the largest party, having democratically secured 40 per cent of the Czech and 30 per cent of the Slovak votes. In February 1948 fourteen ministers of the moderate parties resigned from the government in protest against Communist infiltration of the police and security forces, and at the elections held in May of that year there was a single list of candidates, all of whom were sponsored or approved by the Communist Party. In effect there had been a coup d'état.

For most of the next two decades Czechoslovakia was dominated by the theories and policies of the Soviet Union. Its Presidents – Gottwald, Zapotocky and Novotny – were completely subservient to Moscow, and the people experienced an era of extremely harsh Stalinist rule. In 1956 there was an attempt at de-Stalinization, following Khrushchev's famous speech to the Twentieth Party Congress in Moscow, in which he denounced Stalin's oppressive policies, but this was resisted by the Czechoslovak Communist Party and it was not until the government reshuffle of 1963 that any real relaxation was permitted.

---

The next four years saw the start of the changes which were to culminate in the 'Prague Spring' of 1968. All the churches, and especially the Evangelical Church of the Czech Brethren, played a notable part in this development, but the first open signs of rebellion were seen in the freedom movement started by the Czech Writers' Union in June 1967. In November of that year students demonstrated in support of the writers' claims. Two months later Alexander Dubcek replaced Novotny as leader of the Communist Party, and introduced reforms designed to offer the people 'socialism with a human face'. Although Dubcek had been trained as a Party leader in Moscow, he departed very sharply from the Soviet line once he was in a position of authority. In March 1968 censorship was abolished and the churches were given a freedom of which, since the Communists came to power, they had previously only dreamed. The extent to which they had been infiltrated and manipulated by the pre-Dubcek regime soon became clear. In April Novotny was expelled from the Communist Party. This dramatic change in the political atmosphere of Czechoslovakia was the consequence, not so much of anti-Communist feeling, as of a recognition of the need for reform, which was shared by many within the Communist Party itself.

In July 1968, however, representatives of Russia, East Germany, Hungary, Poland and Bulgaria met in Warsaw where they signed a letter condemning the Czechoslovak reform. This letter was very threatening in its tone, but Dubcek rejected the criticisms and continued his policy. On 21 August Czechoslovakia was invaded by the Russian army, supported by soldiers from the other four countries, supposedly in the interests of peace and to suppress counter-revolution. According to Communist propaganda at the time, Western imperialists, including the Vatican and the World Council of Churches, were preparing a counter-revolution. For six days the invaders were confronted with passive resistance, but gradually the Russians gained control and the Dubcek government was forced to resign. The 'Spring' was over and 'Winter' returned with a vengeance, imposed by a neo-Stalinist regime installed by the Soviet overlord and determined to repress every sign of independence. The churches were now destined to feel once more the full force of repression, and throughout the 1970s they battled against odds as heavy as could be found anywhere in Eastern Europe outside Albania and the Soviet Union itself.

The present population of Czechoslovakia is just over fifteen million. The country has three regions: Bohemia in the west, Slovakia in the east, and Moravia in the centre. Language differences are slight, and since 1969 there has been a federal constitution which enables the Czech (Bohemia and Moravia) and Slovak Republics to exercise a certain amount of autonomy, although they are subordinate to the Federal Assembly. There are minority groups of Hungarians, Germans, Poles and Ukrainians. The present constitution was drawn up during the brief period of liberalization, and provides for the Czechs and Slovaks to work in partnership as 'two equal nations' (the Czechs actually outnumber the Slovaks by about two to one), but the long-standing rivalry between the two peoples shows no sign of abating. The constitution also offers safeguards to certain national minorities.

_____

Since 1948 reliable statistics relating to the churches of Czechoslovakia have been notoriously difficult to obtain. The figures that follow are believed to be accurate, and in some cases it has been possible to check them from a number of different sources, but they should be treated with reserve and regarded as broad indications of proportion rather than as statements of detailed fact.

At the time of the 1948 coup there were said to be more than nine million Roman Catholics in Czechoslovakia, including about 500,000 of the Eastern Rite (Uniates). They were served by 5,779 diocesan priests and 1,163 priests who belonged to religious orders; of these clergy about 400 were Uniates. By 1965 the number of Roman Catholics had fallen to eight million; today's total is unknown. In 1980 there were just over 4,000 Catholic parishes served by 2,691 diocesan priests and 212 priests who belonged to religious orders. In addition, there were 43 lay monks and, according to official Catholic records, 5,115 nuns, but in 1972 all nuns were obliged by the government to work out of sight on farms and in mental hospitals, so they are no longer living in community, though doubtless most of them are trying to live some form of the religious life in their particular circumstances. The two Catholic seminaries had a total of 243 students.

It will be seen from these figures that in the course of just over twenty years the number of active Roman Catholic clergy declined by almost 60 per cent. This decline continued throughout the 1970s and was exacerbated by the State banning about five hundred priests from active ministry.

The largest church after the Roman Catholic is the Czechoslovak National Church, or the Czechoslovak Hussite Church, as it is now called. This came into existence at about the same time as the foundation of the Czechoslovak State, when some 800,000 Roman Catholics used their new-found freedom to demand a vernacular liturgy, a married clergy and the right to doctrinal differences stretching as far as Unitarianism. These demands were rejected by Rome, so a schismatic national Church was founded. In 1977 its membership was said to number about 650,000, located in some 350 parishes and served by a rather smaller number of priests, of whom about eighty are women. There are six bishops, headed by a Bishop Patriarch (Novak), who is *primus inter pares*. During the early years of its existence the Hussite Church was rather frowned upon by the other churches, but it is now involved in the ecumenical movement.

The Evangelical Church of the Czech Brethren came into existence in 1918 as the result of the union of Christians of the Lutheran and Reformed traditions, together with some former Roman Catholics. It draws its inspiration from the old tradition of the Hussites, and now has about 240,000 members who meet in 521 places of worship (about half of which are established congregations, the rest are preaching stations), and are served by 250 ministers, whose number includes 30 women. The church has a presbyterian form of government and is administered on a synodal basis. Local congregations are grouped in seniorates, each averaging twenty churches, and the supreme organ of government is the General Assembly, known as the Synod, which meets every two years. At every level of church life ministers and laity share responsibility, and the lay members of the church are on the whole well trained and vigorous in their witness. About 3,000 of them serve on church committees.

The Slovak Lutheran Church has 369,000 members, 384 places of worship and about 350 ministers, while the Silesian Lutheran Church has about 46,000 members, 41 places of worship and 21 ministers. The Reformed Church of Czechoslovakia, which is Calvinist and of Hungarian origin, has 170,000 members (three-quarters of them Hungarian-speaking, the rest Slovak-speaking), about 300 places of worship and about 150 pastors. The Church of the Brethren has 8,000 members, 29 churches and 30 pastors, and the Unity of Brethren (or Moravian Brethren) also has 8,000 members, but only 18 churches and 20 pastors.

The Baptist Church has just under four thousand members on its rolls, but probably twice as many as this attend its worship regularly. These are spread fairly evenly throughout the country and there are twenty-eight churches besides many other informal places of worship. The largest congregations are in Prague, Brno, and Bratislava, and new church buildings have recently been completed at Cheb, Jablonec, and four other towns. At

Bratislava, where the Baptist church building was severely damaged in an earthquake, the 450-member congregation purchased a former Lutheran church in 1976 which they now use, and which also houses an office for the Baptist centre of all Slovakia. The church throughout Czechoslovakia employs twenty-one full-time ministers, and there are some lay pastors. Ministers are trained at the Comenius Evangelical Faculty in Prague (Church of the Czech Brethren) or at the Slovak Evangelical Faculty (Lutheran) in Bratislava. A notable feature of the life of the Baptist Church is its vigorous youth department, which organizes study conferences and camps, and has a mobile work group consisting of young people who give up their weekends and holidays in order to assist with the building of new churches.

The Methodist Church has just over 1,500 members and a total community of nearly 5,000. These worship in forty-two preaching places and are served by eighteen ministers and six retired ministers. Ministerial candidates are trained at the Comenius and Hus Faculties in Prague, and at the Evangelical Faculty in Bratislava. There are small numbers of Old Catholics and Unitarians, and about 7,000 Seventh Day Adventists.

At the end of the Second World War and after the Sub-Carpathian Ukraine had become part of the USSR, there were about 20,000 Orthodox Christians in Czechoslovakia. For historial reasons these were under the jurisdiction of the Serbian Orthodox Church, though there were in fact no Serbs among them. By 1948 they had been transferred to the jurisdiction of the Moscow Patriarchate, and an Exarch came from Russia to assume the leadership. When, under state pressure, some 500,000 Uniates joined the Orthodox Church a request for 'autocephaly', or complete independence, was made to Moscow and granted in 1951. Present numbers are unknown, but it is believed that no more than 10,000 Uniates remained within the Orthodox Church when they were given freedom to resume their own life in 1968, so the membership of the Orthodox Church is probably 20,000 to 30,000.

There are six theological faculties for the training of priests and ministers: the Comenius Evangelical Faculty (Church of the Czech Brethren), the Hus Czechoslovak Faculty (Hussite Church), and the Cyril-Methodius Roman Catholic Faculty are in Prague and Litomerice; the Slovak Evangelical Faculty (Lutheran) and the Roman Catholic Faculty are in Bratislava, and the Orthodox Faculty is in Presov.

The ecumenical movement began early in the territory which now constitutes Czechoslovakia. In 1905 the 'Unity of Constance' was founded to provide for co-operation between the Protestant churches in their minority and often repressed situation. This movement changed its name to 'Christian Unity' in 1969, and now has the involvement of some progressive Roman Catholics. Soon after the Second Assembly of the World Council of Churches at Evanston in 1954, the Ecumenical Council of Churches in Czechoslovakia was founded. All the main churches of the country, with the exception of the Roman Catholic, now belong to the Council. It is responsible for organizing the Week of Prayer for Christian Unity, and arranges conferences and meetings from time to time. An important element in its work is the fostering of contact between the Czech and Slovak churches, though the establishing of federal government in 1969 has meant that ecumenical work has had to be divided into national sections.

Prague is one of the great historic centres of Jewry, and during the 1930s the Jewish population of Czechoslovakia was in the region of 350,000. About 250,000 of these were killed by the Nazis during the occupation, and many others fled from the country. In 1948 there were about 48,000 Jews in the country, and when the Communists seized power more than half of these emigrated to Israel. By the time of the 'Prague Spring', in which some Jews played an important part, the Jewish community had been reduced to between 12,000 and 15,000, and after the Russian invasion of 1968 many more emigrated, so that the present Jewish population is only about 5,000. There are about ten congregations in Slovakia. There have been no rabbis since the death of the last Chief Rabbi in 1978, though there was a student in training at the Budapest Rabbinical Seminary at the end of 1980. Before the Second World War there were 320 synagogues and prayer houses in Slovakia alone, but now only twenty of these remain. The Jewish State Museum in Prague houses one of the most famous Jewish collections in the world; it is maintained by the government and is an important tourist attraction.

Since 1969 there has been a limited breakthrough in the
production and distribution of Bibles. Prior to the 'Spring' there
was very little Bible production in Czechoslovakia, but between
1969 and 1973 120,000 copies of Czech and Slovak scriptures
were produced. An ecumenical committee is working on a new
Czech translation of the Bible, and 30,000 copies of the Gospels
were printed in 1973. It will be a few years before this project
is completed, but a new translation of the Slovak Bible was ready
for production in 1973. Distribution of Bibles takes place in the
churches, and copies are also on sale in church bookshops in
Prague.

The main churches of Czechoslovakia all have their own
newspapers and magazines, the chief of which are published in
both Czech and Slovak. *Katolicke Noviny* (Catholic News) is a
Catholic weekly, published in Prague in Czech and in Bratislava
in Slovak. Both are intended for the general lay membership of
the Catholic Church. *Duchovni Pastyr* (Spiritual Pastor) is a
monthly magazine for clergy, published in Czech and Slovak.
The Church of the Czech Brethren publishes a monthly
magazine *Cesky Bratr* (Czech Brother), and this has a theological supplement, 'The Collection of Sermons'. This church also
has a monthly for young people *Bratrstvo* (Brotherhood), and
the Synodical Council has a regular press service containing
news items. An ecumenical group, formed in 1905 as Unity of
Constance and now known as Christian Unity, publishes a
weekly paper *Kostnicke Jiskry* (The Sparks of Constance) and
a monthly theological journal, *Christian Review*. In addition to
these church papers, there is *Nase Rodina* (Our Family), which
is the weekly of *Lidova Demokracie* (People's Democracy) – the
organ of the (Christian) People's Party which has a mainly
political content, but also a certain religious perspective. The
Jewish community has a monthly magazine, *Vestnik*
(Messenger), which is published in Czech, and an information
bulletin, published in German. There is also a Jewish calendar.

---

The comprehensive restrictions now being imposed upon the
Christian and Jewish communities in Czechoslovakia are,
unfortunately, no more than a continuation of the general policy
of repression which has characterized the government's attitude
to religious bodies for more than three decades, apart from the

brief 'Spring' of 1968. The scope and effect of these restrictions was clearly indicated in two letters of protest addressed to the President and Federal Assembly of the Czechoslovak Socialist Republic in 1977. The first letter, dated 7 May, was signed by thirty-one members of the Evangelical Church of the Czech Brethren, and included a careful analysis of the problems facing this church in its relations with the State. The second, dated 1 October, was signed by fifty-five Roman Catholics and drew attention to the disabilities being experienced by the Catholic community. The main points of these letters were as follows:

*Parish activities.* Pastors and priests cannot preach or officiate at worship services outside their own parishes unless they have received permission from the State authorities. This permission is often refused, and in consequence the parishes are becoming isolated from each other. Lectures, discussions, cultural activities, concerts, larger meetings of children and youth also need special permission, so that in many places these activities have ceased altogether. Publications activity in parishes is limited to circulars to church members and their contents are by and large censored.

*Pastoral work.* State officials who deal with church affairs often attend pastoral conferences and thus hamper any free expression of opinion. At least one-third, and perhaps as many as half, of the clergy have been visited by State security officials or invited to supply them with information. Clergy who are diligent in visiting church members in their homes are given warnings. They must inform State organs of their contacts with foreign friends. If they meet friends and colleagues in their own homes they are sometimes accused of illegal activity. Meetings of elders are either restricted or forbidden. The State decides which pastors shall be involved in the planning of important church meetings, conventions, synods and elections.

*Control of the clergy.* All priests and pastors need a State licence for the exercise of their ministry. Licences are frequently withdrawn from clergy who have crossed swords with the authorities, even over small matters. Retired clergymen who have to reapply for a licence often fail to obtain one. A priest or pastor without a licence cannot be employed by the Church in a ministerial capacity, he cannot preach sermons or publish articles in the church press, he is not allowed to attend the monthly meetings of clergy. Pressure is put on the Church leadership to dissociate itself from clergy who are without licences. State approval is needed for entry to theological education, and although the number of applicants increased in the 1970s the number of permits granted was reduced from eight hundred to four hundred. Students completing their training in theological faculties and seminaries are sometimes denied licences for parish work.

*Job discrimination.* Lay Christians are rarely entrusted with important posts in finance, the civil service or State administration. Some careers are closed to active church members. Teachers have to swear 'that they will carry out education in the spirit of scientific Marxist teaching'.

*Access to education.* A number of young people are deprived of the possibility of secondary or university education because of their own Christian convictions or those of their parents. Children can attend religious instruction only at a certain age, in a lower class at school, and are often discouraged from attending religious instruction by personal humiliation or threats to their parents.

*Church publishing.* Church journals and papers can be published only in small editions. The State has enforced changes in editorial staffs, some authors are not allowed to publish, and some journals have suffered heavy financial sanctions for publishing articles which have questioned State policies. The effect of all this is that the Church's publications are generally of poor quality.

*Monastic life.* Monastic orders and communities have no legal rights and are not allowed to recruit new members. Monks and nuns are deprived of theological and other specialized education. Limits are placed on the charitable work of religious communities.

Most, if not quite all, of these restrictions are based on decrees promulgated by the government in 1949 and 1950. The constitution adopted in 1960 and amended in 1969 speaks of religious freedom, but leaves ample room for the government to keep believers and religious institutions on the tightest of reins:

> Freedom of confession shall be guaranteed. Every one shall
> have the right to profess any religious faith or to be without

religious conviction, and to practise his religious beliefs insofar as this does not contravene the law. (Article 32/1) Religious faith or conviction shall not constitute grounds for anyone to refuse to fulfil the civic duties laid upon him by law. (Article 32/2)

---

Soon after the coup d'état in February 1948, the Archbishop of Prague, Josef Beran, thanked the Communist Minister of Justice for his promise that the government would do nothing to disturb the good relationship between Church and State, but went on to express four grievances already felt by the Catholic community. These were:

1.  The confiscation by the State of church buildings and institutions.
2.  The depriving of priests, monks and nuns of their normal work.
3.  The suspension of the majority of Catholic publications.
4.  The hampering of Catholic organizations.

During this period the government tried to play down the differences between the State and the Roman Catholic Church and, in common with most countries in Eastern Europe, included in the new constitution clauses which provided for religious freedom and for the equality of all religious organizations. Certain public declarations about religious freedom were also issued by the government, and a Catholic priest, Father Josef Plojhar, was appointed Minister of Health. Plojhar was chairman of the (Catholic) People's Party, which had no independence and slavishly followed the directions of the Communist Party. Government officials attended important church ceremonies and the Church provided liturgical celebrations to mark important events in the developing life of the new Czechoslovakia.

However, this apparent friendship between the government and the Church was superficial. The government, seeking to establish its position in the nation and to secure some credibility in the eyes of the world, had no desire to launch into immediate confrontation with the Catholic Church. The Church for its part recognized the reality of the political situation and was prepared to accept and co-operate with the government at certain levels, in the expectation, or at least the hope, that it would be permitted to continue many of its traditional ecclesiastical activities. But there was not the slightest element of mutual respect or of partnership.

The year 1948 saw the passing of two laws which were designed to undermine two important pillars of Roman Catholic power and influence. The Law Concerning Agrarian Reform led to the confiscation of virtually all church lands – a total of 320,000 hectares – which had for centuries been a major source of income for the Church. The government argued that this law was not an expression of anti-religious feeling but was intended simply to bring all privately-owned land under state control; none the less, the effect was to hit the Church hard and, although the government undertook to continue paying the salaries of the clergy by way of compensation, the scale of payments was set far too low to represent a reasonable bargain. The Law Concerning Education was even more painful for the Church, since it led to the suppression of all Catholic schools and the abolition of religious instruction in schools. In theory the Roman Catholic Church, like the other Christian communities in Czechoslovakia, was to be free to make its own private arrangements for the religious instruction of children and young people, but in practice the pressure brought to bear on parents by the government restricted enrolment for parish classes and courses and made the freedom somewhat illusory.

A year later the government took further steps to restrict the activities of the Church and to reduce its influence. State commissars (the equivalent of Hungary's 'moustached bishops') were appointed to every diocese and, in effect, took over the episcopal administration. Government approval was needed for all church appointments. The clergy were required to obtain government permission for any meetings they desired to convene. Pastoral letters and all other forms of communication within the Church were subject to censorship, and the Church was forbidden to impose ecclesiastical punishments on Catholics who supported the government. All lay organizations were suppressed or restricted, and in many cases their leaders were imprisoned. A schismatic Catholic Action movement was founded, with State support, to encourage Catholics to back the government, and this organization was allowed to publish its own journal, *Catholic News*.

About this time a confidential circular went to all local branches of the Communist Party indicating the immediate aims of the government as far as the Roman Catholic Church was concerned. These involved the removal of all ties between the clergy and the Vatican, the isolation of the bishops from the people, and the incitement of the people against Archbishop Beran.

The actions of the government confirmed the worst fears of the Catholic hierarchy, who were at that time much influenced by Pope Pius XII and shared his horror of Communism. During the early part of 1948 the bishops ordered all priests to avoid involvement in politics, and Archbishop Beran demanded that Father Plojhar should resign from the government. When he refused to comply he was suspended from the priesthood, along with two other priests who had accepted office in the Slovak State government. A notice announcing the suspension of the three priests was nailed to every church door in the country, in defiance of a government order, and a strongly-worded pastoral letter from Archbishop Beran on the subject of Church-State relations was read from every pulpit. Plojhar, who had often been used by the Communist Party to attack the Vatican, was later excommunicated.

In January 1949 the bishops protested against the restrictions being placed on the Church, and in May of the same year issued a pastoral letter which protested against the censorship of books, the closure of church schools and a new regulation which forbade the Church to hold public collections of money for its own and other charitable purposes. When the government announced that it proposed to compile an inventory of all church property, possessions and sources of income, the bishops told the parishes not to supply any information on these points.

On 19 August 1949, the Church consecrated two bishops in Slovakia without obtaining government approval for their appointment and, although the government blocked the roads and cancelled the trains into the cathedral city of Trnava, some hundred priests and 12,000 people attended the consecration. On the same day the bishops wrote to the government suggesting that negotiations between Church and State should be reopened, and laying down their requirements for the talks to begin. These included the restoration of freedom for Archbishop Beran (who was by this time confined to his palace), the removal of the State commissars from the bishops' offices, the ending of persecution of the clergy, the withdrawal of government support for the schismatic Catholic Action, and the ending of all propaganda against the Church. There were no further negotiations.

Towards the end of 1949 the government published a new law governing relations between Church and State. A State Office for Church Affairs was to be established, with a government official responsible for the development of religion in accordance with the constitution. Continuing the tradition of the Austro-Hungarian Empire, a state salary would be paid to the clergy of all denominations, but their appointments must be approved by the State and they would be required to swear an oath of loyalty to the State before an appointment was confirmed. State approval would be required for the budgets of all religious organizations, and the State would take over responsibility for institutions for clergy training. The basis of the new law was that: 'The State has the supervisory authority over the possessions of the Church and of religious communities.'

The form of the oath of loyalty was as follows:

I promise on my honour and conscience that I shall be loyal to the Czechoslovak Republic and its People's Democracy, and that I shall do nothing that is detrimental to its interests, its security and its integrity. As a citizen of the People's Democracy I shall honestly and sincerely carry out all duties which are incumbent upon me in the position which I occupy, and I shall support with all my strength the efforts towards reconstruction which are being made for the welfare of the people.

The bishops refused to take the oath, but advised their priests to take it and to add the sentence: 'If it is not in contradiction to the laws of God and of the Church, and to human rights.' Later this qualification was revised to read: 'After I have become convinced that the government will not demand anything that is in contradiction to the law of God and to human rights.' According to *Catholic News*, the organ of the government-sponsored Catholic Action movement, some 95 per cent of the clergy took the oath with the prescribed qualification, and soon afterwards the bishops told their clergy to accept the state salaries only on the following terms:

I declare that I am ready to accept the salary because it is the law of the State. But with this acceptance of the salary I do not make any promises which are against my priestly conscience or against the laws of the Church. I declare that the spiritual affairs of the Church and the complete freedom of my priestly activities are more important than the material security of my personal life.

Shortly before Christmas 1949 the bishops declared the new state law to be contrary to the law of God and, after objecting to specific provisions in the law, concluded with this warning: 'If the government wants to start a new fight in this country of saints and martyrs, a great number of the faithful will be ready to sacrifice everything for the glory of God and for religious freedom.'

In the event, the resistance of the Roman Catholic Church to the increasingly ruthless pressures of the government proved to be weak, and the state authorities had little difficulty in imposing their will on the Catholic community. A key factor in this process was the removal, during the period 1950–53, of virtually all the bishops who were loyal to Pope Pius XII and determined not to capitulate to Communism. By a variety of devices the government succeeded in leaving dioceses vacant but under the control of compliant vicars-general. Once the strong leadership had gone, the overwhelming majority of the clergy and laity were left bewildered and helpless, and for the most part were incapable of mounting any effective resistance to the government.

All but two of the seminaries were closed, and during the early part of 1950 the religious orders were ruthlessly attacked. After a show trial in which the superiors of ten religious orders were accused and pronounced guilty of subversive activities against the State, soldiers and policemen were sent to every monastery and convent in the country during the night of 13–14 April. The 1,910 monks and 10,660 nuns were forced into lorries and taken to a number of 'concentration monasteries'. Here they were supposed to be free to continue the religious life, but gradually they were secularized. A few were permitted to work in diocesan administrations. Recruitment ceased and, although many monks and nuns remained faithful to their vows in factories and on the farms where they were driven to work, the institutional expressions of monasticism were virtually eliminated.

Next it was the turn of the Uniate Church in Slovakia. This church had a single diocese, Presov, and just over 585,000 members who were served by about four hundred priests, but on 28 April a council attended by five priests and three hundred lay people declared themselves in favour of the Uniate Church returning to the Orthodox Church under the Patriarchate of Moscow. Once this decision was announced, the government moved to enforce it. Within a short time the Uniate bishop (Gojdic) and his suffragan (Hopko), together with about a hundred priests, were arrested and given prison sentences. Bishop Gojdic died in prison in 1960. Eight years later a fellow prisoner, Vasa Petrik, described in the newspaper *Lidova Demokracie* how Bishop Gojdic, 'who was always smiling and strengthening others', had been forced into a four-man team which was yoked to a plough and made to plough the prison fields. The priests who remained free were told in no uncertain terms that they must continue to serve the congregations which were now integrated with the Orthodox Church; refusal to do so would be regarded as attempted sabotage, and in fact those priests who tried to resign were sent to gaol. All the Uniate church buildings and possessions were turned over to the Orthodox Church.

Throughout the period of severe repression in the 1950s and 1960s, the size of local Catholic congregations declined dramatically. The pressures brought to bear on believers provided strong tests of commitment which not all were able to meet. Obstacles placed in the way of religious instruction for children and the discouragement of young people from church membership took their toll and cut off the supply of new life. The acute shortage of priests led to a weakening of local leadership and pastoral care. Intensive campaigns of atheistic propaganda had some effect, and so did the secularism which has characterized the twentieth-century life of the greater part of Europe. However, the decline in church attendance was not evenly spread throughout the country. The most serious effects were felt in the large cities, and particularly in the western areas of the country; in the rural areas of Slovakia church attendance remained comparatively high. But the overall picture was gloomy.

---

The decline of Czechoslovak Catholicism cannot, however, be

accounted for simply in terms of Communist oppression and the growth of secularism. The causes run much deeper, and go back to the Reformation, when large numbers were alienated from Catholicism. The problems created by the Reformation and the Counter-Reformation became increasingly evident during the Nazi occupation of the country, and the Roman Catholic Church was ill-equipped to meet the challenge of Communism. In fact, there were those who saw the Communists as the liberators of Czechoslovakia from an alien and oppressive religious yoke. And some observers believe that the extremely harsh line taken by the new Communist rulers in their dealings with the Catholic Church was not simply an obedient response to directives from Moscow, but represented an emotional expression of resentments which had been smouldering for centuries. Paradoxically, the witness of the Catholic Church during the hard times of the 1950s served to rehabilitate the Church in the eyes of many people, and the courage of Josef Beran made a considerable impact.

Although he was unable to play any active part in the life of his church after 1949, Beran symbolized for the Czechoslovak Catholics their resistance to Communist oppression and their sufferings for the Christian faith. His place in the history of European Catholicism seems assured. Born into a teacher's family, Beran was nurtured in Counter-Reformation piety and was very much a man of the people. Towards the end of his life he came to recognize that the Roman Catholic Church in Czechoslovakia had in a certain sense been required to suffer for its past sins and errors, but the Communists who seized power in 1948 found themselves confronted with a church leader who was fearless and ready to defend the interests of the Catholic community without thought of serious compromise and without care for the cost.

On the Feast of Corpus Christi 1949, he spoke to a large crowd at the monastery of Strahov and warned the people of his approaching arrest: 'I do not know how many more times I shall be able to talk to you in the future ... Whatever may happen, do not believe that I have capitulated. I come before you and swear that I shall never sign an agreement of my own free will which violates the laws of the Church.' Shortly after this a group of demonstrators interrupted his sermon in Prague cathedral and as a result the police moved into the archiepiscopal palace 'to be at his disposal and to protect him against the wrath of the faithful'. The Archbishop was not allowed to leave the palace or to receive any visitors. A State official took over the administration of the archdiocese and all the Archbishop's mail was confiscated. In spite of these strict measures, however, Beran managed to get a letter smuggled out of the palace and this was read in many churches. In it he said:

> He who refuses to betray God cannot be a traitor to his country and to his people. Let all the faithful pray that the nation will return to God, as the prodigal son returned to his father. We are so insignificant and helpless in the midst of these raging and satanic powers. But even though we are powerless we can help through our attitude to keep the evil from our people.

Charges of treason were prepared against him, and the clergy were called upon by the government to denounce both the Archbishop and the Vatican. They refused to comply and passed a resolution which said: 'In loyalty we stand with our bishops and our Archbishop and we shall continue to do so even if we are persecuted.' Later Beran was transferred to Rozelov Castle and eventually to so-called 'concentration monasteries' in a remote part of Southern Moravia-Bohemia. Here he remained until the beginning of 1964, when Pope Paul VI announced his appointment as a cardinal.

The government saw the appointment as an opportunity for getting the intransigent Archbishop out of the country, so permission was given for Beran to go to Rome to receive his cardinal's hat at the traditional ceremony, but on condition that he did not return to Czechoslovakia. It is not clear whether Beran knew of the conditions attached to his release, but on his arrival in Rome he was soon acquainted with the fact that he would not be returning to his homeland. The Second Vatican Council was in session at the time, and on 20 September 1965, Cardinal Beran made a speech on the subject of freedom of conscience which is now considered to have been one of the great speeches of the Council. In it he said:

> In my country the Catholic Church at this time seems to be suffering expiation for defects and sins committed in her name against religious liberty in times gone by, such as in the fifteenth century, with the burning of the priest John Hus, and

in the seventeenth century, with the forced reconversion of a great part of the Czech people to the Catholic faith . . . By such acts, the secular arm, wishing or pretending to serve the Catholic Church, in reality left a hidden wound in the hearts of the people. This trauma was an obstacle to religious progress and offered – and offers still – easy material for agitation to the enemies of the Church.

Cardinal Beran remained in Rome until his death on 17 May 1969.

---

The experience of the Protestant churches of Czechoslovakia since the Communists came to power stands in contrast to that of the Roman Catholic Church. This can be explained by the radically different approach to Church-State relations made by the Protestant churches, and the response which this evoked from the Communist government, which regarded these churches as too small and fragmented to constitute any threat to its authority. Having been obliged to accept a minority position for over two hundred years, during which time their religious freedom was often seriously limited, the Protestant churches thought they had little to lose whatever kind of government came to power. When the Communists declared the equality of all religious bodies in the eyes of the State, this represented for Protestants a notable advance, with an added bonus in the form of greatly reduced Catholic power. Then there was the very important fact that the spiritual heirs of John Hus, particularly within the Church of the Czech Brethren, were far from averse to revolutionary political change. For them salvation had – and still has – a social dimension, and after centuries of repression there was no shortage of Protestant Christians who in the immediate post-war period were prepared to see in socialism a political expression of their own desire for a more just and democratic society. Even so, no Protestant of any stature actually embraced Communism and joined the Party.

The position of the Czechoslovak National Church (or the Czechoslovak Hussite Church, as it is now called) has been somewhat different. Born of a recent schism and designed to express the aspirations of the new nation, in 1948 its leadership was taken over by a handful of pro-Communist clergy who strongly supported the new regime. They were 'rewarded' for their efforts when the government ordered the Faculty of the Church of the Czech Brethren in Prague to relinquish its name Jan Hus to the Czechoslovak National Church; it was at this point that the former was renamed Comenius Faculty. The present Patriarch of the Czechoslovak Hussite Church (Novak) still complies with government requirements and speaks in favour of government policies, but recent reports suggest that the majority of his church members are opposed to the post-1968 regime.

Once the 1949 Church-State law was applied, the Protestant churches found themselves subject to the same restrictions and disabilities as the Roman Catholic Church. Among those imprisoned during this period was Henry Prochazka, a leader of the small Baptist Church who had been influential in Czechoslovakia before the war. He was released from prison in 1955, following a letter to the President from the officers of the World Council of Churches (Bishop George Bell, Dr W. A. Visser 't Hooft and Dr Ernest Payne), but his health was broken and he died in 1961. There were problems over religious education and work among young people. Appointments of church leaders were subject to state approval, and the intensification of atheistic propaganda in the 1950s caused considerable alarm and disappointment. But if there were difficulties over the religious education of the young there were few over the training of the adult laity, and the Protestant churches embarked upon a massive programme of laity education designed to strengthen the internal life of the churches and equip church members for their work within the new social order.

It was during this time that the traditional pattern of the Church's life – particularly as this is expressed at the local level in the regular Sunday worship, the midweek Bible class and youth group, the church meeting and confirmation instruction group – took on new meaning. Professor J. M. Lochman, who was at the time on the staff of the Comenius Faculty and is by no means a conservative churchman, has described the life of the local parishes and congregations:

> Deprived of their institutional 'power', they got a new 'glory' of a free, spontaneous, meaningful community. Their institutional element became important: it was a base – in many respects the only base – for Christian organization and service.

Not all congregations and parishes were capable of realizing this possibility. Some were nearly overwhelmed by the sociological changes in their own environment. Traditional patterns and contexts of service in their habitual environment collapsed, and many found it very difficult to seek and find new possibilities outside those patterns and contexts. This happened especially in the country, where the traditional way of life changed radically because of the upheavals of collectivization. Most of our congregations, however, discovered and grasped a new chance of becoming free communities of nonconforming Christian life. Contacts and encounters with those congregations became for many of us the source of the strongest inspiration for our work as theologians and Christians. I personally could hardly recall in all my ecumenical and ecclesiastical activities an experience which was of stronger encouragement to me than the regular contact with our congregations throughout the country in the '50s and '60s. I visited them Sunday by Sunday, speaking and listening. In all human perplexities, sometimes frustrations, the glory of Christian fellowship and mission kept emerging beyond any doubt. (*The Church in a Marxist Society*, pp. 87–8)

Individual Christians certainly needed such support and encouragement, for they often found themselves in extremely difficult situations where they sometimes had to choose between loyalty to their faith and the well-being of their families and their careers.

The Evangelical Church of the Czech Brethren is not the largest of the Protestant churches of Czechoslovakia, yet there can be no doubt that (since the end of the Second World War) it has easily been the most influential. This is due in large measure to the work of one man, a theologian who became world-renowned for his attempts to integrate Christian belief with the developing Communist life of Eastern Europe: Josef Hromadka.

Hromadka was born in 1889 and, like Cardinal Beran, had a humble beginning. His intellectual gifts were quickly recognized and he owed a great deal to the influence of Thomas Masaryk, who strongly resisted Communism and the policy of revolution but opened the eyes of Hromadka to the significance of Russian literature and philosophy. In 1911 Hromadka spent some time at the college of the United Free Church in Aberdeen, where David S. Cairns was teaching systematic theology. A year earlier Cairns had been involved in the great missionary conference at Edinburgh, and it was through him that Hromadka was introduced to the thought of John R. Mott, J. H. Oldham and other pioneers of the ecumenical movement.

As early as 1918 Hromadka declared that socialism would become the outstanding issue for the Church of the future, and in 1920 he was appointed Professor of Systematic Theology in the Jan Hus Theological Faculty which had just been founded in Prague. Soon after this his attention was drawn to the theological work of Karl Barth, and increasingly he was drawn towards socialism as the appropriate political expression of the Gospel for the new age which he believed to have dawned. He was critical of certain aspects of the Russian revolution but, in general, regarded it as a positive development which, because of its basis in the vision of a more just society in which the poor and wretched of the earth received a proper share of the world's wealth, had profound spiritual implications.

In 1938, shortly after the German army had moved into the country, Hromadka went to America and was unable to return home owing to the outbreak of the Second World War. He spent the next eight years as Professor of Christian Ethics at Princeton Theological Seminary. Towards the end of this time, and on his return to Europe when the war was over, he played a prominent part in the foundation of the World Council of Churches, which he actively supported for the rest of his life.

When he arrived back in Czechoslovakia in 1947 Hromadka saw the Communist rise to power as something to be welcomed, and he advised the other Protestant churches of Eastern Europe to share his optimism about the future. His broad position was that the former Christian West had degenerated to the point of collapse, and that there was no future for the capitalist society which he believed to have arisen through the neglect or distortion of fundamental Christian insights and values. Communism had arisen not as the expression of a particular ideology but as a consequence of man's struggle for justice and freedom. The fact that what the Communists preached and practised in Eastern Europe was atheistic and materialistic was, according to Hromadka, secondary and almost incidental. There was no reason why it should remain anti-religious, and if the churches showed a positive understanding of the Communist interpretation of history and a readiness to become involved in the building of a new society, there was a real possibility that the Christian view of man might come to be recognized as true and as meeting real spiritual needs.

The ability with which Hromadka argued his case and the integrity he displayed in his dealings with politicians earned him considerable respect in government circles, though his critics often accused him of academic naïvety and of being too romantic. His viewpoint was also a useful instrument for those who wished to enlist the support of the Protestant churches for their social policies or who needed a theological stick with which to beat the Roman Catholic Church. But, while Hromadka was sympathetic to the aims of the government, he never became a member of the Communist Party, and was firmly convinced that he must retain his freedom to evaluate the political situation in the light of his Christian faith.

This evaluation frequently led to his criticizing particular government policies, especially when these encroached upon the freedom of individuals or groups. His method was to write to the ministers or officials concerned, rather than indulge in public pronouncements which would have served only to arouse further hostility. During the time of the severest repression in the 1950s he made great efforts to persuade the government to ease the pressure, and in 1958 sent a memorandum to the central committee of the Communist Party in which he questioned the aims of the 'cultural revolution', particularly as this was being applied to Christian teachers and to the life of the churches. Again, the address which Hromadka gave at his reception of the International Lenin Peace Prize in 1958 was a remarkable application of his Christian faith to the life of Communist society. It was about this time that he floated the Christian Peace Conference.

Another result of Hromadka's work and influence was the development of the Christian-Marxist dialogue. He did not hesitate to challenge the atheism of leading Communist thinkers, and this provoked a response from many of them which opened the way to serious dialogue, culminating in an international congress on the subject at Marienbad in 1967. The path which he had chosen was an extremely lonely one and called for great courage. To many within the Church he seemed to have sold out to Communism and betrayed his friends, many of whom were suffering for their faith. On the other hand, the government could only treat him with the greatest reserve, for he had never ceased to be a Christian theologian and thus, in their eyes, he represented the religious element in life which they wished to eliminate.

The ferment of thought in which Hromadka played such an important part proved to be an important factor in the events which led to the brief Dubcek era and the process of liberalization in the spring of 1968. He saw this as a 'true revolution towards a more genuine, more creative and more humane socialism'. The Russian invasion was, therefore, a devastating blow to him, as he made plain in a letter which he sent to all those who were to attend the meeting of the Prague Christian Peace Conference (CPC) in Paris, 1–4 October 1968. Hromadka was at that time President of the CPC, and evidently felt that he owed some explanation of his position and feelings to his friends.

After outlining the basis of his own commitment to socialism and the events which led to the Russian invasion, Hromadka said:

> I am not able to express the depth of our disappointment, our grief, our feelings of outrage, and even betrayal . . . In my mind 21 August is written in much darker colours than 15 March 1939. The Nazis were our chief enemies and always declared quite openly their intentions towards us and the whole of Eastern Europe. But on 21 August our friends and allies invaded our country . . .

There followed a detailed analysis of the consequences of the betrayal, viewed in the light of the Christian faith, and he concluded with a reaffirmation of his continuing commitment to democratic socialism, and his belief in the necessity of an even deeper involvement by Christians in the building of democracy 'in its moral, spiritual, human and cultural depths, in its freedom, justice, personal responsibility, and cultural creativeness'.

A further disappointment awaited Hromadka. With the process of 'normalization' in Czechoslovakia after 1968, there came increasing pressure on the Christian Peace Conference, in which Hromadka had for many years had an enormous intellectual and emotional involvement (see Chapter 13). The pressure was exercised chiefly by the Russians, who apparently saw the CPC leadership's involvement in the 'Prague Spring' as evidence of counter-revolutionary elements on their own doorstep. As a result of Soviet intervention, the secretary-general of the CPC, Dr J. N. Ondra, was in effect dismissed in November 1969, and it was widely suspected that his removal was motivated by political considerations. For Josef Hromadka this was yet another betrayal, probably the most tragic of his life. He died a few weeks later.

Although Hromadka's personal contribution to the life of his church and nation was of the greatest importance, he was by no means an isolated theologian. On the contrary, he was the best-known member of a team of scholars, clerical and lay, whose varied work during a crucial period of their country's history can now be seen as deeply significant. Among them was J. B. Soucek, a pupil of Hromadka, who succeeded him as Dean of the Comenius Faculty. He, too, studied at Aberdeen for a time and served as a parish minister, but from 1933 onwards he taught New Testament Studies and combined his teaching post with a secretaryship in the Synod of the Church of the Czech Brethren. During the war years, when Hromadka was absent in America and the Nazis closed the theological faculties, Soucek played a leading part in the organization and teaching of an underground faculty for the training of clergy. In his thinking he was influenced by the work of Emil Brunner, and to a lesser degree by Karl Barth and Rudolf Bultmann, and on the occasion of his sixtieth birthday he was aptly described by one of his former pupils as 'a theologian of circumspect faith'. In addition to his academic work, the fruits of which are to be seen in many publications and particularly in the new Czech translation of the Bible, Soucek took a lively interest in the ecumenical movement and was involved in the founding of the Conference of European Churches; his influence among students and ministers was extremely important in the events which led up to the 'Spring'.

During the 'Spring' the churches found themselves with almost complete freedom. Clergy and lay people who had been in prison for their beliefs were released and rehabilitated. The women's religious orders were permitted to function openly, and there was a significant increase in admissions to the theological faculties. The church press benefited from the general relaxation of censorship, and Christian speakers were invited to broadcast on the radio. Many public meetings were held to promote Christian-Marxist dialogue and the first of these, held in Prague in April 1968, was attended by more than 3,000 people. The Uniate Church was given the right to exist again, and local congregations were asked to vote on whether they wished to stay within the Orthodox Church or return to their former Uniate life; the overwhelming majority elected to return, and there was great rejoicing when they repossessed Presov cathedral in July 1968. This resurrection of a church after its apparent death was an event of great significance in Czechoslovakia, and hardly less so in the nearby Ukraine where the news brought hope to the repressed Uniates and disquiet to their rulers. This was a time of new hope for all Czechoslovak Christians and in June 1968, Bishop Tomasek, then Apostolic Administrator of the archdiocese of Prague and friend of Hromadka, went as far as to send a telegram to Alexander Dubcek assuring him of the Catholic Church's support if he continued along the path of liberalization. Many churchmen were already giving Dubcek the strongest support, and this not primarily because of the freedom given to the religious communities but because they were highly enthusiastic about the possibility of developing a truly democratic socialism. When the factory sirens and church bells sounded out together in August 1968 in support of the 'Spring' they were expressing feelings which ran deep in the consciousness of the Czechoslovak people, as indeed was President Svoboda later in that year when, on behalf of the State, he thanked the churches for their contribution to the 'Spring' and for their support during the threatening days of the summer.

The Russian invasion brought a serious setback for the churches, as well as for Czechoslovak society as a whole, though it was not until July 1969 that the churches began to feel the effects of 'normalization'. Mme Kadlecova, the head of the State Office for Church Affairs during the Dubcek administration and a person of integrity, was replaced by Karel Hruza who had held the office before her. Hruza was the only pre-'Spring' man to return to office, and he immediately attacked the churches, pointing out that they had influence over more than 60 per cent of the population in some parts of the country and had gained the support of the intelligentsia during 1966–67. He also claimed that the Christian-Marxist dialogue had been turned to the advantage of the churches who represented a vast reservoir of actual, or potential, anti-socialist activity.

---

Since 1969 the pressure on the churches has been unrelenting, and the suffering of the Czechoslovak Christians who have fallen foul of the state authorities has been considerable. On 5 April 1974, for example, Cardinal Stefan Trochta of Litomerice, who was convalescing after three eye operations, was subjected to a six-hour hectoring interview by the District Secretary for Church Affairs. The following day he died of a brain haemorrhage. During the 1970s about five hundred clergy were banned from exercising their ministry; some of these have since died, and over two hundred priests and pastors were known to be banned in 1981. Among them are Father Alojz Tkac, who is now working as a tram conductor; Dr Jaroslav Studeny is employed in a factory after spending three years in prison for distributing religious literature; Professor Ladislav Hejdanek is a nightwatchman; Pastor Jaromir Dus is a lift-attendant in a hotel; and Pastor Jan Simsa is a shepherd. The best-known of the banned clergy is the Slovak bishop Jan Korec, S.J., who has worked as a railway porter, storekeeper and maintenance mechanic, and is regarded as a Christian hero in Slovakia. Bishop Korec was secretly ordained to the priesthood in 1950, and a year later, at the height of the Stalinist terror, was secretly consecrated a bishop. This was discovered in 1960 and he was sentenced to twelve years' imprisonment, during which he contracted tuberculosis. In the Prague Spring he was released from prison and rehabilitated, but in 1974 he was sentenced to serve the remainder of his original prison term. By this time Bishop Korec's health was poor, and his future had become a matter of international concern, so the government tried to expel him from the country. The Vatican was not prepared, however, to transfer him elsewhere and he was then allowed to pursue a secular occupation and live in Bratislava under police supervision. He continues to be harassed by the authorities, and in July 1979 was interrogated by the police for alleged 'illegal pastoral activities' (i.e. holding a prayer meeting), for receiving religious books from abroad, and for informing contacts in the West of his frequent summonses to the police station. When at the end of this particular interrogation Bishop Korec was offered a remote parish in the mountains, he declined and added, 'I would accept it if all Slovak priests who have been denied their ministry were reinstated as well.'

Another well-known priest in trouble in 1979 was Father Josef Zverina, the most able Catholic theologian in Czechoslovakia, who was detained in September of that year, in company with ten other Catholics, and charged with 'obstructing State supervision of the Church'. This appears to have related to the fact that he had written certain material which was being circulated in duplicated form and constituted 'illegal trading'. A survivor of the notorious Dachau concentration camp, Father Zverina has since 1948 spent a total of thirteen years in Communist prisons. He is the author of several major theological books, and during the 'Spring' was appointed Professor of Theology at the Catholic seminary of Litomerice. He was dismissed from this post in 1970 and at the same time lost his state licence to exercise a pastoral ministry. During the early part of 1981 the government began a new tactic when it called up for military service a number of Slovak priests who had previously been exempt, and in some cases were actually medically unfit for military duties.

The plight of the Catholic clergy has aroused concern outside Czechoslovakia, and in February 1980 the Jesuit Generalate in Rome issued a statement expressing anxiety about the harassment and persecution of its members, pointing out that since 1977 the impeding of priests and laymen in the carrying out of ordinary pastoral work had gradually increased. Later in the same year Pope John Paul II referred to the situation in Czechoslovakia in one of his midday addresses in St Peter's Square:

> Let us pray that the Christians in Czechoslovakia may be united in confessing Christ and enjoy full religious freedom in all areas of life, including the possibility of receiving normal theological training in accordance with their priestly or religious vocation... Let us pray also for the well-being of Czech society and the State, which always depends on respect for the rights of all citizens.

---

Although the churches have borne the main brunt of the State's repressive policies since 1968, many other individuals and groups in Czechoslovakia have experienced the ruthless and crushing power of the present regime. In the aftermath of the Prague Spring, about half a million members of the Communist Party were purged and also removed from any responsible positions in society which they may have held. About 180,000 eventually left the country and found refuge elsewhere. Artists, writers, academics and professional people have been particularly hard hit, and in January 1977 some 241 of them, including seven clergy, published a manifesto which they called 'Charter 77'. This began by welcoming the International Declaration on Civil and Political Rights signed by many nations at Helsinki in 1975, but went on to say that the publication of this Declaration, to which the Czech government was a party, served as 'a powerful reminder of the extent to which basic human rights in our country exist, regrettably, on paper alone'. The manifesto then outlined the various ways in which human rights are denied in Czechoslovakia, and said in respect of religious belief and practice:

Freedom of religious confession is continually curtailed by arbitrary official action; by interference with the activity of churchmen, who are constantly threatened by the refusal of the State to permit them the exercise of their functions, or by the withdrawal of such permission; by financial or other transactions against those who express their religious faith in word or action; by constraints on religious training and so forth.

Charter 77 could be circulated only in *samizdat* form, but it quickly attracted another five hundred signatures, of whom thirteen were clergy, and eventually the number of signatories rose to over a thousand. In April 1977 the original sponsors of the Charter issued another statement, known as 'Document 9', which was concerned specifically with the lack of religious freedom, and the clergy associated with Charter 77 also wrote an open letter in which they outlined their attitude to the Charter and which was widely circulated in *samizdat* form.

The government, fearing that the Charter might become the focus of a powerful dissident movement, moved quickly against its signatories and especially against those responsible for writing and promoting it. By the middle of 1978 no fewer than

162 of those who had signed were known to have been dismissed from their posts, another 30 were in exile, and 20 had been tried and sentenced for alleged offences against the State. The government also put pressure on all the religious bodies to condemn the Charter, but this they refused to do. Their public statements about the Charter were couched in very broad terms and did little more than explain that the churches had not been involved in its compilation and distribution. In fact, a number of individual churchmen have been deeply involved in the Charter 77 movement, as it has come to be called. Dr Vaclav Benda, a well-known Catholic philosopher, poet and novelist, became a spokesman for the movement in February 1979. A month later he was arrested and charged with 'subversion of the Republic', for which he was in due course sentenced to four years' imprisonment. At the beginning of 1980 Pastor Milos Rejchrt of the Evangelical Church of the Czech Brethren was nominated as one of three new spokesmen for the movement; he had been deprived of his State licence as long ago as 1972, soon after he had persuaded his church to withdraw from the Christian Peace Conference. But Charter 77 is now very weak, most of its supporters having succumbed to unrelenting State pressure.

---

So-called peace movements have been a problem for the Czechoslovak churches, and especially for the Catholic Church, for more than thirty years. The Peace Movement of Catholic Clergy (MHKD) was founded in 1951 under the leadership of Josef Plojhar. It soon proved to be a typical 'front' organization and, although its general statements about peace were unexceptionable, its ideas and proposals were always very close to those issuing from the Kremlin. The 'peace priests' also became fervent supporters of the government's plans for collectivization and socialization, and with the passage of time MHKD was aligned exclusively with the Communist Party. Pope John XXIII's encyclical *Pacem in Terris* (1963) was misrepresented and exploited by the movement, which had by this time become a divisive force in the Catholic Church and also an instrument of government control. Once the older bishops retired, or had otherwise been disposed of, the government selected vicars capitular for the dioceses from the most influential, hardline members of MHKD. These men assumed office without any

kind of official ecclesiastical recognition, were usually excommunicated by the Vatican and often played havoc with their
cathedral chapters and diocesan officials. During the Prague
Spring the movement was disbanded and replaced by the
Movement for Conciliar Renewal (DKO), but the change was
short-lived, for after the Russian invasion the activities of the
'peace priests' were revived under the name 'Pacem in Terris',
with the former leaders of MHKD in control and chief among
those demanding that supporters of Alexander Dubcek should be
put on trial.

Just how many Catholic priests have belonged to the 'peace'
movement since its inception is impossible to tell. In the early
days the then secretary-general claimed a membership of 1,700,
but since then there have been widely differing reports about the
size of the movement. In 1978 over 250 'peace priests' attended
a meeting in honour of the sixtieth anniversary of the founding
of the Czechoslovak Republic, but the clearest indication of the
present strength of the movement was given by Cardinal
Tomasek of Prague in 1980 when he told the Italian newspaper
*Il Regno* that about one-third of the Catholic clergy were
members. It must not be supposed, however, that all of these are
government supporters, since many priests have joined the
movement at different times in its history, simply in order to win
the approval of the State Office for Church Affairs and thus
remain free to minister to their sorely pressed parishioners. Even
so 'Pacem in Terris' continues to be a problem for the Catholic
Church, as Cardinal Tomasek indicated in his *Il Regno* interview:

> It depends totally, I emphasize totally, on the State. Its
> programme is inspired by slogans of brotherhood and co-oper-
> ation but in reality it does nothing for the Church . . . It has no
> dialogue with the hierarchy. I am in total disagreement with
> it because it does not have the approval of the Vatican. On the
> contrary, I can tell you that the Pope is very worried about
> it.

The Cardinal and the Pope have some other reasons for their
concern, since 'peace priests' hold many key posts in the
Church's educational and publishing work, and have full control
of four dioceses. In 1972 discussions were opened between
representatives of the Vatican and the Czechoslovak govern-

ment, with a view to appointing resident bishops to some of the fourteen dioceses, all but one of which were at that time vacant. Early in 1973 four appointments were made, and the four new bishops were all prominent members of 'Pacem in Terris', one of them (Josef Vrana, appointed to the diocese of Olomouc in Moravia) being president of the movement. Archbishop Casaroli, who was at that time the Vatican's chief negotiator with the Communist countries of Eastern Europe, travelled to Czechoslovakia in order to preside over the consecration of the new bishops, and declared in his sermon at Nitra, 'This is a great day for the Catholic Church in Slovakia and for the country as a whole.' But a number of Slovak Catholics were extremely unhappy about these episcopal appointments and spoke of the Vatican 'spitting on the blood of martyrs'. It seems that the Vatican hoped to secure some reduction of the State's pressure on the Church in return for the concession over the bishops, but in the event the government conceded nothing. Further talks have been held between Vatican and government officials since 1973, but no agreement has been reached over the appointment of further bishops, and nine dioceses remain vacant.

---

At the centre of the conflict between Church and State, occupying a most uncomfortable position, is Cardinal Frantisek Tomasek, Archbishop of Prague. Tomasek, who was born in 1899, became a priest in 1922, having obtained a doctorate in theology at the university of Olomouc. In 1949 he was appointed Bishop of Olomouc but two years later, during the period of fierce Stalinist persecution, he was imprisoned in a labour camp where he remained until 1954. On his release he became parish priest of a small village in Moravia and was obliged to stay there for the next ten years. However, when Cardinal Beran left Czechoslovakia for Rome in 1965, Tomasek was appointed Apostolic Administrator of Prague. In 1976 Pope Paul VI secretly appointed him a cardinal, but in the following year it seemed safe to make the appointment public and in 1978 he was appointed Archbishop of Prague. Tomasek has a very different personality from that of his famous predecessor, and his policy is one of conciliation rather than confrontation. But he is in no sense a collaborator with the government and he has never been associated with the 'peace priests' movement. His aim is to secure the survival of a church which has been harassed and persecuted for the best part of three decades, which has been seriously weakened during this time, and which is now painfully divided. At various times, particularly since 1977, he has been sharply criticized for failing to speak out against government policy and on behalf of those who have been imprisoned or exiled for their faith. Yet those who hear his sermons in the cathedral at Prague are left in no doubt as to his position, and his belief in quiet diplomacy and quiet suffering is in its own way as impressive as the more dramatic forms of martyrdom.

The other Czechoslovak churches are now committed to a similar approach. During the period prior to the Prague Spring a group of mainly young, radical pastors of the Evangelical Church of the Czech Brethren formed the 'New Orientation Group'. They were politically sophisticated and were the new theological counterpart of a generation of young Marxists who helped to pave the way for Dubcek's 'socialism with a human face'. In 1968 members of the Group came to the fore as leaders of their church, and for a time after the Russian invasion they influenced its synods to hold out against Soviet-style 'normalization'. Jan Palac, who achieved world fame in 1969 when he immolated himself in protest against the Russian invasion, was a lay member of the Church of the Czech Brethren; so also were two others who followed his example. At the October 1971 synod of the church three documents were prepared for presentation to the government. These asked for amnesties for Christians who were in prison for their beliefs, for the cessation of attacks on churches and individuals, and for the opening of an honest and sincere dialogue between the government and the churches. The documents were published and provoked a hostile reaction from the government, since when this church has sought to remain faithful within the constraints imposed upon it by the State. Some individual pastors and laymen have identified themselves with the Charter 77 movement, and in 1977 thirty-one Czech Brethren sent a detailed analysis of the problems facing their church to the Federal Assembly of the Republic. When the Fifth Christian Peace Conference was held in Prague in 1978 its members received a number of communications about the situation of Christians in Czechoslovakia, including a letter from twenty-two members of the Church of the Czech Brethren which began, 'We greet you with the words of the apostle: "Remember them that are in bonds, as bound with them".' In general, however, the Protestant churches are keeping quiet, intent upon survival rather than displaying dramatic acts of heroism, but it is significant that a new generation of pastors is somewhat critical of the stance taken by the late Josef Hromadka. They believe that close collaboration with the Communist government of their country has done nothing to further the Christian mission among the Czech and Slovak peoples, and that nothing can be changed while Czechoslovakia remains under the domination of the Soviet Union. A certain distancing from political affairs is therefore the order of the day, with greater concentration on maintaining and strengthening the community life of local congregations and the faith of individual believers.

The early 1980s have, however, brought to the West news of an underground Catholic Church in Slovakia, organized around a renewal movement known as 'Oasis' which is modelled on a similar movement of young Catholics in Poland. The size of this underground church is thought to be between 10,000 and 25,000, and some reports suggest that it may have as many as two hundred secretly ordained priests and four secretly consecrated bishops. There are also said to be secret 'convents' – usually three or four nuns sharing the same apartment – and a secret 'seminary' staffed by theologians who visit ordination candidates in their own homes and provide training there. For obvious reasons, these reports cannot be checked, but in March 1981 a report in *Pravda*, the Slovak Communist Party newspaper, described the movement as 'well organized' and said that it was causing serious concern to the authorities, who had ordered special detachments of the police to search it out and break it up.

Broadly speaking, the Christians of Czechoslovakia can now be divided into three categories, not so much by their traditional denominational allegiances, but rather by their response to heavy State pressure over many years. At either extreme are those who are collaborating with the government to a point at which their Christian faith is in danger of being betrayed, and those whose dissent from the government places their limited freedom, and sometimes their lives, at serious risk. Between the two are the overwhelming majority of Christians who are incapable of heroic deeds, yet remain intensely loyal to their faith and to their churches. The odds are stacked heavily against them, for not only are they and their religious communities subject to continuous pressure by the government, but the educational system of their country and the cultural life of the nation is almost totally infused with atheistic, anti-religious propaganda. After the events of 1968 no one in Czechoslovakia can believe that the road to freedom is likely to be anything other than a long haul. But the Czechoslovak Communist Party has few admirers, and since 1968 many writers and intellectuals have turned to the Christian faith as an alternative to what they now regard as a bankrupt Marxism. The longing for a truly democratic society has not been extinguished, and is to be found at its strongest in the churches.

# Chapter 8

# HUNGARY

On 6 January 1978 the American Secretary of State handed over to the President of the People's Republic of Hungary the ancient crown of St Stephen which had been in American custody since 1945. The ceremony took place in the parliament building in Budapest, and during the following months some hundreds of thousands of Hungarians filed past the crown, which has had a special place in the life of their nation for almost a thousand years.

Stephen, the first king of Hungary, received a crown from Pope Sylvester II in the year 1001, and the golden circle which forms the base of the crown today dates from that time. A strong supporter of the papacy, Stephen was, most unusually, given a crown and the title of king without having to swear suzerainty. Thus the independence of Hungary was affirmed from the earliest days of its nationhood, and the crown was invested with a deep religious significance, for Stephen, who was canonized as a saint in 1083, had asserted that Hungary belonged to the crown and the crown to Mary, the Mother of God.

This doctrine remained part of the coronation oath and was taught in Hungarian schools until the present century, but the crown was seen only at coronations. At other times it was kept in an iron chest to which there were three keys – one held by the monarch, the second by the prime minister, and the third by the head of the Holy Crown's Guard. It was this Guard that handed over the crown to the American military authorities at the end of the Second World War, to prevent it from falling into the hands of Soviet troops.

The American decision to return the crown, after keeping it in Fort Knox for more than three decades, was interpreted as a sign that the government of the United States regarded the Communist regime in Hungary as open enough to justify normal friendly relations between the two nations. Certainly it seemed inappropriate to return it during the years of the cold war, and had it been returned while Cardinal Jozsef Mindszenty was in prison or in exile, considerable offence would have been caused in most parts of the Western world.

Significant changes took place in Hungary during the 1970s. The government led by Janos Kadar remains tough and the country's links with the Soviet Union are close, but the regime is secure enough, and prosperous enough, to allow a degree of personal freedom that is not found everywhere in Eastern Europe. And even though the Hungarian Communists do not exhibit the fierce nationalism of their Romanian neighbours, they are once again expressing pride in their distinctive history and culture, and are prepared to allow national unity to have priority over strict Marxist-Leninist orthodoxy. The return of St Stephen's crown was therefore a matter of considerable religious significance, and the churches of Hungary, though still subject to strict control, now have greater freedom than at any other time since 1945.

A change of government policy in 1970, which coincided with the millenary of the birth of King Stephen, and gave the Church a little more freedom, was intended to indicate to the world that after the years of conflict between State and Church – symbolized internationally by the plight of Cardinal Mindszenty – all was sweetly harmonious again. The revised constitution, ratified in 1972, followed its predecessor in making provision for 'the liberty of conscience of all citizens and the freedom of religious worship', and shortly before the 1973 election Janos Kadar, the First Secretary of the Party, declared 'Religious life is authorized, conditions for the Church are favourable and no one is disadvantaged because of his beliefs'. He went on to express the hope that churchmen, particularly Catholics, would participate in the elections. Officially, this declaration was no more than a repetition of the government's position during the years of most severe repression, but it was well received by the Catholic bishops, who interpreted it as a positive statement which implied criticism of the past as well as promise for the future.

By this time Cardinal Mindszenty was out of the country and, officially at least, had ceased to be an issue between Church and State, but it was not until Pope Paul VI had in 1974 taken the drastic step of declaring vacant the Primatial See of Esztergom that any significant improvement in relations between the State and the Catholic Church became possible. In November 1974 the Vatican sent envoys to Budapest to have preliminary talks with government officials, and these were encouraging enough to warrant the sending of a senior member of the Vatican's Council for the Public Affairs of the Church to have further talks a month later. The main fruit of these conversations appeared in January 1975 when Pope Paul VI announced the appointment of five new bishops to Hungarian sees, and the movement of four of the existing bishops, so that all but two of the eleven dioceses in Hungary now had bishops. Earlier, when Church-State relations were at a low ebb and the government was demanding the right to nominate episcopal candidates, the Pope appointed apostolic administrators rather than bishops. Agreement with the State over names is still required, and the Vatican continues to appoint apostolic administrators in the first instance, confirming them as residential bishops later, but the discussions at the end of 1974 opened the way to the appointment of bishops who are not simply government stooges.

Shortly after the names of the new bishops had been announced, Monsignor Jozsef Cserhati, Bishop of Pecs and secretary of the Hungarian Catholic Bishops' Conference, published an article in the Catholic monthly paper *Vigilia* which indicated a significant change of attitude on the part of the Catholic hierarchy. The article consisted of a careful assessment of the Catholic Church's response to the political and social situation in Hungary during the previous thirty years and, while recognizing the existence of unresolved problems in Church-State relations, Bishop Cserhati went on to say:

> Since the fundamental goal of the socialist state is the advancement and well-being of man, there is no reason why Catholics should not regard our country's spiritual climate as a healthy one, despite their consciousness of living in an ideologically pluralist society and awareness that an ideological struggle is taking place. But even if the various ideologies are ultimately incompatible, this ought not to hinder their respective proponents from feeling united on the major issues facing the Hungarian people.

In November of the same year the President of Hungary visited the Pope, and on 12 February 1976 the appointment of Mgr

Laszlo Lekai as Archbishop of Esztergom and Primate of Hungary was announced. Archbishop Lekai, who had been apostolic administrator of the see of Esztergom since Cardinal Mindszenty's departure from Hungary in 1971 and was himself soon to become a Cardinal, said at the time of his appointment to the Primacy:

> It would be an anachronism for me to present myself as 'first baron' or 'prince primate' of Hungary. The Church must not look backward but must accept reality as it exists . . . The Church has found its place in the socialist society and the authorities allow freedom to profess; nevertheless many questions remain unresolved and it must be hoped that they will be resolved in an atmosphere of peace. Although the world view and ideology of Christians and Marxists are different, we must nevertheless look for ways to work out a common future. We must look not at what divides us but at what unites us.

The change of approach on the part of the Catholic Church could hardly have been more complete, and a new era in Church-State relations was clearly established.

---

Political developments in Hungary after the Second World War followed the pattern common to the whole of Eastern Europe. In 1945 the victorious Allied powers arranged elections. There was no overt interference by the Russians, who occupied the country, and the Smallholders' Party headed a truly representative coalition government which promised to restore the fortunes of a heavily devastated nation. The chairman of the Smallholders' Party was in fact a Catholic priest, Mgr Bela Varga, who became President of the National Assembly, and a Reformed minister, Zoltan Tildy, who was at one time a student at the Presbyterian theological college in Belfast, became President of the Republic. (He presented the college with a silver Communion cup to mark the occasion.) The Communists obtained only 16 per cent of the total vote, but one of their leaders, Laszlo Rajk, was given the powerful post of Minister of the Interior in the new government, and from that point onwards the Communists gained increasing control of the government and the country. At the next elections, in 1947, the Communists secured only 22 per cent of the votes, but they entered into an alliance with other socialist groups, whom they then proceeded to disband, and at the 1949 elections there was a single list of candidates, all of whom had been approved by the Communist Party.

The years that followed were a time of harsh Stalinist rule. Both the President and the Prime Minister were at this time members of the Reformed Church, but the real control was in the hands of the vice-premier, Matyas Rakosi, who became the most hated man in Hungary. Government and Party spies were everywhere, arrests and executions were commonplace, and the ten million people of Hungary found themselves dragooned by a small but ruthless Communist dictatorship. The real size and strength of the Party was demonstrated in 1956 when the liberal revolt led to its disintegration, and Soviet troops had to move into Budapest in order to overthrow the rebels and install another harsh regime. This provoked a large-scale emigration of Hungarians who sought refuge in other countries, fearing for their safety at home or unwilling to submit to a new Communist government imposed by Moscow.

The present Hungarian government is difficult to place in the political stakes of Eastern Europe. Janos Kadar was on the Russian side in the Soviet repression of the 1956 revolt, yet he is now surprisingly popular and has made much use of the slogan, 'Those who are not against us are with us'. Again, Andras Hegedus, who was Premier 1955–56 and a hardline Stalinist, is now well known as a nonconforming Communist, and protested publicly when Russia invaded Czechoslovakia. He was expelled from the Communist Party in 1973. On the other hand, many of those who were supporters of Imre Nagy, the leader of the 1956 revolt, and went to prison for their involvement in it, are now among the strongest supporters of the Kadar regime. Pragmatism is the order of the day at every level of Hungarian society, and the economic reform which has been applied since 1968 has not only brought a noticeable rise in the general standard of living throughout the country, it has made Hungary the only country in Eastern Europe with a favourable trade balance with the West.

Of the three main Christian churches in Hungary, the Roman Catholic is easily the largest. Until 1945 it was, apart from the immediate post-Reformation period, the dominant power in a feudal Hungarian society, owning large areas of land and claiming the allegiance of the nobility and large landowners. The influence of the Catholic hierarchy was very considerable, and during the inter-war years when Admiral Miklos Horthy served as Regent it was natural that the Primate of Hungary should be his deputy. At the last official census, in 1949, there were 6,240,427 Latin-Rite Catholics and just under 250,000 Uniates, who together constituted just over 70 per cent of the total population of the country. This figure may be compared with the situation at the end of the sixteenth century, when the Archbishop of Esztergom reported to the Vatican that there was no more than one Catholic for every thousand Protestants in the country.

Such was the dramatic effect of the Reformation, and the hardly less dramatic effect of the Counter-Reformation which, by the end of the eighteenth century, had reduced the number of Protestants to one-third of the total population. Many Catholic immigrants from Bavaria and Swabia also came to settle in Hungary after the departure of the Turks from central and southern areas. The methods used to secure conversions to Catholicism during this period were often extremely cruel; the memory of them is still alive and leads many Protestants to distrust the Catholic Church. In 1976 services were held in many Lutheran churches throughout Hungary commemorating those who were persecuted and died for their faith during the seventeenth century, and special meetings and services extending over six days were held at Debrecen Theological Academy to mark the three hundredth anniversary of the liberation of twenty-six Hungarian pastors who had been sold as galley slaves for refusing to renounce their Protestant faith. During the same year a 'Cantata in Memory of the Galley Slaves' was given its first performance in Budapest.

---

Although the Catholic Church has always drawn its membership from the whole of Hungary, and has divided the country into eleven dioceses, its greatest strength lies in the area to the west of the Danube. There are now about six million baptized Catholics, representing 65 per cent of Hungary's total population of 10.5 million. In 1980 there were 3,600 Catholic priests, of whom 2,790 were in active ministry, serving about 2,000 Latin-Rite parishes and about 150 Uniate parishes. Priests are trained in five diocesan seminaries, one of which is Uniate, and there is a Catholic theological academy at Budapest. This academy also offers three-year correspondence courses in theology for lay people, together with weekend consultations; 145 students passed an entrance examination and began study in 1978, and another 100 students joined them a year later. In 1980 there were about 250 seminarians in training, and a further 62 were doing their military service. In that year there were 26 monks and 55 nuns – members of the Benedictine, Franciscan and Piarist Orders, and the Sisters of Our Lady – and about 700 elderly members of the dissolved orders living in special retirement homes. Following the nationalization of church schools in 1948, there are only eight Catholic schools in the entire country. These are secondary schools which give a full Catholic education to just under two thousand pupils and are run by members of religious orders who are paid by the State. This is a meagre stake in education, but it is unusual in Eastern Europe for the Church to have any schools.

The Reformed Church of Hungary has, according to its official, published figures, two million baptized members. These constitute just under one-fifth of the population and are distributed among 1,250 self-supporting independent parishes which are mainly in urban areas and in the large rural area east of the River Tisza. The parishes are grouped in twenty-seven seniorates and four church districts. There are 1,250 parish ministers and about 250 assistant ministers. All the governing bodies of the church have equal numbers of pastors and elders, who meet under the joint chairmanship of a pastor and a layman. There is a General Synod of a hundred members, which receives contributions from the parishes for a central church fund, and each church district has a bishop and a lay curator-general who sit side-by-side as co-chairmen of official meetings. This is one of the few churches of the Reformed tradition to have bishops. Clergy are trained in the theological academies at Budapest and Debrecen, which cater for 150 students, and there are also theological institutes at Sarospatak and Papa. At Debrecen, where a woman is professor of New Testament studies, a Doctoral College was established within the academy in 1972. Post-graduate training courses for pastors are held every summer in each of the church's four districts, with visiting lecturers from other parts of the world. The church runs seven old people's homes, one children's home and six homes for handicapped children. It also has two grammar schools.

The Hungarian Evangelical Lutheran Church, again quoting its own figures, has about 400,000 baptized members, i.e. just under 4 per cent of the total population. Of these, some 80,000 live in Budapest, while the rest are dispersed and constitute minorities in most parts of the country; one in every four members lives some distance from his nearest church. There are about three hundred 'mother' parishes grouped in sixteen seniorates and served by about four hundred pastors. In addition, there are about 1,900 scattered groups known as sub-parishes or 'daughter' congregations. The seniorates belong to two church districts, and the supreme administrative body for the whole church is the General Assembly, presided over by a lay General Inspector and a Bishop-President. There is a theological academy in Budapest, and in 1980 this had fifty students, men and women, attending a five-year course. The academy also provides post-graduate courses for pastors, and in January 1980 it started a new theological extension course for lay men and women who are able to attend lectures one weekend a month. Fifty-one students were in the first enrolment and these are being trained for preaching and pastoral work in Lutheran parishes. It has yet to be decided whether or not they will be ordained. The church has eighteen charity institutions, which include homes for the elderly, orphans and people with incurable diseases. In common with other Hungarian churches, the Lutheran Church suffered serious losses of buildings during the Second World War, and since 1945 it has reconstructed 227 church buildings and 140 parsonages, and erected thirty new churches.

The size of the Hungarian Baptist Church, which began to function in its present form in 1873, is variously estimated. Published figures speak of 12,000 members, with 200 churches, but there are sometimes said to be as many as 50,000 adherents. Ten new Baptist churches were built during the 1970s. This church has about five hundred congregations spread throughout the country and these are served by just under a hundred pastors. Not surprisingly, the number of pastors is deemed far too small for the church's needs, and the one Baptist seminary has only ten students. Baptists support two homes for the aged.

Methodism came to Hungary in 1900, when a German Methodist preacher was sent to start work with a German community in the southern part of the country. A preaching place was established in Budapest in 1905. The Methodist Church now has about 1,200 members and adherents who attend services in forty-one places of worship; thirteen of these are prayer rooms or chapels, the remainder are the homes of church members. There are seven pastors and seventeen lay preachers, and one Methodist charity home. General oversight is given by a Swiss bishop, who is also responsible for other small Methodist communities in Yugoslavia, Bulgaria, Czechoslovakia and Poland. During the years before the Communists came to power, the Methodist Church had no legal status in Hungary and frequently complained that it was subject to harassment by the State and by other churches. However, it was officially recognized by the government in 1947. More recently, the church was divided by an internal dispute which led in the end to the formation of a small independent free church run on Methodist lines and calling itself the Hungarian Evangelical Fellowship.

The Hungarian Orthodox Church has about 5,000 members in ten parishes, served by eight priests. There arc also a number of ethnic Orthodox churches, and the total number of Orthodox Christians in Hungary is about 20,000.

The Scottish Mission in Budapest is the focus of an unusual and interesting British presence in Eastern Europe. This goes back to 1841, when two ministers of the Church of Scotland, Dr Alexander Black and Dr Alexander Keith, visited Hungary to explore the possibility of a mission to the Jewish people of Europe. They received encouragement from the Archduchess Marie Dorothea, the Protestant wife of the Viceroy, Archduke Joseph, and soon afterwards the Scottish Mission, led by Dr John Duncan, sailed in from Vienna on the Danube. Ostensibly they were to act as industrial chaplains to the Scottish workmen who were at that time building the Chain Bridge over the Danube, for the Austrian government would not have admitted any Protestant mission, but soon the services they held in the Bela Gasse attracted Hungarians and Germans as well as British residents. A number of Jews also began to attend, and after a time there were so many of them that the Mission centre became known as 'the Synagogue'.

Among these Jews was a prominent Budapest merchant, Israel Saphir, whose family was later to become Christian and play a prominent part in the foundation of the Scottish school. Israel Saphir himself became a Christian in his old age. During the 1930s the Mission became an important centre for work among Jewish refugees who had fled from Nazi oppression, and the Rev. George Knight remained in Budapest until the outbreak of war. The Hungarian pastors and teachers continued their work, as did Jane Haining, the Scottish matron of the Girls' Hostel, who was arrested with the Jewish girls in the home and died with them in a Nazi concentration camp.

After the war a Scottish minister again worked in the Mission for a time. The Communist government eventually nationalized the school, but the church remains and is served by the Rev. John Dobos, a Hungarian pastor who has been on the staff of the Mission for over thirty years and, in addition to the Hungarian services, holds an English service once a month. From the beginning the Church of Scotland has enjoyed close relations with the Hungarian Reformed Church, the two churches recognizing their common Reformation roots. Scottish ministers working in Budapest functioned as 'vicars' of the Superintendent of the Reformed Church, and many Hungarian pastors have studied at Scottish universities under a scholarship scheme sponsored by the Church of Scotland.

Unitarianism in Hungary goes back to the sixteenth century, but most of its people were forcibly converted to Catholicism during the Habsburg era, and it was not until the nineteenth century, after the reunification of Transylvania with Hungary, that the Unitarian Church was re-established. Today there are ten Unitarian congregations and forty–fifty fellowships, which often meet in the parish halls of local Lutheran or Calvinist churches. The Unitarian bishop, Dr Jozsef Ferenc, is a former research scholar of Manchester College, Oxford, and the lay president, Bela Bartok, is the son of the famous musician. Among the other churches, the Adventists have just over 5,000 members and the Pentecostalists just under 5,000. In 1977 the Church of the Nazarene, which has about 3,300 members in 112 congregations or groups, was given full legal recognition by the government. Previously there had been problems arising from this church's uncompromising pacifist stance, but in 1977 its members agreed to accept the duty of military service and the government undertook to draft them only into non-combatant services. These and other small churches, along with the Baptists and Methodists, form a Council of Free Churches, and the leaders of this Council have been involved in the national Ecumenical Council since 1965. The smaller churches also sponsor a joint Pastoral Training Institute for the training of ministers and pastors. Courses are conducted by correspondence and residential weekends, and the final examination and diploma are given by the Reformed theological academy at Debrecen.

In 1941 there were 725,000 Jews in Hungary, many of them refugees from other parts of Nazi-dominated Europe. Today there are about 80,000, most of whom live in Budapest. During the Second World War Adolf Eichmann moved into Budapest's Hotel Majestic and, as a result of his work, over 600,000 Jews were sent to their deaths in concentration camps. There was a further reduction in numbers during the immediate post-war period owing to a declining birth rate and to emigration. About 20,000 Jews left the country soon after the 1956 revolt, but emigration to Israel is now on a greatly reduced scale. In 1978 there were about a hundred synagogues, sixty congregations and twenty-six rabbis affiliated to the Central Board of Hungarian Jewish Communities. The Chief Rabbi, Dr Salgo, celebrated his seventieth birthday in 1980, when he was presented by the government with the Order of the Flag of the Hungarian People's Republic and also with the Memorial Medal of the Patriotic Peace Front. The largest synagogue – in Budapest – has room for more than three thousand worshippers, and the regular Friday evening services are well attended. The National Rabbinical Seminary – the only one in the whole of Eastern Europe – is also in Budapest, and in 1980 it had thirteen Hungarian students, three Russian, and one Czech, though not all of them were going to be rabbis. A number of Jewish secondary schools are still open in different parts of the country, including a co-educational grammar school in Budapest, and religious instruction is given in seventeen talmud torahs by resident or itinerant rabbis and teachers. About a thousand people attend the Budapest talmud torah. There is a Jewish hospital and two old people's homes. In 1980 it was reported that the number of mixed marriages was increasing, and that young people were less interested in maintaining the traditional Jewish way of life. Anti-Semitism is against Hungarian law.

All the main Hungarian churches publish newspapers and journals, some of which have large circulations. The most important of these is *Reformatusok Lapja* (Reformed Paper), the weekly newspaper of the Reformed Church, which is designed for a parish readership and sells over 100,000 copies. The Reformed Church also publishes a monthly magazine, *Reformatus Egyhaz* (Reformed Church), which contains articles on theology and pastoral work and is read mainly by the clergy. *Confessio* is a quarterly magazine read by Reformed pastors and lay people who are concerned about social and cultural issues. The Lutheran Church weekly is *Evangelikus Elet* (Evangelical Life), with a circulation of about 15,000. This prints articles of a devotional character and, in the words of a church spokesman, 'information as regards the decisive problems of the Hungarian people'. There is also a Lutheran theological monthly, *Lelki-pasztor* (Spiritual Pastor), which publishes reports on theological developments in other countries as well as articles by Hungarian scholars. *Diakonia*, which began publication in May 1979, is concerned with Hungary's social and cultural life and examines secular issues from a Lutheran standpoint. A bi-monthly, *Theologiai Szemle* (Theological Review) is published by the Ecumenical Council of Churches.

The most popular Catholic journal is the weekly *Uj Ember* (New Man), which was founded in 1945 and has a circulation of 90,000. Like all such publications, it is subject to severe paper rationing, and the editors claim that they could sell many more copies if more paper were available; every issue is sold out within hours of reaching the streets. The Catholic monthly *Vigilia* (Vigil) has a circulation of about 15,000 and is the third largest among Hungary's cultural magazines. There is also the Catholic quarterly review *Teologia*, which is devoted mainly to academic theology and has a circulation of about 4,000. The two Catholic publishing houses produced a total of twenty books and several school textbooks in 1980.

The Baptists have a weekly, *Bekehirnok* (Herald of Peace), which has a small circulation, and the Jewish community publishes a bi-weekly, *Uj Elet* (New Life). The Hungarian Protestant churches jointly provide a church news service for the secular daily press. *Egyhazi Tudosito* (Church Reporter) gives journalists the full texts or summaries of important speeches by church leaders and documents published by councils and synods, together with items of significant church news, which may find their way into the columns of the daily newspapers. A news service in English and German is also provided for the benefit of foreign journalists.

Copies of the Bible are freely available in Hungary, and scriptures are exported from Hungary to Yugoslavia, Romania and Slovakia for the use of Hungarian-speaking minorities. The work of translation, production and distribution is supervised by the Hungarian Bible Council, which was set up by the Protestant churches and is an associate member of the United Bible Societies. A new Hungarian translation of the Bible, the result of twenty-five years' work, was published in 1975, and 140,000 copies had been sold by 1980. The Reformed Church published a new edition (10,000 copies) of the *Bible Readers' Guide*, with daily Bible readings, in 1979. Religious literature is not generally available in ordinary bookshops, but there is a Catholic and a Protestant bookshop in Budapest and books can be bought in some churches. A religious programme is broadcast by the State radio every Sunday at 7 a.m. and responsibility for this is shared by the various religious bodies according to their size, none getting more than nine to ten hours of air time in a year.

---

Many of Hungary's ancient parish churches are extremely beautiful and have fine painted interiors. A quarter of the church buildings were destroyed or severely damaged during the Second World War; those that remained are invariably in good repair, and after some disastrous floods in 1970 the government gave very substantial grants and interest-free loans for the restoration of nearly fifty church buildings. Since 1945 some 170 Catholic churches have been built: thirty of these are new, the rest replaced weather-damaged or confiscated churches, and all of them are fairly small. Under the terms of the 1948 Church-State agreements, the State's financial commitment in respect of church buildings and personnel ceased in 1968 but, as the churches are very short of money, the government continues to assist in the restoration of historic buildings and to pay about 25 per cent of the salaries of the clergy. There are two fine museums of Christian art which receive a good deal of financial support from the State.

A visitor to Budapest will find many Roman Catholic churches in the city. Mass times are advertised on the notice boards, and some of the churches have a stall in their porches selling rosaries, crucifixes and pictures, usually representative of traditional Catholic piety. The Matthia Church in Budapest, which was the Coronation Church in former times, is crowded on Sundays and, continuing a long tradition, the main mass is generally in Latin, with classical settings led by a fine choir. As in other parts of Eastern Europe, church life tends to be conservative. The framework within which the churches are permitted to work makes large-scale innovation and experiment difficult if not actually impossible. An act of worship conducted along traditional lines holds far fewer risks, for both Church and State, than a service which seeks to express something of contemporary life in the light of the Christian Gospel. In certain places, however, there are signs of considerable musical creativity. Small orchestras are fairly common and some visitors to Hungary have experienced acts of worship in which there was impressive use of drama, poetry and modern beat music. Within the Catholic Church, the teaching of the Second Vatican Council has made little impact and when the debate about clerical celibacy was at its height in the early 1970s the Hungarian bishops sent a message to Pope Paul VI pleading that he should not change the traditional regulations in any way. Some of the more able priests are, however, now being sent to Rome for post-graduate study, and the writings and speeches of some of the bishops, notably Bishop Cserhati of Pecs, make extensive use of the Vatican II teaching on the role of the Church in the modern world. In view of the bitter religious history of Hungary it is not altogether surprising that ecumenical activity involving Catholics and Protestants is slight. But relations between the two groups are improving slowly, and in some places Catholics attend Protestant churches during the Week of Prayer for Christian Unity. In 1980 Bishop Tibor Bartha, president of the Ecumenical Council, and Dr

Jozsef Nagy, president of the Free Church Council, together with other Protestant leaders, had their first-ever official meeting with Cardinal Lekai, the Catholic Primate, to explore future contacts.

One of the most impressive expressions of Christian life in Hungary today is to be found in the Benedictine abbey at Pannonhalma, where the monks are well aware of the implications of Vatican II and manifest a lively ecumenical spirit. An English visitor to the abbey reported:

> I attended mass on St Stephen's Day, 20 August. It was the 10.30 mass at Pannonhalma, which is on top of a hill outside a minute village about fourteen miles from the nearest large town, Gyor. The monastery church was packed with a widely cross-representative congregation, ranging from children to (not very many) aged, but clearly including many young married couples and young people. The monks anticipated that the two other masses that morning would be equally well attended. Only a small percentage could have come from the village, which in any case has its own parish church, so these people clearly made a special effort on a public holiday to get there.

In the Reformed and Lutheran Churches instruction for confirmation is highly organized and carefully directed in content and duration. The period 15 December to 15 April is set aside for the instruction of candidates in the Reformed Church, and since 1972 all candidates have been required to attend a Bible class for twelve months immediately preceding the confirmation course. A syllabus of Bible study for this purpose is provided by the Church's mission department. Special textbooks of religious instruction are also provided for children whose preparation for confirmation is integrated with the religious education they are receiving in school hours.

Since 1949 religious instruction has been given in the Hungarian state educational system on the basis of voluntary enrolment, although the 1948 Church-State agreements said that religious education in schools was to be compulsory. During the Stalinist era the number of children enrolling for religious instruction fell from 86 per cent to 27 per cent in primary schools, and from 80 per cent to 0.7 per cent in secondary schools. After the 1956 revolt the number of enrolments began to rise, but during the last twenty years they have been steadily falling. Since 1975 religious instruction classes, except in large all-ability schools, have had to be held away from school premises, generally in churches, and are taught by local pastors and priests. Children can be withdrawn for this purpose on two occasions every week, one of which must be Sunday. Separate classes may be formed for children in the six to ten and over ten age groups, and acts of worship can be arranged. In the early days State inspectors kept a close watch on teaching material and methods, but the clergy now seem to have much greater freedom in this area of their work.

The disincentives against enrolment for religious instruction are considerable. Children wishing to enrol are often made to feel that they are eccentric and going against the conventions of their school. Parents sometimes fear, and not without reason, that insistence on their child receiving religious instruction may jeopardize future educational prospects, especially when the time for selection for higher education is approaching. In May 1980 Pope John Paul II took the unusual step of addressing a letter to the Catholic community in Hungary urging parents to make use of the law and ask that their children should be given religious instruction in State schools. A year earlier the Catholic bishops issued a pastoral letter asking Catholics to support their own eight secondary schools, which were facing grave financial difficulties. In 1980, however, there was a new development in Hungarian education when it was announced that study of the Bible as literature would be permitted in academic secondary schools. The announcement said that selections from the Bible would be included in the literary curricula of these schools in order to 'expose the students to one of the most splendid masterpieces of literature in ancient times'. It was also emphasized that study of the Bible in this context must not be used to intensify differences between the beliefs of the churches and the atheism of the State. Teachers were warned against textbooks of 'a vulgarizing level' which had at one time been produced in an attempt to refute the Bible. The churches welcomed this development, while recognizing that it is no substitute for classes in religious education.

Another factor in the decline in enrolments for religious instruction is the ever-increasing secularization of Hungarian society. Since 1945 Hungary has been transformed from a largely agrarian society to one in which 83 per cent of the national income comes from industry, transport and tourism, and only 17 per cent from agriculture. The proportion of the population engaged in agriculture has declined from 60 per cent to 17 per cent. Hungarian sociologists have noted that when people move from a village to a city they normally cease attending church, except at major festivals, but if they return to their old village for a weekend in order to visit relatives and friends they attend church on Sunday.

In June 1980 the government newspaper *Magyar Hirrlap* published the results of a survey of religious belief and practice carried out by a social scientist. This indicated that 50–60 per cent of the population hold religious beliefs, and about one-third of all adults attend church regularly. In the villages the proportion of believers rises to 70–85 per cent, while in Budapest it is only 35 per cent. About 86 per cent of children born to Catholic parents are baptized, and 86 per cent of all funerals are conducted by the Church. While these figures are still relatively high, there is general agreement that regular church attendance is significantly lower than in the late 1940s, when it was still as high as 50 per cent. All the churches are experiencing a shortage of vocations to the ordained ministry. The Catholic Church is ordaining only 30 to 40 new priests a year and is losing about a hundred priests every year through death and laicization. Between 1969 and 1975 there was an overall decline of 451 priests. Given the present age structure of the Catholic clergy, the total number of priests will be halved by 1990 unless many more men enter the seminaries. Bishop Tibor Bartha spoke of a serious shortage of ministers in the Reformed Church in 1977, and also of the problems for the Church caused by the movement of people from rural to urban areas.

---

Lying just behind the present ambiguities and contradictions, expressed and implied, in Church-State relations in Hungary is the history of almost a quarter of a century during which the Communist government brought and kept all religious institutions under strict control, and deprived them of the conditions in which they might prosper. In the period immediately following 1945, relations between the churches and the State became increasingly uneasy. The government introduced a new divorce law which allowed divorce by mutual consent. Parish churches (like all other private landowners) were not permitted to own more than 50 to 100 acres of land, in 1946 all Catholic trade unions and all church organizations (again, in company with all other independent groups) were banned, and there was much propaganda directed against the work of the churches and their schools. The first priests were arrested as early as 1945, and in October of the same year the Primate of Hungary, Cardinal Mindszenty, issued three pastoral letters which indicated that open conflict between the Catholic Church and the government was unlikely to be long delayed.

In June 1947 Mgr Bela Varga, a Catholic priest who was President of the National Assembly, had to flee the country, having been accused with others of conspiracy against the State. By the following year six hundred Catholic priests were in prison and eighty-seven had been deported to remote parts of the country. The work of many more priests was inhibited because they were frequently moved from one parish to another. On 16 June 1948 all church schools were nationalized. The great majority of these (3,116) belonged to the Catholic Church and represented more than half of the country's educational system. Cardinal Mindszenty responded by ordering church bells to be tolled throughout the country as a sign of protest, and by excommunicating all the government ministers who were responsible for the new law. He warned the nation that its children would now be exposed to the teachings of Darwin. Later a small number of schools were handed back to the churches and made the subject of special agreements. In May 1948 Vice-Premier Rakosi said that the final settlement of relations between the State and the churches was the most pressing problem in Hungary, and on 7 October of that year an agreement was signed by representatives of the government and of the Reformed Church. A similar agreement was also signed by the Lutheran Church. Those who refused to comply were either forced to resign or sent to prison. These agreements purported to give the two churches freedom to continue and develop their life in return for general support of the State. In the event they, in common with all other religious bodies, were brought under comprehensive State control.

In the case of the Lutheran Church, all the church schools having been nationalized, the four church districts were next reduced to two, at the insistence of Rakosi, and two bishops were retired. As far as the smaller Protestant churches were concerned, they had few privileges to lose in any case, and the agreements with the government offered them some freedoms and financial subsidies which they had not previously enjoyed. The position of the Catholic Church was quite different. Cardinal Mindszenty had been arrested in December 1948, and now, having occupied a highly privileged and influential position in Hungarian society, the Church was forced to sign an agreement which made it subservient to the State. The bishops hesitated before accepting the agreement, but on 30 August 1950, when the government threatened to exile to remote places all the monks and nuns in the country, the hierarchy gave in.

The new constitution of the Hungarian People's Republic had come into force a year earlier, and the section on religion and the churches explicitly guaranteed for all citizens 'Freedom of conscience and the right to a free exercise of religion. In order to ensure the freedom of conscience, the Hungarian People's Republic separates the Church from the State.' But these provisions are qualified by the next article in the constitution, which reads: 'The Hungarian People's Republic guarantees freedom of speech, of the press and of association, as long as this freedom does not interfere with the interests of the working masses.' (Similar provisions were repeated in a revised constitution ratified in 1972, except that 'the freedom of religious worship' was substituted for 'the right to a free exercise of religion'.)

In the event the 1949 guarantees and aspirations were not fully realized. In 1950 all but four of the Catholic Church's sixty-three religious orders, comprising 2,582 monks and 8,956 nuns, were dissolved. The then Minister of Education informed the Hungarian people that 'Hundreds and thousands of monks and nuns are walking through our country and are doing the work of agents of imperialism'. About 350 monks from the dissolved orders were allowed to continue as parish priests, and just over a thousand nuns were permitted to continue as nurses in State-run hospitals or privately. More than two thousand monks and nuns left the country. In the same year the government issued a decree requiring the Catholic Church to obtain the approval of the Presidium for all appointments to bishoprics and other senior ecclesiastical posts. It had in fact been the practice of the Church to obtain government approval for its senior appointments prior to the Second World War, but from 1945 onwards the Vatican ceased consulting the Hungarian government when bishoprics had to be filled. Now it was required to return to the traditional practice and to understand that approval would be forthcoming only for men known to be loyal to the new Hungary.

The year 1951 saw the setting up of a government Office for Church Affairs. This was given the task of keeping the churches under constant surveillance and of maintaining strict control over their activities. State officials were placed in the offices of bishops and church leaders in order to censor all forms of communication and to 'advise' bishops on 'appropriate' forms of action. These were later known as 'moustached bishops'. Earlier, two government nominees – Erno Mihalyfi and Jozsef Darvas – held the office of General Secretary of the Lutheran Church at different times, though neither of them attended church and Darvas openly declared himself to be an atheist. Later both became government ministers and were specially concerned with the nationalization of church schools.

By 1951 all the 'difficult' Catholic bishops, including Archbishop Jozsef Grosz who had signed the 1950 agreement, had been arrested, while the remainder pledged their support for the government after a conference held in July of that year. In their statement the bishops spoke approvingly of the Catholic Priests' Peace Movement, which had come into existence on the initiative of a number of priests who wished to demonstrate their own support of the Communist regime in Hungary and to encourage their fellow clergy to show a like solidarity. Not surprisingly, the Office for Church Affairs quickly showed interest in this movement and offered firm support. No figures are available for the number of priests who have joined the movement, but it was reported in 1978 that 80 per cent of diocesan Vicars-General and Chancellors were members. On the other hand, only two hundred priests, including some from other East European countries, were present at the movement's twenty-fifth anniversary celebrations in 1975. On that occasion the secretary-general, Dr Richard Horvath, who is also a

Member of Parliament and rector of the Franciscan Church in Budapest, said that, as a result of the 'patient and persevering' efforts of the Priests' Peace Movement, the Hungarian Church had been 'fundamentally transformed': all Hungarian priests, under the direction of almost the entire episcopate, had accepted the aims of the movement. Dr Horvath added that a good basis had been established for the gradual development of improved relations between Church and State, and he expressed the view that under the leadership of Cardinal Mindszenty the attitude of the Church to the new social order had been 'uncomprehending and hostile'.

---

Throughout the years of severe repression, which largely coincided with the Stalinist era in the Soviet Union, Cardinal Mindszenty symbolized the Catholic Church's resistance to Hungary's Communist government. Born in 1892, of peasant parents, Jozsef Mindszenty was ordained priest in 1915. His pastoral work, which he combined with involvement in social and educational issues, was interrupted in 1919 when he was arrested during the Bela Kun (Bolshevik) revolution and confined to his home village. On his release he continued a traditional parish ministry until he was appointed Bishop of Veszprem on 4 March 1944. This was only two weeks prior to the German occupation of Hungary and, having spoken out in defence of the Jews and denounced the 'new paganism' of the Nazis, Mindszenty was quickly imprisoned. It is said that he insisted on entering the jail in his full episcopal robes, with a mitre on his head and a pastoral staff in his hand.

The Russian army freed him from prison in March 1945, and after six months back in his diocese of Veszprem Pope Pius XII appointed him Archbishop of Esztergom, Primate of Hungary and a Cardinal. Soon he was in trouble with the Rakosi regime. He denounced all attempts to limit the freedom and influence of the Church, and aroused the anger of the authorities by protesting against the harsh treatment of the Hungarian minority in Czechoslovakia. Following his arrest in 1948, he was charged with treason and currency offences, and at a show trial which aroused worldwide interest he was sentenced to life imprisonment. He was widely believed to have been brainwashed into a confession of guilt, and the Vatican excommunicated everyone connected with the trial.

Mindszenty remained in prison until the 1956 revolt. But his freedom then was short-lived. After four days the Russians put down the rising and the Cardinal was obliged to take refuge in the American legation (later raised to the status of an embassy). Here he occupied a two-roomed apartment for fifteen years, resisting every suggestion that he should leave the country and thus open the way for the appointment of a new Primate of Hungary. His presence there was a constant irritant to the Communist authorities and a vivid reminder to the Church of its persecuted status. In 1971, at the age of seventy-nine and under pressure from Pope Paul VI, he finally left Budapest. Shortly before his departure he wrote a letter to the Pope in which he said that leaving his native land would be 'perhaps the heaviest cross of my life'.

For the next four years Mindszenty lived in exile in Vienna, but he remained Archbishop of Esztergom and Primate of Hungary until 1974. Then, having failed to persuade him to retire, Pope Paul felt obliged to remove him from office. This was an exceedingly painful decision both for the Pope and for the Cardinal. In an affectionate letter to Mindszenty, Pope Paul paid tribute to his heroic past: 'Such serious suffering represented a crown of thorns placed on your head, and this was no less precious than your fidelity to the Church of Christ. We bow to you with profound respect and thank you from the bottom of our heart for the numerous examples of courage which you have shown over so many years to the entire Church.' The Pope assured him that he was acting purely in the pastoral interests of the Hungarian dioceses, particularly the metropolitan see of Esztergom. Mindszenty accepted the decision loyally, but was never convinced that the best interests of the Catholic Church in Hungary had been served by what he saw as an unnecessary and totally inappropriate capitulation to a Communist regime which was alien to the Hungarian tradition, and which would never allow the Church the freedom it needed for the exercising of its apostolic mission. He died in Vienna on 6 May 1975.

Whatever history's final verdict on Mindszenty, his heroic witness against an atheistic and totalitarian government for more than twenty-five years will be remembered as one of the great

human sagas of the twentieth century. As the last of Hungary's
Prince-Primates, he was undoubtedly wedded to a past in which
the Catholic Church was an integral part of Hungarian society
and enjoyed great privilege and power. He showed few signs of
comprehending why Communism had managed to gain a
foothold in Hungary, and he seemed quite unable to accept that
some of the social and economic changes brought about by the
Communists had been of benefit to the Hungarian people as a
whole. He was certain that Communism had to be defeated, not
treated with, and like many of the saints he was very stubborn.
For him, life consisted simply of black and white, without any
grey, and he paid the price of this conviction. It would be
impudent for anyone who had not shared the circumstances of
Mindszenty's 'crown of thorns' to pass judgement on the
courageous decisions he made. Yet his choices provoke certain
questions about the nature of the Christian mission and about the
Christian faith itself. Is the authority of Christ best expressed
when the Church has a position of privilege and authority in
society? Is there a proper autonomy of the secular which enables
God to work through agencies that have no religious sympathies
and may even be hostile to ecclesiastical institutions? Was the
kind of society that characterized Hungary prior to 1945, with
its gross inequalities, a social order that could appropriately be
defended and even suffered for in the name of Christ? At a more
pragmatic level: did the witness of Cardinal Mindszenty make it
more, or less, difficult for the Catholic Church to discharge its
responsibilities to the Hungarian people between 1948 and
1974?

---

There are neither certain nor abstract answers to questions of
this kind, and the witness of the Protestant leadership has been
in marked contrast to that of Cardinal Mindszenty. Soon after
the Cardinal's arrest in 1948 the authorities of the Reformed
Church issued a statement in which they said that they
considered the matter 'as a political and not as a religious
problem', and they asked the government and the foreign
churches 'not to identify the service of the Gospel with political
action appearing in church guise'. Today the leaders of the
Protestant churches appear to find it much less easy to draw so
clear a distinction between the political and the religious, for the

President of the Reformed Church, Bishop Tibor Bartha, and the President of the Lutheran Church, Bishop Zoltan Kaldy, are both deeply involved in the political life of the nation and serve in the Hungarian Parliament. Bishop Bartha is a member of the Presidential Council and, along with Bishop Kaldy, is a member of Parliament's Foreign Relations Committee.

The two church leaders dominate the lives of their churches, and are prominent on most state occasions. They travel widely abroad and both are members of the Central Committee of the World Council of Churches. In July 1972, on the occasion of his sixtieth birthday, Bishop Bartha was awarded the First Class of the Banner Order of the Hungarian People's Republic. This award, which was a national event, was made to Bishop Bartha by the government 'in recognition of his services in working for the good relations developed between the Hungarian State and the Reformed Church as well as his efficient activity in the international peace movement'. In a television interview in 1975, Bishop Kaldy said, 'It is unthinkable to me that anyone would oppose socialism.' He added that he himself spoke to his flock from a socialist platform and he hoped that all the pastors of his church would do the same. A year later Bishop Kaldy and other church leaders issued a declaration:

> Hungarian Lutherans will willingly join the People's Patriotic Front and support its policies, because it stands for unity and socialist patriotism. We do so with a sense of Christian responsibility and a good conscience... We call on all our clergy and all members of our Church to help and support wholeheartedly and with complete conviction the good common cause contained in the programme of the People's Patriotic Front.

Support for socialism is not confined to the leaders of the Reformed and Lutheran Churches. In a review of the period 1945–75, the President of the Baptist Union of Hungary, Janos Laczkovszki, said, 'The liberation opened the way for a socially just life, and Baptist believers have been in a position personally to experience results achieved through progress on the road of socialism. Following the example of our Lord, we regard the proclamation of the Gospel and service as our tasks.'

The concept of service, *diakonia*, has been prominent in the teaching and life of the Hungarian Protestant churches over the last two decades. It recurs constantly in the sermons, speeches and writings of their leaders, together with the related concept of the Servant Church. The second Sunday in Advent is known as Diakonia Sunday in the Lutheran Church, and is the occasion for special sermons and biblical expositions on the importance of service to individuals and to society. The Lutheran Church has a Diakonia Department, and the secretary of this department contributed an article on the subject in the Lutheran Church weekly, *Evangelikus Elet*, in December 1972. He wrote:

> A personal *diakonia* is carried on in the congregation where, beside the pastors, some parishioners are also engaged in visiting each other so that no one in the parish lives in loneliness. They systematically visit the sick, the old people, they help with the work of the parishioners in need, they help to keep the parish buildings in good repair, build footpaths and plant trees alongside them – all such efforts of personal *diakonia* contribute to the sense of fellowship and friend-ship.

There is much here, in both biblical exposition and practice, which Christians in other parts of the world could endorse and from which they might learn. What has not yet emerged in this approach is any suggestion that the proclamation of the Gospel and the service of individuals and of society may, in certain circumstances, involve a critique of political and social struc-tures as well as a questioning of politicians and policy-makers.

Yet brave voices of protest have been heard from within Hungarian Protestantism, though these have always been quickly silenced – generally by the church authorities, acting with or without state prompting. During the early 1950s a movement which called itself the 'Confessing Church' came into existence within the Reformed Church. This movement, which had clergy and laity in its membership, and took its name from the movement of German Christians who opposed the Nazis, was strongly opposed to the policies of the leaders of the Reformed Church, and expressed its objections in a pamphlet published by the Theological Academy of Budapest in 1956. After pointing out that biblical theology requires the Church to scrutinize the actions of governments in the light of the Word of God, the pamphlet said that 'the serving Church' in Hungary had become 'a servile Church'. It concluded by severely criticizing what it called the dictatorial attitudes of the church leaders who allegedly intimidated pastors, forced changes upon local congregations, accused their opponents of heresy, and generally acted in violation of the Reformation heritage.

During the October 1956 revolt a number of leading ministers of the Confessing Church met in the Theological Academy and formed a new administrative council of the Hungarian Reformed Church. One of the council's first actions was to request the resignations of Bishop Bereczky and Bishop Janos Peter, and they recalled to office a somewhat reluctant Bishop Laszlo Ravasz, who had resigned from the presidency of the church in 1947. The new church government was, however, short-lived. With the collapse of the revolt, the old guard returned to power. The appointment of Bishop Ravasz as President was declared null and void, and Bishop Bereczky resumed his office. Janos Peter moved into secular politics, eventually becoming Foreign Secretary, and was succeeded in his diocese by Tibor Bartha, who said during the course of his induction: 'We are firmly convinced that the orientation which has been given to the Church, and the decision of our Church to follow these directions, is a gift of the justifying Word of God, and that the justifying and life-giving Word will bear rich fruit.' The dean of the Theological Academy was removed from office and replaced by a government supporter.

The response of the Lutheran Church to Communist pressures is reflected in the story of the fortunes of Bishop Lajos Ordass, who was the senior bishop of the church at the end of the Second World War. Under his leadership, the Lutheran Church retained a marked degree of independence and autonomy, but in September 1948 he was arrested and charged with failing to register with the government a gift of $5,000 which the church had received from American Lutherans. He was sentenced to two years' imprisonment and, although government supporters in the Lutheran leadership asked him to resign his office, he refused. As a result, the State Office for Church Affairs insisted that the church should set up a special court and reduce Bishop Ordass to the position of an ordinary pastor. Shortly afterwards he was released from prison and went into retirement.

In 1956, however, and after discussions between the Lutheran Church of Hungary and the Lutheran World Federation, it was decided that Bishop Ordass should be rehabilitated. On 5 October of that year he was declared 'absolved' by the Hungarian Supreme Court, and a few days later the decision of the church court which had removed him from his bishopric was declared to have been illegal. During the revolt at the end of October Bishop Ordass resumed the leadership of the Lutheran Church and Bishop Veto, who was well disposed towards the old, repressive Rakosi regime, resigned, including with the announcement of his resignation a confession of guilt. But as soon as the revolt had been suppressed Ordass was again removed, and by 1957 Veto was back in the leadership. In June 1958 the council of the southern diocese, where Ordass was still officially the bishop, declared that he must resign this office, though a number of pastors and lay members of the council said that they were seeking his resignation only because of external pressure. Four months later Bishop Ordass's place was taken by Zoltan Kaldy, the present leader of the Hungarian Lutheran Church, who promised, 'I shall do my best to further develop the good relationship between Church and State so that we can remain faithful servants of our country.'

This account of the words and actions of today's leaders of the main Protestant churches of Hungary may give the impression of men who have too readily come to terms with the demands of the Communist government. There are ample grounds for uneasiness, and searching questions should be asked about the approach of the leaders of two important Protestant communities. It would, however, be unfair to regard Bishops Bartha and Kaldy as men who support the Hungarian government for personal ends. Both bishops have been nurtured in church traditions which encourage co-operation with the secular powers – co-operation which sometimes provides opportunities for influencing governments and authorities with the insights of the Gospel. There seems little doubt that both men are convinced socialists, and though they are certainly not Marxists they sometimes argue that the Communist governments of Hungary – Stalinist and post-1956 – deserve Christian backing after the Church's past support for reactionary regimes. They will also add that freedom to preach the Gospel and to gather for worship, which their churches still enjoy, is something very precious. Some Lutheran churches have as many as five services every

Sunday, and in September 1977 Dr Billy Graham, the American evangelist, spent eight days in Hungary as the guest of the Council of Free Churches. During this time he addressed five meetings, the first of which, at a Baptist youth camp, was attended by 14,000 people. It was estimated that more than 40,000 people heard Dr Graham speak, and at the end of his visit he said, 'People can attend church and freely worship God; there have been no pre-conditions or restrictions to my preaching, and church leaders have talked freely to me about the challenges, opportunities and problems they face.' The Hungarian government found nothing to object to in any of Dr Graham's sermons and speeches.

Just where the pastors of local Protestant churches and their congregations stand in all this is impossible to tell. Some of them are undoubtedly anxious about the degree of compromise involved in the present Church-State relationship, but in Hungary as elsewhere the vocation to martyrdom is quite rare. So the great majority of pastors and people make their Christian witness as best they can, generally going about their business quietly, and accepting the dictatorial demands of their own leaders and of the State Office for Church Affairs. Yet some pastors do find themselves in serious trouble, especially if they display what the authorities regard as excessive zeal or are in any way critical of the leadership in Church or State. The apparent tranquillity of church life is mainly on the surface.

---

So, although Church-State relations have improved during the last decade, the churches of Hungary, and most especially the Catholic Church, still face serious problems. They certainly have greater freedom than at any time since 1945, but this freedom remains circumscribed by the routine demands of a totalitarian government which cannot tolerate open criticism and which is determined to retain control of every aspect of Hungary's national life. All church appointments still require the actual or tacit approval of the government, and the records and utterances of some of those recently appointed to the Catholic episcopate have aroused some suspicion. Priests who attempt to step out of line are likely to be disciplined by their bishops, and in June 1980 the editor-in-chief of the Catholic news agency *Magyar Kurir*, the only agency of its kind in Eastern Europe, was dismissed at short notice by the Bishops' Conference for allegedly relying too heavily on Vatican and other Western sources. The speed with which he was dismissed was unusual. Soon after this a Catholic seminarian at Budapest was refused ordination because of his active membership of an informal church renewal group. When fifteen other seminarians appealed on his behalf, and showed signs of creating public controversy, the ordination was allowed to take place, but the protesters were sent back to their dioceses and banned from further study at the seminary. Ordinary lay Christians are not of course subject to discipline of this kind, but there is evidence of discrimination against practising Christians in education and in appointments to public office unless support for the government has been openly expressed.

Cardinal Laszlo Lekai, the Primate of Hungary, is a quiet and somewhat enigmatic figure. Unlike his world-famous predecessor, he has none of the style of a Prince-Primate, and in meetings and social gatherings is hardly distinguishable from an ordinary parish priest. His outlook is essentially pastoral, and in an interview published in *Uj Ember* in March 1980, on the occasion of his seventieth birthday, the Cardinal outlined the Church's plans for the next few years. These will include special masses for pregnant mothers, during which the importance of religious education in the family will be explained; special services for grandmothers, who will be instructed in their family role, which has become very important now that large numbers of married women in Hungary go out to work; a retreat house is to be built; there is to be increased emphasis on the education of the laity. Survival, rather than confrontation, is the Church's policy, and the government honoured Cardinal Lekai on his birthday by awarding him the Order of the Banner of Rubies of the Hungarian People's Republic in recognition of his 'exceptional efforts to promote good relations between the Hungarian State and the Catholic Church'.

Not everyone inside and outside Hungary is happy with this changed approach, and from time to time there have been rumours that the Catholic hierarchy in Hungary is itself sharply divided. In 1978 the then Primate of Poland, Cardinal Wyszynski, criticized the Hungarian bishops for what he regarded as their too ready acquiescence in the State control of the Church.

About this time there was anxiety in Hungary lest the election of a tough Polish Pope might lead to a more uncompromising policy *vis-à-vis* Hungary in the Vatican, so Archbishop Luigi Poggi, an experienced negotiator in Eastern Europe, was sent from Rome to Budapest with a letter in which Pope John Paul II set out his *Ostpolitik*. The letter began by emphasizing that the policy initiated by Pope Paul VI would be continued, and went on to urge the Hungarian bishops 'not to falter in their loyalty to their proud heritage of faith . . . We wish at all costs that the light of the Gospel of Jesus Christ should radiate through your episcopal activity, that your priests can be active pastorally and that your religious communities and laity can perform their apostolic duties . . . You must bear your apostolic witness in a manner which will have effect and which will enable your national traditions always to be held in honour.'

Meanwhile problems had arisen within Hungary over the appearance of so-called 'basic' or 'base' communities. These communities, which have sprung up in many parts of Western Europe and Latin America, are small, informal groups, generally made up of young people and intellectuals, meeting with or without the leadership of a priest. They worship, pray and study together; they are politically conscious and are often critical of the established order, social and ecclesiastical. Just how many of these groups exist in Hungary is impossible to tell. Estimates vary from a hundred, given in *Herder Correspondence* in June 1977, to two thousand, mentioned by the Hungarian bishops a few months later, and on to four thousand, reported in *The Tablet* in March 1980. Whatever the precise number, the 'basic' communities were condemned as sectarian by the Catholic hierarchy during the winter of 1976–77, and Cardinal Lekai described them as uncanonical. Pope Paul VI also made an oblique critical reference to them when he received the Hungarian hierarchy in Rome in 1977.

As in other parts of the world, the anxiety of the bishops was caused mainly by the spontaneous character of the 'basic' communities and their criticisms of a conservative Church. But in Hungary there was, and is, a potentially explosive political factor, for these informal groups tend to be beyond easy surveillance and some of them are certainly critical of certain aspects of Hungarian socialism and of the present Church-State rapprochement. At one point, in 1977, it was rumoured that twenty-two young priests associated with the movement were to be arrested and put on trial. In 1980, however, the spring meeting of the Hungarian Bishops' Conference was addressed on the subject by its secretary, Bishop Cserhati of Pecs, who pleaded for understanding of the 'basic' communities:

> There are today many, especially young people, who – moved by the Holy Spirit – wish to make use of their charismatic gifts of grace within the community to build up the community. They must be given their due rights in the Church and it is important that their endeavours should find expression within the constitutional framework of the life of the Church.

This statement was welcomed by many Hungarian Catholics, though it was interpreted by some as the beginning of a new attempt to bring the communities under control.

The Catholic Church's change of attitude to the State during the 1970s was matched by a change of attitude to religion on the part of the State. A leading Hungarian Marxist, Jozsef Lukacs, expressed this change when he said:

> We know that the churches and religious sentiment will have a great deal of influence for some time to come. One must be mindful of this. But as Marxists what we are really interested in are the people influenced by this particular phenomenon. The people concern us far more than the nature of religious belief itself.

The First Secretary of the Communist Party, Janos Kadar, has often said in recent years that ideological differences need not prevent Christians and Marxists from working together, and the President of the State Office for Church Affairs, Imre Miklos, saw a positive role for the churches when he presented a paper to a meeting of the World Council of Churches staff in Geneva in 1978. Having acknowledged that the position of Marxists and their relationship with churches is open to change and is not a 'ready-made model', he went on:

> We cannot and must not rank religious people among the enemies of socialism. Large masses of people adhere to religion in one form or another in a socialist society. Their presence and their belonging to some church are an important sociological reality. In the course of building socialism we expect their constructive contribution . . . We respect the

God-believing man who stands with us more than the atheist, nihilistic non-believer who is against us.

It appears therefore that both Church and State in Hungary have discovered each other's strength and staying power during the course of more than thirty years of co-existence, and each has decided that more is to be gained by compromise than by confrontation. The State still holds the reins of power firmly, and the position of all the Hungarian churches is a long way from satisfactory. Yet the government cannot afford to risk another 1956 uprising or even the degree of disturbance manifested in Poland in 1980, so it is expedient to allow the churches a greater measure of freedom and to enlist their support for the causes of socialism and national unity. Had Cardinal Mindszenty lived to witness the present Church-State relationship he would have been horrified. So also, although to a lesser degree, would Matyas Rakosi, the Cardinal's ruthless opponent in 1948.

# Chapter 9

# YUGOSLAVIA

Yugoslavia is the despair of tidy minds. Although it is in many ways the most attractive country in Eastern Europe, Yugoslavia's historical, political, cultural and religious backgrounds combine to create a minefield which even the most sensitive and well-informed commentator can only cross in fear and trembling. The risks are even greater than usual in the early 1980s when the consciousness of the people and the machinery of government are adjusting to the death of the man who emerged from the Second World War as a great hero and during the next thirty-five years became a living myth, dominating the corporate life of a people whose external security and internal development demanded a compelling focus of unity.

In 1945 the Communist partisans led by Josip Broz Tito emerged with political power in their hands and proclaimed a People's Federative Republic. During the early years the new government consolidated their power and dealt with any opposition with the harsh dictatorial methods they had learned during their underground life before the war and in the ruthless wartime fighting which had claimed the lives of a large number of their Party comrades. By the time of his death in May 1980 Tito was presiding, still firmly, over a population of almost 22 million, composed of six republics, six nations (including the recently affirmed Muslim nation), a dozen different national minorities, four principal (and two only slightly less important) languages and two alphabets. Leaders of the religious communities were present in specially reserved places at the President's secular funeral, and three of the special masses for the homeland, said in all Roman Catholic churches at the time, were broadcast by Zagreb television.

Throughout his Presidency, Tito was much preoccupied with maintaining and strengthening the fragile unity of the Federation. The existence of different nations and national minorities, with their own proud histories and deeply-rooted jealousies, makes the resurgence of nationalism, often with religious undertones, an ever-present danger in Yugoslavia. In addition, despite the prevailing political doctrine, wealth is very unevenly distributed. Parts of the underdeveloped south and east are still extremely poor; the illiteracy rate in these regions is high, while in Slovenia, where the standard of living approximates to that of Austria and Northern Italy, nearly everyone is literate.

Though they were for a short time among the most devoted of the Russian satellites, the fact that they had made their own revolution without the help of the Soviet Union – and were a fiercely independent people – led Tito and his colleagues to reject Soviet dominance after the war. Hence the expulsion of the Yugoslav Communist Party from the Cominform in 1948. Stalin confidently expected this dramatic event to lead to the overthrow of Tito and his replacement by a more compliant leader, but he miscalculated the extent to which the repudiation of Soviet overlordship would rally popular support for Tito. Since the 1950s the Yugoslav government has maintained a non-aligned position in international affairs, veering sometimes towards the West and sometimes towards the Soviet bloc, the direction determined by the needs and pressures of the moment. When Tito visited Moscow in June 1956 (his first visit since his clash with Stalin) the document signed by himself and Khrushchev, symbolizing the normalizing of relations between Yugoslavia and the Soviet Union, stated that 'roads to conditions of socialist development are different in different countries'.

Yugoslav socialism has certainly developed its own characteristic form. There was a short period after 1948 when an attempt was made to show that the Yugoslavs were better Communists than anyone else, and an attempt was made to impose collectivization on the peasants, but it was soon dropped. The peasants have retained their sturdy independence, and can own up to ten hectares (about twenty-five acres) of land. Within industry there is a degree of 'workers control' or 'self-management socialism' unique in Eastern Europe, or indeed in any other part of the world. There is also a highly developed tourist industry, not unlike that of Spain, which brings into the country large numbers of Western visitors and a considerable amount of welcome 'hard' currency. During the post-war era a large number of Yugoslav migrant workers and their families have lived in West Germany, and there is a good deal of coming and going between the two countries. For the individual citizen there is greater personal freedom than anywhere else in Eastern Europe, but there is no mistaking the fact that Yugoslavia is a Marxist State, not a social democracy. The effect of all this is to create a society with a strange ambivalence, and a style which is often puzzling to the outsider.

In Yugoslavia religious allegiances are inextricably bound up with national origins. The country came into being after the First World War in the aftermath of the break-up of the Austro-Hungarian Empire. The inhabitants of the constituent territories were all South Slavs, although they were divided by religion and culture. During the war a number of groups had pressed different political and geographical solutions; the most energetic among these groups was the intelligentsia, who had the vision of a country of unified and equal South Slavs, transcending barriers of religion and cultural heritage and, most important of all, uniting the Catholic Croats and the Orthodox Serbs. However, after the creation of the Kingdom of Yugoslavia conflicts between Serbs and Croats sprang up in the wake of the centralizing policy of the Serbian dynasty, and the following twenty years were stormy.

Today the Roman Catholic and Serbian Orthodox Churches dominate the Christian scene, but there is a large Muslim religious community and a handful of Protestants and Jews. Serbia, Montenegro and Macedonia are the main geographical base of Orthodoxy, and to be a Serb is to be Orthodox, though in the coastal regions there are Serbian Catholics. Similarly, the inhabitants of Croatia and Slovenia are nearly all Roman Catholic, though there are important pockets of Orthodoxy along the old military frontier of Croatia, for it was here that the Serbs settled to defend the frontier of the Habsburg dominions against the Turks. The population of Bosnia and Hercegovina is mixed: Catholics who are Croats, Orthodox who are Serbs and Slav Muslims who now have their own 'nationality'. The latter are descendants of those who adopted Islam after the Turkish conquest of the Balkan peninsula in the fourteenth and fifteenth centuries.

---

Accurate statistics about religious allegiances in Yugoslavia are virtually impossible to come by, and figures published by apparently impeccable authorities often show startling variations. It is possible, however, to obtain a good general idea of the size of the religious communities and of the pattern of their organization. In 1964 the Serbian Orthodox Church was about eight million strong and commanded the allegiance of some 40 per cent of the total population. This figure could not have been far wrong and there is no reason to suppose that it has changed significantly. More recent figures indicate that there are about 2,400 Orthodox parishes organized in twenty-two dioceses, served by about 1,400 priests, of whom nearly two hundred are monks. This means that approximately a thousand parishes are without a resident priest, and there is in fact only one priest to every two church buildings. Part of the explanation of the shortage of clergy is to be found in the dreadful massacres of Serbian Orthodox Christians in the 1940s when the ranks of the clergy were decimated; but the shortage goes back to the years before the Second World War, and since 1945 the number of vocations to the priesthood has never been large enough to replace losses. Many of the retired clergy, of whom there are about four hundred, give assistance in the parishes. The Orthodox dioceses each have about a hundred parishes and, in addition to its dioceses in Yugoslavia, the Serbian Orthodox Church has five others abroad. In 1979 there were reported to be seventy students at the Orthodox theological faculty in Belgrade, and there are just under six hundred students in five seminaries. The Orthodox monasteries and convents have been numerically weak in Yugoslavia since the days of the Ottoman Empire, and there are still only two hundred Orthodox monks in the whole country. There was, however, a great revival of women's monasticism after 1919; this survived the Second World War and there are now about seven hundred nuns.

According to figures published in 1981, the Roman Catholic Church had, at the beginning of 1980, 6,942,300 members, comprising 32 per cent of the total population of the country.

These live in 2,782 parishes, organized in fourteen dioceses and one apostolic administration. The parishes are served by about 2,700 secular priests and by about 400 priests who are members of religious orders. There are altogether 4,046 priests in the country, of whom 1,399 are monks. About four hundred Yugoslav priests are living in other countries, serving migrant workers or pursuing studies. There are about 6,500 nuns, living in just over four hundred convents, and another thousand nuns living and working outside Yugoslavia, mainly in West Germany, where some of them receive salaries and send money back to their mother houses. In the monasteries, of which there are about 180, there are, in addition to the priest-monks, about 350 lay brothers. The two Catholic theological faculties, at Zagreb and Ljubljana, had a total of 760 students in 1979, while the eight major seminaries had 560 students. Before a young man can enter a seminary he must have completed the compulsory eight years in a state school, and all priests have attended either Zagreb or Ljubljana theological faculties as well as a seminary. Since 1952 all theological faculties have been separated from their universities, but they have maintained university standards. There was a sharp decline in the number of vocations to the priesthood in the 1970s.

The Protestant churches claim the allegiance of only 0.8 per cent of the population. There are four Evangelical churches, which are members of the Lutheran World Federation, each serving a separate national minority. The largest of these is the Slovak Lutheran Church (of the Augsburg Confession) which has one bishop, twenty-seven parishes, twelve smaller units, twenty ministers and lay preachers and thirty church buildings. Its 51,000 members are of Slovak nationality. The Evangelical Church in Serbia has a mainly Hungarian membership, while the Evangelical Christian Church of the Augsburg Confession in Slovenia, established in 1945, serves about 20,000 Slovenes in thirteen parishes and two smaller units. The Reformed Church (Calvinist) is largely Hungarian and is organized in three seniorates, each of which has between ten and twenty parishes, together with a large number of preaching posts. In 1978 there was a total of forty-three Reformed ministers, and students were training in Vienna, Budapest and Debrecen.

The Baptist Church has been active for more than a century, but it was not until 1923 that a Union was formed in Yugoslavia. Before and during the Second World War, Baptists were subjected to harassment or actual persecution, but since 1945 they have experienced the same degree of freedom as all the other religious bodies. There are now about 3,500 Baptists, in fifty-four localities, each of which has a church or a prayer house. Fifteen other prayer houses are in more isolated communities where numbers are small. There are altogether twenty pastors and lay preachers. A seminary and conference centre are attached to the Baptist church in Novi Sad.

Adventist groups have been active since the beginning of the present century, and these are now organized in four regions as the Adventist Church in Yugoslavia, with 120 full-time ministers serving about three hundred local churches. About seventy Adventist ministerial students attend the Higher Divinity School in Rakovica for a four-year course, and a Secondary Religious School, accommodating a maximum of 120 students, was opened in the 1960s at Marusevac.

The Methodist Church originated with the work of German missionaries whose efforts in Northern Yugoslavia were united with those of Congregational preachers in Macedonia in 1921. There are about 3,700 members in a total Methodist community of about 4,500, with forty preaching stations and thirteen active ministers.

The Pentecostal Church has about seventy-two congregations, with seventy preachers, and the Jehovah's Witnesses have 104 congregations. The Church of the United Brethren has no full-time ministers but its members constitute twenty-four local churches.

A Protestant theological faculty, named after the sixteenth-century reformer, Matija Vlacic Illirik, was opened in 1976. This was founded by the Baptist Union of Yugoslavia and the Evangelical Lutheran Church of Croatia, and confers degrees equivalent to those granted by the Catholic and Orthodox faculties. It is open to students from all the Protestant churches. The Old Catholic Church, established in 1923, has eleven parishes, seven churches and ten priests.

Muslims, both Slav and Albanian, number approximately two

million, just under 10 per cent of the total population. (The Slav
Muslims now have their own 'nationality' but the Albanian
Muslims still regard themselves as being of Albanian nationality.) The Islamic religious community is a highly developed
organization with its hierarchy of councils, assemblies and
seniorates. Sarajevo is the residence of the chief religious
official, the Reis-ul-Ulema, and the Sarajevo Seniorate is the
largest of the four in the country. It has about 1,100 mosques,
over a hundred halls for religious education, three chief imams
and about 750 imams. The Islamic community has been
stimulated by Islamic revival in other parts of the world and
many new mosques were built during the 1970s; altogether,
Yugoslavia has about 2,100 mosques and about 1,600 imams.
Imams are trained in two schools: the Gazi Husrevbeg madrassah in Sarajevo has about 250 students, while the Alaudin
madrassah in Pristina (where the teaching is in Albanian) has
about 130 students. A Muslim theological faculty was opened in
Sarajevo in 1977.

Jewish communities have existed in the area since the
Byzantine era. Although banished many times, they have always
reappeared at the first opportunity, and the Serbian constitution
of 1888 gave them rights of equality. At the outbreak of the
Second World War there were about 76,000 Jews in Yugoslavia,
but no fewer than 60,000 of these were murdered in concentration camps, and of those who survived or returned to the country
after the war about 10,000 have moved to Israel. The rest (six
thousand) are now organized in thirty-five Jewish communities
which belong to a National Federation. This Federation is
primarily a secular body, concerned chiefly with the organization of seminars, cultural activities, and youth camps which are
attended by young Jews from many other parts of Eastern
Europe. Since there are no rabbis in Yugoslavia, the functions
of the rabbis are carried out by older laymen as far as possible,
but it is proving very difficult to maintain the religious life of the
Jewish people.

All the religious communities in Yugoslavia have their own
publications and these total more than a hundred. A notable
feature of church life in the last fifteen years has been the vigour
of the Catholic press, which has sixty-seven publications of

various sorts, including diocesan gazettes. *Glas Koncila* (Voice of the Council) first appeared in 1962 and was intended by the Archbishop of Zagreb to be an information bulletin about the Second Vatican Council. Since then, however, it has developed into a first-class fortnightly newspaper with a circulation of about 120,000. Like all publications in Yugoslavia, a particular issue may be banned by the authorities after publication if it contains something offensive to the government. In 1980 a parish priest in Slovenia was sent to prison for five months for writing a letter to *Glas Koncila* complaining of attacks against priests and church property which, according to the authorities, had never taken place. Even so this newspaper appears to be remarkably free to comment on a wide variety of subjects to do with the Church and the State, and over the years has gradually pushed back the frontier of State toleration. Another popular Catholic publication is *Kana* (Cana), a family colour magazine published in Croatia with a circulation of 53,000. *Druzina* (The Family), circulation 125,000, and *Ognjisce* (The Hearth), circulation 83,000, are the equivalent Catholic newspaper and magazine published in Slovenia. *Svesci* (Notebooks) was started in order to put Yugoslav Catholics in touch with Western theological thinking, and sometimes incurs the wrath of the hierarchy by publishing articles which are considered 'injurious to the faith'. *Aksa* is a weekly Catholic news service in Croat and German.

The Serbian Orthodox Church has ten publications, of which the most important is *Pravoslavlje* (Orthodoxy). This is published fortnightly by the Patriarchate in Belgrade and has a circulation of about 24,000. Another fortnightly is *Vesnik* (The Herald), the journal of the Serbian Priests' Association, which is read mainly by the clergy and sells about 3,500 copies. *Pravoslavni Misionar* (Orthodox Missionary) appears six times a year and has 50,000 subscribers, while *Svetosavsko Zvonce* (The Bells of St Sava) is a monthly magazine with a circulation of 30,000. The other Orthodox magazines tend to be of a specialist theological character or professional journals for the clergy.

The publications of the Protestant churches are somewhat modest, but none of the churches is without its printed organ of communication. The four Evangelical churches all publish a magazine, and the Reformed Church has achieved a circulation of 4,000 with its *Reformatus Elet* (Reformed Life). The official paper of the Baptist Union is the monthly *Glasnik* (Messenger) which sells 3,000 copies, and there is a Baptist fortnightly *Glas Jevandjelja* (Voice of the Gospel) which also has a circulation of 3,000. The Pentecostals publish *Izvori* (Source), a monthly. The Jewish community has a monthly, *Jevrejski* (Jewish Review), which sells 3,500 copies, and also a youth magazine and an almanac. The Supreme Islamic Seniorate publishes a fortnightly, *Glasnik* (Messenger), with a circulation of 15,000, copies of which are sent to Islamic countries together with a summary in Arabic, and *Preporod* (Renaissance), which is the journal of the Islamic Clergy Association.

The Bible circulates freely throughout the country and, in addition to a shop in Belgrade which is run by the United Bible Societies, copies of the new Croat translation of the Bible, prepared by a committee of Roman Catholic and secular scholars, are sold in many other bookshops. New translations are being made in all the principal languages spoken in Yugoslavia, and in 1971 the United Bible Societies decided to transfer the production of all Yugoslav scriptures to Yugoslavia. The translation work is nearly always carried out on an interconfessional basis. The Islamic community publishes its own translations of the Koran.

---

The present legal position of religion and religious communities in Yugoslavia is laid down in a constitution which came into force in February 1974 and varies little from the constitutions of 1946 and 1963.

Religious confession is free and is the individual's private affair.

The religious communities are separated from the State and free to perform their religious affairs and religious rites.

The religious communities may found religious schools only for the training of their own clergy.

Abuse of religion and religious activities for political purposes is unconstitutional.

The social community may give material assistance to the religious communities.

Within the limits determined by law, the religious communities may exercise the right of ownership of real estate. (Article 174)

The dissemination or pursuance of national inequality, as well as incitement to national, racial or religious hatred and intolerance, is unconstitutional and shall be punished. (Article 170)

These provisions were a reaffirmation of those laid down in the constitutions of 1963 and 1946, but this time the individual republics and provinces were required to pass their own enabling laws to replace the earlier federal law. The republics published draft laws during 1975–76 and these were offered for public discussion. The Catholic and Orthodox Churches took the opportunity to make strong representations about certain matters, as a result of which some proposals were modified, and when all the laws were finally enacted it became clear that there were significant local variations. Stella Alexander analysed the laws of Slovenia, Croatia, Serbia, Bosnia and Hercegovina, Macedonia and the Vojvodina Autonomous Province in the Summer 1980 issue of *Religion in Communist Lands*, the journal of Keston College, England:

Some provisions are basic, and common in one wording or another, to all the republican laws. No one's constitutional and other rights may be restricted on the grounds of religious belief or membership of a religious community; but neither may members of religious communities enjoy any special privileges or protection or be exempt from their civil obligations. Citizens may establish religious communities which must be registered with the authorities.

All the republics prohibit the abuse of religion, religious activities and the religious press for political purposes. Coupled with this, Slovenia, Croatia and Serbia prohibit any interference with the holding of religious assemblies. The Macedonian law is more precise and prohibits activities which are against the general or particular interests of society, the spreading of religious intolerance, hatred or discord and the

298 Discretion and Valour

preaching of inflammatory sermons; it also prohibits the disturbance and breaking up of religious assemblies.

All the republics allow religious communities to establish a religious press. The laws in Croatia, Bosnia and Hercegovina and Macedonia give blanket permission, subject to the provisions of the law on the press, but Slovenian law is more precise and specifies that the religious press shall deal with religious instruction, the carrying out of religious rites and activities, and, in general, religious and church matters, and the Serbian law is similar. The proposal of the Catholic bishops that the churches should have access to the mass media, i.e. radio and television, was turned down. All the republics allow persons in hospitals, sanatoria and old people's homes to practise their religion and to receive visits from a priest, so long as house rules are obeyed and other inmates are not disturbed. Visits by a priest to prison inmates are not, and never have been, allowed.

A new feature of the recent laws is the ban on social activities of the churches. The draft law in Croatia banned both social and economic activities of religious communities, and this would have abolished the charitable activities of the Catholic Church, which in Croatia are extensive and important. The bishops protested strongly, and indeed the disappearance of the work of Caritas would have left such a gap that the clause was withdrawn. Now only social activities which do not directly serve religious requirements are banned. Many energetic parish priests organized, for example, sports, excursions and clubs for the young people of the parish, and this has now been virtually stopped.

The founding of priests' associations (which are supported by the government) is specifically provided for in the Croatian, the Serbian and the Macedonian laws. The Catholic Church has always opposed these and the Croatian bishops would have liked to see this clause deleted but were unsuccessful. The State may give financial assistance to religious communities, and all the laws specify that the religious community may spend the funds as it chooses, unless the money is given for specific purposes, in which case it may be required to account for it (i.e. the funds given for the upkeep and restoration of historic buildings and art treasures). All the republics allow religious communities to collect voluntary donations from their adherents on their own premises, and outside their premises with permission; no one may be either forced to contribute or prevented from doing so; priests may also receive fees for religious services (i.e. weddings, funerals, the blessing of a house).

All the republic laws allow the performance of religious rites and ceremonies in churches, temples and mosques, and also in their courtyards and other church buildings. Outside activities require permission. All republics require church premises to be registered; all make provision, either specifically or by reference to the Law on Public Gatherings, for the banning of gatherings for reasons of public order or health. Family religious rites, for example the blessing of a house or the celebration of a family's patron saint's day, are allowed outside religious premises without special permission, and all republics allow religious rites in cemeteries; but all make it illegal to introduce political or other non-religious matter into funeral orations.

Religious communities in all the republics are allowed to found schools for the education and training of priests, pastors and imams. The curriculum and the appointment of teachers are under the control of the religious community, but no one who is not a Yugoslav citizen may teach in a religious school except with the permission of the authorities. Students at religious schools, with the exception of Bosnia and Hercegovina, now have all the rights (social and health insurance, travel concessions) of students at State schools and universities, except the right to shorter and deferred military service until the completion of education. These are concessions which the churches sought for many years and have at last been granted in part.

The religious instruction of children is provided for in all the republics. It must be held on religious premises which are places of public access (i.e. a church or church building), it must not clash with school hours or school-linked activities, and it must have the consent of both parents, and of the child if over fourteen years of age. (The Macedonian draft law was to have contained a clause forbidding religious instruction of children under the age of seventeen, but this was leaked in advance and picked up by *Glas Koncila* – the Catholic fortnightly – and there was such an outcry that the proposal was dropped.) All the republics provide that weddings, christenings and circumcisions can only take place after the civil ceremony or registration of birth.

Violations of the various laws are not criminal offences but 'contraventions'. The penalties vary considerably but none is particularly heavy: the biggest fine is the equivalent of just over US $500 or £220 and the longest prison sentence sixty days. Serious offences such as incitement to religious, national or racial hatred and intolerance are crimes covered by the federal criminal code and can be punished by imprisonment for up to ten years.

---

As far as the day-to-day life of the churches is concerned, this vast apparatus of rules and regulations, though undoubtedly inconvenient and sometimes restrictive, poses less of a threat than does the process of secularization which is now affecting Yugoslavia, as it has for some time been affecting most industrialized Western nations. Roman Catholic churches are generally well attended, but not packed except on major feast days. It is estimated that mass attendance in rural areas is about 50 per cent, but the rate is very much less than this in the cities where only 30 to 40 per cent of Catholic families send their children for religious instruction. On the other hand *Glas Koncila* reported in 1977 that nearly 100 per cent of Catholic families in rural areas and 90 per cent in urban areas have their children baptized. In the villages older women tend to predominate in church congregations, but in the university towns of Catholic Croatia and Slovenia there has in recent years been a considerable increase of students and young people at mass. The Jesuit Church in Zagreb has a special 'Mass for Intellectuals' (so described on the list of services in the church porch) at 11 a.m. on Sunday, and this mass is packed tight with students, who are said to come more from the scientific faculties than from the faculties of philosophy or political science. What is believed to have been the largest crowd (estimated by *Glas Koncila* as 'no smaller than 250,000') ever to have attended a religious event in Yugoslavia assembled at Nin, in Southern Croatia, on 2 September 1979. The occasion was the 1,100th anniversary of the unbroken connection between the Croats and the papacy, and the small town of Nin was chosen for the celebration because it was the seat of the first Croat bishopric. Pope John Paul II sent as his legate Cardinal Franjo Seper, prefect of the Vatican Congregation for the Doctrine of the Faith, who is himself a Croat and was previously Archbishop of Zagreb. Earlier in 1979 more than 10,000 pilgrims from Croatia went to Rome when, for the first time ever, mass was celebrated in Croat at St Peter's. The Pope welcomed the pilgrims with great affection, and praised the Croats for their love and devotion to the Church of Rome and especially for their devotion to Mary, the Mother of God. The pilgrimage slogan was 'The Croat Catholic family prays daily and goes to mass on Sunday' and all Croat Catholics are now being urged to pause for a short time of prayer every evening at nine o'clock – to renew their baptismal covenant with God and commend their actions to Mary.

The election to the papacy of a Polish cardinal who had personal experience of co-existing with Communists was greeted with great enthusiasm by Yugoslav Catholics, and they have another focus of admiration and pride in Mother Teresa of Calcutta, who was born in Skopje, of Albanian parents, and lived there from 1910 to 1928. In 1979 Mother Teresa opened a children's home and a branch of her Missionaries of Charity at Zagreb, and when in the same year she was awarded the Nobel Peace Prize this was widely reported and applauded in the Yugoslav Communist press. Almost all the Catholic parishes have religious instruction for children. This is given on church premises by priests, who are sometimes assisted by nuns, and it was reported in 1978 that in the year 1975 about 530,000 children and young people had attended religious instruction, the highest proportions being in Bosnia and Hercegovina (80 per cent) and Slovenia (60 per cent). Every year about 150 priests, nuns and lay people attend a summer school for catechetics, sponsored by the Yugoslav Bishops' Conference and held each time in a different city. From time to time difficulty is experienced over obtaining permission for new churches to be built, though a new Catholic cathedral was built at Mostar in the late 1970s. In the diocese of Mostar-Duvno some thirty-five of the sixty-nine parishes are served by Franciscan priests, a practice which arose during the Turkish occupation, when for several centuries the Franciscans ministered to the people of Bosnia and Hercegovina, often risking their lives, after most of the secular clergy had fled. After the Second World War, when vocations to the priesthood increased, the Bishop of Mostar-Duvno attempted to displace some of the Franciscans with secular priests, but the people of the parishes concerned refused to accept the diocesan clergy. In 1975 the Franciscans were ordered to vacate four parishes and to prepare to hand over thirteen more. But the provincial board of the Franciscans and the parishes ignored the instruction, appeals were made, threats were issued, priests were suspended and the matter has yet to be finally settled.

The Serbian Orthodox Church is rather less active than the Catholic Church in Yugoslavia. Orthodox believers go to church in very large numbers at the great festivals and on popular saints' days, but their churches are more sparsely attended at other times. Only two dioceses, Belgrade and Backa (Novi Sad), have religious instruction for children in every parish. This is sometimes due to administrative pressures, especially in the poorer, more primitive regions, but generally the lack of children's instruction in Orthodox parishes is due to the shortage of priests or to other claims on the parish priests' time. From time to time Orthodox bishops complain that they cannot obtain permission to build new churches, though it is now clear that the late 1960s was a time of quite extensive church building. Unlike the Catholic Church, which has always refused to accept financial assistance from the State, except in such areas as health and social insurance for its clergy and maintenance of the fabric of historic churches, the Orthodox Church receives some direct subventions from the State, which it regards as compensation for the nationalization of church lands. As in other parts of Eastern Europe, the Church raises a good deal of its income by making and selling candles. The monasteries and churches built by the Serbian kings have remarkable frescoes on their walls and the most important of these, which are a major part of Yugoslavia's artistic heritage, are maintained by the State. Life in the monasteries, especially in the remote rural areas, still has many of the characteristics and the 'feel' of the Middle Ages.

Since the schism of the three Macedonian dioceses in 1967 and the deep trauma which that caused (see page 308), the Serbian Orthodox Church has avoided open conflict with the Communist State, though the late Bishop Vasilije Kostic of Zica, always an outspoken churchman, spent a month in prison in 1971 after preaching a sermon in which he denounced the effects of atheism and the lack of religious teaching for children and young people. More recently, the Holy Synod of the Orthodox Church addressed a petition to the President of the Republic of Serbia in May 1977, asking for greater freedom in ten areas of religious life:

1.  Permission to extend the Belgrade patriarchal cathedral.
2.  Return to the Church of cult objects now in the historical museum in Zagreb.
3.  Return of church registers in State possession for over thirty years.
4.  Permission to build new churches.
5.  Social insurance to be extended to the teaching staff and students at theological seminaries.
6.  End to discrimination against children who take part in religious education.
7.  End to State interference in church affairs.
8.  Directives to forbid all libelling and maligning of clergy in the media.
9.  Burial rituals in accordance with the wishes of the bereaved.
10. Return of confiscated church property.

Patriarch German, who signed this petition, along with two other bishops, was born in 1899. After his ordination to the priesthood, he worked mainly in ecclesiastical courts and when still quite young he became general secretary of the Holy Synod, travelling with Patriarch Vikentije to Greece and Moscow, as well as making a journey of his own to the United States. Government pressure was brought to bear at the time German was elected to succeed Vikentije in the Patriarchate in 1958, but he is by no means a government cipher, as his strong stand against the Macedonian schism, his opposition to the recognition of the priests' associations, and his support for the 1977 petition makes clear. He is generally regarded as a wise spiritual leader. During his years as Patriarch, German has had to deal not only with the Macedonian schism but also with the setting up of a schismatic Serbian Church in North America, this in turn leading to the unfrocking of its leader Bishop Dionisije for uncanonical behaviour. German has travelled widely, visiting all the principal Orthodox churches, and the government has found his friendly exchanges with foreign church leaders, especially in the Middle East, useful to its own policy of non-alignment.

The small Protestant churches in Yugoslavia are more conscious of their recently acquired freedom than of state restriction, and their leaders sometimes lament the fact that they lack the strength to make full use of the freedom they now have. Evangelical groups have made most progress in small, rural communities where the local Orthodox church may be without a priest, and the arrival of an itinerant evangelist from another part of the country is seen as a great event. It is much more difficult to make an impact in the large cities, where the Protestant communities tend to be submerged by the scale and impersonal character of urban life, though there has been some successful work among young people. A coffee bar in Zagreb is in a very attractively decorated basement and is open four nights a week. Young people meet here to listen to music, to read Christian literature and to share in discussions about religious and personal issues. Summer camps at the coast or in the mountains are also arranged for young people, usually during public holidays such as the First of May or the Day of the Republic, and these often attract large numbers. About eight hundred young people attended a Baptist youth conference held in Novi Sad in the spring of 1978. A crusade conducted by the American evangelist, Dr Billy Graham, in Zagreb in 1967 was, however, deemed to be only partially successful. Those attending the crusade meetings were in the main people from the villages who were already Christian, and the main result of a follow-up campaign held three years later with the aid of television seems to have been squabbles among evangelical groups who accused each other of stealing members.

The history of Yugoslavia has not been such as to encourage love and charity among Christians today, especially between Serbs and Croats, but relations between the Serbian Orthodox Church and the Roman Catholic Church are now formally good, and in many individual cases there is real warmth. The culmination of early attempts at rapprochement came in 1968 when Cardinal Seper called on Patriarch German at his summer residence to take leave before going to Rome as prefect of the Congregation for the Doctrine of the Faith. The two leaders prayed briefly together in the Orthodox cathedral, and later lunched together and exchanged gifts. Following this came other acts of friendship, as for example the permission given by the Bishop of Maribor for Orthodox to worship in the Catholic parish church of a nearby resort during the summer months. Officially, leaders and representatives of each of the religious communities, and the Communist chairman and secretary of republican Commissions for Religious Affairs, attend all of each other's ceremonial occasions, such as the installations of bishops and imams and the funerals of leaders. In September 1979 Cardinal König and a delegation from Pro Oriente, a Catholic movement working for closer relations between the churches of East and West, spent several days in Serbia as guests of Patriarch German. This was the first occasion a foreign Catholic bishop had been welcomed by the Orthodox Church since the Second World War. Four ecumenical seminars, at two-year intervals, have been held by the two Catholic theological faculties and the Serbian Orthodox theological faculty; the last one was attended also by the Protestants. The leader of the Pentecostals, Peter Kuzmic, was recently granted a doctorate *summa cum laude* by the Zagreb Catholic theological faculty. An ecumenical movement has also emerged among the Protestant churches. A group of 150 pastors and church leaders, representing six denominations from all parts of the country, met at Easter 1980, and again just after Christmas in the same year, as a result of which an Evangelical Fellowship has been established to foster collaboration between the churches. At the local level, however, many of the old hostilities and suspicions still linger, and Pope John Paul II caused considerable offence to the Serbian Orthodox (for which he later apologized) when in his inaugural address he forgot to mention the Serb language as one of those which had played its part in the propagation of Christianity among the Slavs.

The Muslims, particularly the Slav Muslims of Bosnia and Hercegovina, have recently been affected by the worldwide resurgence of Islam, which has fed Muslim national feelings. The Slav Muslims of Bosnia and Hercegovina and neighbouring territories were officially recognized as a separate nation in January 1968, and given various forms of encouragement. Many now study at Arab universities, large numbers make the annual pilgrimage to Mecca, and at least half of all Muslim children receive religious instruction. New mosques have been built in towns and villages, some with financial contribution from friendly Arab states. But the government is very aware of the dangers which the old rivalries between Muslims and Serbs, and the links between Slav Muslims and Croats, pose to the precarious ethnic balance in Bosnia and Hercegovina, and which are themselves a reflection of the wider strains within the Federation. Early manifestations of an exclusive Muslim nationalism in Bosnia and Hercegovina – directed against Serbs and Croats – were attacked by the authorities in 1978. The editors of *Preporod*, the journal of the Islamic Clergy Association, were censured and eventually replaced for defending the war record of some Slav Muslim leaders; Muslim religious leaders were accused of having fallen for a Khomeini-style Islamic fundamentalism – a surprising charge against men who had taken an enlightened attitude to many social questions affecting Islamic customs. It is evident that the authorities are watching the situation carefully and are determined not to be caught unawares by the emergence of yet another form of nationalism.

---

It is impossible to understand the present religious situation in Yugoslavia without taking account of the wartime sufferings of the country, and in particular of the Orthodox Christians. Following the invasion of the country by the Germans, Italians, Hungarians and Bulgarians in 1941, an Independent State of

Croatia, under Axis patronage, was formed out of Croatia-Slavonia, Bosnia-Hercegovina and parts of Dalmatia. A Serbian puppet state was set up in the territory of inner Serbia, and the rest of the country was carved up between the invaders. The official Yugoslav claim is that during the next four years one in ten of the entire population of the country – a total of 1.7 million – were killed.

The Independent State of Croatia was ruled by a Croat Fascist, Ante Pavelic, and his Ustasa Party. They came to power determined to avenge what they considered to have been the repression of the Croats by the Serbs and to 'purify' the State from Orthodoxy, having themselves proclaimed their devotion to the Catholic Church and the spirit of the crusades. One member of the regime declared: 'We shall convert one-third of the Serbs, expel one-third and kill one-third.' It is impossible to ascertain precise figures, but estimates indicate that, out of a Serbian population in the Independent State of Croatia of roughly two million, at least 300,000 were deported or fled, over 350,000 were killed and about 250,000 were converted under duress to Catholicism, undergoing mass public 're-baptism' to show their new allegiance. This effectively destroyed the Orthodox Church in the area. Among those murdered were three bishops and about 220 priests, while two other bishops were expelled, one was interned and about 330 priests either fled or were deported. Here it is important to remember that the purpose of forcing Orthodox Serbs into the Catholic Church was as much political as religious. Catholics counted as Croats and thus the number of 'official' (i.e. Orthodox) Serbs would drop to an insignificant minority.

The Roman Catholic Church welcomed the creation of an independent Croatia, which freed Croats from the increasingly resented domination of Serbs. Some of the bishops and priests were active supporters of the Ustasa ideology, and a number of priests and friars actually took part in the killings and acts of violence. Archbishop Stepinac of Zagreb, leader of the Catholic hierarchy, protested vehemently to Pavelic in private and, as the war went on, preached publicly against the racist and religious persecution of Serbs, Jews and Gypsies. He also did what he could to intervene in individual cases, but he was increasingly hampered by the ambiguity of his position: he desired the end – an independent Catholic Croatia – but was horrified by the means which the Ustasa used. His actions, during and after the war, were always governed by his determination to defend the Church and its institutions. The Serbs retaliated when they could, and some Orthodox priests joined the Cetniks – the Serbian national resistance movement which owed allegiance to the exiled royalist government – and took their toll of Croats. A small number of Catholic and Orthodox priests fought with the partisans.

These facts, painful and divisive though they still are, must be rehearsed, even at the risk of reviving tragic memories and divisions, in order to give an essential part of the background of the present religious situation in Yugoslavia. It is, for example, hardly surprising if the memory of wartime experience has not yet been erased from the minds of middle-aged and elderly Serbs. Although neither Catholics nor Orthodox now have any intention of proselytizing, many of the old fears and resentments lie only just beneath the surface of national life. The situation is perhaps more easily understood by people who have tried to have a sympathetic understanding of the Irish problem.

---

The greatest threat to the Serbian Orthodox Church has been fragmentation from within. The Macedonians had long resented the Serbian assumption that they were South Serbs and when, at the end of the Second World War, Macedonia became one of the constituent republics of federal Yugoslavia, a strong demand for an autocephalous Macedonian Orthodox Church was made by a group of Macedonian priests, backed by the Communist authorities who saw that this affirmation of Macedonian nationality would strengthen their south-eastern borders against the pressures of Bulgarian irredentism. A long-drawn-out struggle followed. Patriarch Vikentije succeeded, by a mixture of obduracy, evasion and procrastination, in postponing the final decision for years. The government, which had supported the Macedonian clergy from the beginning but had not created the movement, were unwilling to press the Patriarchate beyond a certain point. They finally managed to secure, by a mixture of blandishments and veiled threats, the consent of the Sabor

(Assembly) of the Serbian Orthodox Church to the creation of an autonomous Macedonian Church, still under the jurisdiction of the Serbian Patriarchate. It was an uneasy arrangement and was terminated in 1967 by a unilateral declaration of autocephaly by the Macedonian Orthodox Church, a move which the Serbian Patriarchate refused to recognize but was powerless to stop. Relations between the two churches were severed and no other Orthodox church has recognized the Macedonians, who now flourish under the benevolent wing of the government and have built themselves a large new Metropolitanate in Skopje. Although a number of efforts have been made to restore relations between the two churches, these have come to nothing; there is some evidence that the State authorities would welcome a reconciliation. The Macedonian Orthodox Church has about 250 active and about 50 retired priests.

The schism in the North American dioceses, which finally came to a head in 1964 when the Sabor unfrocked Bishop Dionisije for disgraceful conduct, was a different matter and did not strike at the fundamental unity of the Serbian Orthodox Church in the same way. Dionisije had been under attack by the Yugoslav government ever since the war, for his anti-Communism, and this served to protect him from disciplinary measures by the Patriarchate, lest they appeared to be acting as a tool of the authorities. When the Sabor eventually proceeded against him a certain number of the Serbian Orthodox clergy and about half of the laity in the United States followed him, but many of these have now returned to the jurisdiction of the Serbian Orthodox Patriarchate.

---

Present Church-State relations in Yugoslavia can be traced back to 1943 when, at a meeting in Bosnia, the Communists declared their attitude towards religion in the statutes proclaimed by AVNOJ (the Anti-Fascist Council for the National Liberation of Yugoslavia). These became the basis of the post-war constitution: Article 8 gave equal rights to all citizens without regard to nationality, race or religion; Article 10 guaranteed freedom of religious belief and conscience; Article 11 guaranteed freedom of speech, of the press, of association and assembly 'in the framework of the NOB' (national liberation struggle) to all except those who had served the enemies of the people. They also declared their philosophical attitude to religion, based on Lenin's interpretation of the early Marx and Engels: religion springs from the material conditions of society and is a result of man's alienation from the product of his labour. It is therefore useless to attack it directly, but it will wither away when man's alienation has disappeared; meanwhile it must be separated from the State.

This attitude was declared repeatedly in the speeches and writings of leading Communists; an example is an important speech Dr Bakaric, the Croat Communist leader, made to Zagreb students in 1946, in which he argued that religion is a private matter and should not be opposed unless it interferes outside its own domain. Essentially, the Communist aim was to separate religion from the State and limit its province to religious affairs and the celebration of religious rites. The fact that 'religious affairs' has never been precisely defined has been the cause of a good deal of subsequent difficulty.

This basic philosophical attitude was not, however, always paralleled by the beliefs and actions of hardliners, people who would now be described as Stalinists. They were mainly the less educated and more primitive elements in the Party who simply wanted to 'bash the churches'. And underlying all this are the undocumented, and only to be guessed at, activities of the secret police who (according to the statement of the government minister responsible for them, Rankovic, in a speech in 1951 calling for the strengthening of legality) were subject to no legal controls.

Obviously any church, such as the Roman Catholic Church, which had opposed the partisans during the war and given support to the occupying powers, and some of whose clergy had collaborated openly with the oppressive Ustasa regime, was liable to penal reprisals. In the immediate aftermath of the war retribution against collaborators was swift, ruthless and indiscriminate. Yet it is not easy for those who have never lived in an enemy-occupied country to appreciate the degree to which loyalties are strained during a long period of suffering, and the extent to which fear and sensitivity remain even when the immediate cause has been removed. Certainly any individual or institution whose loyalty to the State was in doubt, or who was suspected of collaboration with the occupying powers, was extremely vulnerable to persecution in post-war Yugoslavia. The fact that the persecution of the churches became much less intense in the 1950s may be explained – in part, though not entirely – by the gradual return to normal peacetime conditions in the country as a whole.

Another cause of great difficulty to the churches was the land reform. Even before the end of the war, when the Communists had already established their government in Belgrade, they passed the Agrarian Reform Law which completed the break-up of estates over a quite moderate size, a process which had begun soon after the First World War. During the years following 1945 the government passed a series of laws on the nationalization and expropriation of buildings and real estate and businesses, for which social, cultural and charitable institutions were to receive no compensation. These laws were intended to alter the basis of land, real estate and industrial ownership, and were not specifically directed against the churches. None the less, as a result of the new legislation the principal religious communities – Catholic, Orthodox and Muslim – lost the major source of their incomes.

From 1945 to the middle 1950s the churches were harassed and persecuted in various ways. Trials in the courts were, however, always on *political* charges: for wartime collaboration, for helping 'enemies of the people' after the war, for inciting national or religious intolerance, and so on. An important reason for the government's hostility to the Roman Catholic Church was the long-drawn-out dispute between Yugoslavia and the Western Allies over Trieste and the Yugoslav boundary with Italy, which dragged on until 1954. The Yugoslav government claimed that the Roman Catholic Church in Yugoslavia was under orders from the Vatican, which supported Italy – a defeated enemy who claimed territory which the Yugoslavs believed to be theirs.

The most famous of the trials was that of Archbishop Stepinac of Zagreb. Born in 1898, Alojzije Stepinac fought in the Austro-Hungarian army during the First World War and was taken prisoner by the Italians. He then volunteered, as did many subjects of the Habsburg Empire, to fight for the Allies. When the war was over he returned to Yugoslavia and it was not until he was twenty-six years of age that he went to Rome to study for the Catholic priesthood. He was ordained in 1930 and served as the Archbishop of Zagreb's master of ceremonies. Four years later he was, to the astonishment of everyone including himself, appointed co-adjutor to the by then ailing Archbishop, and at thirty-six was the youngest bishop in the Catholic Church. Within three years he had succeeded to the archbishopric and was responsible for one of the largest dioceses in Europe. Stepinac was a man of somewhat intense personal piety, but he became much concerned with the Church's social work and merged various Catholic charities into one organization known as Caritas. Before the Second World War he was chairman of a committee to help Jewish refugees from Nazi Germany. As Archbishop of Zagreb, Stepinac soon became disillusioned with the Serbian rule of Yugoslavia, and when the German and Italian armies invaded the country in 1941 he welcomed the setting up of an Independent State of Croatia. In the closing days of the war he issued a pastoral letter denouncing the misdeeds of the partisans, and when Tito and the partisans took control in 1945 the Bishops' Conference, of which Stepinac was president, issued a pastoral letter fiercely denouncing Communism and making considerable claims for the Church in the life of post-war Yugoslavia. The government let it be known that they hoped the Vatican would transfer Stepinac to Rome, and when this met with no response the Archbishop was arrested in September 1946 and put on trial. He was accused, among other things, of supporting the wartime Ustasa regime, of deep involvement in its affairs, and of complicity in the forced conversion of Serbs to Catholicism. He was also said to have been involved in a plot to invite the Anglo-American occupation of Yugoslavia to thwart the aspirations of the partisans. At his trial Stepinac was defended by one of the ablest lawyers in Zagreb, but the defence was greatly hampered by the authorities, and the evidence of important witnesses was disallowed. There is in fact ample evidence that once Stepinac had realized the full significance of Ustasa aims and methods in 1941 he often intervened privately and protested against what was happening. But there was a

certain ambiguity about the Catholic Church's position and when
the war was over Tito was able to make a good deal of capital
out of the fact that the Archbishop's attitude to the Ustasa
massacres had been somewhat restrained in comparison with his
open attacks on the new Communist government. Stepinac was
declared guilty by the court and sentenced to sixteen years'
imprisonment, a lighter sentence than many Catholics had
feared. He spent five years in prison, under conditions more
lenient than those of many of his fellow priests, and was then
allowed to go to his native village of Krasic where he remained,
restricted and under supervision, for the rest of his life. He was
created a Cardinal by Pope Pius XII in 1952, and the government,
regarding this as a snub, responded by breaking off diplomatic
relations with the Holy See. Later, when Stepinac's health was
failing, the authorities were prepared for him to move south to
a warmer climate or to live in exile in Rome, but he refused to
leave his diocese and died in February 1960. At first it seemed
that he would have a simple funeral in the parish church at
Krasic, but on the day before the funeral was due to take place
the government announced that the Cardinal could be buried in
his cathedral at Zagreb. The plans were immediately changed
and Stepinac was buried near the high altar of the cathedral, in
the presence of a huge congregation which filled the building and
overflowed into the square outside. His tomb is now regarded
as a shrine by Yugoslav Catholics, and every year there is a
requiem mass in the cathedral on the anniversary of his death.
This has become the occasion for increasingly outspoken
sermons by the present Archbishop of Zagreb, calling for justice
to be done to his memory. The Serbs, including the Serbian
Orthodox Church, regarded the funeral as a 'posthumous
amnesty' and were displeased.

Much of the post-war persecution of the clergy took the form
of 'administrative' action, often by local officials or Party
members, and during the early years many of the clergy were
subjected to savage physical attacks. Bishops visiting their
dioceses for confirmation were obstructed and in some cases
beaten up by mobs. Pressures – sometimes crude, sometimes
more subtle – were brought to bear on believers not to practise
their faith and not to give their children a religious upbringing.

Young men were discouraged from attending seminaries, and ordinands often had a difficult time during their military service. All of this went on until the mid-1950s, when Tito himself called a halt to the more brutal harassment. In a speech at the end of 1953, he said that physical attacks on bishops and clergy and believers were illegal and unworthy of a socialist nation, and in that same year the Law on the Legal Status of Religious Communities was passed, giving the churches a legal basis for defending their rights. After that the position of the churches improved slowly but steadily.

Tito had made it plain from the outset, however, that, while the churches would be permitted to play their part in the life of the new Yugoslavia, he was determined that they should have the 'right' kind of leaders, i.e. leaders whose loyalty and co-operation could be taken for granted. In the case of Patriarch Gavrilo of the Serbian Orthodox Church, though, it was impossible to bring him to heel, for his war record was impeccable. He had vigorously opposed the Nazi invasion of the country and suffered for it in the notorious Dachau concentration camp. His personal prestige was enormous, but after his death in 1950 the government brought strong pressure to bear on the Church to elect Bishop Vikentije to succeed him in the Patriarchate. Assessments of Vikentije's leadership vary considerably. Some say that he was weak but obstinate, others that he was shrewd and diplomatic. Whatever the final verdict, he led his church through eight difficult years and kept it out of serious trouble with the government, without giving way on the two subjects about which his church felt most strongly: recognition of the government-sponsored priests' associations and the demands of the Macedonian dioceses for independence. In the long run, the avoidance of trouble with the government may have helped the Orthodox Church considerably, because it was necessary at this time for the Church to recover some of its former strength, after the harrowing years of war, rather than become involved in a confrontation with the State. In any event, it lacked resources for a sustained and effective confrontation.

During the Patriarchate of Vikentije and in the early years of his successor, German, the government brought pressure to bear on the churches through the encouragement of priests' associations. There had been associations of Orthodox priests in Serbia since 1889 and these aimed to give the lower clergy some voice in the government of their church, e.g. over the appointment of priests to parishes and the election of bishops. They were generally opposed by the ecclesiastical authorities. Shortly after the end of the war meetings were held of priests who had been partisans or assisted the underground forces, and during the next few years associations were formed or revived in all the republics. On the Catholic side, priests' associations came into existence for the first time, and today the most authentic and important of them are in Slovenia and Bosnia and Hercegovina. The government saw in the priests' associations an opportunity for dividing the churches and bringing pressure to bear on the bishops, so they attempted to secure the enrolment of all the priests in one or other of the associations. Arrangements for health insurance and social security benefits were made only through the associations, while clergy who were in prison were often promised remission of their sentences if they joined an association. However, not all who joined were responding to government pressure or seeking personal advantages. Some priests saw the associations as providing an opportunity for reforming and liberalizing their churches, but unfortunately the credibility of the associations was destroyed by the extent to which the government used them, or attempted to use them, as tools of its own policy. Hence their reforming influence has been somewhat limited, though the Association of Serbian Orthodox Priests has done good work in promoting the idea of a social Gospel. The hierarchies of both the Orthodox and Catholic churches (especially the Catholic) have always been strenuously opposed to the priests' associations, seeing in them not only the danger of state influence but also a growing challenge to their own authority. Today the government deals directly with the hierarchies and no longer needs the associations as intermediaries; their principal function now is that of a professional association for the clergy, concerning themselves with social insurance and similar matters. The Protestants and Muslims also have their associations.

Although the early years of the 1950s saw the churches facing very considerable difficulties and much hardship, the second half of that decade can now be seen as a time when the pressure began to ease. Once again, it is difficult to disentangle what appears to have been a mixture of motives behind the changed attitude towards the churches. Was the State, in the more relaxed atmosphere of the late 1950s – with wartime memories receding into the background – deliberately seeking to implement its declared policy of leaving the churches to order their own affairs? Having failed to break the churches, did the Communists decide that the unity and purposefulness of the nation would be best promoted through tolerance? Or did the government which had broken with Moscow deliberately begin to seek Western support and come to recognize that it would gain little sympathy from the West if its image remained that of the persecutor? Probably it was a mixture of all these factors, and the relaxation of pressure on the churches cannot be seen in isolation from the general easing of repression which began to characterize the whole life of Yugoslavia at this time and which has made the country unique in Eastern Europe.

In 1966 a Protocol was signed by the Vatican and the Yugoslav government and envoys were exchanged. The separation of Church and State was reaffirmed, together with guarantees of freedom of conscience and religion. The Protocol also recognized the Vatican's jurisdiction over the Roman Catholic Church in spiritual, religious and ecclesiastical affairs. But the Vatican agreed that Catholic priests and bishops should not interfere in the political life of the country. Not everyone in Yugoslavia was happy with this Protocol which was negotiated over the heads of the Catholic bishops, who were never consulted at any point and were simply presented with a *fait accompli*. The Catholic clergy were deeply offended by a clause in the agreement which referred to possible 'terrorist activities of priests'.

By 1970 full diplomatic relations between Belgrade and the Holy See were restored, and in the same year President Tito paid an official visit to Pope Paul VI. In his speech to the Pope he said that Yugoslavia respected the independence and sovereignty of all peoples and would like to see all forms of discrimination and exploitation abolished. Pope Paul spoke of Yugoslavia's great

religious traditions, praised the principles underlying the constitutional structure of the country, and promised the President that
he need not fear any interference by the Church in the State's
legitimate field of authority. The meeting was seen not only as
a sign of the Yugoslav government's desire for good relations
with the Roman Catholic Church but also as one of the fruits of
a new Vatican policy aiming at a *modus vivendi* with the
Communist governments of Eastern Europe.

Before another year had passed, however, there was a marked
change in government policy. During 1971 a growing Croat
nationalist sentiment developed into what Tito described as
'national euphoria', and which the government believed to be a
threat to the unity of the Federation. In December of that year
the President struck hard. The leaders of the Croatian League
of Communists – many of them highly regarded in the life of the
country as a whole – were dismissed and replaced by representatives of the more conservative, hardline elements in the
Communist Party. This was followed by the resignation of liberal
leaders in all the republics and their replacement by hardliners,
thus indicating that the change of policy was not only concerned
with nationalism but represented a conservative backlash
against liberalization. The churches, particularly but not exclusively the Catholic Church, did not escape attention in the
crackdown. Several issues of *Glas Koncila* were banned for
including what was alleged to be nationalist propaganda, and
both the editor of the newspaper and a woman journalist on its
staff were given prison sentences (in the case of the editor the
sentence was suspended) in the years between 1973 and 1975.
The secular press launched a fierce attack on Archbishop
Kuharic of Zagreb, the president of the Catholic Bishops'
Conference, accusing him and some other bishops of supporting
the dismissed Croatian Communist leaders. About the same time
the Serbian Orthodox Bishop Vasilije of Zica was sentenced to
thirty days in prison for 'hostile propaganda', and in various
parts of the country schoolteachers were dismissed for attending
church. But there was no all-out attack on the churches, and
during the closing years of Tito's rule it appears to have been
deliberate government policy to include the churches and

believers in the national unity of the country which was being
fostered in every possible way.

---

This continues to be the government's policy now that Tito has
gone. Pressure on the churches is still strong, though it is slightly
easier than it was in 1974. Bishops and other church leaders are
attacked from time to time in the press and in the speeches of
Communist Party officials, the usual line being that they
represent a reactionary 'clericalism' which is aiming to secure
political influence and power. The ethos of the schools is atheist
and there is very little possibility of a known religious believer
holding any significant position in public life. A few priests are
in prison for what are said to be political offences, and local
problems arise occasionally when a government official become
over-zealous in applying a particular interpretation of the law.
On the other hand, the government is clearly trying to draw the
churches into its constant effort to bind the Yugoslav people into
a closer and more stable unity. Thus at the end of 1979 the tough
chairman of the central committee of the League of Communists
of Croatia, Jakov Blazevic, who was actually the public
prosecutor at the trial of Archbishop Stepinac, condemned the
use of hardline administrative methods against believers and the
churches, and went on to say that religious belief must not
become an obstacle to the co-operation of believers in realizing
the common interests of all citizens. Shortly after this, in 1980,
Dr Vladimir Bakaric, a veteran Croatian Communist leader, said
in a newspaper interview that atheism was a movement of the
nineteenth century, and he added:

> We have nothing to do with this for the simple Marxist reason
> that we know the Church cannot be abolished, it lives in
> people's heads ... it is stupid to fight against the Church as
> a religious institution. Our criteria are not 'Are you an atheist
> or not?' but 'Are you for or against socialism? Are you for or
> against world peace?'; everything else takes second place.

During 1980 there was a good deal of public discussion about the
involvement of religious people in the Socialist Alliance, an
umbrella organization that undertakes social as well as political
work, and on 16 March of that year Mitija Ribicic, president of

the Socialist Alliance of Slovenia, said in an interview published in the daily newspaper *Vjesnik*:

> The Socialist Alliance must realize that it is not made up only of people with a Marxist orientation, but that there are many people who are religious, or if they are not religious are still not Marxist-orientated but nevertheless support self-management, the policy of non-alignment and in general are favourable to our system ... Local organizations must adopt a policy of association with these elements. Religion must not be an obstacle to equal participation of people in socialist life and society. We must tell people quite clearly that the private religious life, or attendance at religious rites, is in no sense clericalism.

Statements of this sort indicate that it is possible in Yugoslavia to accept socialism, and to work for the development of a socialist society, without accepting the doctrines of Marxism, and this is precisely what the sixty theologians who belong to the theological association *Krscanska Sadasnjost* (Contemporary Christianity) are now attempting to do. The association was founded when Cardinal Seper was Archbishop of Zagreb and was originally intended to encourage post-Vatican II research, documentation and information. So it remained until July 1977, when under the leadership of Yugoslavia's most able theologian, Dr Tomislav Sagi-Bunic, the members of the group decided to widen the association's aims and register it with the State. The main point of this was to obtain certain tax concessions and social security benefits, but the government welcomed the association as a sign that a religious body was prepared to work along the lines of self-management socialism. The Catholic bishops were not consulted about this move and quickly denounced it, fearing that it represented a divisive movement within the Church and also indicated improper collaboration with the Communist authorities. Archbishop Franic of Split was particularly fierce in his denunciation of the association and has forbidden any of his clergy to join it. Members of the association are not now allowed to hold any posts of responsibility in the Church and this has removed Dr Sagi-Bunic and his colleague, the philosopher Dr V. Bajsic, from their positions as heads of the Catholic theological faculty.

The Catholic bishops are generally conservative in outlook, and this is creating a certain amount of frustration in some dioceses in Croatia where the many younger priests are keen to implement the teaching of Vatican II. Archbishop Kuharic of Zagreb, the president of the Bishops' Conference, is personally conservative but less heavy-handed than some of his colleagues, and he has grown greatly in stature since he became leader of the Catholic Church in Yugoslavia. His approach is pastoral rather than intellectual, but he has kept in touch with the theological association and, though usually discreet, he has on some occasions been outspoken. When, early in 1981, Jakov Blazevic went back on all that he had said a few months previously about not attacking the Church, and launched a most intemperate attack on the late Cardinal Stepinac, following this up with a blunderbuss volley at the present Archbishop of Zagreb for defending Stepinac's memory, Kuharic defended himself promptly and with spirit. He has also spoken out against atheist indoctrination in schools. Some recent appointments to the hierarchy suggest that a different kind of bishop is now beginning to appear in Yugoslavia. Mgr Koksa, for many years rector of the Croatian College in Rome, is now assistant bishop of Zagreb. Mgr Sustar, who succeeded to the Archbishopric of Ljubljana, came from Switzerland where he was originally sent for health reasons and eventually became secretary of the European Conference of Bishops. The experience of these two men is therefore much wider than that of most of the other Catholic bishops. Again, the new Archbishop of Belgrade, Mgr Aloyz Turk, addressed himself to the Serbian Orthodox Church soon after his appointment and placed all his work, his apostolate and ecumenical endeavours under the protection of Mary, the 'most holy Mother of God whom Catholics and Orthodox equally venerate'. He went on to exhort Catholics in Serbia to represent their church worthily by their works of brotherhood and service, co-operation and helpfulness, and called on the two churches to 'see which can do most to build true brotherliness on the road to full unity in Christ'.

    The death of President Tito in May 1980 has inevitably brought a new element of uncertainty into the life of Yugoslavia, and it has yet to be seen how the new form of government, based on a collective nine-man presidency with a rotating leadership, will work. The churches share in this uncertainty, and it is not a new experience for any of them, but they are aware that it is in their own best interest, as well as that of the Yugoslav people as a whole, to avoid conflict and to work for a greater sense of unity within the Federation. The Catholic and Orthodox communities have a great deal to contribute to this quest for social and political unity, and they are better equipped to make their contribution than for many years past.

# Chapter 10

# ALBANIA

Albania is a land of martyrs. In no other country in the world are fundamental human rights so completely denied, and in no other place is the persecution of religious believers so relentless. An official proclamation in the capital, Tirana, in 1967, declared Albania to be 'the first atheist state in the world', and since then all public expressions of religious belief have been illegal. Church buildings and mosques have been destroyed or converted to secular use, religious leaders have been imprisoned or executed, and no visible signs of religious practice are to be found anywhere in the country. The present constitution, drafted in 1976, states the Communist government's position clearly:

> The State recognizes no religion and supports and develops atheist propaganda for the purpose of implanting the scientific materialist world outlook in people. (Article 36)
> The creation of any type of organization of a fascist, anti-democratic, religious or anti-socialist character is prohibited. (Article 54)

And lest any shadow of doubt concerning their attitude should remain, the humourless leaders of the Albanian Communist Party attacked the Soviet Union in August 1977 for allegedly slackening its anti-religious struggle and for treating with 'the chieftain of the world's reactionaries' – Pope Paul VI.

There is a tradition that St Paul preached within Albania's mountainous territory during his travels in Illyricum, and Franciscan missionaries arrived in the middle of the thirteenth century. But from 1467 to 1912 Albania was under Turkish rule, and even after its independence had been proclaimed shortly before the outbreak of the First World War, the nation – which at that time had only about one million inhabitants – was under constant threat from its Greek, Italian and Serbian neighbours. The Italian army eventually invaded Albania on Good Friday 1939, the rest of the world hardly noticing this act of aggression, and the country remained under enemy occupation until the German army withdrew in 1944. The population of this tiny country of 11,000 square miles has doubled since the end of the Second World War and is now about 2.5 million. Three-quarters of the population have been born since the People's Republic was established in 1946, and contraception is officially discouraged. The years of Communist rule have been a time of massive industrialization and agrarian reform. All industry belongs to the State and virtually all land is owned by the State or by State-run co-operatives. The growth rate has been phenomenal, though the country is still very poor.

When the German army withdrew from Albania in November 1944 a provisional government was formed by leaders of the resistance movement who constituted the National Liberation Front. Communists dominated the NLF, and accepted the leadership of Enver Hoxha who had been responsible for the formation of an illegal Communist Party of Albania in 1941. The British, American and Russian governments recognized the provisional government in 1945 after Hoxha had given certain assurances about free elections, but when the elections were held a month later they were far from being free. The NLF changed its name to the Democratic Front and was the only political organization permitted to nominate candidates. Not surprisingly, it obtained 95 per cent of all the votes cast.

During the next three years relations with the new Communist regime in neighbouring Yugoslavia were uneasy, and when Yugoslavia was expelled from the Cominform in 1948 Albania sided with the Soviet Union, with some relief, and began to look to Moscow for inspiration and economic assistance. Russian military advisers moved in and Russians held certain key positions in the life of the country, but there was a break with Moscow and most of the other Warsaw Pact countries in 1961 after the Soviet government had publicly accused Hoxha and his colleagues of pursuing Stalinist policies and they in turn had accused Khrushchev of 'revisionism'. At this point China supported Albania, and from 1962 to 1978 Albania had close economic and political relations with China. These fell apart after the death of Chairman Mao, when the new Chinese leadership began to seek better relations with the West and a stronger alliance with Yugoslavia and Romania in the Balkans.

Albania has no diplomatic relations with either the United States or the Soviet Union and is now completely isolated.

When the last religious census was taken, in 1945, 70 per cent of the population were said to be Muslim, including a large membership of the Bektashi sect, a pantheistic group, 20 per cent Orthodox and 10 per cent Roman Catholic. There were also a handful of Jews. Initially the Hoxha regime aimed simply to reduce the influence of religion and of the churches. Religious instruction of young people was forbidden, all forms of religious communication were censored, the churches were forbidden to undertake social work, the State controlled all church appointments, church lands and revenues were confiscated. The leaders of the religious communities naturally resisted these measures and in consequence were sent to prisons or labour camps. In February 1948 four Roman Catholic bishops were executed, and in the same year Archbishop Nikolla Prenushi of Durres was sentenced to twenty years' imprisonment; he died soon after being sentenced, in unknown circumstances. In August 1949, a few months after two Orthodox bishops had been sent to prison, the Metropolitan of Tirana, Kristofor Kisi, was deposed, for allegedly plotting to make his church into an Eastern-Rite Catholic (Uniate) community under the Vatican. Contrary to the Orthodox tradition, Metropolitan Kisi was replaced by a married priest who was also a Communist sympathizer.

According to the government, it was intended that religion should be a private affair. The constitution of 1946 (revised in 1950, amended in 1953, 1954, 1955, 1958, 1960 and 1963, and replaced in 1976) said:

> All citizens are guaranteed freedom of conscience and of faith. The Church is separated from the State. The religious communities are free in matters of their belief as well as in their outward exercise and practice. It is prohibited to use the Church and religion for political purposes. Political organizations on a religious basis are likewise prohibited. The State may give material aid to religious communities. (Article 18)

But within five years all religious practice was under rigid State control. In 1951 the Catholic Church was forced to sever its links with Rome in order to become a national Church, with its own statute acknowledging its complete subordination to the State. Members of the government and Communist Party officials also embarked on an intensive campaign designed to discredit religious belief and to alienate the people from religious institutions. The religious world outlook and the Communist world outlook were said to be irreconcilable, while the clergy were held up as the enemies of socialism and therefore of the people. The Catholic Church was subjected to special attention, partly because of its international connections, but also because it had, during the long years of Ottoman rule, played an important part in maintaining Albania's national traditions and values.

The campaign against religion continued throughout the 1950s, and the way was thus prepared for the actual suppression of religious institutions in the 1960s. Just why the Albanian government should have embarked upon a policy of complete suppression at a time when most of the other East European governments were beginning to accept that they needed to reach some sort of accommodation with the churches and other religious institutions, is far from clear. One theory is that after their break with Moscow in 1961 the rulers of Albania decided to move quickly towards the creation of a purely totalitarian society – the first of its kind in the world – and this meant breaking away from all outside influences and also obliterating all rival ideologies within the country. Another view is that the Hoxha regime's antagonism to religion owes more to nationalism than to socialism. The Albanians are a proud people and a nineteenth-century slogan, coined by the poet Vaso Pasha, asserts that 'The religion of the Albanians is Albanianism'. Certainly they tend to be very suspicious of foreigners (fewer than 10,000 visitors are admitted annually), which is not altogether surprising in view of their experience of foreign powers in the past. The Atheist Museum in Tirana, which exhibits old Communion hosts in a pyx, monstrance and ciborium taken from a church in 1967, also attempts to show, by means of photographs and documents, that the Muslim, Orthodox and Catholic faiths were used by Turkey, Greece and Italy respectively when these countries were occupying Albania.

Whatever the explanation, an 'ideological and cultural revolution' was initiated in 1967, and soon afterwards the statutes governing relations between the State and the religious communities were annulled. The 2,169 buildings used for public worship were closed, and the Catholic cathedrals in Tirana, Scutari and Durres were defaced. What this was to mean for the Catholic Church in Albania was explained in the official Vatican newspaper *L'Osservatore Romano* on 26 April 1973:

> Places of worship either no longer exist or have been transformed into dance halls, gymnasia or offices of various kinds. Scutari cathedral has become the 'Sports Palace', a swimming pool with showers has been constructed in place of the presbytery and sacristy; the artistic bell-tower that soared above it has been razed to the ground. The ancient canonry chapel at Scutari, used as a baptistry, among other things, has become a warehouse for tyres. The church of St Nicholas in the Catholic district of Rusi has been transformed into flats for factory workers. The church of the Stigmatine Sisters has become a lecture hall, the one of the Institute of the Sisters of St Elizabeth is used as the headquarters of the political police. The national sanctuary of Our Lady of Scutari, 'Protectress of Albania', has been pulled down. On its ruins there now rises a column surmounted by the red star.

In 1939 there were 203 Catholic priests in Albania, of whom 62 were foreign, and there were also 165 monks and nuns, of whom 76 were foreign. By 1971 only fourteen priests were known about, twelve of them in prison camps, the other two in hiding. Within two years the number in prison had been reduced to thirteen, when Father Shtjefen Kurti was executed by a firing squad for baptizing a child at Lushnje in South Albania. Father Kurti was in fact first sentenced to death in 1945, having been charged with 'spying for the Vatican'. This sentence was commuted to life imprisonment, and eighteen years later he was released from prison. He then returned to parish work, but when the government declared all religious practices to be illegal he took a secular job as a clerk in a co-operative. Soon after this soldiers arrived to destroy Father Kurti's parish church, and he fought them with his fists. For this offence he was sentenced to a further sixteen years' imprisonment, but he continued to exercise his priesthood secretly, and during the early part of 1973 a woman prisoner asked him to baptize her child. The ceremony took place privately, but news of it reached the authorities who once again put the seventy-year-old priest on trial and later handed him over to a military firing squad. Albanian radio said that he had been executed for spying on behalf of the Vatican, the United States and Britain. Reports reaching the West in November 1980 stated that Bishop Coba, formerly Apostolic Administrator of the Catholic diocese of Scutari, who had been in a prison camp for many years, was murdered there on Easter Day 1979 for having said mass in contravention of prison regulations.

In 1975 the entire hierarchy of the Orthodox Church and most of the Orthodox clergy were believed to be in prison, the head of the Albanian Orthodox Church, Archbishop Damian, having died there in 1973 at the age of eighty. Nothing is known of the whereabouts of the Muslim leadership.

Although the government's efforts to destroy institutional religion in Albania have been entirely successful, its campaign against personal religious belief and private religious practice appears to have achieved a good deal less than the Communist Party hoped for. On 1 June 1975 the Albanian Communist Party newspaper *Zeri i Popullit* reported disapprovingly that in some areas of the country 'there have been occasions when religious services have been held, such as baptism or circumcision; or worshippers have requested masses from ex-priests. They have celebrated the Easter Vigil, the Feast of St Nicholas and Easter; in some areas Ramadan and Lent are kept.' The report went on to describe certain disguised religious activities: 'Instead of a cross, a laurel branch is used; baptism is celebrated in other ways – by gifts; suppers and dinners are held for the "spirits of the dead".' The clandestine manufacture of new religious objects was also noted: 'Crosses from cloth; rosaries from olive stones, which are also peddled; blessings are found in the dowry of brides.' The newspaper, which had complained in 1973 that even some secretaries of Communist Party organizations and bureaux had 'fallen into religious positions', called for an intensification of the struggle against 'religious remnants'. In the same issue of the newspaper, Dr Arif Gashi, a Communist Party specialist on religion, referred to the impact which religious ideology was still having on young people, especially when family influence remained strong.

A year later, in 1976, the newspaper *Bashkimi* complained that a decline in 'revolutionary vigilance' had led to the reactivation of certain religious ceremonies in several districts, and in 1977 a series of scientific meetings on the theme 'The Struggle against Religion' were held throughout the country. Among Muslims fasting for Ramadan is still commonly observed, and in some districts Muslim graves still face Mecca. In July 1975 the official Communist Party organ *Rruga e Partisi* noted that some women in rural areas were not doing any washing on Fridays, and asked why some girls who were supposed to have embroidery lessons on Fridays were not taking up their needles on that day. The government promulgated a new anti-religious decree in May 1979, which states that any person involved in underground religious activity can be sent to a prison camp without trial.

Whether the government's efforts to destroy religious belief and practice completely will eventually be successful is impossible to predict. Students of Albanian history recall that during the four and a half centuries of Turkish rule some of those who had been more or less forcibly converted to Islam persisted in secret Christian practices and belief. After thirty years of anti-religious propaganda and ruthless repression under Communism in the present century, there is mounting evidence that the Albanian religious consciousness is more resilient than the state authorities anticipated.

# Chapter 11

# BULGARIA

The history of Christianity in Bulgaria is long, chequered and often unhappy. There were Christian missionaries in the territory now known as Bulgaria in the sixth and seventh centuries, but others had been there before them, as the remarkably preserved fourth- and fifth-century church of St George in Sofia vividly testifies. It was however St Cyril and St Methodius, the 'apostles of the Slavs', and their disciples who were responsible for the conversion of the people as a whole in the ninth century and at the same time were laying the foundations of the Slavonic script which was destined to have a profound influence on the culture and liturgy of Eastern Europe. Soon after it had been reported to Pope Nicholas I, in about 862, that 'a great majority of the Bulgarians are converted to Christianity' a dispute arose as to whether the Bulgarian Church was to be within the jurisdiction of Rome or Constantinople. A Council held at Constantinople in 870 decided that Bulgaria should belong to the Orthodox East, and in 919 the church of the country was considered sufficiently important to be raised to a Patriarchate. This distinction was short-lived, for in 1018 Bulgaria came under Byzantine domination and the Patriarchate was suppressed, though the church retained its autocephalous status as the Archbishopric of Ochrid. The re-establishment of the Bulgarian State in 1186 led to the restoration of the Patriarchate in 1235, but this lasted for only just over 150 years, as Bulgaria fell to the Turkish Ottoman Empire in 1393 and remained within it for almost five centuries.

During the long years of the 'Ottoman yoke' many Bulgarians emigrated to Russia and other Balkan countries; at the same time a considerable number of Turks came to live in Bulgaria. Many churches were destroyed or converted into mosques, and the discovery in the present century of small churches dug into the earth in Sofia is a reminder of times of severe repression. Greek leadership and Greek ecclesiastical control were imposed by the Ottoman rulers, and in some periods there were campaigns to convert the people to Islam. But the church retained its independent spirit, and the monasteries became important centres not only of Christian faith but also of Bulgarian national identity. They carried out educational work, and travelling monks helped to keep alive the faith and spirit of the nation in many isolated communities. It was in fact a history of the Slav-Bulgarian people by an eighteenth-century monk, St Paissi of Hilandar, which helped to bring about the Bulgarian revival in the nineteenth century, and the uprising in 1876, which was followed by the Russo-Turkish war of liberation, was plotted in certain monasteries. This war broke the Turkish stranglehold on Bulgaria and led to the birth, in 1878, of the modern Bulgarian State. The Orthodox Church was an integral part of this State and a Bulgarian Exarchate, given independence once more, had been achieved in 1870.

During the next seventy years the country experienced successes and disasters which have left their mark on it ever since. The first and most traumatic disappointment occurred at birth. Russia had planned a 'Great Bulgaria', extending far west and embracing Macedonia and Salonica, nominally still tributary to the Sultan but expected to be suitably grateful to its liberators. This was disallowed by the other leading powers, and a much reduced scheme took its place. Building on this, Bulgaria not only enlarged its borders without war but by the end of the nineteenth century was generally regarded as the most prosperous, efficient and progressive of the Balkan States. It became formally independent in 1908. This achievement was seriously damaged by the outcome of the Second Balkan War (1913) and the First World War. In the First Balkan War (1912) Bulgaria was a leading member of the Balkan Alliance against the Turks and won impressive victories in the field, but owing again to rivalries between the Great Powers, the division of the territorial spoils previously agreed between the allies was upset and Bulgaria attacked her partners and was defeated. Hoping to recoup her losses, she came into the First World War on the side of the Central Powers in 1915, only to lose the modest access to the Aegean which was all the earlier war had brought her.

The interwar years were a time of unrest and disorder. The

leader of the radical Agrarian government was assassinated in 1923, and during a period of political instability government was by coups rather than consent. In the end King Boris took matters into his own hands and, after getting rid of the military and other extremists who had seized power, he set up an authoritarian regime of his own in 1935. Still hoping to secure the lost territories, Bulgaria moved into the Second World War on the side of the German-Italian axis in 1941, and was rewarded by being allowed to occupy part of Yugoslavia. But the people as a whole became increasingly uneasy about this alliance, particularly when Germany invaded Russia. In spite of pressure from Hitler, no Bulgarian troops were sent to Russia, with whom Bulgaria remained in theory at peace until the very end of the war, when a Russian declaration of war became necessary in order to justify the entry of the Red Army into the country. By the time the Russian troops arrived, there were revolutionary forces ready to seize power and open the way for a post-war Communist government. The monarchy was abolished in 1946 and the following year a new constitution, modelled on that of the USSR, was adopted. Since then, Bulgaria has been one of the Soviet Union's most faithful satellites. The reason for this is to be found not simply in post-war power politics but also in the deep gratitude felt by the Bulgarian people for the part played by Russia in freeing their country from the Turks.

Today Bulgaria has a population of about nine million, of whom 650,000 are Turks, 200,000 Gypsies, 30,000 Armenians and 5,000 Jews. The country is still largely agrarian but it is becoming industrialized and under Communism great efforts have been made in this direction. Some 98.5 per cent of all arable land is owned by the State, and the peasant farming of the past has been replaced by large collective farms. There is now hardly any illiteracy among people under sixty years of age. In 1971 the Communist Party was said to have a membership of about 700,000.

---

Reliable figures about religious belief and practice in Bulgaria are not easy to come by, and tend to vary according to the source of the information, but statistics published in 1975 by the Ecumenical Department of the Holy Synod of the Bulgarian Orthodox Church in a booklet *Churches and Religions in the*

*People's Republic of Bulgaria* agree with some other, independently published, figures and are probably fairly accurate. The number of Orthodox Christians is about six million, i.e. just under 75 per cent of the total population. In the case of older people this generally means that they were baptized in the Orthodox Church and may perhaps attend the liturgy regularly, at least at great festivals. As far as young people are concerned, their connection with the church is likely to be more tenuous, though many of them still regard the Orthodox Church as 'our church', even if they rarely attend apart from family occasions such as weddings and funerals. There are about 3,700 Orthodox churches and chapels in 2,600 parishes, served by just over 1,500 priests. (In 1938 there were 2,486 priests.) Many of the 120 monastic communities are very small, and the monks and nuns number about four hundred. The country is divided into eleven dioceses, the bishops of which have the title Metropolitan. Each bishop is assisted by a council of elected priests and laymen, and the Holy Synod – which is the supreme spiritual authority for the whole church – consists of all the metropolitans. There is also a permanent synod of five, of which the Patriarch is an *ex officio* member, and the bishops are elected to it for a period of four years. Clergy are trained at the Academy of St Clement of Ochrid, which was until 1950 a constituent part of the University of Sofia and has room for about 120 students. There is also a theological seminary at the Cerepish monastery, about forty-five miles from Sofia, which can accommodate two hundred students; it announced that forty-five places were available for the year 1976–77, thirty of these for students under the age of seventeen who would have a five-year course, followed by military service, and fifteen for students under thirty-five years of age who would attend for three years.

The Roman Catholic Church has always been regarded as a foreign element in Bulgaria, though it played its full part in the country's struggle for freedom in the nineteenth century. In 1975 the number of Latin-Rite Catholics was reported as being in the region of 50,000, worshipping in thirty churches and served by two bishops and about fifty priests. A government official said in 1972 that there were four Catholic monasteries with 113 nuns and some monks, but by 1980 the number of nuns had declined to seventy. Eastern-Rite (Uniate) Catholics number about 10,000 in twenty-five parishes, served by twenty priests and headed by a bishop who is known as an Apostolic Exarch. In contrast with Communist policy in other parts of Eastern Europe, no attempt has been made to absorb the Uniates into the Orthodox Church.

The Protestant churches are small communities and trace their origins to the work of foreign missions in the latter part of the nineteenth century. The Congregational Church came from America in the early 1860s, and within ten years had translated the Bible into Bulgarian. This church now has about 5,000 members in fifty-two churches or communities, served by the same number of pastors. The Methodist Church came from America in the late 1850s, and today it has about 1,300 members, fifteen churches and fifteen pastors. The Baptist Church was founded in 1871 by missionaries from Russia, but it has made little progress and has only 650 members in ten churches and nine communities. Representatives of the Baptist World Alliance, making their first post-war visit to Bulgaria in 1978, noted a shortage of places of worship and a very elderly church leadership. The Seventh Day Adventists came from the Crimean peninsula in 1891, and they now have about 3,000 members and forty pastors. Easily the largest and most active of the Protestant communities is the Pentecostal Church, which began its mission in 1921 when émigré Russian Pentecostals came to Bulgaria from the United States. It now has about 10,000 members and 120 churches, with a presence in all the main towns and a Pentecostal Union with its headquarters in Sofia. The so-called Tinchevists, named after their founder Stoyan Tinchev, are Pentecostals who separated from the mainstream church in 1928 because they do not believe it is right to have church buildings or any kind of ecclesiastical organization; they also reject all forms of medical aid. There is no Protestant theological seminary, but a few Protestant students are sometimes admitted to the Orthodox theological academy.

There have been Armenian Christians in Bulgaria since the seventh century, with comings and goings among them across the years, the last influx being in 1922 when 20,000 came from Turkey. Today there are about 20,000 baptized Armenians, twelve churches and ten priests, under an archbishop for Romania and Bulgaria who resides in Bucharest.

After Orthodox Christians, the Muslims are the largest religious group in Bulgaria, and they live mainly in the north-east of the country and in the Rhodope region. Altogether they number about 800,000, or just under 10 per cent of the population. The great majority of these are Muslim Turks who have 1,180 mosques and about 500 imams. The Muslim Bulgarians (Pomaks) have 120 mosques and about 100 imams. There is a Chief Mufti and one madrassah (Koranic school) for the training of imams. As recently as 1956 the two Muslim communities were served by 2,715 imams.

In pre-war Bulgaria there were about 50,000 Jews, the majority of whom survived the war, thanks mainly to King Boris, who had the Bulgarian Jews scattered into remote villages. The Bulgarian Orthodox Church also played a significant part in the protection of the Jews, and made a courageous stand against anti-Semitism. There were actually more Jews in Bulgaria in 1945 than there had been in the 1930s. Between 1948 and 1955, however, over 40,000 of them emigrated to Israel, and today there are only about 5,000 left, of whom 3,000 live in Sofia, 600 at Plovdiv and the rest are distributed throughout the country. There is a central synagogue at Sofia and others at Plovdiv, Ruse and Varna, but there are no rabbis; lay people carry out their functions.

Publishers of religious literature experience difficulty in securing adequate supplies of paper, and the circulations of magazines and periodicals are consequently quite small. The Holy Synod of the Orthodox Church publishes *Tsarkoven Vestnik* (Church Gazette) weekly, and this contains news of church life in the dioceses and parishes, together with articles on religious themes and an arts section. *Douhvna Kultura* (Spiritual Culture) is a monthly magazine concerned with religion, philosophy, science and art. The Academy of St Clement of Ochrid publishes a yearbook containing articles on academic theology, written mainly by the teaching staff of the Academy. The recently created Church Historical Institute has also published a series of academic studies. The other churches have few opportunities for publishing their own material. The Baptists have a small periodical, and the Pentecostals and Methodists produce a limited number of calendars every year. There are no Catholic publications, and a common complaint among Protestant pastors is that they have no aids to their preaching and teaching ministry apart from books published prior to the Second World War. The Jewish community publishes a bi-monthly, *Jewish News*, and also a yearbook.

In 1972 a new translation of the New Testament and the Psalms into Bulgarian was completed. This was the result of seven years' work by Orthodox scholars, who asked Roman Catholic and Protestant theologians to read and comment on their translation at different stages, in the hope that the final version would be acceptable to all the Christian churches in Bulgaria. The new translation has not yet been published, however, as it was thought best to publish first a text which is only a slight revision of the traditional version of the Bible. The United Bible Societies provided paper for 30,000 copies of this slight revision, which appeared in 1981. Copies of the Bible are not available in bookshops, and the Bulgarian Orthodox Church is not over-concerned about Bible distribution, though most of the people who wish to have a Bible seem to have acquired one from somewhere. No difficulty is experienced when other books are sent to church libraries through official channels, such as the World Council of Churches, the Vatican and the Society for Promoting Christian Knowledge.

---

Today the Orthodox Church enjoys far greater freedom than it could ever have thought possible during the Stalinist era. This freedom is hedged around by many restrictions imposed by a harsh, atheistic government, and the situation is a long way from ideal. But the Orthodox clergy are free to order their parishes on the traditional pattern, with regular celebrations of the liturgy and as much pastoral work as they have energy or inclination to tackle. Organized work among young people is still not permitted; nor is political and social comment from the pulpit. In the towns and larger villages, however, the church often has a parish fellowship open to Christians of all ages, which provides opportunities for teaching, pastoral and restricted social work. This is an important part of the church's life.

Easter processions continue to be popular, and in recent years it has been rare for any of these to be interrupted by militant Communists. A visitor to the Cathedral of St Alexander Nevsky at Easter 1973 noted the presence of several hundred young people in the congregation. Very large numbers attend the regular concerts of fine music given by the St Alexander Nevsky choir, and there is a remarkable exhibition of icons in the cathedral crypt. After the Russians, the Bulgarians have the best church choirs in the Orthodox world. A growing number of people are reported to be visiting the monasteries on feast days, and also for baptisms and marriages.

Another English visitor to Bulgaria reported in 1973:

I used to go fairly frequently to the cathedral of St Alexander Nevsky in Sofia, and perhaps got something of the feel of things there. There was always a modest crowd of people for the Vigil Service on Saturday nights (Vespers and Matins) which included quite a high proportion of young people. But most of them gave the appearance of being casual or curious visitors, who had little understanding of what was going on. Archimandrite Dometian, Chief Secretary of the Holy Synod, and now Bishop of the Orthodox diocese of Akron, Ohio, said that there is a vast amount of ignorance among young people about the basic facts of Christianity. The numbers of regular worshippers seemed small.

There was usually a fair congregation for the liturgy on such occasions as I was able to go. But since that was generally on feast days, when the Patriarch was celebrating, that is perhaps not a fair picture. I was told that there is always a reasonable congregation where the Patriarch is, but that the other churches in Sofia were less well attended.

One of the other churches I occasionally went to was a small church in the centre of the city, which was a hive of activity. There were generally several priests on duty, and always numbers of people, either confessing, or talking with a priest, or attending special, short prayer services, probably for the dead. That was a balancing contrast to the cathedral, where the impression was generally that of a splendid performance, with good singing, attended by the faithful and elderly few, with many sightseers. I was never able to go to St Nedelya on a Sunday. One weekday liturgy I went to had a very poor congregation. I was told that that church was much in demand for weddings.

Of the monasteries, I visited Rila, the great national monastery of Bulgaria. It is very much a tourist attraction, with about ten or a dozen monks, as far as I could see. I did not have the opportunity of getting to know any of the monks personally, and so cannot say what quality of life is lived behind the touristic façade. The other was Bachkovo, in south-east Bulgaria, with about twenty monks. There is certainly an impressive atmosphere there, and the present Abbot gives the impression of being a genuine monk.

There is no direct evidence of Party members attending church, though it is said that some of them do and that in some places these encounter greater hostility from church members than from Party officials. In quite a lot of districts, priests play a prominent part in the organizing of social work, and occasionally find themselves acting as treasurer of the local co-operative. A few priests also serve on local councils. As in other parts of Eastern Europe, conflicts sometimes arise not because of government policy but when a local official takes the law into his own hands, or when a local priest and Party official do not find it easy to co-exist in the same community. In these instances someone from the Ministry of Cults visits the area and tries to sort things out. Hooliganism or destruction of church buildings is regarded as a serious crime by the State, with severe punishment for those found guilty.

Evangelistic activity is frowned on by the Communist authorities, and in December 1978 the Burgas local newspaper *Chernomorski Front* published an attack on the proselytizing activities of believers in general and of three Christians in particular. Yanko Hristo Zlatev, a member of the Orthodox Church and a planner at a Burgas cable factory, was accused of distributing material copied from religious books. Yulia Yaneva Dolchinkova, a middle-aged nurse who attends the Orthodox church of SS Cyril and Methodius in Burgas, was said to be sharing her faith with other people. Dinyo Rusev Mitev, described as an 'evangelist', has a small private workshop full of religious pictures, and it was reported that he shares his faith with those who visit the workshop. The author of the newspaper article went on to assert that, while the Bulgarian constitution gives individuals the right to hold personal beliefs, it does not permit individuals to share their beliefs with others.

The Orthodox Church is financed from a variety of sources, and in addition to the offerings of believers the Holy Synod receives 13 per cent of its annual income from government grants. The church has also been given an exclusive monopoly for the making of candles, crosses, icons and other religious articles. According to the booklet published in 1975 by the Holy Synod, the synodal candle workshop in Sofia, whose products are sold in churches and monasteries throughout the country, provides 58 per cent of the Bulgarian Orthodox Church's income, while a further 12 per cent comes from church utensils and souvenirs made in the synodal foundry. The church still owns about 3,500 hectares of land in the dioceses, which is either cultivated by the church or rented to co-operatives and state farms. There are eighty-one monastic farms, and the one at Bachkovo monastery is said to be the largest privately owned farm in the country. The State gives substantial grants every year for the repair and restoration of ancient churches and monasteries, chiefly, it seems, because of their value as tourist attractions and as evidence of the country's artistic heritage. Concern for this heritage was expressed in an article published in the Young Communist newspaper *Narodna Mladezh* on 27 July 1977. The writer complained that the Kuriliski monastery, founded in the tenth century, had lost its identity after being taken over by the local psychiatric hospital, while the Iskretski monastery had become part of a sanatorium, and the Podgumerski monastery had been turned into an asylum. Other monasteries which had been either demolished or allowed to fall into ruin were also mentioned.

Generally speaking, church buildings are no longer closed by government decree, but in 1978 reports reaching London indicated that several Protestant churches had been closed and confiscated by the government. The Baptist church in Russe, the Congregational church in Burgas, and the Methodist churches in Vidin and Gorna Mitropolia were mentioned, and it was suggested that the government was now aiming to reduce the Protestant presence to one interdenominational church in each place. In some ways, however, the non-Orthodox churches now have greater freedom than they enjoyed in the pre-Communist days, when it was impossible to be married outside the Orthodox Church and education was also in Orthodox hands. In theory these churches are, like the Orthodox, entitled to state subventions, but so far none has actually applied to the government for financial assistance. Since the late 1970s the Pentecostal Church has been experiencing a noticeable revival, and the number of young people attending church has increased considerably. The worship, held twice on Sundays and twice during the week, is lively, and in some places 'baptism in the Holy Spirit' and healings have been reported. Evangelistic campaigns are not allowed. Most of the pastors are untrained, yet the church is growing and its leaders appear to have less difficulty than most other non-Orthodox churchmen in obtaining permission to travel abroad for conferences and meetings. Meetings in homes are also being arranged by Pentecostals who are perhaps unhappy with their local official church or wish to experience a less-structured form of Christian fellowship. Some other 'underground' groups have been formed by the Christian Brethren, who are unable to register with the State because they have no official pastor; many of their members do not wish to have the church registered anyway.

The ecumenical movement is still in its early stages although some progress is being made. The delegation of the Bulgarian Orthodox Church to the World Council of Churches Assembly in Nairobi in 1975 was accompanied by a Congregationalist pastor, who was a fraternal delegate representing the Protestant churches in Bulgaria. Representatives of various Bulgarian churches were reported to have met for an ecumenical prayer meeting in the chapel of Sofia theological academy in February 1978, and during the following year a group of Bulgarian Orthodox clergy, led by Metropolitan Pankratij of Stara Zagora, visited Pope John Paul II in Rome and, in conveying the greetings of Patriarch Maxim, expressed appreciation that the Pope was a fellow Slav. A distinguished Bulgarian Orthodox theologian, Professor Todor Sabev, is now Deputy General Secretary of the World Council of Churches.

---

During the period immediately following the Second World War, when the Bulgarian churches were faced with the problems of major reconstruction, they were not greatly hampered by the new government. The Communists were busy engineering the conversion of the coalition Fatherland Front government into a Communist regime, and largely ignored the churches. They were also anxious to redeem the reputation of Bulgaria in the eyes of the international community, and recognized that the repression of religious bodies would not endear them to those nations who placed high value on freedom and toleration.

This did not prevent the government from making it clear that the Christian faith and the churches would no longer have a privileged position in the life of the Bulgarian nation. Prayers and religious education were removed from school curricula. Religious services were abolished in the army, and it was announced that dialectical materialism was to be the official philosophy of the State.

The attitude of the new regime was expressed plainly by Georgi Dimitrov, the former Secretary of the Communist International, and the hero of the 1933 Reichstag fire trial, who returned from the Soviet Union in 1946 and became the founder of Bulgaria's Communist State. In a speech made soon after he took office, and in the presence of Patriarch Alexii of Moscow, who was in Bulgaria for the millennium of the national saint, Ivan of Rila, Dimitrov said that the church had great historic merits for it had preserved the Bulgarian national consciousness during the long years of Turkish rule; unfortunately, the present Synod of the church included some 'old men of ossified brains and extremely conservative views'. None the less, there was a role for the church in the new Bulgaria provided it became 'a truly people's, republican and progressive church'. To illustrate what he meant, he called on the Exarch and the clergy to stop praying for the old monarchy which had been abolished and to cease glorifying 'that which the people reject'.

Some of the Orthodox clergy responded to this challenge by forming a league and then calling for a general council of the Bulgarian Church. They said it was necessary to draft a new, and more democratic, constitution for the church. There was also a need for the church to become more active in the life of the nation through the promotion of social work. At the same time, they urged the government to reintroduce religious education into the schools (allowing priests to carry out the instruction) and they strongly opposed the threatened closure of the theological faculty in the University of Sofia. The government was, however, in no mood to make concessions.

In October 1946, Dimitrov – who had himself had a Christian upbringing – produced a draft constitution for a Bulgarian

People's Republic. This closely resembled the Soviet model, and provided for the complete separation of Church and State. It also proposed that all education should be secular and that only civil marriages should be regarded as legal. The Synod of the Orthodox Church objected to these proposals, but in December of the following year they became law. The new constitution contained, however, a clause guaranteeing freedom of conscience, religion and religious rites and forbidding the preaching of racial, national and religious hatred. The use of the church or of religion for political ends was prohibited, but the church was given an assurance that state subsidies would be continued if these were needed.

During this time the Orthodox Church was led by Bishop Stefan of Sofia, who had been elected Exarch in 1945. One of the first tasks awaiting his election was the healing of the schism between the Bulgarian Church and the Patriarchate of Constantinople which went back to 1872. This he accomplished by getting Alexii, the recently elected Patriarch of the Russian Orthodox Church, to persuade the Ecumenical Patriarch to recognize Stefan as head of the Bulgarian Church. A feature of Stefan's leadership was the cultivation of close ties between the Bulgarian and Russian Orthodox Churches, and in 1948 the Synod of the Bulgarian Church acknowledged, in response to certain government accusations, that in the organizing of its life the views and practice of the Russian Orthodox Church had been taken into account. Here it may be recalled that during the ninth and tenth centuries the Bulgarian Orthodox Church had a crucial role as a 'pilot project' for Slav Orthodoxy and thus opened the way for the momentous conversion of Russia. The Church Slavonic of the Russian liturgy has its roots in Old Bulgarian.

Under Stefan the church tried hard to accommodate itself to the new regime. Although the Synod had objected very strongly to certain parts of Dimitrov's draft constitution, especially the separation of Church and State, once this had become law Stefan said that it contained some 'constructive stipulations'. The Synod also urged the Bulgarian people to support the government in 'all useful undertakings', which it specified as charitable work, justice and social and economic progress. But 1948 saw the beginning of a campaign of repressive measures against the church, which lasted until the end of 1952 and reflected a general trend throughout Eastern Europe. Exarch Stefan was ready to compromise with the government over certain matters, but was not prepared to lead a complete sell-out. He complained about Communist encroachment on ecclesiastical and political freedom, on the religious education of young people and on freedom of conscience. He also suggested a plebiscite of the whole Bulgarian people on the question of their rights and freedoms, and in October 1948 resigned from the offices of Exarch and Metropolitan of Sofia. The official announcement of his departure mentioned failing health, and a statement issued by the Holy Synod accused him of being autocratic and arbitrary. It is now clear that Stefan was forced out of office and exiled to the village of Banya, in the Karlova region, where he remained until his death in 1957 at the age of seventy-nine. On Good Friday 1952 the former Exarch addressed a powerful message to the Bulgarian people, in which he reminded them of the way in which the church had been, and remained, 'the beacon, the soul, the strength, the hope and the conscience of the nation'. He then accused the government of seeking to eradicate the Christian faith from Bulgaria's heart by every possible means, and of 'subjugating the holy national church to Communism's political and propagandist aims'. He went on to accuse the metropolitans of the church of a 'Judas-like betrayal', involving the hatching up of a plot with a representative of the Communist Party, after a visit to Sofia by the Soviet Foreign Minister which had led to his (Stefan's) downfall and exile.

With Stefan out of the way, the government was quickly able to secure the close co-operation of the church. No appointment was made to the Exarchate, but during the next two years three different metropolitans served as acting chairman of the Holy Synod. On the day following Stefan's resignation in 1948, the Synod sent a message to the government praising its 'statesman-like wisdom'. In the same month the Synod authorized the clergy to join pro-Communist organizations and accepted the government's decision to end religious education in schools. At the same time it supported the policy of collective farming, and urged the people to show respect for the authorities. The clergy were told that in future they must refrain from political and social comment in their sermons. A year later, to the great astonishment of many Christians inside and outside Bulgaria, the Synod urged the clergy to hold special services in honour of Stalin's seventieth birthday. The clergy as a whole showed little enthusiasm for this recommendation, and some of those who objected or simply failed to conform were arrested and sent to labour camps. Recruitment to the pro-Communist Union of Orthodox Priests also proved disappointing to the authorities.

A new law promulgated in 1949 followed the by now familiar East European pattern of affirming freedom of religious belief and practice, but at the same time bringing the churches under firm state control. It stated: 'All citizens of the People's Republic of Bulgaria are guaranteed freedom of conscience and religion' (Article 1), and went on, 'The Bulgarian Orthodox Church is the traditional confession of the Bulgarian people; inseparable from its history, the Bulgarian Orthodox Church can as such be, in its form, content and spirit, a people's democratic church' (Article 3). The price of this so-called freedom and status was to be extremely steep. The Minister of Foreign Affairs, oddly enough, was made responsible for supervising the churches and he was given considerable powers, including the withdrawal of recognition from a particular church (Article 6), the removal or suspension of a minister of religion deemed to have infringed the laws, public order and morality, or to have worked against 'the democratic regime of the State' (Article 12), and the suspension of the dissemination of pastoral letters, circular letters and 'publications of a social character' (Article 15). The churches were required to submit their budgets to the Ministry of Foreign Affairs, and to have their financial affairs supervised by the financial bodies of the State (Article 13). Criticism of Bulgaria's Communist rulers was forbidden on pain of imprisonment or 'more severe penalties' (Article 28). Thus armed, the government took over the church's hospitals, orphanages and similar institutions, together with all church-organized youth and educational work. A number of churches were closed, and some monasteries practically became tourist hotels. Senior church appointments required the approval of the State. The theological faculty was detached from the University of Sofia, and compelled to add Marxism to its curriculum. The senior secretary of the Holy Synod was dismissed, and the leader of the Orthodox Brotherhood (a fellowship of laymen and laywomen in the parishes) was arrested. Some priests were put on trial and a few were executed.

Action against non-Orthodox churches and other religions was even more severe. All churches with international headquarters outside Bulgaria were ordered to close. The Baptists, Congregationalists and Methodists, who had American connections, responded by severing their links with their overseas brethren, while relations between Sofia and the Holy See were officially terminated. Only Bulgarian nationals were permitted to hold office in any church or to serve as priests or pastors. In February 1949 fifteen prominent Protestant ministers were tried in Sofia. Among them were the leaders of the Methodist, Baptist, Congregational and Pentecostal Churches, as well as the leader of the Supreme Council of Evangelicals. They were charged with high treason, espionage, unlawful foreign exchange transactions and attempts to undermine the Communist government. In the course of the trial they all made 'confessions of guilt', and after being sentenced to terms of imprisonment ranging from life to one year they all thanked the judge for the 'mild punishment' they had been given. Protests against the trial and the sentences were lodged by the governments of the United States, Britain, Canada, Australia and New Zealand, and the matter was raised in the General Assembly of the United Nations, all without effect. In 1950 the Roman Catholic Bishop of Nikopolis (Mgr Eugene Bossilkov) was arrested, together with thirty priests and nuns, and after a long trial he and three of the priests, including the head of the Catholic seminary at Plovdiv, were sentenced to death. Pope Pius XII protested publicly about the 'wave of terror' against Bulgarian Catholics, but nothing further was heard of Bishop Bossilkov until 1975, when a Vatican delegation to Bulgaria was told that he had died in prison shortly after being sentenced. He was well known in Britain as a member of the Passionist Order. While all this was taking place a large number of Muslims went to Turkey as the result of a special Turko-Bulgarian agreement, and many of them suffered great hardship during their journey and subsequent resettlement. A large number of Jews also left Bulgaria and settled in Israel.

The endurance of persecution appears to have stimulated the Orthodox Church to increased activity. Although its sphere of influence was severely restricted, good use was made of those areas of religious life in which freedom remained. Religious instruction, usually within the context of the liturgy, was provided in many parishes for the children of Christian parents. The clergy were diligent in caring for their people. Lapsed Christians were encouraged to return to the liturgy. The Church made it clear to the State – by the vigour of its life, rather than by episcopal pronouncement – that it had no intention of being destroyed. With the slight but significant easing of the repressive State policy in 1953, following the death of Stalin, came a demand for the revival of the Bulgarian Patriarchate which had been suppressed in the fourteenth century. The government gave a good deal of encouragement to those making this demand, seeing in it an opportunity for asserting Bulgaria's independence and integrity as a nation. Metropolitan Kiril of Plovdiv, the third of the acting chairmen of the Holy Synod, was duly elected Patriarch, but his election was not accepted by the Patriarchate of Constantinople, and it was not until 1961 that the re-establishing of the Bulgarian Patriarchate was officially recognized by the Orthodox world as a whole.

Kiril was a remarkable scholar, linguist and preacher, as well as a man of strong character, and for nearly twenty years provided the Bulgarian Orthodox Church with outstanding leadership. His accession to the Patriarchate made little difference to his literary output, and, although he was carrying a heavy burden of leadership, he published eight major works during his period of office. These were mainly on historical subjects, which were his special interest, and they proved to be particularly useful in that they avoided any criticism of the existing government, yet showed that the church had over the years become an integral part of Bulgarian life and culture. Throughout his tenure of the Patriarchate he was concerned to stress that Church and State occupied common ground in their desire to encourage 'patriotic service'. History, he argued, demonstrated the Church's patriotic stand in the past, and its present support of the government was not the result of state pressure or coercion but simply the continuation of a long tradition. Kiril was one of the most learned bishops in the Orthodox world, and his scholarship was recognized by the Bulgarian Academy of Sciences, of which he became an

academician in 1970. At the time of his death in 1971 he was
engaged in writing a massive history of the Exarchate.

Had Kiril lived a few months longer he would have seen the new
Bulgarian constitution designed for the next stage in the building
of 'the advanced socialist society'. The secular character of the
Bulgarian State is again strongly emphasized:

> Citizens are guaranteed freedom of conscience and of religion.
> They have the right to perform religious rites and carry out
> anti-religious propaganda. The Church is separated from the
> State. The legal status, questions of material support and the
> right of self-government of the various religious communities
> are regulated by law. It is prohibited to misuse the Church and
> religion for political purposes or to form political organi-
> zations on a religious basis. Religion cannot be used to justify
> the refusal to accept the duties imposed by the constitution
> and the laws. (Article 53)
>
> Marriage and the family are placed under the protection of the
> State. Only civil marriage is valid. (Article 38)
>
> Education of youth in a Communist spirit is a duty for the
> whole of society. (Article 39)

These provisions in the constitution find expression in government policy today. Atheist education is compulsory in Bulgarian
schools and there are 'Young Atheist' clubs which are, according
to the newspaper *Chernomorski Front* of 27 October 1978,
'schools for the training of active atheists, able to carry out their
own atheistic work among both their peers and their elders'.
Secular funeral rites have been introduced as an alternative to
religious ceremonies, and families who opt for the secular rather
than the religious receive a telegram of sympathy on their
bereavement from the town council; a member of the council or
the head of the deceased's place of work delivers a speech at the
funeral, and Communist symbols, such as the red flag and the
five-pointed star, are used. A State Council document entitled
'Basic Directions on Developing and Perfecting the Holiday and
Ceremonial System in the People's Republic of Bulgaria',
published in May 1978, did, however, concede that there is still
a place for some of the symbols inherited from 'the old culture'
once they have been 'freed from mysticism and ambiguity'.
Statistics published by the government in June 1977 indicated

that some 45 per cent of the people who had died during 1976 were buried with secular ceremonies, and that 50 per cent of the children born in that year were named with secular ceremonies. In the town of Burgas, 230 of the 590 people who died during the first six months of 1978 had secular funerals. Even these State figures, which do not always agree with those of the Church, indicate that quite a large number of Bulgarians are still going to their churches for important occasions in their family life. In the case of births, the number of children baptized is almost certainly higher than 50 per cent, since it is well known that mothers and grandmothers take children to church secretly after name-giving by the State authorities.

---

The Roman Catholic community in Bulgaria is small and its members are mainly elderly and poor. In 1980 only three priests were under the age of fifty and, since all the presbyteries have been confiscated by the government, the clergy are obliged to live in their churches or in huts. A thaw in relations between Bulgaria and the Vatican came in 1975 when, in the course of an official visit to Italy, President Todor Zhivkov had an audience with Pope Paul VI. At this meeting Zhivkov agreed that bishops should be appointed to the two Latin-Rite dioceses which had, officially, been without bishops since 1962. One of those nominated was Bishop Bogdan Dobranov, who had actually been secretly consecrated as a bishop by Pope John XXIII in 1959. The other, Bishop Vasco Seirekov, died in 1977 – worn out, it was said, by heroic pastoral work in the large northern diocese of Nikopolis. He was replaced in 1979 by Father Samuel Dzhundrin, who had been given twelve years' imprisonment in 1952. Not long after the President's papal audience, thirty Catholics, including eight priests and seven nuns, went on a Holy Year pilgrimage to Rome, and became the first Bulgarians to have left their country on a pilgrimage for over thirty years. In the following year, 1976, Archbishop Casaroli, the then Vatican 'foreign minister', spent a week in Bulgaria, the first four days of which were given to visiting the Catholic dioceses and the rest to conversations with President Zhivkov and government officials. The Archbishop described these conversations as 'open and cordial', and shortly before leaving Bulgaria said, 'I have no illusions but I return to Rome with hopes.' The hopes of the Bulgarian Catholics have been greatly raised by the presence in Rome of a Slav pope who shows great concern for their plight.

The Pentecostal Church – at least, those of its members who are specially enthusiastic and active – have less ground for hope. In September 1979 five of their number, including the Treasurer of the Pentecostal Union, were put on trial and accused of receiving goods and currency from foreign sources, that is from missionary societies abroad. Reports in the Bulgarian press stressed that the trial was not to be regarded as an attack on the Pentecostal Church, the president of which made a statement in court to the effect that the church did not approve of the defendants' activities. Prison sentences of three to six years and heavy fines were imposed, though these were reduced after appeals and pressure from the West. On a strict interpretation of the law, the five Pentecostals were undoubtedly guilty of certain offences, but government officials had previously turned a blind eye to the receiving of modest amounts of money and goods from abroad, and it seemed hardly a coincidence that five of the most active Pentecostals were singled out for harsh treatment. As in the case of the other churches, the State is prepared to be 'tolerant' provided the Pentecostal Church orders its life quietly and within the prescribed limits. But as soon as individuals or congregations show signs of fervour and active witness they are likely to be harassed, discriminated against, and sometimes severely punished.

The more overt signs of Orthodox activity are to be seen in the Church's involvement in the Christian Peace Conference and in other peace movements inspired by Moscow. Bulgarian political leaders were present in 1975 when the present Patriarch, Maxim, was enthroned, and a Holy Synod document described him at the time as 'a devoted pupil and follower of the peacemaking activities and patriotism of the Russian Orthodox Church under whose beneficial power and traditions he has been during his five years of service at the Bulgarian Church Mission in Moscow'. His attitude to the State is markedly different from that of his predecessor, Kiril. Two other Orthodox metropolitans and some professors from the theological academy are also involved in the Christian Peace Movement, and a special office has been created at the Holy Synod to promote peacemaking and ecumenical activities. After the Moscow World Peace Forum of Religious Workers held in 1977, follow-up conferences of the clergy were held in all the dioceses of Bulgaria. A few months later, in January 1978, representatives of all the Bulgarian churches, and of the Jewish and Muslim communities, attended a protest meeting in Sofia against the neutron bomb, and issued a statement expressing the solidarity of believers with secular society in condemning the bomb. The churches were also much involved in a 'World Peace Parliament' held in Sofia in 1980.

With the exception of the Pentecostal Church, which is in any case very small, all the Bulgarian churches appear to have lost ground since the Communists came to power in 1946. During the early years of Communist rule they were exposed to state pressure more fierce than anything experienced elsewhere in Eastern Europe, apart from in the Soviet Union and Albania. Today they have very little room for manoeuvre. And while it is certainly true that the religious policy of the present harsh government is modelled on that of the Soviet Union, it also seems to be the case that the Church is not really strong enough to require the State to treat it more circumspectly. The causes of the apparent weariness of the Orthodox Church lie deep in Bulgarian history, and they pre-date both the Communist revolution and the compliant church leadership today. When President Zhivkov received the Patriarch in 1978 on the twenty-fifth anniversary of the re-establishment of the Bulgarian Patriarchate, he thanked the Church for its patriotic activity, its share in the struggle for world peace and its links with the Russian Orthodox Church, which had contributed to Bulgarian-Soviet friendship. Admirable though this contribution may seem to Bulgaria's present rulers, it hardly exhausts the Christian witness in a secular society, and in the long run the Bulgarian people may come to expect more of their national church. In the meantime, and bearing in mind the experience of five centuries of alien rule, which ended only just over a hundred years ago, survival is everything. And the Bulgarian churches still have ample reserves of faith and courage.

# Chapter 12

# ROMANIA

The dome of the Grand National Assembly building in Bucharest is surmounted by an eagle, in the beak of which is a cross. This is the only parliament building in Eastern Europe to be marked with a Christian symbol. Its origin, obviously, lies in the pre-Communist past, but there is no shortage of ladders in Romania's capital and the symbol could easily be removed if President Ceausescu found it offensive or considered it inappropriate. Such an action would, however, scandalize the overwhelming majority of the Romanian people, including many members of the Communist Party, for whom the Christian religion and the history of the nation are inseparable. A leading Marxist intellectual speaks quite naturally of the Romanian Orthodox Church as 'our church'. And this in a country which, in spite of its carefully nurtured friendship with the West, is ruled by one of the most ruthless Communist governments in Eastern Europe. From almost every point of view, Romania is an enigma. Ambiguities and contradictions abound, and are, by unspoken agreement, generally ignored.

The Communists came to power in 1947 after two years of manoeuvring for supremacy in the left-wing coalition which replaced a Fascist regime in 1945. Since then the hold of the rulers has relaxed a little but remains firm. Critics of the government are quickly rounded up by the police, and either sent to prison or despatched to the airport for deportation. Yet it is hard to think of any other East European country in which it would have been possible in 1972 to televise the village funeral of the father of the First Secretary of the Communist Party, with the full rites of the Church conducted by a bishop and thirteen priests.

President Ceausescu is committed to a massive programme of industrialization in a country which is still predominantly agricultural and where three-quarters of its 22 million people are peasants. As recently as 1948, 23 per cent of the population was illiterate and, although the educational and economic policies of the Communist government have transformed the lives of the ordinary people, it is still necessary to think of Romania as a developing country with an ethos and charm unknown in most parts of Western Europe for more than two centuries. In order to achieve an annual growth rate of 9 to 10 per cent for the remaining years of the present century, Western capitalist enterprises have been invited into the country to share with the government in joint industrial ventures. Romania is the only East European country that belongs to the International Monetary Fund. The workers are required to contribute to the nation's economic well-being with regular unpaid overtime, and it is not unknown for thousands of clerks to be moved, by Presidential decree, from their desks to construction work.

The President is equally committed to maintaining the independence of his country and to preserving Romania's national identity. During the immediate post-Second World War era Soviet army units and political and economic 'advisers' were in Romania exercising control, but, as a result of skilful diplomatic moves on the part of the Romanians, Soviet troops were withdrawn in 1958. Since 1969 Romania has refused to take part in joint military manoeuvres with Soviet and other Warsaw Pact armies, and in October 1976 Ceausescu stated that the Romanian nation 'would fight solely in defence of its independence and sovereignty against any attempt at domination and oppression'. Earlier in the same year, at a conference of Communist and Workers' Parties in East Berlin, he had contradicted the Marxist-Leninist concept of 'proletarian internationalism' and asserted that it was 'completely wrong to believe that the national idea has concluded its historic mission'. When Soviet forces invaded Afghanistan at the end of 1979, Ceausescu broadcast a New Year message to the Romanian people and, although he did not mention Afghanistan by name, he called for 'the withdrawal of foreign troops within their national borders, the dismantling of military bases and the dissolution of military blocs'. In January of the following year the United Nations General Assembly censured the Soviet Union for its action against Afghanistan, and – alone among the Warsaw Pact delegations – the Romanian representative was absent from the Assembly, and therefore failed to vote against the motion of censure. Also significant is the fact that the new Romanian national anthem *Te Slavim, Romania, Pamint Stramosesc* (We Glorify You, Romania, Our Ancestral Land) omits the words of the 1948 anthem glorifying 'the everlasting Soviet-Romanian brotherhood-in-arms'.

In the sphere of religion there is a depth of spirituality and an attachment to the Church such as has not been experienced in the West since the end of the Middle Ages. Religion is intertwined with the day-to-day life of the people and with the national culture. The only other Christian parallels are to be found in Poland, and to a lesser degree in Spain and Eire. Parish churches are always crowded for the Sunday liturgy of the Romanian Orthodox Church, and they are never empty during the week. People of all ages drop into the local churches whenever they are near, to venerate an icon or to light a candle or to have a few moments of rest and reflection. They do not see these as special 'religious' actions, for devotion is a normal part of life, like eating and sleeping, and the church building is a second home, a place where the Romanian belongs.

It is therefore not difficult to see why the post-war Communist governments have decided against an all-out confrontation with the Romanian Orthodox Church and have settled for a form of co-existence. The size of the Party is in fact quite small, and the leaders themselves do not find it easy to dispense with their own cultural roots. Even the most devoted disciple of Marx has difficulty in believing that the religion of the Romanian people will inevitably wither away as their social conditions improve. Indeed, President Ceausescu has warned Party members that the Church 'might be around for centuries'. Moreover the Romanian Orthodox Church has an extremely important, indeed a crucial, part to play in the expression and development of national independence.

Romania did not become an independent state until 1859, and since then it has been affected – usually adversely – by the tides of European power-politics and war. But there were Christians in the Roman province of Dacia, to which the present frontiers of Romania approximate, as early as the fourth century. A bishop was resident in Tomi (Constanza), and the Church had links with St John Chrysostom of Constantinople. The allegiance of the Romanian people to the Orthodox East is the result of

Bulgarian influence and domination from the ninth to the eleventh centuries, but the Latin elements of the earlier era survived and are still expressed in the Romanian language and in the language of the Church. Romania is sometimes described as a Latin island in a sea of Slavs. The acceptance of the faith of the Orthodox East was to be of crucial importance during the centuries of Turkish domination, which by the early years of the sixteenth century had embraced the provinces of Moldavia and Wallachia. The Orthodox faith played a critical part in keeping alive the heart of the nation over a long period of alien rule. Unlike the other parts of South-East Europe which were conquered by the Turks, the Romanian lands were not subject to direct Turkish rule but were left as vassal states under Christian princes approved by Constantinople. As such they remained free to organize their own religious life without Muslim interference, even the building of mosques and attempts at conversion being forbidden. Moldavia and Wallachia, although economically exploited and constantly a battleground between Turkey and Russia, were thus able to remain Orthodox princedoms. In Transylvania, on the other hand, and especially after its liberation by Austria, the large Romanian population was the object of political, social and religious discrimination by the Catholic and Protestant Hungarian ruling classes, and of Catholic missionary campaigns launched from Vienna and Budapest. Orthodoxy thus became increasingly the badge of Romanian national identity. There are still some Muslims in the Dobrogea province but hardly any mosques north of the Danube. Between 1859 and 1914 Romania was almost entirely Orthodox, and other churches only came into the national picture with the acquisition of Transylvania after the First World War. The Eastern-Rite Catholics (Uniates) were mainly from Transylvania, while the Latin-Rite Catholics and Lutherans were German-speaking, and the Calvinists Hungarian-speaking. The way in which these religious groups are treated by the Communist government today is not unrelated to their ethnic origins and to their potential threat to Romanian national unity. All of them are disadvantaged, to a greater or lesser degree.

---

When the Romanian Orthodox Church applied for membership of the World Council of Churches in 1961 it gave its total membership as 13 million. Today about 17 million (just over 80 per cent of Romania's total population of 22 million) regard themselves as Orthodox Christians. The Church itself is organized according to the synodical pattern of Eastern Orthodoxy and is divided into five metropolitanates, each of which has two or more subordinate bishoprics. There are thirteen dioceses in all, each comprising 600 to 1,600 parishes which are grouped in deaneries. In 1980 there were 8,100 parishes altogether and about 11,000 places of worship, served by 9,100 priests and about 100 deacons. Parishes, naturally, vary considerably in size. In general, approval is not given for the formation of a new parish unless there are at least five hundred Orthodox families in a town area, or four hundred families in a village, though exceptions to this rule are made in special circumstances. In September 1975 it was reported that eighty new churches and chapels had been built 'in recent times'.

There are two Orthodox theological institutes of university status, in Bucharest and Sibiu. During the academic year 1980–81 there were 1,500 full-time students at these institutes. Standards are comparatively high, and their students, who are required to learn at least two foreign languages, are recruited by competition from seminaries. The Bucharest institute offers part-time courses in theology to students of other disciplines at Bucharest University. The institutes also provide refresher courses for parish clergy. These are usually held in a monastery and last from four to eight weeks; parish clergy are expected to attend every five years. The majority of the clergy are trained in the six cantors' schools and seminaries, one of which is reserved for older candidates for the priesthood. There is room for just over 1,500 students in the schools and seminaries, and in recent years the number of candidates for admission has exceeded the available places. The course for church cantors is designed for those who will lead the elaborate music of the liturgy, and lasts for two years. The normal procedure is for ordination candidates to be enrolled at an early age – sometimes as young as fourteen – and all attend the cantors' course. Those who are not going forward to the priesthood leave at the end of two years with their musical qualifications, while the rest remain for a further three years and are prepared for ordination. Graduates of the seminaries are, however, permitted to serve only in village parishes. Priests for city and suburban parishes are drawn exclusively from those who have graduated at either of the theological institutes.

Priests are paid on the same salary scale as the secular teachers. The State makes a substantial contribution to the stipends of the Orthodox parish clergy (as it does to the ministers of all recognized churches), and also assists in the payment of bishops, diocesan administrators, theological teachers and some members of monastic communities. There is also a church-administered sickness, disability, pensions and social insurance scheme which guarantees the clergy benefits similar to those that go to other Romanian citizens. A number of monasteries provide rest and recreation homes for the clergy; some of these homes are free, others make a nominal charge. In 1975 it was reported that there were 122 Orthodox monastic foundations with a total number of about 2,200 religious, of whom about 1,500 were nuns and the rest monks. These figures show a sharp decline from those of 1956, when there were 200 monasteries with over 7,000 monks and nuns.

The highest authority in the Romanian Orthodox Church is the Holy Synod, which is composed of the Patriarch, as President, and all the active metropolitans, archbishops and bishops. The National Church Assembly meets once or twice a year when it deals with administrative and financial matters; it is made up of the members of the Holy Synod and one priest and two laymen from each diocese. The National Church Council is the executive organ of the Holy Synod and of the National Church Assembly. In practice, however, and contrary to the Orthodox tradition, much power is vested in the Patriarch who is allowed to intervene in the internal affairs of dioceses, with or without the approval of their bishops, and has authority in a wide range of church affairs. The development of this highly centralized form of church government dates from 1948, when the Orthodox Church was required to submit a statute to the State and to make provision for a greater central control.

Romania has just over 1.3 million Roman Catholics, who constitute about 6 per cent of the total population. About 85 per cent of these are of Hungarian and German stock and are to be found in Transylvania, but there are five diocesan adminis-trations covering the country as a whole. Only one of these, Alba

Iulia, has a bishop; the others have apostolic administrators –
priests who have the pastoral responsibility of a bishop and can
administer confirmation, but not ordination. Their appointments
can be terminated whenever the Pope wishes, but in practice
they hold office indefinitely. Of the priests 60 per cent are over
sixty years of age. The Vatican does not publish statistics
relating to Romania, but the number of parishes is believed to
be about 650. There are theological seminaries at Alba Iulia and
Iasi. Since the Roman Catholic Church has not submitted a
statute for approval by the State it is tolerated but not officially
recognized, though a Roman Catholic priest sits in the Grand
National Assembly.

The largest Protestant church in Romania is the Hungarian
Reformed Church, which has about 700,000 members. In spite
of its name, the membership of this church consists entirely of
citizens of Romania, although the worship is in fact conducted
in Hungarian. The Lutheran Church is established in the
German- and Hungarian-speaking areas of Transylvania, where
it has about 200,000 members in 250 parishes served by 220
pastors. Some of the Lutheran congregations are very small, and
quite often church members are dispersed over a wide area.
Even so, a strong community life is maintained and, in addition
to the regular worship, there are Bible study groups, confirmation classes for young people, and catechism instruction for
children. Ministers of the Reformed and Lutheran Churches are
trained at the United Protestant Theological Institute, which has
sections at Cluj-Napoca and Sibiu.

According to an official government estimate, there are about
200,000 Pentecostals in Romania and their numbers have grown
rapidly in recent years. They meet for worship in a thousand
churches or groups, and during the late 1970s new churches were
built at Bucharest, Oradea, Timisoara, Maramures and Arad, the
latter being built by church members and seating 1,500 people.
A Bible School for the training of pastors was opened in 1976,
with an intake of twenty students. The leadership of the
Pentecostal churches is on good terms with the state authorities,
and emphasizes its lack of concern for political matters, but
individual Pentecostal groups are sometimes harassed and
obstructed by the police when their evangelistic activities
become too public. Among the other evangelical groups, the

Brethren have about 120,000 members, and there are some Seventh Day Adventists – a 'reformed' group of which are often in trouble with the state authorities.

The Baptist Church has been active in Romania since the 1850s, when small groups of missionaries came from Germany, Hungary and the Ukraine, and it has grown rapidly during the present century. In the early years of the century there were just a few hundred Baptists, and a Union of local churches was not formed until 1920, but in 1935 there were over 58,000 and in 1965 there were 65,000. In 1980 the official statistics indicated 160,000 Baptists with 662 churches, but unofficially the total membership is believed to be in excess of 300,000. These years of growth have included some periods of severe persecution long before the Communists arrived on the scene. In the 1920s, for instance, the Baptists were forbidden to hold worship services or to conduct burials, ministers were arrested and imprisoned, and church property was often seized. There was a period of comparative freedom from 1928 to 1937, but the next seven years were a time of fierce repression. Between December 1938 and April 1939 all Baptist churches were closed, and only after the American Baptists and the Baptist World Alliance had protested to King Carol's dictatorial government were the Baptists given any relief. The churches were closed again 1942–44, under the Nazi occupation, and when the Communists came to power after the war the Baptists were singled out for specially harsh pressure – probably because they and the Eastern-Rite Catholics are the only non-Orthodox churches in Romania to have made significant progress in winning the allegiance of ethnic Romanians. The phenomenal increase in Baptist membership has not been matched by comparable increases in the number of ordained ministers or of church buildings. Nor has the church recovered from the dismissal of pastors and the closure of many of its buildings during 1960–61. There are only 170 full-time pastors, and the great majority of local churches depend on lay preachers and travelling teams of pastors. The Baptist seminary in Bucharest, which was closed by government decree from 1968 to 1971, has room for eighty students, but the State imposes a quota of twenty students a year, so the seminary is only half full.

In 1968 the Unitarian Church celebrated the four hundredth

anniversary of its foundation in Transylvania by Bishop Francis David. During the sixteenth century there were over four hundred Unitarian congregations, but these suffered severe persecution under the Habsburgs and in 1939 there were 112 congregations, with about fifty other smaller groups. Today the total membership of the Unitarian Church in Romania is about 80,000 (all Hungarian-speaking) in about 130 congregations. The local churches are organized in eight districts, each presided over by a dean, and the chief consistory at Cluj-Napoca has a bishop and two lay presidents. This easily constitutes the largest Unitarian presence in Eastern Europe. Ministers are trained in a theological college which was founded in Cluj-Napoca in 1568 and is now part of the university there. There are said to be enough ministers to serve the local congregations and a sufficient supply of ordination candidates. The Francis David Association, which was established in 1884 for the promotion of religion and moral culture, has a large number of branches and about 1,500 members.

The Jewish community in Romania is now the largest in Eastern Europe outside the Soviet Union, and is recognized by the State as an ethnic minority entitled to its own language and culture. In 1939 the Jewish population of Romania was over 800,000, but this fell to about 400,000 in 1941 when Northern Bukovina and Bessarabia were ceded to the Soviet Union and Upper Transylvania to Hungary. Unlike the majority of Jews in Europe, most of those who remained in truncated Romania managed to survive the war, but more than 300,000 emigrated to Israel when the war was over, and this process continues. There are now about 35,000 Jews in Romania, of whom nearly half live in Bucharest. The sixty-eight local Jewish Communities are united in the Federation of Jewish communities, whose President, Dr Moses Rosen, has been Chief Rabbi of Romania since 1948, and holds a seat in the Grand National Assembly. Throughout the country there are 130 synagogues open for worship on the High Holy Days; the sixteen synagogues in Bucharest usually have daily services. There are, however, now only three rabbis in Romania, compared with 600 in 1948 and thirty-six in 1958. The rabbinical seminaries and Yiddish schools are all closed, but there are twenty talmud torahs for young people, and in many towns there are special classes in Jewish studies and the Hebrew language. The Yiddish State Theatre in Bucharest flourishes, with the aid of a state subsidy, and there is a Jewish museum and a library of about 70,000 volumes. The Federation undertakes much welfare work among elderly and housebound Jews, and there are nine old people's homes and hostels. Kosher restaurants are to be found in most of the main towns. Jews play a prominent part in the political, economic and intellectual life of the country and, according to Romanian law, anti-Semitism is an offence.

There is a long tradition of Bible translation and printing in Romania, and the first complete Bible was printed in 1688. The most recent translation appeared in 1968, and 100,000 copies were printed by the Orthodox Patriarchate's press on paper supplied by the United Bible Societies. This press is almost three hundred years old and its output is considerable: 200,000 copies of Orthodox Bibles have been printed since 1971, with paper and binding materials provided by the United Bible Societies, and in 1981 25,000 shorter Bibles and 15,000 books of Psalms were printed. In spite of this, Bibles remain in short supply and are normally distributed, on a quota system, through the local congregations. A number of Bibles and scriptures printed at the Patriarchate are shared with the non-Orthodox churches, but the Protestants have to rely mainly on imported Bibles, and the government exercises strict control of all imported literature. However, the United Bible Societies were able to supply Baptists with 5,000 Bibles and the Adventists with 3,000 Bibles in 1977; 7,500 Bibles and New Testaments went to Pentecostals and Lutherans in 1978; 4,000 German scriptures, Bibles and New Testaments and some scholarly editions were imported in 1979; 10,000 Bibles in Hungarian were supplied to the Reformed Church by the United Bible Societies and the Reformed Alliance in 1980; and small quantities of Braille gospels are regularly supplied.

Theological periodicals are of a higher academic standard than in most other parts of Eastern Europe. The Patriarchate publishes three journals: *Biserica Ortodoxa Romana* (Romanian Orthodox Church), first published in 1882, is a monthly review concerned mainly with the way in which the life of the church is organized; it has a circulation of about 5,000. *Ortodoxia* is a quarterly journal devoted to Orthodox theology, and has a circulation of 10,000. *Studii Teologice* (Theological Studies) is concerned with theological education and is published ten times a year by the theological institutes; its circulation is about 5,000. The five metropolitanates also produce their own magazines which are read mainly by the clergy and have circulations of between 1,000 and 2,000. In addition to these journals, there is a fairly considerable output of commentaries and sermon outlines for preachers, and an assortment of calendars and almanacs for the use of local churches. A quarterly bulletin of Romanian Orthodox Church news is published in English. The libraries of the theological institutes and most of the monasteries are good and some are up-to-date. In 1978 Patriarch Justin launched a project for the publishing of ninety volumes of patristic texts covering the first eight centuries of Christian history. Two years earlier, Father Dumitru Staniloae, one of the world's leading Orthodox theologians and a prolific writer, edited the fifth volume of the *Philocalia* – the influential anthology of Orthodox spirituality compiled in the eighteenth century – and more recently he has published a long-awaited three-volume study of Orthodox dogmatic theology.

---

For the Romanian Orthodox Christian the family home is a place of deep devotion. Parish priests are kept busy officiating at the many domestic blessing ceremonies. They sprinkle houses with blessed water at certain seasons of the year. Household implements are blessed. So, naturally, are the sick and the dying. Provision for all these occasions is made in the official books of ritual authorized by the Patriarchate, and priests are expected to carry out the ceremonies in the prescribed form, for they are an integral part of the corporate life of the Christian community. Since religious education is forbidden in schools and can, in theory, be given only in the context of worship, the priests also spend a good deal of time – especially on Saturday – conducting services for children, during which careful instruction is given.

The great Christian festivals are still occasions of national celebration, as an observer reported in 1972:

On Good Friday I went, accompanied by some students, to the Orthodox cathedral [at Sibiu] where, in the night, the body of Jesus is laid symbolically to rest. Around the large cathedral and packed inside it were thousands of people, well over half of them children and teenagers, singing, praying, carrying candles and waiting to be blessed by the Bishop.

But that was as nothing compared to Bucharest on Easter Eve. The Parliament Square, where the beautiful, small patriarchal cathedral stands, was solid with young people, happy and yet reverently waiting for the Patriarch to emerge at midnight to proclaim the Risen Christ. I watched the scene from the steps of the Patriarch's house, together with British and Egyptian diplomats. It was in some ways, although much more intimate, like St Peter's Square in Rome on Easter Sunday, but the crowds had not come from all over the world; they were ordinary people and specially young people from Bucharest itself – not necessarily all committed Christians, but devoutly caught up in the mystery of the proclamation of Christ's victory over death.

At 2 a.m. I set off alone to wander through the streets, stopping as I went at many of the town's 240 or so Orthodox churches, all crowded, as were the streets around, with celebrating people carrying candles and greeting each other: 'Christ is risen – He is risen indeed!' Even later in Easter week, specially in shops and restaurants, total strangers were still in the most matter-of-fact way greeting each other with these words. I was greeted with them (not dressed as a priest) by the butcher selling sausages early one morning.

On Easter Monday Bucharest's largest church was again well filled for the ordination of a priest, even though it was an ordinary working day. Three hours of liturgy was devoutly followed even by the many young children present; school holidays were on.

A year later, Brian Cooper, a Baptist journalist, was also in Bucharest for Easter and after describing, in *The British Weekly*, the scene in Parliament Square during the Patriarchal proclamation of the Resurrection, he continued:

I called in at over a dozen churches that night – at tiny St Spiridon's, ablaze with light and warm with a sense of real felt Christian joy; at the Cretulescu church, the tourists' favourite, with its serene icons, where worshippers were still coming in at half past four in the morning; at several local parish churches, where priests and people were exchanging Easter greetings, eating blessed bread together, giving painted Easter eggs, and worshipping and then chatting deep into the small hours.

Orthodox Easter in Communist Romania is not just what happens early on Sunday: Orthodox fasting throughout Lent leads up to Palm Sunday, or Flower Sunday as the Romanians term it. At the large Catholic-style Domnitsa Balasa church, opposite the Ministry of Justice, I had worshipped with more than a thousand others as Bishop Antonie, who was at that time in charge of Romanian Orthodoxy's Ecumenical Relations Department, celebrated the three-hour liturgy.

Most believers go to confession and receive Holy Communion at the major festivals and on certain saints' days and commemorations of the Blessed Virgin Mary. Two Saturdays in the year are observed as times of special remembrance of the departed. On the day before the Sunday of the Last Judgement, *Mosii* (Ancestors), and on Whitsun Eve, the churches and cemeteries are crowded with people who are remembering the souls of departed relatives and friends. The women, who are identified with those who discovered the empty tomb in the Garden of the Resurrection, play a special part in these ceremonies.

Each diocese has its own candle and match factory, as well as workshops for the production of lamps, icons, chalices, metal crosses and other devotional items. Sales of these objects are considerable, and parishes are allowed to keep part of the profit from anything they sell locally. The dioceses also have their own vineyards for the production of wine for the liturgy. In the parishes there is a council made up of laymen and the priest or priests, which is elected every four years by a general parish assembly and is responsible for the overall administration of the parish and for financial matters. Women are not permitted to serve on the council or to take part in the general parish assembly, but they can belong to committees, especially those concerned with pastoral work.

Although the number of Orthodox monks and nuns has been greatly reduced since 1956, the monasteries continue to play an important part in Romanian life. Most of them are in the provinces of Moldavia and Wallachia, and the large ones are really monastic villages. At Agapia and Varatec, for example, where each community has about 350 nuns, there is a central church surrounded by a complex of other buildings, housing the administrative centre, workshops, a library and accommodation for official guests. The nuns live in rows of bungalow-type houses, each accommodating four or five members of the Community who enjoy quite a lot of freedom in the ordering of their corporate life. Beyond these houses, and hardly distinguishable from them, are the homes of ordinary village people, some of whom share in the life of the monastery by working on its extensive land. Large monasteries of this kind play an important part in the social and commercial life of a whole neighbourhood, and at the great Christian festivals they are visited by large numbers of pilgrims – including members of the Communist Party – from the towns. The monastery at Putna, where Stephen the Great, the most famous of Romania's medieval princes, is buried is a national shrine as well as the home of an active religious community. Where a monastic church is of historical or artistic interest, as is generally the case, the State provides substantial sums of money for its maintenance. Several monasteries have registered as co-operatives and have workshops for weaving and carpet-making, and when monks and nuns are engaged in productive work or serve as guides to their historic churches they receive salaries from the State, as do the heads of all religious houses in Romania. The average age of the nuns is high, and many of them are simple peasants, but the Abbesses of Agapia and Varatec are very able women, with considerable theological and administrative skills. The present age structure of the women's communities is closely related to the fact that they are no longer permitted to recruit very young girls, and the government has decreed that no one can be professed as a nun unless she has first received some form of professional training. There are also reports from time to time of government obstruction of monastic life, but it is difficult to determine whether particular incidents are the result of deliberate government policy or a consequence of high-handed local bureaucracy. The attractive ministry of a particular monk can lead to government action against him and his monastery.

The large crowds at church services and the evident devotion of the people are by no means confined to Orthodoxy. The other churches attract a degree of support which is now virtually unknown in Western Europe. In 1972 a priest of the Church of England described a Good Friday visit to 'the huge gothic church of the German-speaking Lutherans [in Sibiu] where the over-flowing congregation heard a sermon by the Lutheran Bishop of Munich, West Germany. "Was this a very special occasion for so many to have come?" I asked. My question caused astonishment – "Our people are always in church, and not only for festivals." "Is it then that there are not enough churches as in the Soviet Union?" – "Not that either, not a single church has been closed down".' Journalist Brian Cooper also visited the Nicolae Titulescu Baptist Church in Bucharest, where 'more than a thousand people crammed into the church building and hundreds stood in the courtyard for the Easter Sunday services and prayer meeting'. During the course of a visit to the United States in 1980, Pastor Klein, Dean of the Protestant Theological Institute at Sibiu, described how Romanian Lutherans prepare for worship:

> On the day before the celebration of the Eucharist villagers meet in groups at various houses to ask forgiveness from anyone they have wronged. If people have had a quarrel or have done wrong, they shake hands and say 'Forgive me if I have offended you'. And the other answers, 'You are forgiven with all my heart. Go in the name of God.' When this is done to the group's satisfaction, the senior member goes to the pastor and tells him that all are reconciled. Those who do not ask or grant forgiveness are usually barred from Communion. In that case, often the whole community will work to get them reconciled. People go to Holy Communion as entire neighbourhoods. An entire community goes and this makes a difference in how they live together.

---

During the years prior to the Second World War the Orthodox Church enjoyed a privileged position as Romania's national Church. Its bishops had considerable social and political influence, and the parish clergy played an important part in local affairs. There was rarely any conflict between the Church and the organs of secular government: officially the State had final authority over church appointments and legislation but in practice the Church had all the freedom it desired. This 'symphony' of Church and State ended abruptly when the Communists came to power in 1947. The new regime was hostile to religious faith and to ecclesiastical influence; it demanded sole authority over the lives of the Romanian people. Yet the Orthodox Church had been close to the ordinary people in their earlier struggles, and could still count on the devoted allegiance of the overwhelming majority of the population. So the Communist government adopted a policy designed to control the Church, rather than to destroy it, and the Orthodox Church, which had weathered other storms in previous centuries, was ready to submit to the authority of a hostile government, and to support its domestic and foreign policies, in exchange for freedom to celebrate the liturgy, to train priests and to maintain pastoral work in the parishes.

The founders of the People's Republic (as it was then called) took account of religion and the churches in a section of their 1948 constitution entitled 'The Law for the General Regime of the Cults'. This said that all citizens were guaranteed freedom of conscience, and prohibited discrimination between citizens on religious grounds. Religious cults were to be free to practise their rites and to organize their own domestic life without interference from outside bodies. This degree of freedom was, however, circumscribed by the requirement that all religions must be recognized by the Presidium of the Grand National Assembly, which could 'for good and sufficient reasons' withdraw recognition (Article 13). Each religion must submit to the state authorities 'for examination and approval' a statute regulating its institutional life (Article 14). All local religious communities, parishes, congregations, associations, societies and groups must be registered with the appropriate state authority (Articles 17 and 18). Assemblies other than for worship, for example, meetings, lectures, congresses, may be convened only with the approval of the authorities (Article 24). Pastoral letters and 'circulars of general interest' must be submitted to the censor before distribution (Article 25). All church budgets are to be subject to inspection and control by the State (Article 32).

The constitution which now operates was framed in 1965 and reaffirms the broad attitude of the State to religious institutions expressed in 1948. Article 30 reads:

Freedom of conscience is guaranteed to all the citizens of the Romanian Socialist Republic. Anybody is free to share or not to share a religious belief. The freedom of exercising a religious cult is guaranteed. The religious cults organize and function freely. The way of organization and functioning of the religious cults is regulated by law.

It is clear from this article that freedom to express and practise religious beliefs is conditional upon conformity to the laws of the State, a point emphasized by President Ceausescu in a speech in 1979:

Religious freedom is for those cults recognized by the law, but the cults have to respect the laws of the country and help build a socialist State. Romanians cannot close their eyes to any infringement of the law under the pretext of Christianity.

Experience over the course of three decades has shown that the laws of the State can be used not only to restrict the freedom of the churches quite considerably but also to disrupt, and in one particular case to destroy, their own institutional life.

From the beginning of the Communist era, relations between the government and the Roman Catholic Church were very difficult. The Hungarian and German origins of this church in Transylvania were seen as a threat, potential if not actual, to Romanian unity, and the church's links with the Vatican were regarded as a sign that the loyalty of the Catholic community lay elsewhere than in Romania. In 1948 the old concordat with the Holy See was denounced, and the government began the cruel process of coercing the Eastern-Rite (Uniate) Catholics back to the Orthodox Church.

It was during the years 1696–1700 that a substantial number of Romanian Orthodox Christians severed their links with Constantinople and accepted the jurisdiction of the Papal See of Rome. There are Orthodox Christians who believe that this move was due not to any real desire on the part of Romanians to link themselves with the Catholic West, but rather to political pressures applied by alien powers. They argue that ordinary Romanian Christians never accepted the breach with the Church of their forefathers, and longed for the day when they could be free from bondage to Rome. On the other hand, there are Romanians who believe that the movement to Rome was the consequence of a genuine desire to be united with the traditional see of Peter and at the same time to be free of the corruptions which they perceived within the Orthodox Church. Whatever the rights and wrongs of the situation, it created feelings of deep bitterness among the Romanian people and, from time to time, persecution leading to bloodshed.

The events of 1948 and the years that have followed may, therefore, be seen as the latest move in an unhappy story. The Romanian government, having severed its own links with Rome, decreed that the 1.5 million Uniates were to return to the Orthodox fold, and that the Uniate Church in Romania had ceased to exist. Uniate monasteries and seminaries were closed, and parish churches were handed over to the Orthodox Church. The Catholic hierarchy protested strongly, and in consequence all six bishops were arrested and imprisoned. All have since died. On their imprisonment six more bishops were secretly ordained by a papal envoy, Archbishop Gerald O'Hara, but they were soon arrested and were eventually released from prison on condition that they exercised no further ministry. One of their number, Bishop Juliu Hirtea, died in 1978. Between 1948 and 1970 over fifty Catholic priests were killed, two hundred disappeared, two hundred served prison sentences and another two hundred were sent to labour camps. Some prominent members of the Orthodox Church spoke out against the action of the government, and a number of Orthodox priests were sent to prison for refusing to take over Catholic churches, but the ruthless policy was not seriously hindered, and there is no longer an organized Uniate Church in Romania. A large wall painting in the hall of the Holy Synod at the Patriarchate in Bucharest shows the Uniate leaders submitting to Orthodox authority at Alba Iulia. In 1951 the government attempted to establish a national Catholic Church, which would be independent of Rome, but there was no enthusiasm for this and it was not successful.

Ten years after the beginning of the measures against the Uniates, it was the turn of the Orthodox Church itself to feel the repressive hand of the Communist government. By this time Romania was very much under the influence of the Soviet Union, and it is not impossible to believe that the Romanian government's change of policy regarding religion was dictated from Moscow. Whatever the explanation, the Orthodox Church found itself faced for the first time since the end of the war with a government that was openly hostile to its work and ruthless in the persecution of its leaders. The sinister ambiguity of Article 27 of the 1948 constitution was thus heavily underlined: 'Under state control, the Romanian Orthodox Church is autonomous and unified in its organization.' Between 1958 and 1963 about 1,500 priests, monks and lay people were arrested, but the main thrust of the persecution was directed against the monasteries, which were at that time flourishing and increasing in number. In addition to the monks who were imprisoned, more than two thousand were compelled to leave the religious life and over half the monasteries were closed. In 1959 the three monastic seminaries were closed, thus creating serious problems over the training of novices.

A statute regulating the Baptist Church was agreed in 1951, and in 1954 the government produced a set of restrictive regulations, 'The Regularization of Religious Services', which the Baptist Union was instructed to implement. These provided for a considerable reduction in the number of church buildings and services, central control of forms of worship and of the appointment of pastors, submission of lists of candidates for baptism to local Inspectors of Cults, whose approval had to be obtained before baptism could be administered, and financial supervision by the Department of Cults. The leaders of the Baptist Union refused to implement the new regulations, and as a result the government withdrew its recognition of the leaders and instructed the church to organize a congress at which new leaders could be chosen. This congress was held in the autumn of 1955 in the presence of a government representative who imposed his choice of senior officials on the delegates. It was made clear that the State would withdraw its recognition of the Baptist Church if the congress did not comply with the government's requirements. As in the case of the other churches, the government had decided to bring the Baptists to heel, not by external repression, though the means for this were available if required, but by internal control, so that the church's own organization would become the chief instrument of restriction.

Among the Christian groups in Romania that were not accorded recognition by the Communist authorities, The Lord's Army has an unusual history and a special significance. The decade following the First World War saw the development of a small mission movement in the Romanian Orthodox Church led by a priest, Father Tudor Popescu, which ultimately laid the foundation for the Christian Brethren Church in Romania. Then in 1923 another revival movement began in the north of Romania, initiated by a gifted priest, Father Josif Trifa. Initially the movement, which was known as The Lord's Army and owed some of its inspiration to the Oxford Group in Britain, had the official support of the Orthodox hierarchy. The main activities were hymn singing, Bible study, and evangelical preaching by clergy and laity. In some parts of the country, especially in the Ardeal region, the movement attracted considerable support; so much so that Metropolitan Nicolae Balan of Ardeal was appointed to supervise its activities on behalf of the Holy Synod. Father Trifa objected to this attempt to institutionalize the movement, and as a result of the ensuing quarrel he was removed from the priesthood in 1935. The Lord's Army continued to thrive for some years and, although resistant to absorption into the structure of the Orthodox Church, its leaders and members retained their allegiance to the Church. According to official Orthodox spokesmen today, The Lord's Army no longer exists, having eventually separated itself from the Church and lost all its members by natural attrition. The facts appear to be somewhat different: the apparent demise of The Lord's Army in the 1950s was due almost entirely to fierce repression by the government. In the early part of 1948 it was announced that the movement had been dissolved, and a few months later its main leaders were arrested and imprisoned. They were released in 1952 but, together with some other leaders, were committed to prison again in the same year. The Lord's Army had an underground existence throughout the 1950s and '60s: from time to time police searches were carried out, and its leaders and members were either fined or sent to prison. With the dissident revival movement of the late 1970s, The Lord's Army appears to have taken on a new lease of life, and a report from the Christian Committee for the Defence of Religious Rights in Romania in August 1978 said that thirty leaders of the movement had held a Fraternal Council in Brasov in November 1976. The same report claimed that The Lord's Army now had at least half a million members and that its leaders had appealed to the Orthodox Patriarchate to bring the movement 'under its protection'. Some members, however, prefer greater alignment with the evangelical churches.

During the years between the Communist accession to power and his death in 1977, the Romanian Orthodox Church benefited greatly from the outstanding leadership of Justinian, who was elected Patriarch in 1948. Like many East European church leaders of his generation, Justinian came from a peasant background, and after his ordination to the priesthood in 1924 served in a number of rural parishes where he was much disturbed by the poverty of the people. In 1930 he published a pamphlet in which he argued, from the Bible and the early Christian Fathers, that the clergy should be concerned for the material, as well as the spiritual, well-being of their parishioners. At the end of the Second World War he was appointed episcopal vicar at Iasi, in Moldavia, where he was responsible for organizing the Church's contribution to the reconstruction of a badly devastated province. On 28 December 1947 he was elected Metropolitan of Moldavia and Suceava, and two days later, when King Michael abdicated and a People's Republic was proclaimed, Justinian welcomed 'the enthronement of social justice'. In a New Year address he said:

> This New Year finds Romania in new social conditions – the People's Republic of Romania. The Church is not bound by finite institutions, created by men for their needs of the moment. The Church is created by the Eternal God. In this present age she will support social justice, patriotism and seek after man's salvation. She must not remain closed, isolated within herself, but be permanently vibrant in order to revolutionize the religious life of her community.

Within six months Justinian had been elected Patriarch, and his own socialist sympathies facilitated his good relations with the State during the greater part of his Patriarchate, though he was subject to strong pressure during the difficult years between 1958 and 1962. In some quarters his attitude to the State was interpreted as one of complete surrender, but during his time the Orthodox Church retained enough freedom to be able to carry out a number of substantial reforms.

Justinian was himself a notable reformer. One of his special concerns was to encourage parishes to become involved in social work, an unusual emphasis in the Orthodox Church. He was not content that his clergy should merely preside at the liturgy and carry out traditional teaching and pastoral work: they ought to help their congregations to participate in the building of the new People's Republic. Here he exposed himself to the charge of promoting the aims of Communism, and the socialist element in some of the clergy refresher courses was – and still is – so pronounced that opponents have described them as courses in political indoctrination. Yet there is ample evidence to show that Justinian saw some form of socialism and a deep social commitment as a normal expression of the Christian faith. Justinian was also responsible for improving theological education so that the Romanian clergy are now among the best trained in the Orthodox churches. His most impressive reform, however, was concerned with monastic life. In 1950 he initiated many changes in the old monasteries, based on his own understanding of the religious life as combining deep spirituality and active service of society. Monks and nuns were required to learn a trade, and the monasteries were instructed to provide facilities for them to work, either on some project of the religious community or in meeting some needs of society at large.

The Vice-President of the Council of State, together with other state officials and church leaders of all denominations, were present at Justinian's national funeral in 1977. In a message of condolence to the Holy Synod, the Council of State described him as 'an outstanding servant of the Church who kept his clergy in step with the construction of the new Romania'.

---

Nine years earlier, in February 1968, President Ceausescu had acknowledged the contribution of the Orthodox Church to the building of a more prosperous Romania at an official reception for church leaders in Bucharest. This reception, which was without precedent and took the guests by surprise, can now be seen as marking a turning point in Church-State relations in Romania and the beginning of an attempt by the government to 'normalize' these relations. Since then the government has adopted a more relaxed attitude to the churches, especially to the Romanian Orthodox Church, and the leaders of this church have good reason for regarding themselves as privileged when they hear of the plight of Orthodox Christians in other parts of Eastern Europe. But such freedom as the churches enjoy is conditional upon their not stepping outside the narrow boundaries drawn around them by the State. Pressure on the churches noticeably increased after the 1977 earthquake, when many more Romanians began to attend worship services regularly. Six representatives of the major churches, including the Patriarch, now have seats in the Grand National Assembly, which meets twice a year, and all of the fourteen recognized denominations are represented in the United Socialist Front. This offers them little in the way of power or even of influence, since political decisions are all taken by the government or by the Communist Party without reference to parliamentary processes. On the other hand, the government has very considerable power over the churches. Its Department of Cults exercises general supervision of religious matters, and it is impossible for a church leader, or even the priest or pastor of a local church, to be appointed without the Department's approval. The Department also has its full-time inspectors in every province and district – ostensibly to 'assist' the local churches, but in practice to exercise firm control of their activities. This does not necessarily involve much direct intervention in church affairs, since the religious communities, particularly the Orthodox Church, have discovered over the years just how much the Department will tolerate. But any parish or local church attempting to move out of line is quickly and firmly dealt with.

In these circumstances it can hardly be a matter for surprise that the Baptist Church has been, and still is, beset with serious and painful problems. Throughout the 1970s this church displayed the signs of genuine renewal, and among the fruits was a substantial increase in membership. In 1977 the General Secretary of the Baptist Union reported that during the period 1973–76 there had been an annual increase of 20,000. More recent evidence indicates that this church is continuing to grow rapidly, but there are now three main causes of tension. The first of these relates to the need for the church to erect new buildings, or enlarge existing buildings, to accommodate the influx of new members. All building work in Romania is subject to government licence, and in the case of new churches this is not always forthcoming, and there are in any case always long delays. In some places church members have become impatient and started building or renovation without the necessary permission; heavy fines have resulted. The enthusiasm of other Baptists has led them to engage in evangelistic activity outside their church buildings and, again, the police have intervened, sometimes violently. At another level, the renewal of Baptist life has caused some of the church's more thoughtful and articulate members to question the basis of the present relationship between the Baptist Union and the State, and the apparent readiness of church officials to act as instruments of the Department of Cults' repressive policies.

The first signs of open Baptist dissent appeared in 1973 when Pastor Josif Ton, then a teacher at his church's seminary in Bucharest, published an essay entitled 'The Present Situation of the Baptist Church in Romania'. Pastor Ton belongs to the evangelical wing of the Baptist Church, he is a professional theologian who studied at Oxford from 1969 to 1972, and his combination of courage and evident spirituality has made him one of Romania's outstanding Christian leaders, with great influence among the younger pastors. In his essay he denounced, as a betrayal of Baptist principles, the decision of the 1955 Congress to implement the government's restrictive regulations, and he called attention to the ways in which the church's life and mission had been hampered in consequence. He called for an end to the regulations. This essay found its way to Britain where it was published in English and proved to be a source of embarrassment to the Romanian authorities in both Church and State.

In 1974 Pastor Ton published another, longer, paper on 'The Place of the Christian in Socialism'. This was addressed to the Romanian people as a whole and to the Communist rulers in particular, and in it Ton argued that the government's propagation of atheism was actually hindering the creation of a new socialist society. Socialism needed men and women transformed by Christ. The essay was a powerful apologia for the Christian faith, but the Baptist Union Council publicly dissociated itself from Ton's action in publishing his two papers. By this time he had been moved from his teaching post to the pastorate of a small church in Ploesti. In the same year the government gave the Baptist seminary permission to raise the number of its students from twelve to forty in four years, and the grip on the church's administration and pastoral appointments was eased slightly.

These concessions were not, however, sufficient to quell the growing restlessness in the Baptist Church. Some fifty pastors

had followed Pastor Ton's example by presenting a memorandum to the State Council of Ministers asking for greater
religious freedom, and a group of Baptists, Pentecostals and
Brethren protested against the imprisonment of Vasile Roscol,
who had been found guilty of distributing Bibles and other
religious literature. A new spirit was abroad, and in November
1975 the President of the Baptist Union, Pastor Nicolae Covaci,
announced his retirement from office. He gave three reasons for
his decision: (1) The lack of co-operation by the State was
causing discontent in Baptist ranks (he instanced the unwillingness of the Department of Cults to allow the reopening of
churches closed during the years of repression, and its refusal
to permit the repair or expansion of flourishing churches); (2) A
freedom movement growing within the church threatened its
unity; (3) The Union Council had refused to conduct open
elections, i.e. without lists of approved candidates, and it had
declined to recognize the validity of Paul Barbatei's nomination
as a future President. (Barbatei was eventually elected as
General Secretary.) A period of uncertainty followed this
dramatic and unprecedented announcement, and the Baptist
Congress which should have been held in the early part of 1976
was delayed. When it eventually assembled in February 1977 the
fifty delegates from the six constituent Associations were told
by the General Secretary that the delay had been caused by the
activities of Pastor Ton and others who had 'stirred up factions
in the church and damaged the name of Baptists in society'. The
Director of the seminary also spoke of the difficulties created by
protest demonstrations in 1976, when his students had demanded
the return of Ton and another pastor to the teaching staff. In fact,
the delay was almost certainly caused by problems with the
Department of Cults over the candidates for election to various
offices.

The Congress itself was apparently a remarkable occasion.
Besides the elected delegates there were several hundred guests
from the Romanian Baptist Church and abroad, and members of
the public were permitted to listen from the gallery. More than
two thousand people were present and there was much frank
speaking, in the course of which pastors referred to the problems
they were facing because of government regulations. One pastor
said that, while the Department of Cults usually gave permission

for the extension or alteration of church buildings, plans were often obstructed by the local authorities. He advised churches to appeal directly to President Ceausescu in such cases. Pastor Ton said that the harsh treatment of individual believers and congregations was often explained in terms of local police action, rather than of state policy, but the scale on which incidents were being reported was so great that the new Baptist Union Council would have to ask the State to define again its attitude to Baptists.

Most of those elected to the Union Council were new, and difficulty was experienced with the Department of Cults over the appointment of Pastor Vasile Talos as Assistant General Secretary of the Union. Within a month of the Congress, Pastors Ton and Pavel Nicolescu, and laymen Aurel Popescu, Dmitri Dumitrescu (Baptists), Constantin Caraman (Pentecostal) and Silvia Cioata (Brethren) were circulating a document with a detailed account of discrimination against religious belivers in three areas of Romanian life: education, employment and the right of free association. This document appeared shortly after a secular human rights group led by the writer Paul Goma had issued a Romanian response to the Czech 'Charter 77', and on 3 April 1977 the police arrested Goma and his supporters, together with Ton and five other evangelicals. The secular dissidents were eventually obliged to leave Romania, while the Baptists were handed over to their own church for punishment. Two of them – Pavel Nicolescu and Aurel Popescu – were banned from preaching, but Josif Ton escaped with a warning, a difference of treatment that was to lead to a division among the Baptist dissidents.

In April 1978 Nicolescu and Dimitrie Ianculovici formed the Christian Committee for the Defence of Religious Freedom and Freedom of Conscience (ALRC). This called for 'free religion in a free state' and published a document listing twenty-four well-known points at which religious freedom was needed in Romania. Although the ALRC had an evangelical Baptist beginning it has always shown concern for repressed Orthodox believers, especially members of The Lord's Army, and for Uniate Catholics. Its reports and documents call attention to all Christians who have fallen foul of the state authorities. Ton and Popescu declared their support for the Committee but declined an invitation to join, on the grounds that they felt called to concentrate on preaching and teaching the Gospel. By the end of 1978, however, Popescu had been expelled from the Baptist Church, together with Nicolescu and the other Baptist members of ALRC. The letter from the Baptist Union announcing these expulsions said that the conduct of the dissidents 'could place our denomination in an unfavourable position *vis-à-vis* the state authorities and other denominations in our country, thus seriously injuring the prestige of the Baptist denomination and the trust which it must enjoy before the State'. Once again Ton escaped punishment and, having achieved some kind of reconciliation with the leadership of the Baptist Church, began to preach to large congregations in Oradea and Cluj-Napoca. In 1981, however, he decided to leave for the West in order to engage in editorial work and writing for the Baptist community in Romania, and the Romanian authorities gave Ton and his family their passports on condition that they left the country for good. They are now settled in the United States.

During 1979 a number of Baptists and Pentecostals, including Dimitrie Ianculovici and some other members of the ALRC, were arrested and imprisoned for criticizing the government or for receiving literature from abroad. Most of these were given an early release by the summer of 1980, and then expelled from Romania. Of the seventeen believers thought to be still in prison at that time, four were Adventists who had refused military duties on the Sabbath; another eight were Adventists who had managed to print, mainly on state printing presses, 10,000 copies of each of fourteen different religious titles. In October 1980 several evangelical believers of German ethnic origin were arrested for distributing Bibles in the Soviet Union; five of them were imprisoned for periods of two to four years, and 22,000 Bibles were confiscated. Two years earlier Amnesty International appealed to President Ceausescu to release all human rights activists and stated that it had detailed information from numerous sources confirming that religious believers (among others) were being confined to psychiatric hospitals solely for exercising their human rights.

While dissident evangelical Christians are the most dissatisfied with present Church-State relations in Romania, other churches and individuals have voiced unhappiness about their lack of freedom. The Catholic Church is flourishing in some areas, particularly in Moldavia and Muntenia, and in December 1978 a group of priests and laity appealed to Pope John Paul II to intervene with the Romanian government on their behalf. They pointed out that their parishes are often undermanned or served by very old priests, and that they are inadequately supplied with literature and other materials. Among the group's requests were the right to print their own literature, to found religious communities and lay associations, to restore Catholic educational establishments, and to go on pilgrimages to Rome, Lourdes and other shrines. Earlier in 1978 a priest, Father Peter Mares, had appealed to President Ceausescu to allow more Catholic churches to be built and to permit Catholic public festivals. He also asked that vacancies in the Catholic hierarchy be filled and the Uniate Church re-established. He has since been expelled from the country. Another priest, sixty-seven-year-old Father Michael Godo, was fined 140,000 lei and sent to prison for six years in 1980 for collecting money to build a new church. A committee for the restoration of the Uniate Church appeared briefly in Bucharest in 1980 and tried to persuade President Ceausescu that, since the forced integration of the Uniates with the Orthodox in 1948 was due to pressure from the Soviet Union, it would now be appropriate to allow the Uniates to reappear and to make their contribution to Romanian unity and independence. The President was not persuaded.

On the whole the Orthodox bishops and priests seem content with their lot. Whether many of them are strained by a conflict between public duty and private conscience is impossible to tell, but every now and then evidence appears of priests who are not prepared to accept the official line and who suffer as a result. Father Stefan Gavril, for example, was ordained in 1969 and four years later complained (1) that the orientation courses for priests were of limited value because they dealt only with political and social problems; there was a great need for spiritual teaching, too; (2) that the social work of the Church was too dominated by the materialist philosophy of the Communist government and took no account of Christian theology; (3) that the holding of cultural and civil activities on Sunday morning in his locality was preventing members of his congregation from attending the liturgy freely. In May 1974 Father Gavril was removed from the priesthood, and the Diocesan Council gave the following reasons for his unfrocking: (a) he had interpreted the scriptures in a sectarian manner, taking passages out of context and contrary to traditional interpretation; (b) he had refused to pray for the state authorities; (c) he had refused to attend orientation courses laid down by the church authorities; (d) he had been unco-operative with the local State authorities.

Another Orthodox priest, Father Gheorghe Calciu Dumitreasa, was in prison for seventeen years during the Stalinist era for alleged terrorist-fascist activity. On release from prison he studied and taught French for a time. He then turned to theology and in 1973, still a layman, was appointed a professor of theology in the Orthodox theological seminary in Bucharest. Here he was very popular among the students, and after his ordination to the priesthood he became critical of Church-State policy. In the autumn of 1977 he protested against the demolition of a church building, and a few months later attacked atheism in a sermon at the Patriarchal cathedral. In other sermons he opposed the conscription of theological students, and discrimination against young Christians in schools and at work. He demanded free access for all to the monastic life, and complained that state officials were not treating priests with dignity. This led to his expulsion from the seminary, and he then began a private seminar at which various aspects of religious life in Romania were discussed. On 10 March 1979 Father Calciu was arrested and sentenced to ten years' imprisonment; in November 1980 it was reported that he had been removed from solitary confinement and transferred to the prison infirmary, as he had embarked on a three-week hunger strike.

The punishment of religious believers is quite consistent with the government's policy that churches and other religious bodies shall be free to express their beliefs only within clearly defined constraints and always subject to state regulation. The State itself remains officially atheist, and in 1979 the government reaffirmed its policy that in schools and universities students should be encouraged to 'form a Marxist dialectical worldview based on the truths of science, and should acquire an attitude that fights against the concepts of retrograde mentalities'. Many journals and magazines contain articles attacking religious belief, and in August 1978 President Ceausescu told the Central

Committee of the Communist Party about the 'conclusive evidence' that the world is 'purely material'. He added that this 'evidence' should be used as a weapon against 'mysticism'. Teams of lecturers, known as cultural-scientific brigades, sometimes go out to the villages to engage the people in debate about religion and atheism, though with mixed results. There are some signs of a decline in religious belief and practice in Bucharest and other large towns, but even in these places all the churches reported large increases in attendance after the disastrous earthquake in March 1977.

The Romanian churches are very much alive. None of them is finding life easy under a hostile and often ruthless government, and some Romanian Christians are witnessing to their faith at great personal cost. The Cross still stands over Romania and, as symbolized on the dome of the Grand National Assembly building, it is in the beak of the state eagle. Patriarch Justin who was unanimously elected to the leadership of the Romanian Orthodox Church in 1977, following the death of Patriarch Justinian, has a style quite different from that of his distinguished predecessor. He studied in Greece and Poland and had a good deal of international experience during the 1930s. Until the 1950s he was an academic and then became a bishop, ascending the episcopal ladder very quickly to the senior position of Archbishop of Iasi and Metropolitan of Moldavia and Suceava, which he occupied until his election to the Patriarchate. Justin is very much a Prince of the Church, autocratic and more at ease with high officials in the State than with ordinary people. He seems to have no great difficulty with the present Church-State 'solution'. Meetings between all the church leaders now take place frequently, and there are regular interconfessional theological conferences, but the future of the Christian religion in Romania remains in the hands of the Orthodox Church, with its immense resources and its deep relationship with the Romanian people. At the moment it aims to conserve these resources and protect this relationship, in the firm belief – supported by past experience – that external circumstances will change sooner or later. There is an old Romanian proverb: 'The river flows but the stones remain'; to which an Orthodox bishop adds: 'And *we* are the stones.'

# Chapter 13

# THE WORLD CHURCH AND THE CHRISTIANS OF EASTERN EUROPE

The main barrier to close relations between the Christians of Eastern Europe and those Christians who live in other parts of the world was erected long before the Communists came to power. The Great Schism of 1054 was an expression of a profound difference of approach to the Christian faith which had already manifested itself in the thought and practice of the churches of the Orthodox East and the Catholic West. Its effect was to encourage institutionalization and polarization of these differences, and to ensure that for nearly nine centuries the Christians of the two traditions would remain apart. As a consequence of isolation, each tradition developed in its own characteristic way, and with the passing of every century the barrier to understanding grew higher. This remains the fundamental problem in the relations of East and West.

Having asserted this, however, it is necessary, as with so much in this book, to make a number of important qualifications. Within Eastern Europe – Poland, Lithuania, Slovakia, Hungary and Yugoslavia – there are large and important Christian communities which do not embrace the tradition of the Christian East but are an integral part of the worldwide communion which finds its focus in the papal see of Rome. Furthermore, Eastern Europe also has – in Hungary, East Germany and the Czech lands – significant Protestant communities which are of Western origin and stand on common ground with the churches of the West. It is also necessary to note that Orthodoxy is no longer confined exclusively to the East. One of the effects of the 1917 Revolution was to drive many Orthodox Christians out of Russia and into places of refuge in the West where they were able to share their insights with other Christians and, in some instances, establish centres of Orthodoxy which were to interact with Western churches. Here may be mentioned the remarkable work of the Orthodox seminary of St Sergius in Paris, especially in the persons of Sergius Bulgakov and Georges Florovsky, the growth of the Orthodox Church in the United States, and the widely appreciated ministry of Archbishop Anthony Bloom in the United Kingdom.

During the latter years of the Tsarist era in Russia there was some personal contact between a few Christians of Russia and of the West, but after the Revolution the Russian Orthodox Church was forced even further into isolation. Quite apart from the difficulties of leaving or entering the country, particularly after 1929, the Russian Church was more than fully occupied with finding ways of survival under relentless persecution. The Western churches could do no more than pray for their suffering brethren, and in the case of the Roman Catholic Church make such changes to its administrative and diplomatic arrangements as the new situation demanded, or would permit.

## THE VATICAN

In due course the Vatican also felt moved to make certain pronouncements about the nature of Communism and about the policies of the Soviet government. Papal concern about the growth of Communism had first been expressed by Pius IX in the nineteenth century, but it became the task of Pius XI to make the position of the Roman Catholic Church clear beyond all doubt. In his encyclical *Divini Redemptoris*, delivered in March 1937, he declared, 'Communism is intrinsically wrong and no one who would save Christian civilization may collaborate with it in any field whatsoever.' Twelve years later, during the time of the 'cold war', and after the rest of Eastern Europe had come under Soviet influence, Roman Catholics were reminded that this judgement still stood, when the Holy Office issued a decree which stated that anyone who freely and consciously joined or collaborated with the Communists or their allies would be excommunicated.

The feelings of hostility were mutual. Seen through Communist eyes, the pronouncements of the Vatican confirmed the reactionary nature of a Church which had never condemned Nazis and Fascists with comparable vigour. When Pius XI set aside a day of special prayer for the Russian people in 1930, Stalin responded by describing this as 'a clerical crusade led by the Pope against the Soviet Union'. Shortly afterwards Molotov informed the Russians that Roman Catholic priests were 'spies serving on the anti-Soviet general staff', and that the Vatican had been 'trying to intervene actively in international affairs – to intervene of course in defence of capitalists and landlords, the imperialists, the incendiaries of war'. These accusations formed part of the common currency of anti-Catholic propaganda which was to continue for three decades, and which grew particularly intense during the 'cold war' when Pius XII was described as 'the Pope of the Atlantic Alliance'; even Patriarch Alexii of Moscow felt constrained to say in 1939, 'The Pope revealed his anti-Christian face in all its ugliness by his recent decrees excommunicating Communists.' In view of this remark, it is a relief to note that twenty years later the Moscow Patriarchate authorized Roman Catholics to receive communion in Russian Orthodox churches.

Relations between the Vatican and the Kremlin did not begin to improve until the early 1960s, but then the thaw was rapid. Chiefly responsible for this was John XXIII, the peasant pope whose career as a papal diplomat had given him wide knowledge of the world outside the Vatican, and whose brief tenure of the chair of St Peter was to initiate a revolution in the Roman Catholic Church. A few weeks before his death in 1963, Pope John issued his encyclical *Pacem in Terris*, which was to become a manifesto of a new spirit. In it he clearly implied that, while Communists were in error in many respects, they had many redeeming features and, whatever their faults, it was necessary to live in peace and harmony with them. When examined in detail the encyclical made few concessions to Communism, but its chief effect was to change the atmosphere in which relations between Moscow and Rome were conducted.

The reasons for the Vatican's apparent *volte-face* appear to be twofold. First – and in this context the point is often forgotten – Pope John was possessed by a burning love of his fellow human beings. He was never a man for issuing condemnations, preferring to dwell on the more positive elements in human nature. *Pacem in Terris* was an expression of this. But there was another factor: John's career as a diplomat had taught him that the Church must come to terms with reality. In the 1920s and 1930s it was possible to question whether the Communist regime in the Soviet Union would survive, and during the Second World War the country came very close to defeat. But by the 1960s it was clear that the Soviet Union was firmly established as one of the world's super-powers, and that a change of regime was far from imminent. If, therefore, tolerable conditions were to be achieved for the Roman Catholics of Eastern Europe some kind of accommodation had to be reached with the Communist governments of those countries in which there were sizeable Catholic communities.

By this time the Soviet government and some of its satellite regimes in other parts of Eastern Europe were anxious to present a more favourable image to the rest of the world. Moreover, the large Communist Parties of France and Italy could not afford the alienation of the Catholic workers' vote. The policy of religious persecution was widely known to the Vatican and was naturally regarded as a particularly sinister aspect of Communist power. An interview given by Khrushchev to an American journalist in December 1962 also provided evidence that the many papal pronouncements on peace had slightly changed the Vatican's image in Communist eyes. To Norman Cousins, Editor of *Saturday Review*, he said: 'The Pope and I have differences of opinion on many questions, but we are united in our desire for peace. I would like to have contacts with the Pope. I believe it is true that the Pope and I have things in common, because we are both of humble origin.'

Pope John's new foreign policy was continued and considerably developed throughout the reign of Pope Paul VI. Paul was by nature a cautious man but during his fifteen years as Pope the Holy See was involved in much diplomatic activity in Eastern Europe, and several heads of Communist States or their Foreign Ministers paid official visits to the Vatican. These visits were usually much more than ceremonial occasions: they involved serious discussions and often negotiations around a table, and sometimes the fruits appeared quite quickly in the form of some concession to the Church in the country concerned or the appointment of bishops to long-vacant dioceses. It became clear that the Vatican's *Ostpolitik* included flexibility and a degree of compromise, though the politicians from Eastern Europe discovered that Vatican diplomacy was shrewd and subtle, and conceded nothing that was not to the Church's ultimate advantage. The key figure in the negotiations of this period was Archbishop Agostino Casaroli, who, as secretary of the Vatican Council for the Public Affairs of the Church, was responsible for implementing the Church's foreign policy. He travelled widely in Eastern Europe, where his considerable ability and diplomatic skill earned him great respect, though some would say that he burned his fingers in Czechoslovakia. He was in Moscow several times, was deeply involved in the negotiations about diocesan boundaries and appointments in the disputed territories of Poland, was at the centre of the discussions that led to the Vatican's recognition of the frontiers of the German Democratic Republic, and represented the Vatican at the Conference on European Security and Co-operation at Helsinki. The difficult matter of Cardinal Mindszenty's departure from Hungary and removal from Hungary's Primatial See of Esztergom was handled mainly by Cardinal Franz König, the Archbishop of Vienna, who played an important, though largely hidden, role in Eastern Europe, partly as President of the Vatican Secretariat for Non-Believers, but perhaps chiefly because of his proximity to a world that begins only thirty miles from his ancient residence.

All this activity did not pass without comment in the Catholic Church at large, and some of the comment was critical. There were those who argued that negotiations with Communist governments should be left in the hands of the hierarchies in the countries concerned. The fear of a policy split between the Polish bishops and the Vatican was both real and constant. The appointment by the Vatican of 'peace priests' to some vacant sees in Czechoslovakia caused great resentment among the hard-pressed Catholics of that country. Then there were those, mainly on the liberal left, who complained that Vatican policy should not be confined to religious and church interests in Eastern Europe, but extend to broader issues related to the political and civil liberty of the people as a whole. At the other end of the political scale, some believed that the Vatican's *Ostpolitik*, combined with the general Western policy of *détente*, simply played into the hands of the countries in the Soviet bloc which continued to expand their influence and power under the cover of an apparent willingness to negotiate and make concessions. A few expressed the view that it was no longer appropriate for the Church to engage in diplomacy, and that it should seek to exert influence in society with the tools of the Gospel rather than those of power politics.

Whatever the final verdict on these issues, there can be no doubt that without the *Ostpolitik* of the 1960s and 1970s there would have been no Polish pope in the 1980s. The election of Cardinal Karol Wojtyla of Krakow as Pope John Paul II on 16 October 1978 was an event of profound international significance, and its impact was felt most powerfully in Eastern Europe. Overnight the situation was changed. Catholics who had become depressed by the long struggle against totalitarian governments were suddenly elated by the news that a man who shared their faith and had shared to the full in their struggle was now the chief pastor of the universal Church. To many of them this breaking of a 455-year-old tradition seemed no less than miraculous. The Communist governments of Eastern Europe also found themselves dealing with Catholic communities which had not only had their morale raised remarkably, but which also had a leader who knew their situation at first hand and could claim the attention and sympathy of the international community.

The significance of all this was not lost on the East European governments, all of whom, with the exception of Albania and Romania, sent delegations or their Italian ambassadors to Pope John Paul's inaugural mass. A few days before this ceremony the new Pope despatched a telegram to the government and Party leaders of Poland in which he expressed his intention to continue the Vatican's *Ostpolitik* 'in the spirit of the dialogue which was begun by my great predecessors, whose name I bear'. And as evidence that he meant what he said about continuity, Pope John Paul quickly promoted Archbishop Casaroli to be Cardinal Secretary of State (in effect, the Pope's chief minister), and Mgr Achille Silvestrini, who had been very close to Casaroli in the Council for the Public Affairs of the Church, succeeded him as its secretary. The Council was further strengthened by the appointment of Mgr Andryss Backis, a priest of Lithuanian origin, to one of its senior posts, while the experienced Archbishop Luigi Poggi was asked to keep his suitcase packed in readiness for immediate journeys to Eastern Europe should the need arise.

During the course of his own visit to Poland in 1979, Pope John Paul summed up his *Ostpolitik* when he said, 'The Church does not demand any privileges for its activities, but only what is essential for its mission.' And a few days later he made it clear that freedom of speech was one of the essentials: in a (restricted) broadcast speech he said, 'I do hope that the Slav peoples can hear me, because I cannot imagine that any Polish or Slav ear would be unable to hear words spoken by a Polish pope, a Slav. I hope that they can hear me, because we live in an age when the freedom to exchange information is precisely defined, as is the exchange of cultural values.' This oblique reference to the Helsinki Declaration constituted a challenge to all the governments of Eastern Europe, and the representatives of these governments who call at the Vatican now find themselves dealing with a pope who has a crystal-clear vision of what is necessary for the living of a truly human life and who is prepared to concede nothing that will make the living of such a life more difficult for those, in all parts of the world, for whom he feels responsible. There is of course no question of a return to the hostile atmosphere of the times of Pius XII, but John Paul II's *Ostpolitik* is a tough one – with rather more emphasis on valour than on discretion – and, having charted a particular course, he will not easily be diverted from it.

WORLD COUNCIL OF CHURCHES
The involvement of the East European churches in the World Council of Churches goes back to the First Assembly of the Council at Amsterdam in 1948. Present at this Assembly were representatives of the Evangelical and Reformed Churches of Slovakia, the Lutheran and Reformed Churches of Hungary, the Evangelical Church of the Augsburg Confession in Poland and the Evangelical Church of the Czech Brethren, whose well-known theologian, Josef Hromadka, together with representatives of the two Hungarian churches, was elected to the WCC Central Committee. Clearly this could be regarded as only a modest beginning of ecumenical contact, and a good deal of groundwork had to be done before there was further development at the institutional level. In 1948 a Conference of Orthodox Churches held in Moscow had decided 'to decline participation in the ecumenical movement in its present form', and was very

critical of the infant WCC, accusing it of trying to form an 'ecumenical Church', of engaging in political and social activity, and of reducing the Christian faith to a point at which it was 'accessible even to devils'.

In 1951 a Quaker mission went to the USSR, and the Baptist Union of Great Britain and Ireland sent a letter to the Russian Baptists. At Christmas of the same year Martin Niemöller, the German church leader, visited Moscow. The next move came in 1954 when a delegation of British Baptists visited the Soviet Union, and in the following year both Russian Baptists and representatives of the Russian Orthodox Church came to Britain at the invitation of the British Council of Churches. American Baptists visited the Soviet Union in 1955, and in 1956 a group from the National Council of Churches of the USA also made the journey. An Anglican-Orthodox Theological Conference was held in the same year. The next significant move forward came in 1958 when a group of Russian Christians met representatives of the World Council of Churches at Utrecht, and some Russian Orthodox leaders attended the Lambeth Conference. A year later Father Vitaly Borovoy and another Russian priest were at the WCC Central Committee in Rhodes, and a few months after this an official WCC delegation went to the Moscow Patriarchate. Metropolitan Nikodim was in London and Geneva in 1960, and so, after much patient work, the way was open for the Orthodox to join the World Council.

At the Third Assembly in New Delhi in 1961 the Russian Orthodox Church and the Romanian Orthodox Church joined, and some of their representatives were appointed to the new Central Committee. The three main Protestant churches of Romania also had delegates at New Delhi. When the Central Committee met in Paris in 1962 the Russian and Hungarian Baptists, the Estonian Lutheran Church, the Evangelical Lutheran Church of Latvia, together with the Armenian Church and the Georgian Orthodox Church, all joined. Then, at the Fourth Assembly at Uppsala in 1968, the Serbian Orthodox Church and the Bulgarian Orthodox Church, the Evangelical Reformed Church of Poland and the Reformed Christian Church in Slovakia and the Slovak Evangelical Church of the Augsburg Confession also came into membership.

Throughout the 1960s East European, and notably Russian,

participation in the work of the WCC increased, but Uppsala 1968 was the first Assembly at which their large and active delegations could really make their presence felt. They were also present in strength at the Fifth Assembly in Nairobi in 1975, and although they often vote as a bloc this is not always the case and the Orthodox participants in the work of the WCC are by no means a monochrome group. One of their number, His Holiness Ilia II, Catholicos and Patriarch of All Georgia, is a member of the Presidium. Archbishop Kirill (USSR) and Bishop Antonie (Romania) have seats on the Executive Committee, and altogether there are eight Orthodox members on the Central Committee. Father Vitaly Borovoy is now the official representative of the Moscow Patriarchate at the WCC's headquarters in Geneva. Besides the Orthodox, eleven representatives of other East European churches, including Bishop Tibor Bartha of the Hungarian Reformed Church, and the Rev. Alexii Bychkov of the Russian Baptist Church, are members of the Central Committee, and there are five East Europeans on the executive staff of the Council, including Professor Todor Sabev (Bulgaria) who is a Deputy General Secretary. Numerous meetings of WCC committees and groups have been held in Eastern Europe.

That the contribution made by the East European churches has widened and enriched the WCC is hardly open to question. They have, in company with the churches of Africa, Asia and Latin America, helped to change the image of the World Council from that of a West European-North American élite to that of a truly worldwide community. But the involvement of the East European churches, and of the Russian Orthodox Church in particular, has brought with it a problem inasmuch that for over two decades the WCC, while being acutely critical of unjust regimes in Southern Africa and Latin America and other parts of the world, has found it difficult to make any public criticism of what has been happening in Eastern Europe. There have been, it may be added, similar problems in respect of Greece and Indonesia. Not surprisingly, this has led to charges of 'selective indignation' and the matter came to a head at the Nairobi Assembly in 1975.

Two days before the Assembly opened, the General Secretary of the WCC, Dr Philip Potter, received a letter from two Orthodox Christians in Moscow, Father Gleb Yakunin and Lev

Regelson. This took the form of an appeal to the Assembly and, after describing some of the persecution being experienced by Russian believers, it asked for help. The appeal was published in the Assembly's daily newspaper and evoked a defensive response from representatives of the Russian Orthodox and Evangelical Christians-Baptists who were present in Nairobi. Coming soon after the Helsinki Accords on Security and Co-operation in Europe, with its strong emphasis on human rights, the letter from Moscow and the issue of human rights and religious freedom in the Soviet Union became the great unofficial talking point of the Assembly. But it was not until shortly before the close of the proceedings that opportunity was found for a public debate on the matter. This proved to be a confused and often highly emotional event. The Russian delegates found themselves in an extremely difficult position, and at one stage it was feared that they might withdraw from the WCC; but they remained and, after much discussion, the Assembly passed a resolution requesting the General Secretary to ensure that 'the question of religious liberty be the subject of intense consultations with the member churches of the signatory states of the Helsinki Agreement and the first report be presented at the next Central Committee meeting of August 1976'. Since then a number of consultations and conferences have considered the question of religious freedom in the context of human rights, and a Human Rights Advisory Group has been set up within the WCC. With the encouragement of the WCC, a Churches' Human Rights Programme for the Implementation of the Helsinki Final Act has also been sponsored by the Conference of European Churches, the National Council of Churches of Christ in the USA, and the Canadian Council of Churches.

The WCC has from its earliest days been deeply concerned about matters related to freedom, justice and other basic human rights. It has also been at pains to assert the importance of religious freedom, sometimes when this has been restricted by the influence of a dominant church, and all its Assemblies have made strong pronouncements about these issues. But in making pronouncements about the denial of human rights in particular places, the WCC has to take account of three factors. The first of these is that it is a Council of Churches and not the central organization of one worldwide Christian community. Its public statements must therefore command the general support of its constituent churches, and only in quite extraordinary circumstances could the WCC make a statement about a particular country which did not have the support of that country's own churches. Secondly, the primary responsibility for the Christian witness lies with local and national churches who must be allowed to make their own decisions about the character of this witness, without external interference. In some circumstances local and national churches may welcome external assistance, as in the case of the Evangelical Church of the Czech Brethren, who asked the WCC to condemn the invasion of Czechoslovakia by Warsaw Pact forces in 1968. This the WCC promptly did, but during the Amin reign of terror in Uganda in the 1970s the Ugandan churches asked the WCC to remain silent, which it did until compelled to join in the universal condemnation of the murder of Archbishop Janani Luwum in 1977. The churches of Eastern Europe insist that they, and they alone, should negotiate with their respective Communist governments, and that the WCC should not intervene. Just how much negotiation over human rights matters actually takes place is impossible to tell, since any conversations and their consequences must be cloaked in secrecy, but there is clear evidence that the East European churches are not inactive in this area, and that concessions from governments are sometimes obtained.

The WCC is also required to consider seriously what courses of action will be most helpful to those whose human rights are being infringed. Publicity is sometimes a valuable antidote to oppression, but not always. In some circumstances it can actually make matters worse, and again the views of those who are at the receiving end of persecution have to be given great weight. In the case of the Soviet Union this presents the WCC with a special difficulty since it receives contrary advice from the official churches, who request silence, and groups of dissident Christians who ask for maximum publicity. It was no doubt the dilemma created by this situation which led the WCC to address a letter to the Moscow Patriarchate in 1980 expressing concern about the trials of Father Gleb Yakunin, Father Dimitri Dudko, and others. The letter was courteous in tone and tentative in its assertions, but the element of concern was clear, and the significance of the letter lay in the fact that, unlike other correspondence between Geneva and Moscow on particular human rights issues, it was intended for ultimate publication. A prompt reply was received from Metropolitan Juvenaly, at that time head of the Patriarchate's Department of External Church Relations and himself a member of the WCC's Central Committee. Again the tone was courteous and, although Juvenaly tried to reassure the WCC by suggesting that the trials were of individuals who had contravened Soviet law and were not to be taken as examples of general repression, he described the WCC's approach as 'positive' and said that the WCC's concern had been conveyed to the Council for Religious Affairs. One result of this correspondence appears to be that in future the Moscow Patriarchate will receive much fuller information from the government when any Orthodox Christians are facing trial. In the meantime, the WCC will continue its present policy over Eastern Europe and continue to live with the uncomfortable fact that, in the public eye, its witness for human rights is in serious imbalance.

CONFERENCE OF EUROPEAN CHURCHES
In the late 1950s a number of West European church leaders, who had little inclination towards ecumenical encounter with the East, nevertheless came to see the great need for all the European churches to meet and talk. This led to the convening of a Conference of European Churches at Nyborg, in Denmark, in 1959. A small number of East Europeans were present, including one Russian Orthodox delegate, the lay theologian Professor Pariiski. Since then, and with minimal structure, the CEC has met seven times and brought together the leaders of virtually all Europe's non-Roman Catholic churches, large and small, East and West. No longer are the East European churches a small minority. Under its Welsh Baptist General Secretary, Dr Glen Garfield Williams – a man of consummate diplomatic and pastoral skill – the CEC has become a genuine forum of East-West encounter for church leaders. Its originally apolitical agenda has given way to discussion of, among other things, the common responsibility of the churches of East and West for peace, justice and development. In 1980 a human rights programme was established in conjunction with the American

and Canadian churches, and this is specially concerned with the implementation of the Helsinki Final Act; the secretary of the programme is based in Geneva, and the East German Protestant churches have a leading role.

The first seven Assemblies of the CEC were held in Western Europe, but the eighth was held at Maleme, in Crete, and the East European countries were well represented there, among both speakers and delegates. In effect the CEC has become a European regional gathering of the World Council of Churches, with the addition of churches too small to send delegates to WCC meetings. The late Lutheran Archbishop Jan Kiivit of Estonia was an eminent and greatly valued member of the CEC's first presidium. Today the Russian Orthodox Church is represented in the presidium by Metropolitan Alexii of Tallinn, and the Lutheran Church of the German Democratic Republic by Bishop Werner Krusche of Magdeburg. The Study Director is Professor Dumitru Popescu, of the Romanian Orthodox Church, who succeeded Professor Gyula Nagy of Hungary. Roman Catholic observers have become active participants in the Assemblies, and in November 1981 forty representatives of the CEC and forty representatives of the European Conference of Catholic Bishops met in Denmark.

Participation in the ecumenical movement has meant a great deal to the Protestant churches of Eastern Europe who, through their involvement in the WCC, the CEC and in world confessional bodies like the Baptist World Alliance and the Lutheran World Federation, have been made to feel part of a world family of Christians. It is not always easy, and in some instances has proved impossible, to secure fully representative delegations to ecumenical gatherings, but in spite of this a certain amount of information about the world Church, including information about religious conditions in other East European countries, is getting through to local churches. Within Eastern Europe itself the ecumenical movement is still weak. In certain places significant developments in local ecumenism are taking place, but most of this is of an informal kind, and is not generally advertised, since movements in this direction are often severely discouraged by governments. When church leaders meet officially it is usually in a context where they are expected to toe the Communist Party line.

CHRISTIAN PEACE CONFERENCE

There has, however, been one specifically and uniquely East European expression of ecumenism which was of considerable importance from 1958 to 1968. It centred from start to finish on Prague, and began when Josef Hromadka and a group of Czech Christians decided it was time for Christians in East and West to make their distinctive contribution to the quest for world peace. The word 'peace' had always been important in the vocabulary of the Soviet Communist Party, though during the 'cold war' it became a questionable word in the West and, not surprisingly, was regarded with mixed feelings by many Christians of the East. With a mixture of prophetic vision and naïvety – and more than a pinch of Quixotic foolhardiness – Hromadka and his friends sought permission to convene a conference, and to found a movement to be known as the 'Christian Peace Conference'. It was to be understood that its terms of reference would be East European, as would its style of work, but the movement was to be open to all Christians who were prepared to work for the ending of the 'cold war' and for justice and peace.

In 1958 permission was given for Western Christians and representatives of the churches of Eastern Europe to meet in Prague for a preliminary consultation. The authorities of Eastern Europe, including obviously the Soviet government, were ready to allow this experiment provided 'reliable people' remained in control. Like did not meet like. From Eastern Europe, East Germany excepted, there were only – and could only be – representatives of the official Protestant and Orthodox churches, while from the West there came some independently-minded young people, avant-garde Christian individuals and prophetic churchmen, such as Martin Niemöller, who were not afraid to be labelled as Soviet fellow-travellers yet were determined to maintain their spiritual and intellectual independence of East and West alike. (The East German churches, interestingly, did not follow the general Eastern pattern, and they declined affiliation to the CPC. It was left to sympathetic individuals to form a regional group. Nor did the Yugoslav churches at any time join the CPC.)

The Czech founders did not, in the event, invite the considerable number of well-known, uncritical conformists to

Moscow's policies. They wanted genuinely free Western Christians who were prepared to work within the constraints of East European realities. So there were no cold warriors and few fellow-travellers. Until the mid-1960s official Western churches stood almost totally aloof, but from the beginning there was unofficial German, Dutch, French and British participation. The German-born Quaker theologian, Richard Ullman, 'represented' Britain on the first executive organ of the movement, and until his death expressed Western participation at its best and most critical. Of like quality was Professor Charles West, of Princeton Theological Seminary in the USA.

The first All Christian Peace Assembly was held in Prague in 1961. Some thousand Christians attended – including for the first and last time a delegation from China – and, in the context of post-Stalinist hopes, everything relating to peace was debated more openly than was customary in Prague, though still within strictly circumscribed limits. The final documents were only distinguishable from official East European propaganda by those who knew how to read between the lines and how to interpret the finest nuances. Yet in the often heated debates of the CPC the Soviet and other delegations were learning their first ecumenical lessons which would later stand them in good stead in the WCC, the CEC and other ecumenical bodies.

Clearly, without the support of the USSR and the Russian Orthodox Church the CPC could not have functioned. But its atmosphere in the earlier years was in fact determined more by Central European Protestantism, with the German participants the most influential. The Roman Catholic Church was never represented, except in token ways, and at the outset there were still strong anti-Catholic tendencies. These disappeared after Pope John, but rather half-hearted attempts to integrate Roman Catholics never came to anything.

In 1964 the second Assembly brought together several thousand Christians from every continent. Debates became increasingly open, and, although the content and style of the official documents left no one in doubt as to where they had been written, they hardly ever emerged from discussion unchanged. There was considerable give and take and growing trust, always tempered by the knowledge that many of the East European participants were not free agents. The fruits were real:

Christians from East and West came to know and often trust each other, and many who came from the Third World were given their first glimpse of European church life. Through the CPC the Russian, and some other East European, churches strengthened their links with Christians in many parts of Africa, Asia and Latin America.

The 1964 Assembly confirmed the structures of the movement and planned for the future with hope. But these hopes were never quite fulfilled, for the CPC was not equipped to become an effective world movement. Nevertheless, in spite of the tensions, which gradually increased as the Czech climate became more liberal, the CPC held its 1968 Assembly in even greater hopes. These were rudely dashed by the Soviet invasion of Czechoslovakia in August of that year. Attempts to persuade the working committee of CPC to condemn the invasion failed, the Czech General Secretary, Dr Jaroslav Ondra, was in effect dismissed, the president, Josef Hromadka, resigned broken-hearted. Nearly all the leading members of the CPC from the West were in effect barred from making any further creative contribution. Metropolitan Nikodim of the USSR and Bishop Tibor Bartha of Hungary took charge, the old statutes of the movement were largely ignored and a new 'normalized' CPC emerged. In 1971 the Evangelical Church of the Czech Brethren withdrew from membership.

Today the CPC is still based on Prague and remains active under the presidency of Bishop Karoly Toth of Hungary, an able church leader who is particularly concerned with the theological roots of peace. The movement is well organized and draws most of its finance from the Russian Orthodox Church. Metropolitan Philaret of Kiev is chairman of the Continuation Committee, and the Russian influence is still very marked, but during the 1970s the CPC expanded to include churchmen from many other parts of the world. There are now strong regional groups in Africa, Asia and Latin America, and the effect of this has been to widen the horizons of the CPC and, from time to time, to depart a little from the Moscow-inspired line. Thus when the leadership of the CPC issued a statement supporting the Soviet invasion of Afghanistan in 1979 this was objected to by several CPC groups in Asia, Western Europe and especially the USA, who issued statements of their own. However, no statement was issued about the plight of imprisoned Czechoslovak Christians when the CPC held its fifth Assembly in Prague in 1978, even though local churchmen drew the attention of delegates to the lack of justice on the doorstep of their own meeting place. The CPC's limitations remain as obvious as ever.

RESEARCH AND STUDY CENTRES

Until the middle of the 1970s very few Western church members were aware of what was happening to their fellow Christians in Eastern Europe. The years of cold war and much misleading talk of an iron curtain created an impression that the countries of Eastern Europe were remote and inaccessible, although in fact none of their capitals is more than two to three hours' flying time from London, and all of them have been ready to welcome some visitors from the West. The 1960s saw the publication of a number of specialist academic studies of particular aspects of religious life in the Soviet Union, of which the most important was Walter Kolarz's *Religion in the Soviet Union*, published in London in 1961. This was followed in 1962 by the publication in Stuttgart of *Christen hinter dem Eisernen Vorhang* by Kurt Hutten, translated and published in the United States as *Iron Curtain Christians* in 1967, and the first general study of religious conditions in the whole of Eastern Europe.

These studies were not widely read, and information in the West was largely confined to press handouts issued by the embassies of East European nations, which suggested that under Communism the churches were flourishing as never before, and to the literature of anti-Communist organizations which alleged that religion was repressed throughout Eastern Europe and that the churches had been driven to an underground, catacomb-like existence. In this obviously unsatisfactory situation, the Rev. Michael Bourdeaux, an Anglican priest who had spent some time in the Soviet Union during his student years and was fluent in Russian, began a pioneering research venture in Britain. His own books about the Soviet Union, *Opium of the People, Religious Ferment in Russia*, and *Patriarch and Prophets*, established his reputation as a careful scholar, and in 1970, without much official encouragement and with the slenderest of resources, he opened the Centre for the Study of Religion and Communism at Chislehurst, in Kent. Over the years the work of the Centre grew and in 1978, having moved to Keston, also in Kent, it was renamed Keston College. The College now enjoys the patronage of the Archbishop of Canterbury, the Cardinal Archbishop of Westminster and the Chief Rabbi of Great Britain. It has a Council of Management made up of distinguished scholars and churchmen, and in all parts of the world many authorities on religion in Eastern Europe have identified themselves with its work. The chief function of the College remains that of research, carried out by a staff of sixteen and a number of volunteers who scrutinize the press of Eastern Europe, accumulate large quantities of *samizdat*, visit Eastern Europe whenever possible, meet visitors to Britain and liaise with researchers in other institutions. But the College is concerned also with the dissemination of information about religious conditions in Eastern Europe, and this is carried out through contact with the secular and church media, the publication of *Keston News Service*, a journal, *Religion in Communist Lands*, and a newsletter, *The Right to Believe*. The fact that Keston College often highlights the plight of Christians suffering persecution sometimes gives the impression, occasionally leading to an accusation, of anti-Communist, right-wing leanings. There is no foundation for this, and the College's financial support, which falls well below its needs, comes only from untainted sources.

Closely associated with Keston College is the Society for the Study of Religion under Communism, whose headquarters are in Wheaton, Illinois. This is a much smaller organization than Keston College, but it undertakes a certain amount of research and publishing. Its directors and advisers include the following: Executive Secretary, Alan Scarfe; Honorary President, the Rev. Michael Bourdeaux; Directors, Dr Thomas E. Bird, the Rev. Peter J. Deyneka, Jr, Peter J. Dyck, Sister Ann Gillen, Myrna L. Grant, Dr Donald P. Kommers, the Rev. Charles L. Manto, Dr Vasyl Markus, Dr Jerry G. Pankhurst, Paul Snezek, Dr Theofanis G. Stavrou, Dr Paul D. Steeves; Council of Advisers and Sponsors, Dr Alexander Bennigsen, Dr Harold J. Berman, Dr Andrew Q. Blane, Henry S. Dakin, Dr Milorad M. Drachkovitch, Dr Dennis J. Dunn, Father Victor Potapov, Robert B. Reekie, Ginetta Sagan, Dr Donald W. Treadgold, Dr James E. Wood.

The Research Centre for Religion and Human Rights in Closed

Societies (475 Riverside Drive, New York) focuses on all people, of whatever religion, persecuted by totalitarian regimes, and is also concerned about political dissidents. The research centre was started in 1972, but its quarterly magazine RCDA (*Religion in Communist Dominated Areas*) was launched ten years earlier by Dr Paul Anderson and the Rev. Blahoslav Hruby, under the sponsorship of the National Council of Churches in the USA. Information is received from a variety of published and underground sources, and disseminated through the magazine, press releases, lectures and briefings. Blahoslav Hruby, who was born in Czechoslovakia, is now the Executive Director and is assisted by two full-time staff members and fifteen volunteers, who are specialists in various aspects of religion and Communism. Financial backing comes from foundations, denominations, local churches and individuals. The President is C. H. Kallaur, the Vice-Presidents are the Rev. Ralph Mortensen and James E. Wilson, and the Secretary is the Rev. Gareth Miller. There is a large inter-faith board of directors and council of advisers.

Institut Glaube in der 2. Welt (Faith in the Second World) is based in Zurich, Switzerland, with aims and methods similar to those of Keston College. It was started in 1972, largely under the inspiration of a Swiss pastor, Eugen Voss, who remains its Director. A staff of six full-time and one half-time workers, together with a number of free-lance contributors, accumulate and analyse information about religion in Eastern Europe which is then passed to the mass media, churches, international bodies and other interested institutions. The institute has its own publications: *G2W*, which appears monthly and sometimes has additional issues devoted to particular subjects or countries; and *ID–G2W*, which is a monthly news service; besides these regular publications there are from time to time special studies and books. Like Keston College, Institut Glaube in der 2. Welt is fully ecumenical, and its patrons include the Cardinal Archbishops of Vienna and Munich, the Bishop of the Protestant Church in Munich, and the Russian Orthodox Church-in-exile Archbishop of Berlin and West Germany. Financial contributions come from churches and church bodies, groups and individuals, and membership subscriptions.

BIBLES

Another area of growing concern among the churches of East and West, which increasingly involves co-operation between the different Christian communities, is that of translating, producing and distributing copies of the Bible. The United Bible Societies are heavily committed to this work, and bring to it very considerable experience and expertise. Individual Christians in the West who have opportunities for visiting Eastern Europe sometimes wonder whether they should take Bibles with them and what their attitude should be towards the various organizations whose aim is to get Bibles into Eastern Europe, sometimes clandestinely and sometimes openly. The United Bible Societies made their own position clear in 1973 when their European Regional Committee, meeting in the German Democratic Republic, passed a resolution which stated:

(1) The Committee emphasizes that all support given to the work by UBS member Bible Societies is provided through legal channels; (2) The Committee wishes to place on record its dissociation from Bible work done by illegal means. Furthermore, the Committee dissociates itself from any scripture distribution linked with political propaganda; (3) In maintaining this course, the Committee hopes that Bible work in East European countries can effectively continue.

With the exception of Albania, translation work in today's languages is being done, or has recently been completed, in all countries of Eastern Europe. Local production of scriptures, in some cases on a fairly considerable scale, is now taking place in the German Democratic Republic, Hungary, Poland, Romania, Yugoslavia and Czechoslovakia, though some scriptures are still exported to the last four of these countries, and in most instances the UBS provide paper for the printing of Bibles. Bulgaria is a special case inasmuch as there appears to be no widespread demand for the Bible, and the Bulgarian government makes it difficult for copies to be imported, but the UBS recently provided paper for a modest reprinting of the Bible by the Bulgarian Orthodox Church.

No doubt some copies of the Albanian translation of the Bible produced in Yugoslavia do go across the border into Albania, but it would be dangerous for any Western visitor to Albania to take copies of the scriptures into Albanian with him. The Soviet law on the importation of Bibles is not clear. It has been maintained that even under the present law the importing of Bibles is legal, and no official answer has been given to this contention. In practice, the Soviet authorities make no difficulty for visitors who carry in their luggage a single copy of the Bible in Russian or in some other language spoken in the Soviet Union. Scriptures are in desperately short supply in the Soviet Union, and the Christians there are always grateful when a visitor leaves behind a copy of the Bible in Russian or some other Soviet language. But anyone who attempts to import a larger number of Bibles without obtaining prior permission is likely to find himself in trouble.

The introduction of Bibles into Eastern Europe raises again the issue which surfaces whenever any aspect of religious conditions in Eastern Europe is seriously considered. Does the path of religious commitment call chiefly for discretion – the readiness to accommodate responsibly and to accept less than the ideal, even though there be no guarantee of better opportunities tomorrow? Or does the path of discipleship call chiefly for valour – defiance of the law, the authorities and the status quo, even though the price may be suffering and possibly death? Consciously or unconsciously, this dilemma faces every religious believer in Eastern Europe. In other forms, and with varying degrees of intensity, it faces religious people everywhere. Christian believers, whose faith is rooted in a person who identified himself completely with humanity and yet was finally 'despised and rejected of men', can never evade the issue wherever they may be. The tension between discretion and valour, between involvement and withdrawal, is part of daily life.

The tragedy of the ancient division between East and West, reinforced by the events of the twentieth century, is that Christians of differing traditions have been prevented from sharing their insights and experiences concerning this essential element in human existence. The real ecumenical encounter between East and West still lies in the future. When it comes Christians of Western Europe will receive much from the vast treasury of Eastern spirituality and experience, and not least from that which has been added in recent years. Christians of Eastern Europe may perhaps receive something in return from those in the West who have also endeavoured to walk faithfully in a world of rapid and often bewildering change. Doubtless both will be astonished to discover how much they already hold in common.

# For Further Reading

Many of these books are out of print but should be available through libraries. A great deal of published material is available in periodicals only. *Religion in Communist Dominated Areas* is published monthly by the Research Centre for Religion and Human Rights in Closed Societies (475 Riverside Drive, New York, NY 10015, USA), and *Religion in Communist Lands* is published quarterly by Keston College (Keston College, Heathfield Road, Keston, Kent, BR2 6BA, England). It is possible to subscribe to the monthly *Journal of the Moscow Patriarchate* (Box No. 624, Moscow G-435, USSR).

Alexander, Stella, *Church and State in Yugoslavia since 1945*, Cambridge University Press, England, 1979.

Bociurkiw, Bohdan R., and Strong, John W., eds., *Religion and Atheism in the USSR and Eastern Europe*, Macmillan, London and New York, 1975.

Bourdeaux, Michael, *Faith on Trial in Russia*, Hodder & Stoughton, London; Harper & Row, New York; 1971.
  – *Land of Crosses* (Lithuania), Keston College, England, 1979.
  – *Patriarch and Prophets*, Macmillan, London; Praeger, New York; 1970.
  – *Religious Ferment in Russia*, Macmillan, London; St Martin's, New York; 1968.
  – et al., eds., *Religious Liberty in the Soviet Union: WCC and USSR, a Post-Nairobi Documentation*, Keston College, England, 1976.

Dunn, Dennis J., *Détente and Papal-Communist Relations, 1962–1978*, Westview Press, Boulder, Colorado, 1979.
  – ed., *Religion and Modernization in the USSR*, Westview Press, Boulder, Colorado, 1977.

Every, George, *Understanding Eastern Christianity*, SCM Press, London, 1980.

Fletcher, William C., *Russian Orthodox Church Underground*, Oxford University Press, New York, 1971.

Girardi, Giulio, *Marxism and Christianity*, Gill, Dublin; Macmillan, New York; 1968.

Gollwitzer, Helmut, *The Christian Faith and the Marxist Criticism of Religion*, St Andrew Press, Edinburgh; Scribner's, New York; 1970.

Hamel, Johannes, *A Christian in East Germany*, SCM Press, London; Association Press, New York; 1960.

Hayward, M., and Fletcher, W.C., eds., *Religion and the Soviet State*, Pall Mall Press, London; Praeger, New York; 1969.

Hebblethwaite, Peter, *The Christian-Marxist Dialogue and Beyond*, Darton, Longman & Todd, London; Paulist Press, New York; 1977.

Hebley, Johannes A., *Protestants in Russia*, Christian Journals, Belfast; Eerdmans, Grand Rapids, Michigan; 1976.

   – *The Russians and the World Council of Churches*, Christian Journals, Belfast, 1979.

Hromadka, Josef, *Impact of History on Theology: Thoughts of a Czech Pastor*, SCM Press, London; Fides/Claretian, Notre Dame, Indiana; 1970.

Kolarz, Walter, *Religion in the Soviet Union*, Macmillan, London; St Martin's, New York; 1961.

Lawrence, John, *A History of Russia*, Mentor Books, New York, 1969.

   – *Russians Observed*, Hodder & Stoughton, London; University of Nebraska Press, Lincoln, Nebraska; 1969.

*Lenin on Religion*, Lawrence & Wishart, London, n.d.

Lochman, Jan M., *The Church in a Marxist Society: A Czechoslovak View*, SCM Press, London; Harper & Row, New York; 1970.

Marshall, Richard H., et al., *Aspects of Religion in the Soviet Union 1917–67*, University of Chicago Press, Chicago, 1971.

*Marx and Engels on Religion*, Progress Publishers, Moscow, 1972.

Mindszenty, Jozsef, Cardinal, *Memoirs*, Macmillan, New York; Weidenfeld & Nicolson, London; 1975.

Pascal, Pierre, *The Religion of the Russian People*, Mowbrays, London, 1976.

Rogers, Edward, *The Christian Approach to the Communist*, Edinburgh House, London, 1959.

Rothenberg, Joshua, *The Jewish Religion in the Soviet Union*, KTAV, New York, 1971.

Sawatsky, Walter, *Soviet Evangelicals since World War II*, Herald Press, Kitchener, Ontario and Scottdale, Penn., 1981.

Vins, Georgi, *Three Generations of Suffering*, Hodder & Stoughton, London, 1975. (US title: *Georgi Vins: Testament from Prison*, David C. Cook, Elgin, Illinois, 1975.)

Ware, Timothy, *The Orthodox Church*, Pelican, London; Penguin, New York; 1963.

Weingartner, Erich, ed., *Church Within Socialism*, IODC International, Rome, 1976.

Whale, John, ed., *The Pope from Poland*, Collins, London, 1980. (US title: *The Man Who Leads the Church*, Harper & Row, San Francisco, 1980.)

Wyszynski, Stefan, Cardinal, *A Strong Man Armed* (Sermons), Chapman & Hall, London, 1966.

Yakunin, Gleb, and Regelson, Lev, *Letters from Moscow: Religion and Human Rights in the USSR*, Keston College, England; H.S. Dakin Co., San Francisco; 1978.

# Index